Child Development in Cultural Context

Child Development in Cultural Context

Edited by
Jaan Valsiner
University of North Carolina at Chapel Hill

Hogrefe and Huber Publishers
Toronto • Lewiston, N.Y. • Göttingen • Bern

Library of Congress Cataloging-in-Publication Data

Child Development in Cultural Context.

Includes bibliographies and index.
1. Child psychology--Cross-cultural studies.
2. Developmental psychology--Cross-cultural studies.
3. Ethnopsychology. I. Valsiner, Jaan. [DNLM:
1. Anthropology, Cultural. 2. Child Development.
3. Child Psychology. WS 105 C9677]
BF722.C85 1989   155.4   87-8799
ISBN 0-88937-015-X

Canadian Cataloguing in Publication Data

Main entry under title:
Child development in cultural context.

Bibliography: p.
Includes index.
ISBN 0-88937-015-X

1. Child psychology - Cross-cultural studies.
I. Valsiner, Jaan.

BF721.C84 1989   155.4   C87-093824-X

Printed in the United States

ISBN 0-88937-015-X   Toronto · Lewiston, N.Y. · Göttingen · Bern
ISBN 3-8017-0274-X   Göttingen · Bern · Toronto · Lewiston, N.Y.

Table of Contents

PART III. CULTURE AND SOCIAL-COGNITIVE DEVELOPMENT

vi

List of Contributors

Anna Emilia Berti, Department of Developmental Psychology and Socialization, Universita degli Studi di Padova, Via Beato Pellegrino 26, I-35137 Padova, Italy

Anna Silvia Bombi, Department of Developmental Psychology and Socialization, Universita degli Studi di Roma, Via Degli Apuli 8, I-00185 Rome, Italy

Elizette da Costa, Institute of Child Psychology, University of London, London, Great Britain

Douglas A. Davis, Department of Psychology, Haverford College, Haverford, PA 19041, U.S.A.

Paula E. Hill, Department of Psychology, University of Michigan, Ann Arbor, MI 48105, U.S.A.

Thomas Kindermann, Fachbereich Gerontopsychologie (M. Baltes, Director), Freie Universitat Berlin, Berlin (West). Currently: Research Associate, Graduate School of Education, University of Rochester, Rochester, NY, U.S.A.

Ellen S. Peisner, Developmental Psychology Program, Department of Psychology, University of North Carolina at Chapel Hill, Davie Hall 013A, Chapel Hill, NC 27514, U.S.A.

Debra Skinner, Department of Sociology and Anthropology, Peace College, Raleigh, NC, U.S.A.

Barbara Van Steenburgh Reid, Medical Anthropology Program, University of California at San Francisco, 1350 Seventh Avenue, San Francisco, CA 94143, U.S.A.

Jaan Valsiner, Developmental Psychology Program, Department of Psychology, University of North Carolina at Chapel Hill, Davie Hall 013A, Chapel Hill, NC 27514, U.S.A.

Eileen B. Wilson-Oyelaran, Department of Psychology, University of Ife, Ile-Ife, Oyo State, Nigeria

Mei-Ha Wong, Committee on Human Development, University of Chicago, Chicago, IL 60637 , U.S.A.

Robert H. Woodson, Department of Psychology, University of Texas at Austin, Austin, TX 78712, U.S.A.

General Introduction

How Can Developmental Psychology Become "Culture Inclusive"?

Jaan Valsiner

Developmental psychology has emerged in the context of Western societies in conjunction with the social expectations of these societies, and has remained intellectually indebted to their traditions. In the realm of practical applications of the knowledge of child development, the practical needs and social norms of the Western countries have dominated the field (see Cirillo & Wapner, 1986; Kessen, 1979). This has led to a peculiar state of affairs in developmental psychology, where the development of children in Western industrialized countries has come to be considered the "norm" for all children of the human species, independent of the economic and cultural environments which they inhabit.

This limited interest by developmental psychology in child development under different cultural conditions is not based solely on an ethnocentric and pragmatic narrow focus. It is also fortified by the assumption of nativism (genetic determinism) that has been widespread in the discipline. If child development is viewed as a lawful unfolding of genetically pre-programmed behavioral and cognitive functions over time, independent of the environment, then there is little perceivable need for studying that unfolding under different environmental and cultural conditions. Even when some role of the environment is acknowledged, actual comparative-cultural emphasis in research may still remain of secondary importance (see, for instance: Piaget, 1966).

In contrast, developmental research that views development as a joint function of the organism and its environment should in principle be interested in the comparative-cultural study of development. As the study of child development stands, that has not been the case. It is in the area of animal behavioral development where the emphasis on interaction with environment as the motor of development has been fostered (e.g., Gottlieb, 1976; Kuo, 1967). Among the psychologists who have adhered to the basic idea of organism-environment interdependence at the human level, some have been only occasionally interested in development (e.g., Brunswick, 1952; Lewin, 1936, 1938), and others have not emphasized the *cultural* organization of children's environments (e.g., Bronfenbrenner, 1979; Cairns, 1979; Magnusson, 1981, 1985; Sameroff, 1975). The uneasiness that developmental psychologists feel about applying the concept of culture in their theoretical system is understandable. "Culture" carries with it a multiplicity of meanings, which can lead to justified reluctance to use it in any explanatory function (see Valsiner, 1988). However, psychology cannot avoid addressing the issue of culture directly, since "all empirical psychology is folk psychology to some degree, profoundly influenced by cultural assumptions that scientists share with nonscientists of the same background, and all folk psychology is empirical to some degree, embodying folk wisdom effective in a specific milieu" (LeVine, Caron, & New, 1980, p. 77).

Although the term "culture" has been ill-defined, efforts to study children's development in conjunction with culture have at times been productive. These efforts have originated from the fields of cultural anthropology and cross-cultural psychology. In the context of their major interest in culture, anthropologists at times pay attention to children's development and upbringing (e.g., Barry, Child, & Bacon, 1959; Benedict, 1938; Hogbin, 1946; Lebra, 1984; Mead, 1928; Middleton, 1970; Scheper-Hughes, 1985; Schwartz, 1976; Super & Harkness, 1980; Williams, 1958, 1969; and others). In the context of anthropological studies of education, research on the cultural structuring of children's developmental environments has become enhanced (see Spindler, 1974). Furthermore, careful investigations of the symbolic environments within which human development takes place have recently appeared (Leis,

1982; Lutz, 1983; Obeyesekere, 1981, 1985). However, anthropology's major interest remains in the domain of culture, and children have been of interest mainly as targets on which the uses of cultural socialization practices can be studied. Anthropological interest in children has not been developmental in its core.

Within psychology, cultural aspects of child development have become a topic of interest in the subdiscipline of psychology called *cross-cultural psychology* (see Adler, 1982; Curran, 1984; Cole & Bruner, 1971; Deregowski, Dziurawiec, & Annis, 1983; Jahoda, 1982; Munroe, Munroe, & Whiting, 1981; Poortinga, 1977; Rath, Asthana, Sinha & Sinha, 1982; Serpell, 1976). Cross-cultural research in psychology has usually carried the traditional methodology of comparing samples of subjects to the cross-cultural realm. Thus, the majority of such studies have treated culture as an entity to be compared with other, similar entities (e.g., see Field, Sostek, Vietze, & Leidermann, 1981). As a result, performance of samples of children on tasks administered in different cultures is usually compared at the level of aggregate statistical data (averages) that can be interpreted as pertaining to the populations (cultures) compared in a given study. Usually, such empirical research is inconsequential for understanding how the *process* of development takes place within a culture. Investigation of that process would require an analysis of interdependence of culture and child development within individual cases of child development, studied longitudinally. Contemporary prevailing research traditions in psychology, which emphasize large samples and statistical aggregation of data across individual cases, are epistemologically inappropriate for the study of the culture-child development interdependence at the level of individual cases (see Valsiner, 1986).

The emphasis on culture as an *organizer* of an individual child's development has rarely been present in the history of developmental psychology. It is mostly in the framework of the cultural-historical thought of Soviet psychology at the end of the 1920s that the organizational role of the culture in the *development* of human action and reasoning was consistently emphasized (Luria, 1974; Vygotsky, 1929, 1982; Vygotsky & Luria, 1930). A similar emphasis was present in the theoretical framework of child-environment interaction advanced by Mikhail Basov, a contemporary of Vygotsky's (Basov, 1931). However, as often happens in the history of science, the creative search by the cultural-historical school for adequate models uniting culture and psychology became transformed into a very different framework in the USSR, and was perceived by European and American psychologists in a highly selective manner (Valsiner, 1987a). Nevertheless, some recent developments in contemporary psychology have led towards an increasing interest in the organizer's role of culture in cognitive development research (Scribner & Cole, 1981; Wagner & Stevenson, 1982). In the realm of social psychology, some recent efforts towards linking that discipline with cultural history are noteworthy (Harre, 1979; Gergen, 1982; Gergen & Gergen, 1984). However, these developments have not penetrated the core of contemporary developmental psychology, which remains remarkably separate from issues of cultural organization of childhood in different societies (see Jahoda, 1986). This is an obvious shortcoming of the discipline, since the majority of children around the world grow up under life conditions that are very different from the European or North American middle-class standards of living, presuppositions, and beliefs. Instead of being culture-blind, or merely cross-cultural in its emphasis, developmental psychology needs to become *culture-inclusive* — in the sense of considering the cultural organization of child development simultaneously with the study of its cognitive, affective, and behavioral phenomena.

This book is devoted to the task of demonstrating how contemporary developmental psychology could be advanced towards the goal of becoming culture-inclusive. Each chapter covers a particular aspect of inclusion of cultural factors into our efforts to understand how child development takes place. It is one of the aims of this volume to demonstrate that integration of developmental psychology and cultural anthropology for the purpose of the study of child development is not only possible but inevitable, if our knowledge is to become adequate to the reality of child development.

CULTURE-INCLUSIVENESS IN DEVELOPMENTAL PSYCHOLOGY

Culture as the organizer of human cognition and conduct is intertwined with every higher psychological function, as it emerges in ontogeny (Vygotsky, 1982). Any effort to make developmental psychology culture-inclusive necessarily starts from the investigator's own doorstep — his or her own background culture. It is the cultural interdependence of psychological phenomena and their cultural contexts in Western societies that are as important for culture-inclusive developmental psychology, as is similar research in cultures that differ greatly from the occidental ones. Within any other culture, children's individual developmental trajectories are guided by cultural organization of the environment (Valsiner, 1987b). At the same time, children are active in modifying the cultural environment in which they live. Culture and personality are interlocked in a reciprocal relationship: culture guides each individual child's development, while the activities that the child is involved in have an impact upon changing the previous form of the culture.

This reciprocal relationship between culture and individual development sets up unique demands for empirical methodology. Research methodology in developmental psychology is adequate to developmental phenomena when it is made up to study the organism-environment exchange processes (Valsiner & Benigni, 1986). In case of human development, this general methodological requirement entails development of empirical methodologies that document the *process of interaction* between the child and his/her environment. In this book, a particular effort in that direction is presented (see Chapter 1).

FROM CONTEXT-FREE KNOWLEDGE TO CONTEXT-BOUND APPLICATION

The limitations of contemporary developmental psychology become especially drastic when efforts are made to apply know-how of Western psychologies in the context of Third World countries. Contributors to this book deal with this issue in different ways. Eileen B. Wilson-Oyelaran (Chapter 2) outlines the background and consequences of the importation of Western psychology in the context of an African country. The assumption (often comfortably used by Western scientists) that psychology should live up to the standards of an "objective" scientific discipline (e.g., see Toulmin & Leary, 1985) is as fragile as were the efforts of nuclear scientists in the 1940s to stop the use of their discoveries in the making of nuclear bombs. Western psychological theories and methods usually become inappropriate when transposed to non-western cultural contexts (Sinha, 1986; Wilson, 1984; see also chapter 4, this volume). At a minimum, such applications overlook important areas of psychological phenomenology that are relevant in those cultures but absent in Western ones, such as children's development in polygamic families, described in Chapter 3.

The difficulty of application of Western culture-specific knowledge of child development to other countries is often further complicated by the ambivalent attitude of Third World psychologists themselves towards Western theories and practices. On the one hand, many of them try to "import" Western theories and methods, in the hope that such importation will advance the science of psychology in their own country. That hope is certainly misplaced in the case of those areas of psychology (especially child development) that are particularly closely intertwined with the culture. Such "cargo cult" equivalent of Western importations can easily reach major proportions, especially when the importers have themselves been trained in European or American universities, and succeed in gaining governmental support in their own country. The impact of such success is questionable in two respects. First, the real social problems of these countries may remain unsolved, despite all the efforts of the psychologists. The causes for such failures can be found in the mismatch between the imported know-how and the cultural conditions to which it becomes applied. Second, the wholesale importation of Western ideas directs the attention of psychologists away from studying relevant research issues from the historical traditions of their own culture. Fortunately, some efforts to develop culturally adequate developmental psychology on the basis of knowledge of the indigenous culture can be found in various Third World countries (e.g., Akiwowo, 1986; Makoju, 1986; Sannoh, 1986; D. Sinha, 1981, 1986; Soetan, 1986). Such efforts, together with similar approaches that have emerged at the intersection of developmental psychology and anthropology in the West (e.g., Rogoff & Lave, 1984; C. Sinha, 1985), constitute a first practical step towards making developmental psychology culture-inclusive.

SUMMARY:
CULTURE-INCLUSIVENESS OF PSYCHOLOGICAL DEVELOPMENT

To recapitulate, the general network of ideas that substantiates the need for culture-inclusive developmental psychology is quite straightforward. Development is necessarily a *context-bound process* that characterizes the biological world, and is organismic in its structure. Organisms interact with their environments, and develop as a result of that interaction. In the special case of the human species, any environment that the developing child encounters is organized culturally, and serves to regulate that child's psychological development (Heidmets, 1985). Children's interactions with adults, older siblings, and peers constitute episodes of continuous experience with social organization. Therefore, cultural background constitutes an inseparable part of the phenomena that developmental psychologists study.

However, the need for "taking culture into account" in the study of child development is easier said than done. In most of the existing empirical studies that have claimed to take culture into account, "culture" has usually been reduced to the status of an independent variable. More accurately, it is actually used as an "index variable," since varying the culture of subjects in a psychological study in the sense of a traditional experimental paradigm is impossible. Given the use of culture as an index variable, cross-cultural research has produced empirical data that simply reflect differences between generic accounts of child development in different cultures. However, such studies have very rarely explicated the ways in which a *given* cultural system structures the process of child development. In other words, existing research has focused on the *inter*-cultural aspects of child development, leaving the *intra*-cultural interdependence between cultural guidance and actual child development largely outside its sphere of interests. This oversight is the target of the present volume. *Culture-inclusive developmental psychology is a research paradigm that is primarily directed towards explaining how culture organizes the conditions for children's development, and how children assimilate these conditions, and simultaneously accommodate to them.* Cross-cultural comparisons are of secondary importance for culture-inclusive developmental psychology. Rather, of main interest is how the cultural organization of the environment creates opportunities for children's development;

gradually guiding them towards becoming adults with a knowledge base that is sufficient for functioning within their own society. It is this reciprocal causal system that is the focus of the present book.

REFERENCES

Adler, L.L. (Ed.), (1982). *Cross-cultural research at issue.* New York: Academic Press.

Akiwowo, A. (1986). Oral tradition as a source of psychological knowledge. In E.B. Wilson (Ed.), *Psychology and society* (pp. 57-74). Ile-Ife: University of Ife Press.

Barry, H., Child, I.L., & Bacon, M.K. (1959). Relation of child training to subsistence economy. *American Anthropologist, 61*, 51-63.

Basov, M. (1931). *General foundations of pedology.* Moscow-Leningrad: Gosizdat (in Russian).

Benedict, R. (1938). Continuities and discontinuities in cultural conditioning. Psychiatry, 1, 161-167.

Bronfenbrenner, U. (1979). *The ecology of human development.* Cambridge, MA: Harvard University Press.

Brunswick, E. (1952). *The conceptual framework of psychology.* Chicago: University of Chicago Press.

Cairns, R.B. (1979). *Social development.* San Francisco: W.H. Freeman.

Cirillo, L., & Wapner, S. (Eds.) (1986). *Value presuppositions in theories of human development.* Hillsdale, NJ: Erlbaum.

Cole, M., & Bruner, J.S. (1971). Cultural differences and inferences about psychological processes. *American Psychologist, 26,10,* 867-876.

Curran, H.V. (Ed.) (1984). *Nigerian children: Developmental perspectives.* London: Routledge & Kegan Paul.

Deregowski, J.B., Dziurawiec, S., & Annis, R.C. (Eds.) (1983). *Expiscations in cross-cultural psychology.* Lisse: Swets & Zeitlinger.

Field, T.M., Sostek, A.M., Vietze, P., & Leidermann, P.H. (Eds.) (1981). *Culture and early interactions.* Hillsdale, NJ: Erlbaum.

Gergen, K.J. (1982). *Toward transformation in social knowledge.* New York: Springer.

Gergen, K.J., & Gergen, M.M. (Eds.) (1984). *Historical social psychology.* Hillsdale, NJ: Erlbaum.

Gottlieb, G. (1976). The role of experience in the development of behavior and the nervous system. In G. Gottlieb (Ed.), *Studies on the development of behavior and the nervous system. Vol. 3. Neural and behavioral specificity* (pp. 25-54). New York: Academic Press.

Harre, R. (1979). *Social being: A theory for social psychology.* Totowa, NJ: Rowman & Littlefield.

Heidmets, M. (1985). Environment as the mediator of human relationships: Historical and ontogenetic aspects. In T. Garling & J. Valsiner (Eds.), *Children within environments: Toward a psychology of accident prevention* (pp. 217-227). New York: Plenum.

Hogbin, I. (1946). A New Guinea childhood. *Oceania, 16,* 275-296.

Jahoda, G. (1982). *Psychology and anthropology: A psychological perspective.* London: Academic Press.

Jahoda, G. (1986). A cross-cultural perspective on developmental psychology. *International Journal of Behavioral Development, 9,* 417-437.

Kessen, W. (1979). The American child and other cultural inventions. *American Psychologist, 34,* 10, 815-820.

Kuo, Z-Y. (1967). *The dynamics of behavior development.* New York: Random House.

Leis, N.B. (1982). The not-so-supernatural power of Ijaw children. In S. Ottenberg (Ed.), *African religious groups and beliefs* (pp. 151-169). Meerut: Folklore Institute.

Lebra, T.S. (1984). *Japanese women: Constraint and fulfillment.* Honolulu: University of Hawaii Press.

LeVine, R.A., Caron, J., & New, R. (1980). Anthropology and child development. *New directions for child development, No. 8,* 71-86.

Lewin, K. (1936). *Principles of topological psychology*. New York: McGraw-Hill.

Lewin, K. (1938). *The conceptual representation and measurement of psychological forces*. Durham, N.C.: Duke University Press.

Luria, A.R. (1974). *On the history of cognitive processes*. Moscow: Nauka (in Russian).

Lutz, C. (1983). Parental goals, ethnopsychology, and the development of emotional meaning. *Ethos, 11*, 4, 246-262

Magnusson, D. (Ed.) (1981). *Toward a psychology of situations*. Hillsdale, NJ: Erlbaum.

Magnusson, D. (1985). Implications of an interactional paradigm for research on human development. *International Journal of Behavioral Development, 8*, 115-137.

Makoju, G.A.E. (1986). Traditional Igbo concept of children: A psychological perspective. In E.B. Wilson (Ed.), *Psychology and society* (pp. 85-94). Ile-Ife: University of Ife Press.

Mead, M. (1928). *Coming of age in Samoa*. New York: Morrow.

Middleton, J. (Ed.) (1970). *From child to adult*. New York: Natural History Press.

Munroe, R.H., Munroe, R.L., & Whiting, B.B. (Eds.) (1981). *Handbook of cross-cultural human development*. New York: Garland Press.

Obeyesekere, G. (1981). *Medusa's hair: An essay on personal symbols and religious experience*. Chicago: University of Chicago Press.

Obeyesekere, G. (1985). Symbolic foods: Pregnancy cravings and the envious female. *International Journal of Psychology, 20*, 637-662.

Piaget, J. (1966). Necessité et signification des récherches comparatives en psychologie génétique. *International Journal of Psychology*, 3-13.

Poortinga, Y. H. (Ed.) (1977). *Basic problems in cross-cultural psychology*. Lisse: Swets & Zeitlinger.

Rath, R., Asthana, H.S., Sinha, D., & Sinha, J.B.H. (Eds.) (1982). *Diversity and unity in cross-cultural psychology*. Lisse: Swets & Zeitlinger.

Rogoff, B., & Lave, J. (Eds.) (1984). *Everyday cognition: Its development in social context*. Cambridge, MA: Harvard University Press.

Sameroff, A. (1975). Transactional models in early social relations. *Human Development, 18*, 65-79.

Sannoh, B.O. (1986). Traditional Yoruba child psychology. In E.B. Wilson (Ed.), *Psychology and society* (pp. 96-106). Ile-Ife: University of Ife Press.

Scribner, S., & Cole, M. (1981). *The psychology of literacy*. Cambridge, MA: Harvard University Press.

Scheper-Hughes, N. (1985). Culture, scarcity, and maternal thinking: Maternal detachment and infant survival in a Brazilian shantytown. *Ethos, 13*, 291-317.

Schwartz, T. (Ed.) (1976). *Socialization as cultural communication*. Berkeley: University of California Press.

Serpell, R. (1976). *Culture's influence on behaviour*. London: Methuen.

Sinha, C. (1985). A socio-naturalistic approach to human development. In G. Butterworth, J. Rutkowska, & M. Scaife (Eds.), *Evolution and developmental psychology* (pp. 159-181). New York: St. Martin's Press.

Sinha, D. (Ed.) (1981). *Socialization of the Indian child*. New Delhi: Concept Publishing House.

Sinha, D. (1986). *Psychology in a Third World country: The Indian experience*. New Delhi: Sage Publications.

Soetan, A.O. (1986). The psychology of traditional moral education. In E.B. Wilson (Ed.), *Psychology and society* (pp. 75-84). Ile-Ife: University of Ife Press.

Spindler, G.D. (Ed.) (1974). *Education and cultural process: Toward an anthropology of education*. New York: Holt, Rinehardt, & Winston.

Super, C.M., & Harkness, S. (Eds.) (1980). Anthropological perspectives on child development. *New directions for child development, No. 8*.

Toulmin, S., & Leary, D.E. (1985). The cult of empiricism, and beyond. In S. Koch & D.E. Leary (Eds.), *A century of psychology as science* (pp. 594-616). New York: McGraw-Hill.

Valsiner, J. (Ed.) (1986). *The individual subject and scientific psychology.* New York: Plenum.

Valsiner, J. (1987a). *Developmental psychology in USSR.* Brighton: Harvester Press.

Valsiner, J. (1987b). *Culture and the development of children's action.* Chichester: Wiley.

Valsiner, J. (1988). Ontogeny of co-construction of culture within socially organized environmental settings. In J. Valsiner (Ed.), *Child development within culturally structured environments. Vol. 2. Social co-construction and environmental guidance in development.* Norwood, NJ: Ablex.

Valsiner, J., & Benigni, L. (1986). Naturalistic research and ecological thinking in the study of child development. *Developmental Review, 6,* 203-223.

Vygotsky, L.S. (1929). The problem of the cultural development of the child. *Journal of Genetic Psychology, 36,* 415-434.

Vygotsky, L.S. (1982). The historical sense of the crisis in psychology. In L.S. Vygotsky, *Sobranie sochinenii. Vol. 1. Voprosy teorii i istorii psikhologii* (pp. 292-436). Moscow: Pedagogika (in Russian).

Vygotsky, L.S.,& Luria, A.R. (1930). *Studies in the history of behavior.* Moscow: Gosizdat (in Russian).

Wagner, D.A., & Stevenson, H.W. (Eds.) (1982).*Cultural perspectives on child development.* San Francisco: W.H. Freeman.

Williams, T.R. (1958). The structure of the socialization process in Papago Indian society. *Social Forces, 36,* 251-256.

Williams, T.R. (1969). *A Borneo childhood.* New York: Holt, Rinehardt, & Winston.

Wilson, E.B. (1984). Contributions of psychology to the underdevelopment of Africa. *Odu: A journal of West-African studies, New series, No. 25,* 70-81.

Part One:

Theoretical and International Perspectives

Introduction

Contributions to Part One of this book discuss a number of issues that culture-inclusive developmental psychology needs to address. In Chapter 1, an example is given of how quantitative and qualitative data derivation strategies can be devised in ways that integrate the culturally structured context of conduct into the process of empirical analysis. However, not only are presently available developmental psychology methodologies limited in their scope of applicability, but the major theoretical perspectives of this discipline bear the birthmarks of Western cultures. In Chapters 2 and 4, authors discuss the limitations of straightforward application of Western psychological theories and practices in Africa and Asia. Chapter 3 presents an analysis of a topic that is perhaps the best single example of Western culture-centrism: many cultures around the world allow, practice, or have practiced one or another form of polygamy, yet very little is known about the conditions for children's development that polygamous marriages create. Almost all the research interests of western psychologists who study family socialization are devoted to the special case of the Western monogamic tradition. Issues of polygamy are discussed at cocktail parties rather than in conference halls, and usually from the basis of Western misperceptions.

Finally, contemporary Western developmental psychology has also been largely dissociated from its own cultural history. This is not surprising, since psychologists have often tried to avoid connections with the "softness" of history in favor of the "hard science" role model of classical physics. In the study of children's development, however, losing track of the history of the cultures within which this discipline has emerged is detrimental: the search for new ideas can become limited to what is available in the common sense of a given culture at a given time, rather than striving towards generalities that would explain more than those phenomena peculiar to the present. In Chapter 5, then, a cultural-historical analysis of childhood discipline is presented. It explores how discipline has always been seen in Western cultural history as a psychological task that involves both behavioral and cognitive components: behavioral means of reward or punishment will work only if they are applied in the context of the child's internalized (or internalizing) understanding of the nature of the disciplinary situation.

Taken together, the contributions to Part One outline the major domains within which a movement towards culture-inclusive developmental psychology could take place: advancement of new empirical methodology; empirical research in non-Western cultures in conjunction with ethnographic knowledge about these cultures; and the use of a cultural-historical perspective in developing new theoretical systems and conducting empirical research.

Chapter 1

Research Strategies in Culture-Inclusive Developmental Psychology

Thomas Kindermann and Jaan Valsiner

INTRODUCTION

The contributions to this volume tackle the need for making developmental psychology "culture-inclusive." This goal can be accomplished in different ways. On the one hand, it is suggested that it can be reached by introducing cultural relativity into the field's theoretical endeavors. The basic understanding that theories of child development are culture-bound can steer psychologists away from the temptations of "cultural imperialism," which often takes the subtle form of exporting the latest fashions of child psychologists from one country or culture to another (see Wilson, this volume).

However, overcoming culture-bound thinking in developmental theory is not enough. Progress in a second direction — that of dealing with the methodology of empirical research — has to be made as well. This type of progress depends heavily on changing the existing meta-theoretical backprocesses of child development. We will also provide an empirical example of how the same observational material — mother-child interaction in the home context on occasions of dressing the child — can be analyzed in two different ways, both of which are context-sensitive in their approach.

One of these approaches is based on the traditions of social learning theories. It derives data about child development and its interactive context in *quantitative* terms. The second, *qualitative* approach entails empirical analyses that preserve the structural nature of the phenomena and can yield information about the change of that structure in development.

Both strategies of empirical analysis make it possible to arrive at explanations of child development that capture relevant aspects of reality. Therefore, both have their place in culture-inclusive developmental research, provided that they are applied in ways that address the interdependence of the phenomena and their contexts.

13

THE NATURE OF CHILD DEVELOPMENT AND ITS SCIENTIFIC STUDY

Developmental psychology is in double jeopardy with respect to its empirical methodology. Not only has it traditionally been culture-exclusive, but it has largely been oriented towards issues of children's psychological *status quo* at any given time, rather than addressing issues of development *per se* (see Benigni & Valsiner, 1985).

A number of implicit methodological issues have guided empirical research on child development. The "scientific methods" of sciences that are not oriented towards the study of development have often been imported into child psychology, with the predictable result that developmental processes remain "hidden behind the data" (Valsiner,1987a). We will outline a number of methodological problems of developmental research, the *solution* of which is necessary for the advancement of culture-inclusive developmental psychology.

THEORY, METHODS, AND REALITY: THE STATUS OF "THE DATA"

Any effort to apply some research methods to the study of reality for the sake of scientific theories requires explication of what is meant by "theory," "method," "apply," and "reality." The notion that methods can be applied involves separating the set of theories from the set of methods into supposedly independent entities. When such separation is assumed, researchers often conclude that there exists almost unlimited freedom to combine methods with reality to produce data.

We intend to show in this chapter that such freedom is largely an intellectual illusion.

It is usual for psychologists to refer to their empirical activities as "collection of data," implying that "the data" are objectively existing entities that somehow can be "collected," and which stand separately from the theoretical presuppositions of their collectors. In contrast, we advocate the position that data are *constructed* — by *deriving* selected generalized knowledge from the phenomena observed, in accordance with the theoretical presuppositions (explicit or implicit) of the researcher. According to this view, researchers actively construct data as they work purposefully within their invented mental reconstructions of reality (i.e., trying to prove, disprove, falsify, or improve the theories through some intervention in the particular aspect of reality that is being studied). The construction of data is an interactive process, determined both by the agent (the scientist) and the object (reality), and depends upon the means that the agent uses to interact with the object (i.e., the methods).

The view that researchers are engaged in construction of representations of their object phenomena is not totally alien to psychology (Gergen, 1982, 1985a, b; Gergen & Gergen, 1984; Harre, 1981; Scarr, 1985; Smedslund, 1978, 1979) or other sciences (Mitroff, 1974; Tweney, Doherty & Mynatt, 1981). However, there have been very few, if any, efforts to analyze the practical implications that the constructivist nature of scientific endeavours should have for a scientific method that would be specifically appropriate for developmental psychology.

In a broad sense, theory determines what kind of evidence should be looked for and what aspects of reality are assumed to be worthwhile. It is in the context of theories that decisions concerning the *kind* of methods to be used are made. Often, these decisions must start from the first basic distinction between two kinds of methods, quantitative and qualitative.

QUANTITATIVE AND QUALITATIVE METHODOLOGIES

The assumption that some aspect of reality (psychological phenomena) is quantitative (or quantifiable), or qualitative, supercedes the construction of matching kinds of methods for studying that aspect. Given this assumption, the application of quantification to psychological phenomena is itself a cultural-historical product (see Cohen, 1982). This becomes evident if we look at the cultural history of theories of probability, which are based on the practical needs of gambling and forecasting of historical or everyday events (Byrne, 1968; Cassedy, 1969, 1984; Rankin, 1966). Everyday language includes idiosyncratically coded possibilities for communicating inexact ideas that refer to quantified reality.

However, even in the case of quantification in science the results of investigations usually are interpreted by a logical process of *disquantification* — making qualitative inference on the basis of quantitative data (Valsiner, 1986). This is well illustrated in the analysis of the logic of inductive inference (cf. Niiniluoto, 1981, 1982; Salmon, 1970). At the most general level, it involves the transition from thinking in straight numerical terms ("76 out of 100 subjects are P") to the use of fuzzy quantifiers with hedges ("very many subjects are P"), to a generic (homogenizing) statement ("The population is P").

This cognitive process discounts the variability that is present in reality. For example, consider a statement about a democratic election — "51% of voters elected X to become Prime Minister." This statement retains the information that 49% voted for other candidates. However, in further discourse that information may be discarded, and the statement transformed into a more general and (ostensibly) qualitative statement: "The people elected X to become Prime Minister." In this transformation, the qualitative generalization, based on quantitative reality acquires connotations that are in fact absent in reality.

In contrast, qualitative research methodology implies an emphasis on the structural organization of phenomena and tries to retain this throughout the process of data derivation. The heritage of Gestalt traditions (e.g., Ash, 1985) is clearly evident in efforts to devise scientific generalities along qualitative lines. However, the process is complicated by the lack of explicit understanding of how to derive general qualitative statements from empirical materials, which include high variability of forms from one case to the next. Despite a few efforts to solve that problem in the history of psychology (see Lewin, 1931), no satisfactory solutions have been reached up to the present time. A solution appears to be particularly complicated in the case of developmental research, which presupposes constant re-organization of qualitative structures of any phenomena that are studied over time.

Both quantitative and qualitative methodologies have their complications when they are applied in the framework of developmental psychology. The developmental perspective leads to the question of how adequately quantitative accounts can reflect the actual processes of development. Few examples exist from other sciences that developmental psychology could use, because the majority of these sciences study non-developmental phenomena. There are exceptions: In some areas of contemporary physics and social sciences (e.g., Prigogine, 1980; Shotter, 1983; Zeleny, 1981), the issue of transition from quantitative fluctuation to novel qualitative structure has been the object of investigation. However, the application of formal models that have been used in contemporary physical analyses to account for emergence of novel structure through quantitative changes requires that the reality of the quantitative dimensions on which the qualitative change is based be realistically demonstrated. This proves difficult (if not impossible) in the case of child development, where psychological phenomena involve transition from one structural state to another under conditions of active participation of the child and its "social others." In other words — the requirement of independent quantitative parameters that may underlie developmental change in structure cannot be granted. Thus, developmental psychology must address the issue of structural change in primarily qualitative terms, while allowing quantitative aspects of these qualities to be of only secondary concern.

Efforts to establish credible qualitative methodologies in psychology usually meet with stubborn opposition from proponents of quantitative methodologies. The everyday discourse of psychologists often flavors the concept of "qualitative methods" with associations that cast doubts on its status as science. This may be caused by equating "scientific" with "quantitative" in our common sense meaning system, further supported by widespread claims in textbooks of statistics. For example, in a popular book, Hayes (1973, p.82) refers to categorical data (the grouping of individual observations into qualitatively different classes) as "measurement at its most primitive level." Some researchers make even stronger claims, blaming the "soft" nature of psychology on those practitioners, such as clinicians, who refuse to follow the teachings of the "hard" methodologists of quantitative persuasion (Eysenck, 1985, p.112).

The controversy between quantitative and qualitative methodological perspectives will not be resolved by persuasion or by the establishment of consensus among scientists. Instead of arguing endlessly about the possibility or impossibility of scientifically viable qualitative approaches, a more relativistic stance may be useful, which examines *the fit between the perceivable organization of the object of investigation and the investigator's theoretical system.* Thus, if some phenomenon is organized in an unstructured (and, therefore quantifiable) form, a quantitative study of is "scientific." Efforts to explain such phenomena in qualitative terms would be "non-scientific" *on the grounds that the explanatory system does not fit the phenomenon.*

Likewise, a quantified approach to the study of a phenomenon that is organized as a complex qualitative structural form is "non-scientific" on similar grounds: Again, there exists a misfit between the organization of the phenomenon and the investigator's theoretical system. Thus, a refusal to measure simple reaction time quantitatively when the goal of an investigation is intimately connected with the concept of reaction time would amount to what is pejoratively denoted as soft science. However, the highly quantitative and standardized tradition of measuring "intelligence" by intelligence tests is equally "soft," since intelligence is a structured phenomenon that is reflected in person-environment interactions rather than in any aggregated result of answers to a test. This feature of intelligence provides "hard science" credibility to the non-standardized, "clinical" investigations of children's cognitive development for which Jean Piaget and Lev Vygotsky are well known. In fact, efforts to standardize or quantify Vygotsky's and Piaget's methods do not add to their scientific value.

Difficulties with the qualitative approaches start with the loose and multiple uses of the term. In psychology, the term "qualitative" often seems to involve anything from humanistic descriptions of moral-emotional turmoil in one's friends, or what is apologetically called "anecdotal evidence," up to Piaget's logical-structural analyses. Furthermore, the term "qualitative data" is used synonymously with the term categorical data, implying a low measurement level (cf. the quote from Hayes, 1973, above) in the quantitative hierarchy of statistics. Even more, quantification-based statistical methods are sometimes employed in order to extract so-called qualitative structures from quantitative data (see Cairns, 1986). Factor analysis, for example, uses the variance-covariance relationships between different measures to extract more or less independent factorial structures. It is important to point out that any "qualitative" structure derived from quantitatively constructed data *characterizes only those data, and not the phe-nomenon from which the data were derived.* Thus, a factor-analytic "structure" of intelligence, based on the statistical analysis of IQ test scores, is a structure of these scores (distributed in the given sample of subjects), and not of the actual cognitive processes that each of the subjects used while responding to the items on the test.

QUALITATIVE STRUCTURE OF PHENOMENA: UNITS OF ANALYSIS

From our perspective, theorizing in psychology over the last century has been going in circles. The contributions of Gestalt psychology seem to be largely forgotten in contemporary psychology. However, in a continuation of its traditions, we suggest a return to the concept of *structure* as the basis for defining the qualitative method in psychology. We propose to include in the class of qualitative approaches the theoretical perspectives aimed at constructing abstract models of the *structure* of the psychological *processes* through logical structures (e.g., Piaget), dialectical processes (e.g., Vygotsky), temporal unfolding of events in problem-solving (e.g., research traditions of Simon, Wertheimer, and Duncker), or using analogies with computer programs (e.g., syntactic pattern recognition in artificial intelligence).

The structural emphasis in the definition of the qualitative method leads to two questions: What is the unit of analysis implied in psychological theories, and what should it be be if we apply methods to phenomena in trying to model reality?

The question of psychological units is an old problem, extensively addressed in the first quarter of this century, and is closely related to efforts to differentiate qualitative from quantitative perspectives on phenomena. Koehler (1925, 1971; see also Basov, 1929; Vygotsky, 1960; for a comparison see Chapter V in Valsiner, 1987b) introduced the separation between *real* and *differential* elements of a structure. Real elements are units that are naturally existing and limited by natural forces (e.g., atomic components of water). In contrast, differential elements are products of quantitative minimization of a given phenomenon (e.g., very small water drops); these are rather arbitrarily formed, limited only by the technical inability to separate them further. Only the real or "objective" units can form structures with qualitatively new properties. Differential elements are "minimal wholes," containing the same characteristics as the whole structure.

When we examine psychological theories, both of these different realms can be distinguished. Some theories are based on dimensions and continua, as in personality psychology and intelligence research. They rely on artificially separated elements (e.g., test items) that are summed so as to result in an individual score. On the other hand, there are theories that rely on the postulate of real elements that form different structures or "gestalts," and do not allow summative treatment at all (e.g., Piaget). The idea of a continuum is rendered inapplicable in this framework. The whole structure is not equal to the sum of its parts; linearity in the composition of structures is assumed to be not possible; and different structures are not comparable with one another.

This reminiscence from Gestalt psychology is especially relevant for a developmental framework. In developmental psychology, it is necessary to view target phenomena in terms of reorganization of real elements and not as an increase or decrease of differential ones. According to these notions, the complex nature of open systems makes non-linearity the rule and linearity a rare exception. Therefore, development cannot be conceived as a process of moving inside a continuum but as a dialectical interchange between parts of the developing organism on the one hand, and conditions of the environment on the other. Instead of movement on a continuum, of concepts of increase or decrease, developmental reality is characterized by *transformations of the structural relationship of organisms and their environment.* Hence, we would argue that a qualitative developmental perspective employs a *process orientation,* and that a description of the qualitative structure of a developmental process is an explanation of outcomes stemming from that process.

DERIVATION OF DATA: THE EXAMPLE OF A SKULL

What we have discussed thus far points to the simple rule that *all data are constructed (derived) on the basis of phenomena in accordance with the investigator's theoretical inclinations.* As an illustration, let us consider the example of a paleoanthropologist who finds a skull. The skull is obviously not a "datum" in its contemporary sense. It is a fossil object, a crystallized phenomenon, comparable to videotapes or behavior transcripts that can be analyzed in different ways. Actions of the investigator construct "data" on the basis of both the characteristics of the object and the investigator's own ways of thinking — that is, application of methods to the phenomenon is the process by which the data are constructed, and these will depend on the interests and theoretical perspectives of the researcher.

Thus, qualitative comparisons based on anatomical shape may be employed in order to determine the skull's potential position in biological taxonomies/evolution, i.e., its relation to skulls of other species. In a different vein, detailed quantitative (anthropometric) measurement strategies can be employed in order to determine age and physical appearance of the individual at the time of its death and the extent of similarity to other skulls of the same species. However, it is usually the case that combining both qualitative and quantitative strategies is essential. For instance, even in dating the historical period to which the skull belonged, different methods can be employed in order to create a data base. These may be chemical (quantitative) or geochronological (e.g., qualitative — using the surrounding ecology of the finding as time-reference).

In fact, our hypothetical example of the study of an excavated skull has real-life background behind it, if we peep into the history of anthropology: History of physical anthropology shows that very different conclusions have been drawn by researchers with various theoretical backgrounds from the same object of study. At the turn of the century, paleoanthropologists had constructed a data base showing that *Homo neandertalensis* obviously belonged to a different species than *Homo sapiens* (Boule 1913; Smith, 1924). Based on taxonomical backgrounds, their anatomical and anthropometrical comparisons showed incompatible differences between that skull and those of our species. However, based on

knowledge of intra-individual development and pathology (Cave & Straus, 1957; Wolpoff, 1971, Reader, 1981), *H. neandertalensis* now is believed to belong to our species (although representing an extinct sub-type). This is based on a theory that differences in the shape of Neanderthal bones can be reconstructed as a result of severe arthritis, rather than reflecting substantive qualitative interspecies differences.

When investigators presuppose that all qualitatively different specimens in a class of phenomena differ from one another on the basis of only quantitative parameters, they superimpose a quantitative framework upon the phenomena, so that all qualitative differences are reduced to some combination of quantitative variables. If, on the other hand, they consider every specimen to be qualitatively unique, the consideration of quantitative differences is eliminated from the constructed data. These two strategies of data construction can be observed in the anatomical (qualitative) and anthropometric (quantitative) approaches to the study of the class membership (human versus non-human) of an excavated skull.

IMPLICATIONS OF THE DEVELOPMENTAL VIEW: PAST, PRESENT, AND FUTURE

Development is a complicated process. It could be said that one's future-oriented actions at any given time canalize development in some direction so as to preemptively prepare one to act in specific ways in future encounters with the environment. In contrast to the past-oriented ethos in psychology, which emphasizes the direct (mirror image) role of early experience in later life, we posit that one's immediate experience at a given time provides feed-forward signals that act as canalization aids (via memory) towards different future life courses.

The distinction of the PAST→ PRESENT and PRESENT→FUTURE linkages of human action-in-development may seem at first to be two semantic ways of expressing the issue of the accumulative life history of individuals. After all, what is PRESENT at a certain time becomes PAST the next time moment, and what was previously FUTURE becomes PRESENT. However, there is a substantial difference. The FUTURE at *any* moment cannot be observed in its exact form, since that form does not yet exist, and will come into existence as the PRESENT through the individual's active construction processes. In contrast, the PAST can be described, by way of its recollection in the PRESENT. This recollection includes partial retrieval of information *in accordance with the retrieval demands of the PRESENT, and in conjunction with the perspective on the FUTURE as it is contemplated at PRESENT.* That means that the retrospective account of one's personal life course is integrated into the PRESENT-to-FUTURE oriented actions of the person at any given time. The *prospective* perspective includes the *retrospective* one as the information base for further development. In this sense, one's past history and future development (or "would-be" or "could-be" history) cannot be separated.

In contrast, the purely PAST→ PRESENT perspective (e.g., the evolutionary theory in biology) separates the retrospective and prospective aspects of development and treats the former as the explanation basis of the PRESENT outcomes, not considering that the PRES-ENT outcomes are perhaps a means to some events in the FUTURE. Thus, the PAST→PRESENT and PRESENT → FUTURE perspectives are not just equivalent versions of some developmental process flowing according to its own course and independently of the organism's active influence. Both perspectives would be equivalent only if development were conceptualized as a predetermined and environment-independent unfolding of the organism's life course where the organism cannot actively participate in that unfolding. *As soon as we assume that the organism has some active input to its own development, the two perspectives cease to be equivalent descriptions of the process of development.* This specific feature of developmental phenomena was well captured by James Mark Baldwin (1906) in his second basic postulate of developmental sciences:

..that series of events only is truly genetic which cannot be constructed before it has happened, and which cannot be exhausted by reading backwards after it has happened (p. 21).

Thus, any reconstruction of the PAST → PRESENT connection can be seen to be in service of some PRESENT→FUTURE goal-oriented connection, and hence would not exhaust the explanation of the previous life course.

STUDY OF DEVELOPMENT AND THE "SACRED COW" OF REPLICABILITY

The temporal uncertainty involved in development along the line of past, present, and future connections leads to the necessity of rethinking a basic canon of empirical science — that of replicability of findings — for developmental research. Replicability is one of the basic axioms of psychological research; although highly cherished, it is rarely achieved. However, the greater the difficulties in replication of findings, the more actively do psychologists defend the *principle* that replicability is crucial. In this sense, replicability is the "sacred cow" of the psychologist's culture — it wanders around on the landscape of empirical psychology and is honored by the inhabitants, who do not permit it to be modified lest the sacrosanct nature of science be violated. However, it is often the case that psychologists do not make explicit what is meant by replicability in their discipline.

The issue of replicability of empirical research results is perhaps one of the most complicated that developmental psychology has to face. Borrowing from the non-developmental traditions of physics and psychology, developmental psychology has overlooked a basic paradox: *Replicability of particular empirical outcomes over time is possible only if there is no development, i.e., if the phenomenon remains the same over time. However, if we expect that the phenomena that we study undergo development along multiple possible trajectories, replicability in the traditional sense cannot be achieved.*

This paradox emerges only when development is the target of investigation. In classical physics and traditional psychology, which share a disinterest in developmental phenomena, it could not occur. In concrete terms, if an investigator in one laboratory devises an experiment to look at a certain non-developmental problem, that experiment is ex-

pected to be replicable by other investigators in different laboratories, provided the procedure is well described and conditions in each replication well controlled. Failure to replicate the findings would undermine the scientific credibility of the data of the original experiment, and the generalizations that were linked to those data.

The situation is very different when we look at developmental phenomena. Development is inherent in systems (organisms) that are intertwined with their environments. Developing organisms are *open* systems; that is, selected aspects of their organization are not strictly pre-programmed, but are left to be formed in the organism-environment interaction (this even occurs at the biochemical level — see Stent, 1985). The same result can be obtained by development along different pathways; likewise, development along similar lines may lead to different outcomes.

In other words, the classical emphasis on replicability of outcomes may be inappropriate for developmental psychology. Instead, what our methods may attempt to replicate is the *work of the same underlying process mechanism which may lead to variable outcomes from one trial to the next* (see Gould, 1986, for a discussion of similar necessities in biology; Blurton-Jones & Woodson, 1979, for a discussion of reliability and validity in psychological observations).

Replicability in developmental research may thus be based on various and discordant findings of empirical studies of organisms. Consider, for instance, a hypothetical developmental process that involves transformation of a "beginning" state of a structure into an "end" state, via different possible pathways and with the disintegration of the beginning state in

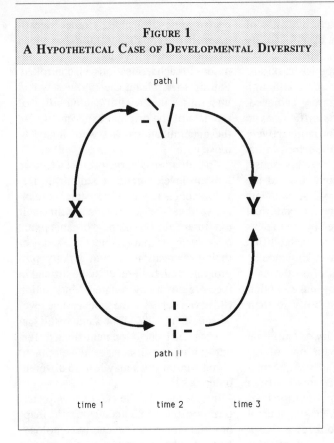

FIGURE 1
A HYPOTHETICAL CASE OF DEVELOPMENTAL DIVERSITY

path I

X

Y

path II

time 1   time 2   time 3

tion from X to Y can proceed along either Path I or Path II, but there is no information available that would predict which path will be followed in any particular case. Furthermore, investigators looking at the development of Y out of X start from having no knowledge about the presence of more than one developmental path. Finally, the exhaustiveness of any set of paths in the transition is never guaranteed: The investigators are in no position to know, even after realizing that Paths I and II exist, that these two constitute the set of all possible paths between X and Y.

Let us now analyze the ways in which replicability of empirical research can be applied to this hypothetical case. As far as the non-developmental side of the study is concerned, different investigators would have little trouble replicating one another's findings at times 1 and 3, i.e., at times where the disintegration of the structure (X) has not yet started, or when the development of Y has already ended. All specimens would provide them with "replicated" findings of Xs or Ys. However, if they choose to look at the phenomena *developmentally*, comparing their transition from time 1 to time 2, they would be faced with discrepant findings. On some occasions X becomes a bunch of linear parts; on others, point-like elements. One

the process of development. A schematic description of such a case is given in Figure 1.

As shown here, a structure (X) can develop into a new structure (Y) through two different paths (I and II), both of which involve the full disintegration of X prior to its reintegration as Y. The two paths, however, differ in the particular form that the intermediate "material" for the development of the new structure takes. In the case of Path I, the original X becomes Y via the emergence of linear parts of X, from which Y is subsequently built. In the case of Path II, X disintegrates into elements, which later become united into Y. Different cases of transi-

researcher may see changes along Path I more frequently than along Path II; another may observe the opposite. If these two investigators assume unilinearity of development, and agree on the rule of generalization that "the most frequently observed case is the modal case," then their generalizations set the two paths up against each other as "the" way in which X develops into Y. The investigators, disagreeing on the "normal" developmental trajectory, can subsequently become involved in lengthy discussions to prove their cases. What may surface as "failure to replicate" in such research may actually be an indication of multilinearity of the development, where both paths can be equally normal.

This description of a hypothetical development of Y out of X remains rather formal, since it stays at the level of the observable phenomena, viewed in transition. It does not address the issue of the *processes* that lead to such multilinear pictures of development. Such processes can generate a multitude of various observable phenomena, many of which have little in common when observed at any single time. The particular outcomes generated by these processes may depend strongly on the given conditions, which in their turn change.

As a result, the same (context-bound) process generates a vast variety of outcomes (e.g., see Jerne, 1985). If only some of these outcomes are taken by researchers to verify the presence of the assumed process, then the presence of the other outcomes (generated by the same process, but under new conditions) can easily be labelled a "failure to replicate" the effect of that process. Since in the case of development, processes are open to generating novel outcomes, the "replication failure" at the level of out-comes need not necessarily imply the absence of the work of the underlying processes. There exists, however, no inferential thought system that is capable of capturing the replicability of the effects of processes in the hide-and-seek game that the outcomes of those processes play with the investigators of development.

Perhaps a simple example of a failure to replicate an empirical finding will clarify this complicated issue. In a study of child-environment relationships in natural home conditions, the second author tested the proposition that parents selectively limit toddlers' access to some aspects of their environments. Parents were asked a direct question about which objects their child was not allowed to play with. The majority of the respondents had no difficulty mentioning some items — in this sense, the proposition was found to be true, and replicated across the majority of cases. One parent, however, denied the existence of anything in the environment that her child was not allowed to play with. Taken at face value, her case could be seen as a failure to replicate the proposition. That divergent subject, however, added on her own initiative: "...because we have taken everything of that kind away." Thus, the preemptive solution to the child's "access problem" resulted in negation of the proposition of "limitation of access" — but it did not constitute a "replication failure." In developmental research, past events may lead to observable phenomena in the present that differ from other cases (which have different past histories). It is because of the *normal* diversity in the developmental trajectories of organisms that the canon of replicability needs to be adjusted to the nature of developmental phenomena.

SUMMARY: DEVELOPMENTAL THEORIES AND STRATEGIES FOR EMPIRICAL RESEARCH

We have briefly outlined the complications embedded in research methodology that any context-bound emphasis on developmental research has to face. First, the empirical data are derived (not collected) entities, and are constructed by the investigator on the basis of his or her theory and in accordance with the empirical phenomenon under study. Second, we have argued that the label "scientific" is applicable only in cases in which data are derived from a phenomenon without losing the quality of the latter. This requirement brought us to the third point — in developmental psychology, *because of the qualitative (structural) nature of most of the phenomena studied,* qualitative (structural) data derivation strategies fit the criterion of "science" more often than quantitative traditions. The latter may of course be appropriate, as our empirical examples will demonstrate, but only if the particular theory upon which an investigator's work is based makes quantification feasible.

Fourth, the emphasis on the qualitative nature of developmental phenomena led us to the issue of units of analysis. Unlike non-developmental psychologists, researchers in the field of developmental psychology need to study the process of transformation of the structural relationship of the person and the environment. The latter is made meaningful by one's culture from the very moment of birth. Children become related with the environment, and assimilate culture as their relations with that environment are transformed into novel states. The emphasis on transformation brought the fifth issue into focus — the relationship between

the past, present, and future, from the perspective of the developing individual. Finally, the irreversibility of time in development led us to call for a reformulation of what "replicability" means in developmental research. We argued in favor of replicability of evidence that a certain developmental process is at work, even if the empirical phenomena generated by the process are vastly diverse.

The rest of this chapter is meant to provide an illustration of how empirical research in culture-inclusive developmental psychology can proceed. We will analyze the same observed episodes of parent-child interaction (everyday dressing situations) from two perspectives, both of which are examples of context-inclusive developmental research. One strategy uses quantitative aggregation of behavioral data along the lines of social learning theories. Here, the parent's responsiveness to the child's behavior becomes the context for the child's development, and the physical environment of the ongoing interaction is not considered. In a sense, however, the parent's responsiveness *is* one aspect of cultural context, and therefore our example of how developmental "macroprocesses" can be studied in quantitative ways is informative. The second strategy entails an analysis of the parent's goal-directed actions in the context of particular conditions under which interactions take place. This involves more particularistic analysis of the ongoing sequence of behavioral phenomena, and no quantification and aggregation of data over particular episodes is involved. Both strategies fit the general goals of culture-inclusive developmental research, albeit differently — depending on the particular theoretical frameworks used in the data derivation process.

EMPIRICAL EXAMPLES: TWO WAYS OF LOOKING AT MOTHER-TODDLER JOINT ACTION WHILE DRESSING

The present study was based on a social learning paradigm which was developed to examine elderly people's interactions with social partners in institutions (Baltes, Kindermann & Reisenzein, 1986; Baltes, Reisenzein, & Kindermann, 1985; Baltes & Reisenzein 1986). The theoretical issues involved the link between people's independent and dependent actions, and the support (or lack of it) from their social environments. A quantitative data derivation process was appropriate in this theoretical framework. In the present study, this approach was adapted for use with mother-child interactions. As we intend to demonstrate here, a quantified analysis of the transaction process requires the construction of data that fit the traditions of the social learning paradigm. (The results of this study are presented in greater detail elsewhere; see Kindermann, 1985, 1986; Kindermann & Skinner, in press).

Subjects and Method

Six children, two each at the ages of 9, 12, and 21 months, were videotaped interacting with their mothers in their natural home setting over a period of about 100 days. One of the 9- and one of the 12-month-old children were girls; the 9-month-old had a sibling over four years of age. Both 21-month-old children were boys and had siblings older than four.

The age groups were selected to represent different developmental points in the process of learning to dress: Starting at 21 months of age, children are ex-pected to show marked success in learning to dress themselves. Younger children were included to provide information about the period before learning had started.

Mother-child interactions were videotaped continuously for a one-hour period during times that the mothers had previously reported high probability of body-care and dressing (e.g., in the morning, evening, or after a nap). Each dyad was observed eight times. Adjacent observation days were paired to form four measurement points. The first two measurement points were separated by about one week, between the second and third measurement point was a two-month interval, and the last two measurement points were separated by about two weeks. At each point in time, mothers were additionally asked about their perceptions of and expectations for their children's development.

Observations from the study are here analyzed from two perspectives. Perspective 1 entails a quantitative analysis of the structure of the child-adult relationship and its change over time. Here, the child's behavior is treated as the object of investigation, and its relationship with parental behavior (as the context for child's behavior) is investigated. This perspective illustrates one possible way of making observational research on child-adult interaction context-inclusive: It is the relatedness of the object phenomenon and its social context that is under investigation. Data are derived in accordance with such distribution of the roles of context and the object. This perspective makes it appropriate to aggregate data over the time dimension, and to discount the remainder of the situation in which the mother and child interact (e.g., the material environment of the interactions).

In contrast, Perspective 2 treats these material and cultural conditions of mother-child joint action as context, and views the ongoing step-by-step action as the object of investigation. Aggregation of such qualitative data over the time of observation becomes theoretically inappropriate, whereas the consistency of the *process structure* of the joint action from one setting to another is of high relevance. On the following pages we illustrate the ways in which empirical data are derived from observations for the purposes of these two perspectives.

Perspective 1. A Learning-Theoretic Context-Inclusive Analysis

The quantitative procedure of data derivation. Videotapes were subjected to a molar level accumulative analysis of the mothers' and children's behaviors during the dressing occasions. The videotapes were coded by trained observers using a system based on that employed in the studies with elderly people (cf. Baltes & Reisenzein, 1986; Baltes, Kindermann & Reisenzein, 1986; Barton, Baltes, & Orzech, 1980). The system is exhaustive and contains 12 mutually exclusive categories for open observable behavior, six for children and six for mothers. Out of these 12, four categories were used: "independent" and "dependent" behaviors for children, and "independence supportive" and "dependence supportive" behaviors for mothers.

Coding of the videotapes proceeded in the course of natural occurences of behavioral events. Simultaneously, a marker was added to each coded behavior, indicating whether or not it belonged to body-care and dressing routines. In a later step, all behaviors that were not directly related to dressing routines were excluded

from further consideration. Thus, out of nearly 24,000 behaviors coded, the analysis of dresssing occasions included about 5,500 events.

The results are described in two parts. First, behavior *frequencies* are examined, both the relative amount of behavior observed in the four categories during dressing occasions, and changes in the frequencies of these behaviors over time. As expected, no changes were seen for the children who were not learning to dress, namely the ones that were 9 and 12 month old at the beginning of observations. Also, as expected, their behavior frequencies matched the starting distributions of the children who were 21 months old in the beginning of the study. Both independent (child) and independence supportive (mother) behaviors were relatively infrequent, whereas both dependent (child) and dependence supportive (mother) behaviors were very frequent. Only among the 21-month old children did these latter frequencies decline over time. In addition, for this group only, initially rare independent (child) and independence supportive (mother) behaviors increased over time. In other words, at age 21 months and afterwards, the respective predominance of behaviors changed.

The examination of relative frequencies (and their changes over time) can be called an enumerative strategy of data construction. It may be doubtful that it comes close to the reality of developmental processes. In fact, its correspondence even to learning theory is limited — their only link seems to be the concept of "behavior." The observer is tempted to interpret these data according to a learning-theory scheme: Independent behaviors must increase because they are obviously reinforced more often, and dependent behaviors decrease because they are increasingly less reinforced.

However, this straightforward interpretive scheme may not be adequate and may be deficient both in terms of precision and in terms of suitability for learning-theoretical interpretations. As Gewirtz (1969) and Sears (1972) have pointed out, a learning-theoretical reconstruction of interaction requires identification of the *interactional details* in terms of antecedent-consequent relationships. This amounts to the identification of the temporal contingency structure of the interactions. Thus, the mother's behavioral reactions to the child's behaviors are considered to represent the social context of the developmental process.

Given the need to study the temporal structure of the interaction process, the second part of quantitative data derivation involved the analysis of the *contingency structure* of mother-child interactions and its change over the time of the study. This analysis represents transitions from the child's behavior to the mother's behavior in the flow of natural interactions. Conditional probabilities were computed for determining the likelihood of behavior sequences (Lag-Sequential Analysis — Bakeman, 1978; Sackett, Holm, Crowley, & Henkins, 1979). Four behavior sequences were of special interest:

1. In the instances when the child acted in an independent fashion, how likely is the mother to react in:

1.1. an independence supportive way, or
1.2. a dependence supportive way.

2. Following the child's dependent behavior, how likely is the mother to react in:

2.1. a dependence supportive way, or
2.2. an independence supportive way.

Data-analytic strategies that use conditional probabilities can be regarded as one quantitative way to help identify structures (e.g., reinforcement schedules) in the behavioral flow. In the present study, our analysis showed (see Figure 2), that for the 9-13- and 12-16-month-old children, their (frequent) dependent behaviors were consistently followed by their mothers' dependence supportive behavior, and their (infrequent) independent behaviors were also followed by this maternal behavior, but somewhat less consistently. However, independence-supportive maternal behavior was not contingent upon either independent or dependent behavior of the children. This pattern of the mothers' consistent dependence-supportive contingencies for both child behavior classes might be described as a "nurturant" interaction pattern.

However, the 21-25-month-old children experienced this contingency pattern only at the first two measurement points. After 22 months of age, there was a marked decline in maternal dependence supportiveness following the child's independent behavior, and a minor decline following dependent behavior. Parallel to this, there was a steady increase of maternal independence supportiveness following the child's independent behavior. Thus, a pattern evolved in which the child's dependent and independent behaviors were followed by the mother's corresponding supportive behavior: Independent behavior met with independence supportive maternal behaviors, and dependent behavior with dependence-supportive ones.

FIGURE 2
EARLY PATTERN OF MOTHERS' PREDOMINANT DEPENDENCE SUPPORTIVENESS CONTINGENCIES IN INTERACTIONS WITH YOUNGER CHILDREN (POOLED DATA) AND CHANGES TO MORE RECIPROCAL PATTERNS IN THE LEARNING PHASE OF DRESSING

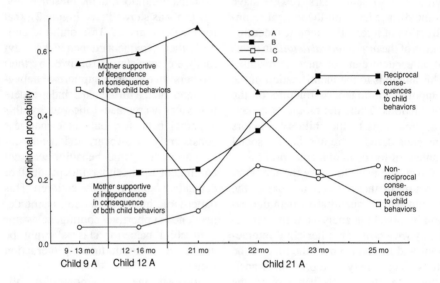

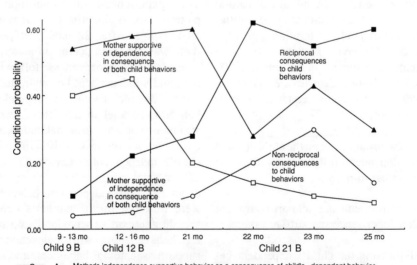

Taken together, these changes may represent a transition from a nurturant towards a more reciprocal and congruent interaction pattern. Additional information from interviews with mothers revealed that they recognized when their children were beginning to learn how to dress themselves, and wanted to arrange opportunities for them to be able to attempt the task alone.

Discussion of quantitative results. What do these results imply for the issues addressed here? First, regarding the criterion of the fit of quantitative strategies to both theory and reality, we want to highlight the qualitative aspects that are inherent in this particular quantitative approach.

Behaviors — defined as single events in the interactional flow of each partner — serve as the units of analysis. Moreover, by using a single-subject approach, potential inter-individual differences can be taken into account. By narrowing down the target of observations to the domain of a clearly defined task, it is expected that the learning schedules will be revealed more clearly. These qualitative differentiations are emphasized in learning theory, especially in the case of dependent behaviors. Sears (1972), for example, pointed out that "...further use of the term 'dependency' as a higher level construct seems unwise" (p.8), and thus argued for a more specific approach.

From a learning theoretical perspective, further differentiations in the definition of behaviors are not considered important. Not included, for example, are inferences about unobservable properties of behaviors (such as warmth or emotional tone); these are considered irrelevant and are ignored. Even descriptions of the material ecology of dressing (e.g., the kinds of clothes involved) are regarded as not important. Instead, every action is assumed to belong to a class of behavior (i.e., "dependent" or "independent"), wherein all elements are assumed to contain the very same properties. Within each of the classes, every behavior is regarded as identical to every other.

In regard to developmental processes, the goal of a learning-theoretical reconstruction requires a further differentiation concerning the structure of the interactions — namely, the temporal contingency of maternal behaviors in response to child behaviors. In this strategy of analysis, the mother's actions are practically differentiated according to the child's behaviors that precede them; and child behaviors are regarded as functionally different, depending on which maternal behaviors respond to them at a given point in development. This strategy is again based on a quantitative approach, but at the same time is aimed at identifying structural characteristics of the interactions.

Through analyses of contingency patterns, the development of learning to dress can be described more precisely than on the basis of behavior frequencies. Dependence supportiveness of the mothers was seen to be indiscriminate prior to the onset of the learning task. However, as soon as mothers realize that their children are beginning to learn, a reciprocal interaction pattern emerges in which the child's independent behavior is followed by the mother's independence supportive reaction, and the child's dependent behavior is followed by her dependence supportive reaction. The interactional style thus changes from a mother-controlled dependence supportive pattern, towards a supportive pattern that is selectively contingent upon the nature of the child's behavior.

Perspective 2: Joint Action Within its Environment as "Context"

As described, the results involving behavioral frequencies fit the general ontogenetic picture of children's learning. However, they provide a rather misleading picture of the actual interaction process. For instance, one might hasten to conclude that the child's accomplishment is *produced* by the mother's decrease of dependent and increase of independent supportive behavior. Conditional probability analyses show that this is not the case. Both classes of child behavior are subject to consistent corresponding support in the learning phase, and this new structure of interaction emerges in congruence with the mothers' expectations and goals.

What about the fit between the method and developmental reality? First, the method of using conditional probabilities in assessing the interactional ecology is well suited to behavioral theory. Second, the question about the fit between behavioral theory and reality — that is, whether behaviors are real elements of interactions, whether they are the only real elements, or whether they are just artifically minimized differential ones — is not one we want to give an answer to. This might be more a matter of theoretical beliefs. Actually, one of the sharpest rivals, action theory, claims that behavior is not the only "real element," but that goals of individuals and cultural meanings assigned to behavior are necessary ingredients too. Behaviorists, on the other hand, claim that it is not goals or meaning but functionality that rules learning and maintenance of behavior. Furthermore, developmentalists share the belief that goals and understanding of cultural meanings (as well as functional proper-

ties) change over time. Thus, the tracing of interaction patterns over time that consist of the very same elements leads to a narrow representation of reality.

Given the fit between behavioral theory and the method used, what could be concluded about the fit between the method and reality? It is obvious that construction of mere frequency data gives a very incomplete picture of reality. In terms of the interactional reality, it is essentially necessary to account for the structure in the behavioral flow of the interactants. Mathematically, all relative frequencies (treated as probabilities) are conditional. They are determined by the restrictions imposed, the current environmental conditions, or the specific subjects. The present approach adds further qualifying markers into the interactional flow as additional conditions for the interacting individuals, developmental levels, and task domains.

Furthermore, an important aspect of children's learning to dress themselves cannot be addressed in this approach. Children do get dressed every day, regardless of which behaviors they show, and irrespective of how their mothers manage the interactions. All of these interactions lead to the same result. What is purposefully left out of consideration when the quantitative approach is used is the *composition* of the joint action process as it occurs in different particular forms every day.

The temporal structure of the composition of joint action can take many forms, even when the material ecology (e.g., the setting and the articles of clothing involved) remains the same from one occasion to another. For instance, in the morning the mother may be in a hurry, and as a result the child is given little opportunity to protest against having a shirt put on. However, in the evening she may be less pressured and the child may have multiple opportunities to resist being dressed in the same shirt.

The uniqueness of every particular interaction in the context of dressing tasks leads to the necessity of finding the basic temporal structure that can be seen as a general representation of the interaction process within its context. Components of the process structure — the interactive behaviors of both child and adult, and the environmental structures where the interaction takes place — are treated as *structurally* (rather than probabilistically) linked with one another. The nature of these linkages is examined through qualitative analyses that complement the quantitative study of children's learning in the course of joint action.

Goal-directedness and equifinality in adult-child joint action. When considering the temporal organization of joint action, we have to acknowledge that situations are constructed by individuals with certain goals and that these goals often change over a very short time frame. For example, the mother's initial goal (i.e., to get the child dressed) may change into another (e.g., enjoy playing "catch me" with the child). After a while, she returns to the initial, dressing-goal. Thus, at every moment, her goal-structure can include multiple intentions, each of which can change at the next moment.

Furthermore, beyond variability of the goal structure, we have to assume that the very same goals can be attained by different means. This assumption follows the lead of the principle of equifinality in biology (Bertalanffy, 1981). There is great variability in the process of how joint action process leads to the same end result (e.g., child is dressed).

Both characteristics — change of goal structure and equifinality — result in a feature of flexibility in the situation constructed by either partner. Additionally, there is the fact of evolution of the problem itself and development of the persons dealing with it over time. With humans, the open systems involved develop as self-regulated, as we construct our goals, attempt to attain these by different means, reconstruct the goals if their attainment is not possible, and — participate in our own development as a result.

From the mother's side this leads to a situation of very complex problem solving. She keeps various concurrent goals in mind, and is actively involved in the child's developing understanding of the "script" of how to get dressed. This multiplicity of goals in her action plan may be arranged along an imaginary time axis, including her view of her child's past, present state, and future ideals of behavior. It is important to realize that our observational material allows us to describe the sequence of behavioral actions integrated in the act of dressing, in which the mother's goal system involving these different time-frames are hidden.

Thus, the dressing event may be triggered by an immediate environmentally-tied need (e.g., the room temperature is too cold for the child to run around naked, or the presence of another adult — the observer — may set up pressure to get the child dressed). However, as soon as the beginning of the event is triggered due to the mother's cognitive decision regarding the immediate goal of getting the child dressed, she may construct additional (complementary) goals to be pursued in the process. For example, she may set up the goal of *teaching the child*

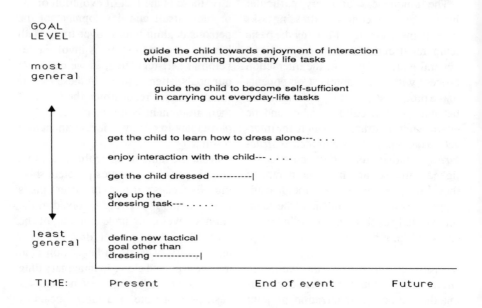

how to dress him -or herself. In this case, we can expect to observe actions on her part that may actually slow down the process of reaching the immediate goal, getting the child dressed, but which are expected to provide an experience that the mother judges to be within the child's "Zone of Proximal Development" (cf. Vygotsky, 1956, 1960). Spending some time getting the child into a given item of clothing may serve the goal of teaching the child how to manage this particular function in the future: i.e., it relates to accomplishments that are expected to take place later. Thus, we observe that the mother takes more time than is necessary to just get the child dressed, by explaining what to do, and giving time for the child to act on its own. The exact age by which the mother expects the child to be able to do this may be unspecifiable (although in many cultures for many tasks this is determined by folk beliefs — cf. Harkness & Super, 1983).

Some other goals may also be integrated into the dressing event. For example, the mother may use the additional immediate goal of *enjoying interactions* in the course of dressing the child. We can then observe mother-toddler play at some points in the temporal structure of the event. Even more, she may relate the *immediate* enjoyment goal with the general goal of preparing the child for enjoyment of various aspects of life (e.g., "socialization for fun").

All these and possible other goals make up the mother's *goal-structure,* in which several different goals are interrelated both across levels of generality (synchronically) and time of expected attainment (diachronically). Figure 3 represents an example of a goal structure at a certain time moment — the beginning of a hypothetical dressing event.

Consideration of the mother's goal structure is important for two general reasons. First, it illustrates that she deals with multiple-criterion problem-solving in joint action with the child on tasks as seemingly simple as dressing. Second, it illustrates the *teleogenetic* nature of her cognitive planning — once she and the child enter into the event of dressing, she sets up both immediate *and* more long-term goals to be pursued in the course of that event. Thus, she is both *goal-oriented and goal-constructing*, as the abstract characteristics of the psychological phenomena outlined above illustrate.

The next important stipulation stems from the *goal-reconstructive* nature of both the mother's and child's psychological functioning: The partners not only construct their goal structures at the beginning of an event, *but also rearrange these structures in the course of the event.* For instance, the mother can abandon the goal of teaching if the child refuses to be taught, or if she is too rushed. She can also add new goals which hold subordi-

TABLE 1
INTERACTIONAL TRANSCRIPT SHOWING MOTHER'S EFFORT OF DIRECTING CHILD'S ATTENTION TOWARDS TASK-COMPATIBLE OBJECTS

Child has been undressed in the bathroom, during which time he has shown interest in a tube of cream. Mother has removed it in order to give him a bath.

Mother: Asks the child to get out of the bathtub to be dried
Child: Climbs out.
Mother: Covers child with a towel and carries him over to another room. She takes the tube with her.
Both: Engage in social/verbal play.
Mother: Puts child on the back on the bed and starts to dry him.
Child: Complains.
Mother: Hands the tube to child.
Child: Takes it and plays with it while mother dries and dresses him.
BOTH: Are engaged in playful interaction.
Mother: Takes shirt and pulls it over child's head.
Child: Takes tube in both hands.
Mother: Takes child's first arm.
Child: Changes tube to second hand.
Mother: Pulls first arm into sleeve.
Child: Takes tube in both hands again.
Mother: Takes second arm.
Child: Changes tube to first hand.
Mother: Pulls second arm into sleeve.

nate positions in the goal structure: For instance, in order to reach the immediate goal of getting the child dressed, she may provide a plaything that redirects his or her attention for the time necessary for the mother to accomplish the operation (see Table 1).

This transcript of a dressing episode illuminates the importance of how the mother makes use of objects in the immediate environment, together with evaluating the child's interests at a given time. In the example given, the cream tube is not actually a toy in the cultural system of meanings; however, it can become a tool for the mother to redirect the child's interest. Thus, at bathtime the she removes the tube from the child's vicinity, but when taking him to be dried and dressed she remembers to take it with her, and gives it to him when it is advantageous for her to redirect his attention.

By re-organizing the goal structure, it is possible to change the whole setting and, in effect, terminate one particular interaction by transforming it into another situation. For example, if the child resists the dressing efforts and insists upon just playing (e.g., "try to catch me"), and the mother feels the dressing can be postponed in lieu of the child's orientation towards play, she may herself *drop the dressing goal* from the goal structure. As a result, the dressing effort stops, and is substituted by joint play that serves the immediate purpose of enjoyment, and the future goal of "getting to enjoy life" in general. The mother need not return to the dressing goal if she considers it inappropriate (e.g., consider mothers with children on beaches, where bundling the child up would be counterproductive to the goal of exposing the child to the sun and water).

The child's knowledge base: Scripting the dressing event. A similar picture of goal-structure setting and re-construction can be assumed to be present on the side of the child. In this case, however, the picture is more complicated since we have no reason to assume that the child's goal-structure is well differentiated. In fact, we can assume that it is currently undergoing development in concordance with the mother's. The asymmetry of these processes (i.e., the adult sets the primary agenda for defining the structure of the event) leads to joint actions that coordinate the mother's and child's (differentiating) goal structures. Based on these, the younger person is provided with the procedural knowledge that is necessary for the development of a differentiated "script."

The fact that at the end of the second year of life the child already possesses knowledge about the "script" of the dressing procedure becomes evident in observations of both the mother's and child's use of knowledge of the other partner's actions and of their *expectancies* related to further actions. At some points in the observed sequence of events the observer can specify a sudden change in the child's action that fits the mother's expectancy. In one of the examples given in Tables 2 and 3, we see that the child's behavior in anticipation of the mother's next step actually leads to a readjustment of her intentions.

The child's "help" in relevant moments of the dressing sequence (putting an arm into a sleeve, or lifting a foot to allow a sock to be put on) reveals a knowledge of what he or she is expected to do at a given time. Obviously, this knowledge is a result of past experience. Likewise, the mother may act in accordance with the child's expectancies, such as providing a dis-

TABLE 2
TWO INTERACTIONAL TRANSCRIPTS SHOWING CHILD'S EXPECTATIONS OF MOTHER'S NEXT BEHAVIOR AND MOTHER'S ADJUSTMENT TO THAT

EXAMPLE 1: Child is lying on the bed, being dressed. Diapers are already changed.

Mother: Pulls overall over child's head.
Child: Passive.
Mother: Puts first arm into sleeve.
Child: Passive.
Mother: Puts second arm into sleeve.
Child: Helps.
Mother: Tries to arrange suit in an orderly way
Child: Lifts legs.
Mother: Stops, looks at child.
Child: Looks.
Mother: Takes advantage of this situation and buttons lower part of the suit.

EXAMPLE 2: Both mother and child are in the kitchen, child is partly dressed, mother kneels on the floor nearby.

Mother: Announces that socks will be put on and makes child sit on her knees.
Child: Pulls table near.
Mother: Arranges socks.
Child: Lifts first foot while holding table.
Mother: Praises child and puts on sock.

---

tracting object that the child expects to get at the given moment in the temporal structure of the procedure. Of course, all observational information we can have about these expectancies comes from (a) looking for sudden changes in the partners' action as compared to their previous actions, which (b) occur in temporal positions dictated by the needs of the task and/or primary goals implied in the task. We can assume that we observe the emerging structure of the "script," wrought by the joint action of the partners in the context of a daily task.

The material ecology of dressing. Being able to dress oneself without help requires both sufficient motor coordination and a cognitive script that specifies what to do, in what order, and how to do it, given the structural properties of clothes. If we consider a person who, although cognitively and motorically developed, was never exposed to daily dressing objects (underwear, pullovers, shirts, trousers, skirts, socks), we might perceive dressing as a problem-solving task of matching objects with body features. For children, learning to dress involves such

TABLE 3
CONDENSED TRANSCRIPT OF A DRESSING INTERACTION INVOLVING A CHILD OF 21 MONTHS AND HIS MOTHER

Child lies in bed; mother initiates dressing by coming in with undershirt and asking for co-operation, but child resists by covering himself with blanket.

Mother: Comes near and attracts child's attention to undershirt by looking through its holes and talking while child watches. Pulls undershirt over child's head; child lets this happen. Takes one arm after another and pulls it into sleeve while talking. Child responds only verbally and lets dressing happen.
Mother: Asks child to get out of bed; tells him about things outside. Child covers himself again. Mother asks again, child nods but does not do anything. Mother suggests that he follow her to the kitchen, and leaves.

(About 4 minutes later)
Mother: Comes in with T-shirt, arranges and plays with it. Child sits in bed and watches.
Mother: Tries to pull shirt over child's head, but child resists and counteracts with arms. Mother takes shirt away and again looks towards child through its holes. Child hides his eyes behind his hands.
Mother: Tries to pull shirt again over child's head; child resists, cries and tries to get it off again. Mother tries to keep it halfway over his head and tries to talk him into letting this part of dressing happen, but child gets shirt off.
Mother: Holds it, laughs, and asks child if he doesn't want to be dressed. Rearranges shirt, asks child to get up but he does not. Re-arranges some playing objects and child's bottle in the bed, and asks him again to get up.
Mother: Takes T-shirt and goes some steps away. Asks child to get up and come dress in the kitchen. Child shows her some other clothing objects.
Mother: Takes them, comes near, takes bottle and toy bunny out of bed, and turns to go. Child climbs out of bed and follows her.

(In the kitchen)
Mother: Asks for diaper change. Child turns away and plays with painting utensils nearby. Mother takes them away, asks him to come to her and tells him about how cold it is outside and what they will do there later, while arranging the T-shirt. Child comes near, listens and watches.
Mother: Leans over when he is near, pulls shirt over his head and guides one arm into sleeve. Child cooperates and tries to climb onto her.
Mother: Meanwhile takes second arm and guides it into T-shirt, takes pullover sweater. Child climbs onto mother and turns around.
Mother: Pulls sweater over child's head, turns him around, takes arms one after another and guides them into sleeves, while child lets her do so.
Mother: Takes diapers and prepares them. Child stands up, observes and waits.
Mother: Gives child one side of diaper to hold, puts diaper underneath him and fixes it while child holds his side. Afterwards, mother arranges the clothes now on, child turns around and both engage socially.
Mother: Asks child to sit down, turns him around and makes him sit on her knees. Child pulls table standing nearby nearer towards himself.
Mother: Asks child to lift feet and puts on trousers when he does so. Child is meanwhile interested in observer, and stands up.
Mother: Announces that socks will be put on and makes child sit on her knees again. Child pulls table near again.
Mother: Arranges socks while child looks. Child lifts first foot in advance.
Mother: Praises that and dresses sock, while child tries to help. The same follows with the second sock.
Mother: Asks child to go get his shoes. Child leaves, but in the next half hour of interaction, no putting on of the shoes is observed.

a matching task. There are objects, for example, that have four openings (undershirt or pullover), three (trousers), or one (socks, shoes). When we observe children trying to dress alone, we can observe nearly all possible ways of trying to fit one's arms and legs into objects with several openings.

One basic step is the task of detecting what clothing item is used for what part of the body. The purposes of some items can be easily detected, but the functions of others (e.g., shirts or shorts) pose a more complicated problem.

Even when the right place of an item of clothing is identified, the child faces the problem of size differences of the openings: Which part of the body fits which opening? Finally, the majority of "multi-opening" clothing has two different sides, one for the front of the body and one for the back. The child who dresses alone must make a decision about the appropriateness of the front/back placement of a shirt before trying to put it on.

Taken together, the structure of relevant knowledge about a given item of clothing is rather complex. It makes dressing an extremely complicated problem solving task, in which decisions on how to place an item appropriately set the stage for the sequence of actual dressing actions. These actions have to be carried out in a strict sequential order: In order to be accomplished, all single subtasks have to be solved, and in the proper sequence (e.g., undershirt before shirt).

Cultural ecology of dressing. In addition to the form of the clothing determining the particular task demands, there exist cultural rules about how the dressing process is organized. The first clothing object for children in contemporary Western cultures is diapers, the use of which is replaced by underwear, in conjunction with completion of toilet-training. The course of toilet training is deeply rooted in the cultural expectancies of the adults (DeVries & DeVries, 1977; Wolfenstein, 1955), and is surely interconnected with norms for dressing. Furthermore, children's clothing is itself constructed in accordance with the adults' cultural norms of covering different parts of the body under different circumstances (Benigni & Valsiner, 1984). The ways of how the child is being dressed for different occasions (e.g., for a birthday party, compared with everyday occasions) prepares the child from an early age to become knowledgeable about the culture's norms of body-exposure in different social settings. Related to this differentiation is the way in which caregivers react to clothes being dirtied — the child has to learn that this is less acceptable for some clothing than for other.

These issues pertain to the child's relation to clothes, rather than to the process of dressing *per se.* In that latter realm, it is the culturally mediated time-organization of the adults that relates to the process of dressing. An impatient parent who needs to be somewhere by 9:00 a.m. sharp would deal with a child who sabotages dressing efforts differently from one whose schedule is more flexible.

Summary: Background of the complexity of dressing events. Luckily for children faced with a dressing task, caregivers can serve as expert helpers. Parents make sure that dressing takes place at all, and assist in its completion. They decide which kinds of clothes are appropriate at a given level of development and are reasonably good at adjusting to the demands of the occasion. As far as teaching the art of dressing is concerned, they help reduce the complexity of the problem to a level that matches the child's developmental status. However, parents are not just supervisors: they also have their own goals, such as wanting the child to be dressed in a way that is culturally acceptable, or getting on with their own day. Thus, they can choose the level of difficulty of the dressing process by opting for simpler clothing items (e.g., overalls but not tuxedos for children's everyday wear), the amount of time they want to invest, and the hour at which it is to be done. The problem experienced daily by many parents, though, is that children do not necessarily agree with these goals, which makes parent-child interaction in dressing situations a very useful research target for developmental psychologists.

Analysis of the Temporal Structure of Joint Action in Dressing Situations

In our present empirical context we are interested in observing interaction occasions on which instrumental and distractive actions of the mother and the child are involved. Different episodes of adult-child interaction in dressing situations proceed by different routes. However, the ultimate "end state" of the goal-oriented action sequence remains the same — sooner or later, and in one way or another, the child gets dressed. When we observe the variability in how that end state is reached, from one occasion to the next, we are not aimed at observing recurrence of the particular behavioral form of that dressing process. Instead, we are interested in the general organizational mechanisms that lead to a variety of ways in which the child is being dressed on particular occasions, while the same end state is guaranteed by these mechanisms.

In other words — our task is to reveal the organizational order that is responsible for the seeming chaos observable in particular cases of the mother's efforts to dress the child. As was described above in more general terms, we seek the replicability of the work of these organizational mechanisms, rather than of the forms of the products that these mechanisms generate and that are highly variable from one occasion to the next.

Components of the process description. The process of getting dressed is generally not continous and cannot be described as a monotonic increase in the number of clothing items to be put on. Likewise, the process of learning of how to do it alone is not a continuous process of the child's gain in knowledge. Rather, on the most general level by viewing dressing as problem-solving by joint action, we can distinguish three major portions of the process that recur repeatedly, while the appearance of particulars of action is highly variable and context-bound. Although in these components both mother and child may take very active roles, in our focus on canalized development we will center on the mother's role in canalizing the child's learning how to dress.

Figure 4 describes the general structure of the process. First, there is the component of *task initiation* (1). Actually, every newly introduced clothing item can be viewed as a new initiation, so that the general macroprocess of getting dressed is partitioned into several smaller tasks. Dressing can be initiated by either partner, depending on the development of the child. The initiation can consist of verbal requests or of one partner simply approaching the other with items of clothing. Often initiations include a process

FIGURE 4
COMPONENTS OF A JOINT-ACTION VIEW ON THE CONNECTIVE TEMPORAL STRUCTURE
IN MICROPROCESSES OF DRESSING

Mother's actions in organizing the microprocess   Child's actions

(may occur at
any time during
the task)

1. INITIATION
Sets up the primary task; or sets up a secondary
task (which is conditional for the primary task);
or demands actions from the child (in order to   passive
prepare for the task)

co-
2. DRESSING PROCEDURE   operates
Attracts attention (towards dressing objects,
consequences of being dressed, or for redirection
T   of the child's attention from objects that undermine   watches
the accomplishment of the dressing task)
Starts dressing (makes use of the child's body   helps
I   position and/or present behavior, demands dressing-   mother
related action from the child)
M   Dresses the child (as well as praises the child
for the contribution — real or imaginary — to   anticipates
E   the previous step)   next step

3. END OF THE MICROPROCESS   resists
If the child is dressed, move to other tasks (or no tasks)
If the dressing is unsuccessful, give up   refuses

4. NEGOTIATION AND/OR INITIATION OF SUBTASKS:
---- sets up secondary task (eventual re-run of the episode)   counter-
--------verbal instruction (after microprocess)   acts
-----------tactical negotiation
---------------tactical redefinition of the task
Social Filler / Leaves the child

of negotiation based on individual's goals about how interactions will proceed. These decisions will prestructure subsequent interaction.

Furthermore, we can distinguish major tasks (such as putting on shirts or trousers) from *subtasks* that either partner wants either as prerequisites or as consequences. Examples could be the parent's request to get up, after first clothing items have been put on in bed; the request to go and get the shoes, before both partners put them on the child's feet by joint effort. It can also be that the child introduces subtasks either in order to evade the general task or to make it more interesting or convenient; for example, sudden thirst or hunger can arise that has to be satisfied, or a teddy bear needs attention.

Second, there is the actual *dressing routine* (2). This component may contain, for example, attempts by the mother to direct the child's attention towards an initiated dressing routine, to get the child into the clothing, and to give instructions and negotiations of how the task may be accomplished. The mother's behavior in this component will actually be dependent on her goal structure, the demands of the dressing objects, and the child's reactions to her efforts.

Inside this component we may see reruns of the same procedures depending on the affordances of the specific dressing-items (e.g., two sleeves of one pullover), on the child's behavior (e.g., the mother succeeds in putting the pullover on, but only after a number of her attempts have been blocked), or on her change of the goal structure (e.g., "Try it again to learn to do it yourself"). Furthermore, this component can be enriched by simultaneous social interchange, while dressing takes place.

Third, there is the *end state* (3) of a run of a task or subtask. The interaction process has arrived at its immediate goal state, and can now proceed further.

Fourth, the last component (4) is the step of *negotiation and/or setup of a new task or subtask*. This component actually represents the simultaneous ending conditions of one task and the starting conditions for a new one. It is designed to include this bidirectional function. Mother and child will procede to the next step of dressing after the former step is sufficiently completed and the child is not yet fully dressed. However, they might also change their efforts towards a new clothing item (set-up of a new task) after an unsuccessful attempt in a specific subtask and/or might re-run the whole procedure in a different way. Similarly, they might jump over to dressing procedures that normally occur later in the sequence by just dismissing earlier steps. Mothers might even try to negotiate with their children, to construct conditions more promising for accomplishment of the subtask — but they would not alter the final goal that the child get dressed eventually. For instance, the whole dressing procedure might be transferred to another room or postponed to a later time.

Description of a particular dyad. Although generally it has to be assumed that both partners may be engaged in all components of the process depicted in Figure 4, an example reflecting the actual complexity of the interactional processes is in order. It is taken from the study analyzed above in quantitative terms. Parts of the videotaped materials, namely the morning observations of one child at the age of 21 months (21A, see Figure 1) were reviewed starting from points in the interaction process where either the mother initiated dressing for the first time verbally or just approached the child with dressing items. On this occasion, the mother was not under time pressure, and indicated in a subsequent interview that she currently perceived the child to just be starting to learn how to dress himself to some extent and expected progress in the near future.

The results: Flow chart of the microprocesses. Figures 5 and 6 give an exhaustive temporal description of this dressing interaction. Generally, in the example described, two major task versions can be recognized: "Dressing the child in bed" (A) and "Dressing the child in the kitchen" (B). The second version followed the first as a consequence of the mother's giving up the effort of getting the taks accomplished within setting A.

Both of these general versions are partitioned into several single tasks and related subtasks: Successful putting on of the undershirt in version A (1) and the unsuccessful attempts to put on the T-shirt (2-1, 2-2, 2-3, 2-4) are related to the initiation of the subtask to get out of bed: Once the undershirt is on, the subtask is set up, but not attained until after attempts to put the T-shirt on in bed are postponed. This initial lack of success while the child is still in bed is finally followed (3) by repetition of the subtask (getting up), and by tactical negotiation to get dressed in the kitchen (where breakfast would take place later).

In version B, the continued attempt to get the T-shirt on is delayed by the mother's decision to change the diapers (4). However, getting the T-shirt on (5) is successfully accomplished, and even the pullover (6) is put on, before the subsequent diaper-change (7). Getting the trousers on (8), and then socks (9) lead to the last step of the dressing procedure, the shoes. This step, although initiated by the mother's request for the subtasks of "go and get them" (9n) — was never accomplished in the entire 30 minutes of observation that followed.

At a more detailed level, we recognize certain nodes in the flow chart that recur repeatedly. These *nodes of similar action* are depicted as instrumental acts of the mother which are essential to accomplish the dressing of the child. Therefore, the similarity of these nodes between different episodes of interaction is given by the structural conditions of the taks in the given setting, rather than by particular action preferences of the interactants.

Let us read the flow charts more thoroughly. When initiating the task, the mother might ask for action from the child (8b: "sit down"; 3b: "get up") or might approach the child nonverbally with clothing items in her hand (1: comes in with undershirt). Following that, she might approach the child immediately in such a way as to direct his attention towards the items or the procedure (1d; 2d; 5d; 6d; 9d), or towards the positive consequences of being dressed (4d). She might also (see the transcript in Table 1) provide interesting objects that catch the child's attention in a way that is compatible with dressing, or remove objects that might be distracting (3d). Of course, she also might leave this step out (8).

The attempts to direct the child's attention toward dressing are very often successful in that either the child watches (1e; 2-1e; 2-4e; 7e) or actively tries to cooperate (by coming near or trying to handle the object of interest: 5e). The child might even anticipate the next step in the procedure and take the initiative (9). Attempts to direct attention might be

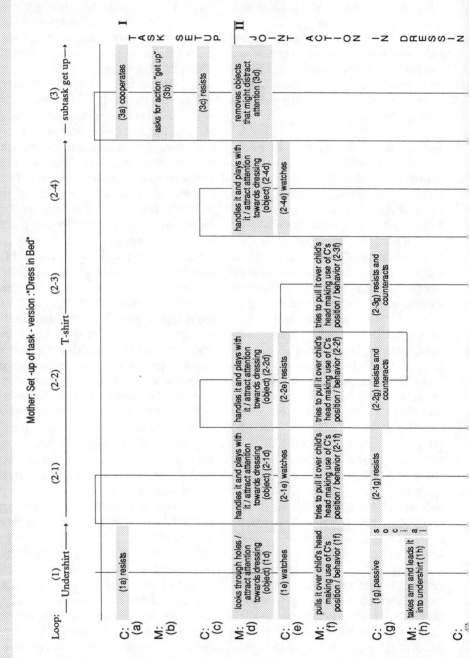

FIGURE 5
FLOWCHART OF SEQUENCES OF MICROPROCESSES IN DRESSING OF A CHILD 21MONTHS OF AGE

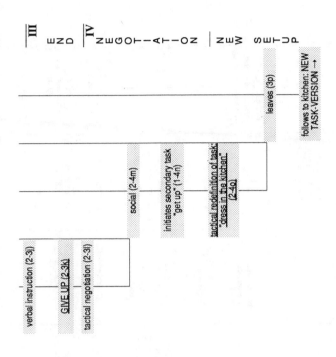

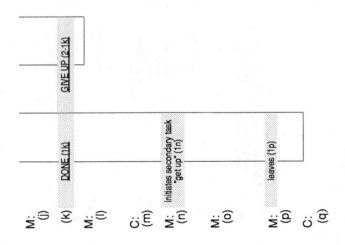

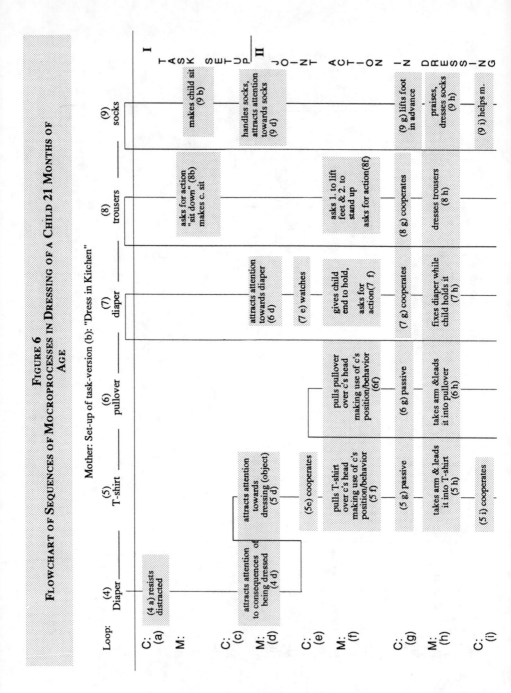

FIGURE 6

FLOWCHART OF SEQUENCES OF MACROPROCESSES IN DRESSING OF A CHILD 21 MONTHS OF AGE

Research Strategies in Developmental Psychology

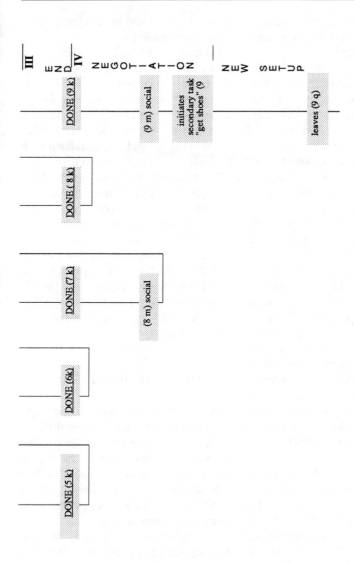

unsuccessful however, as seen in the re-runs of putting on the T-shirt in version A (Dressing in bed: 2-2e).

After attempts to direct the child's attention, an actual dressing attempt by the mother usually follows. This occurs either by the mother taking advantage of a position or a behavior of the child (e.g, the child reaching out his arms when mother is near; see 1f; 2-1f; 2-2f; 2-3f; 5f; 6f), or by asking for a specific behavior (7f; 8f). Passivity of the child, while mother does this, seems to be followed by the mother's trying to do the job without active involvement of the child (5g; 6g) — simultaneously some kind of social interaction might take place (1g). In the case described here, the mother's asking for action in the task is always followed by the appropriate behavior of the child (7g; 8g). It seems reasonable to expect that this reciprocity actually represents developmental adjustment in both partners' behavior (even more, given the results of the quantitative molar analyses, that mothers adjust their behavior according to task difficulty and level of competence of the child).

In the episodes depicted, the child's resistance leads to re-runs of the same task, either directly (2-2g) or after some intermediate steps (2-1g; 2-3g). A first retreat move by the mother (taking the pullover off again: 2-1k) can be the first intermediate step. Verbal instruction ("We have to dress now and you should let me do it": 2-3j) can be a second intermediate step prior to tactical negotiation ("How should we do it?": 2-3l), but the whole task can also be reformulated out of tactical reasons ("OK, let's dress in the kitchen": 2-4o). Whether single tasks can be totally dismissed, will depend on the broader environmental conditions. In most cases, they will just be delayed or tactically reformulated.

Cooperation of the child leads to success in dressing at this point (5i; 7g; 8g; 9i). Later in development, this might not necessarily be the case, when active involvement of the child and "wanting to do it alone" (Geppert & Kuester, 1983) is more likely to lead to complications in the task than to easy accomplishment.

The end-states of the tasks, either success (1k; 5k to 9k) or failure (2-1k; 2-3k) — both refer to an adult's perspective: Not getting dressed can be a great success for the child — can lead to the initiation of secondary tasks (1n; 9n; 2-4n) or new tasks. Failure, however, is very likely to result in re-runs of the same task (as in 2-1 and 2-2), unless repeated failures lead to tactical shifts in the mother's attempts (as in 2-3 and 2-4).

GENERAL DISCUSSION

The same observed psychological phenomenon can be viewed from different perspectives, leading to different data derivation strategies. Some of these strategies involve quantification, others favor a description of the qualitative structure of actions and their changes over time. Both approaches are appropriate for research efforts whose goal is to make developmental psychology explicitly culture-inclusive. Quantitative research is based on a theoretical perspective that operates on the basis of quantified theoretical constructs (e.g., support of behaviors by reinforcement schedules), whereas qualitative research is based on theoretical frameworks that assume that the developing organism and its environment are structured entities linked through dynamic bonds.

The present analysis used the example of mother-toddler interaction while dressing as the target phenomenon. One major line of thought throughout our theoretical consideration and empirical examples can be delineated as the question: What are reasonable units of observation in developmental research? The decision to select a unit with a specific scope implies certain decisions about what are qualitative and what are quantitative differences between units. It is worth considering a philosophical and quite general statement: All things in all of time and space are inextricably connected with one another. Any decisions, classifications, or organizations discovered in the universe are arbitrary. *The world is a complex, continuous, single event* (Meyer, 1967).

Following along those lines, the work of a researcher can be viewed as the enterprise of defining units that, according to particular theoretical considerations, allow a representation of a "reality" that provides some kind of structure, organization, and orderliness inside the phenomenon. We certainly believe that decisions made about units are arbitrary, and therefore should be made in such a way that the outcomes give a sufficient representation of the reality under study. We also contend that methods have to be constructed in concert with the different needs of isolating certain units and their properties according to different theories. Methods that actually help to derive data that represent aspects of reality and theory at the same time are relevant for developmental research. Currently popular traditions of empirical research in psychology have largely neglected this dual focus. However, dealing with these issues is inevitable if we aim to make developmental psychology context-inclusive.

ACKNOWLEDGEMENTS The empirical research on which this chapter is based was conducted by the first author as a part of the research project *Dependence and independence in the elderly: The role of social interactions* (Margaret M. Baltes, Principal Investigator) at the Free University of Berlin. The quantitative components of the study were conducted under supervision of Margaret and Paul Baltes. The authors would like to thank Ellen Skinner for her critique of an earlier version of this chapter. The preparation of the manuscript was made possible by a travel grant that was awarded to the first author by the Volkswagen Foundation. A preliminary version of this chapter was presented at the symposium "Combining qualitative and quantitative methods: Experiences with a dual approach for the study of development-in-context in infancy and early childhood" (M.H. van Ijzendoorn & K. Kreppner, conveners), at the Second European Conference on Developmental Psychology, Rome, September 10-13, 1986. The first author is now at the Graduate School of Education and Human Development and the Department of Psychology, University of Rochester, Rochester, NY, USA.

REFERENCES

Ash, M.G. (1985). Gestalt psychology: Origins in Germany and the reception in the United States. In C. Buxton (Ed.), *Points of view in the modern history of psychology* (pp. 295-344). Orlando, FL: Academic Press.

Bakeman, R. (1987). Untangling streams of behavior: Sequential analyses of observation data. In G. P. Sackett (Ed.), *Observing behavior: Data collection and analysis methods* (Vol. 2, pp. 63-78). Baltimore, MD: University Park Press.

Baldwin, J.M. (1906). *Thought and things: A study of the development and meaning of thought*, Vol.1.London:Swan Sonnenschein.

Baltes, M.M., Kindermann, T. & Reisenzein, R. (1986). Unselbständiges und selbständiges Verhalten im Alter: Die soziale

Umwelt als Einflussgrösse. *Zeitschrift für Gerontologie, 19*, 14-24.

Baltes, M.M. & Reisenzein, R. (1986). The social world in long-term care institutions: Psychosocial control toward dependency? In M.M. Baltes & P.B. Baltes (Eds.), *The psychology of control and aging* (pp. 315-343). Hillsdale, NJ: Erlbaum.

Baltes, M.M., Reisenzein, & Kindermann, T. (1985). *Interaction patterns related to dependent and independent behaviors: A comparison between institutionalized elderly and children.* Poster at the Eighth Biennial Meetings of the International Society for the Study of Behavioral Development, Tours, France, July 6-10.

Barton, E.M., Baltes, M.M. & Orzech, M.J. (1980). On the etiology of dependence during morning care: The role of staff behavior. *Journal of Personality and Social Psychology, 38*,423-431.

Basov, M. (1929). Structural Analysis in Psychology from the standpoint of behavior. *Journal of Genetic Psychology, 36*, 267-289.

Benigni, L. & Valsiner, J. (1984). Il corpo del neonato e i suoi confini sociali. In L.Gandini (Ed.), *Dimmi come lo vesti* (pp. 89-135). Milano: Emme Edizioni.

Benigni, L., & Valsiner, J. (1985). Developmental psychology without the study of developmental processes? *ISSBD Newsletter, No.1.*

Bertalanffy, L. (1981). *A systems view of man.* Boulder, CO: Westview Press.

Blurton-Jones, G. & Woodson, R.H. (1979). Describing behavior: The ecologist's perspective. In M.E. Lamb, S.J. Suomi & G.R. Stephenson (Eds.), *Social interaction analysis: Methodological issues* (pp. 97-118). Madison, WI: University of Wisconsin Press.

Boule, M. (1913). L'homme fossile de La Chapelle-aux-Saints. *Annales de Paléontologie, 6.*

Byrne, E.F. (1968). *Probability and opinion.* The Hague: Martinus Nijhoff.

Cairns, R.B. (1986). Phenomena lost: Issues in the study of development. In J. Valsiner

(Ed.), *The individual subject and scientific psychology* (pp. 97-112). New York: Plenum.

Cassedy, J.H. (1969). *Demography in early America: Beginnings of the statistical mind, 1600-1800.* Cambridge, MA: Harvard University Press.

Cassedy, J.H. (1984). *American medicine and statistical thinking, 1800-1860.* Cambridge, MA: Harvard University Press.

Cave, A.J.E. & Straus, W.L.Jr. (1957). Pathology and posture of Neandertal Man. Quarterly Review of Biology, 32, 348-363.

Cohen, P.C. (1982). *A calculating people: The spread of numeracy in early America.* Chicago: University of Chicago Press.

DeVries, M.W. & DeVries, R. (1977). Cultural relativity of toilet-training readiness: A perspective from East Africa. *Pediatrics, 60 (2),*170-177.

Eysenck, H.J. (1985). The place of theory in a world of facts. In K.B. Madsen & L.P. Mos (Eds.), *Annals of theoretical psychology.* Vol. 3 (pp.103-114). New York: Plenum.

Geppert, U. & Kuester, U. (1983). The emergence of "Wanting to do it oneself": A precursor of achievement motivation. *International Journal of Behavioral Development, 6,* 355-369.

Gergen, K. (1982). *Toward transformation of social knowledge.* New York: Springer.

Gergen, K. (1985a). The social constructionist movement in modern psychology. *American Psychologist, 40 (3),* 266-275.

Gergen, K. (1985b). Social constructionist ideology: context and implication. In K.Gergen & K.E. Davis (Eds.), *The social construction of the person* (pp. 3-18). New York: Springer.

Gergen, M. & Gergen, K., Eds. (1984). *Historical social psychology.* Hillsdale: Erlbaum.

Gewirtz, J.L. (1969). Mechanisms of social learning: Some roles of stimulation and behavior in early human development. In D.A. Goslin (Ed.), *Handbook of socialization theory and research* (pp. 57-212). Chicago: Rand McNally.

Gould, S.J. (1986) Evolution and the triumph

of homology, or why history matters. *American Scientist, 74,* 60-69.

Harkness, S., & Super, C.M. (1983). The cultural construction of child development. *Ethos, 11,* 4, 221-231.

Harre, R. (1981). Rituals, rhetoric and social cognition. In J.P. Forgas (Ed.), *Social cognition* (pp. 211-224). London: Academic Press.

Hayes, W.L. (1973). *Statistics for the social sciences.* New York: Holt, Rinehart & Winston.

Jerne, N.K. (1985). The generative grammar of the immune system. *Science, 229,* 1057-1059.

Kindermann, T. (1985). *A learning theoretical perspective on dependent and independent behaviors in children.* Poster at the Eighth Biennial Meetings of the International Society for the Study of Behavioral Development, Tours, France, July 6-10.

Kindermann, T. (1986). *Entwicklungsbedingungen selbständigen und unselbständigen Verhaltens in der frühen Kindheit: Sozial-ökologische Analyse alltäglicher Mutter-Kind-Interaktionen.* Unpublished Doctoral Dissertation, Freie Universitaet Berlin.

Kindermann, T., & Skinner, E. (in press). Developmental tasks as organizers of children's ecologies: Mother contingencies as children learn to walk, eat, and dress. In J. Valsiner (Ed.), *Child development within culturally structured environments. Vol. 2. Social co-construction and environmental guidance in development.* Norwood, NJ: Ablex.

Kohler, W. (1925). An aspect of Gestalt Psychology. In C. Murchison (Ed.), *Psychologies of 1925.* (pp.163-195). Worcester, MA: Clark University Press.

Koehler, W. (1971). *The selected papers of W. Kohler.* New York: Liveright.

Lewin, K. (1931). The conflict between Aristotelian and Galileian modes of thought in contemporary psychology. *Journal of General Psychology, 5,* 141-177.

Meyer, L.B. (1967). *Music, the arts, and ideas.*

Chicago, IL: University of Chicago Press.

Mitroff, I. (1974). Norms and counter-norms in a select group of Apollo moon scientists: A case study on the ambivalence of scientists. *American Sociological Review, 39,* 579-596.

Niiniluoto, I. (1981). Statistical explanation reconsidered. *Synthese, 48,* 437-472.

Niiniluoto, I. (1982). Statistical explanation. In G. Floistad (Ed.), *Contemporary philosophy. Vol.2. Philosophy of science* (pp.157-187). The Hague: Martinus Nijhoff.

Prigogine, I. (1980). *From being to becoming.* San Francisco: Freeman.

Rankin, B. (1966). The history of probability and the changing concept of the individual. *Journal of the History of Ideas, 27,* 483-504.

Reader, J. (1981). *Missing links: The hunt for earliest man.* Boston: Little, Brown.

Sackett, G.P., Holm, R., Crowley, C., & Henkins, A. (1979). A Fortran program for lag sequential analysis of contingency and cyclicity in behavioral interaction data. *Behavior Research Methods and Instrumentation, 11,* 366-378.

Salmon, W. (1970). Statistical explanation. In R.G. Colodny (Ed.), *The nature and function of scientific theories* (pp.173-231). Pittsburgh: University of Pittsburgh Press.

Scarr, S. (1985). Constructing psychology: Making facts and fables for our times. *American Psychologist, 40,* 499-512.

Sears, R.R. (1972). Dependency, attachment, and frustration. In J.L. Gewirtz (Ed.), *Attachment and dependency* (pp. 1-27). New York: Wiley.

Shotter, J. (1983). "Duality of structure" and "intentionality" in an ecological psychology. *Journal for the Theory of Social Behaviour, 13,* 19-43.

Smedslund, J. (1978). Bandura's theory of self-efficacy: A set of common-sense theorems. *Scandinavian Journal of Psychology, 19,* 1-14.

Smedslund, J. (1979). Between the analytic and the arbitrary: A case study of psychological research. *Scandinavian Journal of Psychology, 20,* 129-140.

Smith, G. E. (1924). *The evolution of man.* London.

Stent, G.S. (1985). Hermeneutics and the analysis of complex biological systems. In D.J. Depew & B.H. Weber (Eds.), *Evolution at a crossroads* (pp. 209-226). Cambridge, MA: MIT Press.

Tweney, R.D., Doherty, M.E., & Mynatt, C.R. (1981). *On scientific thinking.* New York: Columbia University Press.

Valsiner, J. (1986). Between groups and individuals: Psychologists' and laypersons' interpretations of correlational findings. In J. Valsiner (Ed.), *The individual subject and scientific psychology* (pp.113-152). New York: Plenum.

Valsiner, J. (1987a). *Culture and the development of children's action.* Chichester: Wiley.

Valsiner, J. (1987b) *Developmental psychology in the Soviet Union.* Brighton: Harvester Press.

Vygotsky, L. (1956). *Izbrannyie psikhologicheskie issledovania. Myshlenie i rech.* Moscow: APN Press.

Vygotsky, L. (1960). *Razvitie vyshikh psikhicheskih funktsii.* Moscow: APN Press.

Wolfenstein, M. (1955). Fun morality: An analysis of recent American child-training literature. In M. Mead & M. Wolfenstein (Eds.), *Childhood in contemporary cultures.* Chicago: University of Chicago Press.

Wolpoff, M.A. (1971). The single species hypothesis. *Man, 6,* 601-614.

Zeleny, M., Ed. (1981). *Autopoiesis, dissipative structures, and spontaneous social orders.* Boulder, CO: Westview Press.

Not in Text

Saxe, G. (1982). Culture and the development of numerical cognition: Studies among the Oksapmin of Papua New Guinea. In C.J. Brainerd (Ed.), *Children's logical and mathematical cognition* (pp.157-176). New York: Springer.

Vygotsky, L. (1981). Istoricheskii smysl psikhologicheskogo krizisa. In L.S. Vygotsky, *Sobranie sochinenii.* Vol.1 (pp. 292-436). Moscow: Pedagogika.

Chapter 2

Towards Contextual Sensitivity in Developmental Psychology

A Nigerian Perspective

Eileen B. Wilson-Oyelaran

INTRODUCTION

As with all academic and professional activity, psychology operates in particular social/historical contexts, which in turn have significant impact on the development of theory and method in the discipline. In order to apprehend more clearly the problems inherent in the study of child psychology in a non-western milieu, an examination of the context in which the discipline operates is a necessity. In this chapter we will examine both the social context of psychology in Nigeria, and its implications for the study of the developing child.

In Africa, political independence has had relatively limited effect on the power relations that existed between former colonies and their colonial masters. Ostensibly, control of the economy and the body politic is vested in a few members of the national elite, military or civilian. In actual fact however, political and economic decisions are largely determined by western industrialized nations through their agencies such as transnational corporations, the World Bank, and the International Monetary Fund (IMF). These institutions severally and collectively articulate policies that increase the control western nations (particularly the United States, Britain, France, and West Germany) have over the economies of developing African countries.[1]

---

[1] For a thorough discussion of the neo-colonial situation and limitations of political independence in Africa, the reader should consult the following:

B. Onimode, *Imperialism and underdevelopment in Nigeria: The dialectics of poverty*. London: Zed Press, 1982.
NES, *Poverty in Nigeria*. Proc. of the 1975 Annual Conference of the Nigerian Economics Society.
S. Osoba, Deepening Crisis of the Nigerian Bourgeoisie, *Rev. of African Political Economy, 13*, 1978.
B. Beckman, Neo-Colonialism, Capitalism and the State in Nigeria. In H. Bernstein & B. K. Campbell (Eds.), *Contradictions of Accumulation in Africa* (Beverly Hills: Sage Publications 1985).
Toyin Falola & Julius Ihonvbere, *The Rise and Fall of Nigeria's Second Republic*, 1979-84. London: Zed Press, 1985.

Thus, despite political independence, most African nations maintain a relationship of continued dependence on western industrial powers. All local institutions — political, economic, educational, and sociocultural — are affected by this circumstance, and there is hardly any aspect of life or experience that is not significantly influenced by it.

DEPENDENCY AND PSYCHOLOGY IN AFRICA

It is within this neocolonial milieu that psychology as a systematic discipline has grown up in most African countries. Consequently, the predominant characteristic of the discipline has been its inordinate dependence on modern psychology as it is articulated and practiced in occidental societies. The nature of this dependency is highlighted by three interrelated features: development of professional personnel, inappropriate application of theory and concepts, and transfer of methodology and technology.

Training of Professional Personnel

A majority of Nigerian psychologists have received their degrees in the United States or Britain; thus, it is not surprising that their training equips them for the practice of psychology in western cultures. Characteristically, it rarely addresses alternatives that may be relevant to someone who will operate in a non-western, non-urban, developing society (Moghaddam & Taylor, 1986). The theoretical constructs, research questions, and methodologies on which these practitioners are nurtured are congruent with the dominant value systems and sociocultural reality of western societies, where a high premium is placed on individualism, material acquisition, objectivity, and logical-rational inquiry.[2]

Developmental theories reflect this preoccupation. For example, in Piaget's theory of genetic epistemology, one of the most forceful and heuristic theories of cognitive development, logical abstract thinking as reflected in the construct of formal operations is considered the most advanced stage of intellectual functioning. Similarly, Kohlberg's (1969) theory of moral development carefully combines the predominant values of individualism, objectivity, and formal logical reasoning. The result is a paradigm of moral development in which the highest stages (Post-conventional Stages 5 and 6) are attained when one is able to make moral judgments based on abstract principles, rather than being affected by the prevailing social context. In Stage 5, moral decisions are based on the principles of individual rights and respect for the law; in Stage 6, they are based on universal principles including the intrinsic value of human life and respect for the individual. Attainment of the Post-conventional stages is dependent on the ability to carry out logical-rational abstract reasoning. Moral decisions in which universal principles are set aside because of the exigencies of the situation are seen as reflecting a less developed stage of functioning.

As Gilligan (1982) has succinctly noted, Kohlberg's view of moral maturity may

> . . . reflect a conception of adulthood that is itself out of balance, favoring the separateness of the individual self over connection with others (p. 17).

---

[2] The author recognizes the increasingly multi-cultural nature of these societies. This discussion, however, emphasizes the most dominant world view.

It must be recognized that Kohlberg's conception reflects the dominant western view of the world, emphasizing both objective decisions devoid of social context and primacy of the individual over the person-in-relation-to-others. However, it may not reflect the dominant views in other societies.

Just as students trained in the West receive exposure to theoretical constructs that reflect that society's dominant value system, their exposure to research questions is also intimately culture-linked. Emphasis on the mother-child dyad as a unit of investigation provides an example.

Perception of the mother-child dyad as significant in emotional, cognitive, and verbal development (Bowlby, 1969; Feshbach, 1973; Gordon, 1969; Hess and Shipman, 1965) should not be considered a natural outgrowth of the "universal" importance of mothers in the developmental process. Rather, it is the result of the evolution in the West from a largely agrarian extended family situation to a primarily urban nuclear arrangement. In the former situation, most family members engage in agricultural production and the rearing of young children is the purview of whoever is not so engaged, e.g., siblings and the aged. In contrast, in the contemporary urban nuclear context the dominant mythology[3] recognizes the father as principal breadwinner and the mother as homemaker whose primary responsibility is childcare. In addition, it is assumed that the reproductive pattern within nuclear families insures that not more than two children below school-age are in her care simultaneously.

---

[3] The choice of this term is deliberate. The family structure and functions being described pertain primarily to middle-class Anglo-American families. A majority of society may not fit this pattern; however, this description of the family is projected as both prevalent and normal.

It is within this social context, rather than as a universal phenomenon, that the conceptualization of the mother-child dyad as a significant factor in development must be understood. Such an assumption may not be appropriate in other societies where, as is the case in Nigeria, the family structure reflects a different type of organization.

The above examples highlight the primary difficulty associated wtih the fact that most Nigerian psychologists have been trained in societies that are socially, culturally, and historically different from their own. The theories and research questions on which they have been schooled are of limited utility in a culture where the value system is different; where the populace is primarily rural and illiterate; and where the formal discipline of psychology has not evolved with the society but rather has been imported and imposed on it. Thus, their educational experience provides few opportunities for reflection concerning alternative theories, questions, and methods that might be better suited for their own country.

Inappropriate Application of Theory and Method

In the absence of contextually relevant theoretical frameworks, the psychologist becomes a victim of conceptual incarceration (Nobels, 1977). He or she is a captive of concepts, constructs, methods, and paradigms that are considered appropriate for analysis in the Euro-American social context. Thus, research questions and theories developed in the West are continually employed to analyze the Nigerian social and psychological experience with only minor modifications.

"Locus of control" research (Rotter, 1966) provides one example. The underlying assumption of this construct is that individuals develop generalized beliefs about whether desired outcomes are a result of one's own behavior or a function of external forces. Such an assumption presupposes an epistemological framework where causation is represented in the contrastive form of an "either/or" mutually exclusive category. While this system of logic is dominant in occidental societies, there is considerable evidence that alternative systems operate elsewhere (Kluckhohn & Strodtbeck, 1961). One such alternative is the "both/and" system (Dixon & Foster, 1971). The premise here is that the world is not experienced in mutually exclusive categories; therefore, outcomes are a function of *both* internal and external forces, which interact in very subtle ways. Furthermore, any attempt to contrast the two is unnecessary and meaningless. In societies where this alternative logic predominates, locus of control is irrelevant as a theoretical proposition. The construct cannot explain or help us to hypothesize about behavior or the formation of expectancies within these particular contexts, and the assessment techniques used in the examination of the construct are insensitive to explanations of causation within the system of "both/and" logic: consequently, the data can only misrepresent the views of the individuals assessed and further confound attempts at explanation. Despite its questionable relevance, the locus of control construct is often employed in Nigeria (Anazonwu & Ugwuegbu, 1986; Dada, 1986; Galejs & D'Silva, 1982). This tendency to employ psychological theories and constructs inappropriately has been the rule rather than the exception.

Transfer of Technology

Dependency in psychology is further manifested not only by the importation of inappropriate theories, but also by the transfer of various types of technology, including assessment techniques and laboratory equipment. Intelligence tests as well as personality and aptitude inventories are imported and utilized on Nigerian children. Considerable effort has been made to modify some of these instruments through restandardization, translation, or adaptation of items; however, such modifications still assume that the assessment techniques, the social context in which assessment occurs, and the underlying constructs being measured have validity in Nigeria. Because these theories dominate the discipline they are often assumed to be universal, when in fact they are bound to the specific social context in which they evolved.

Dependency and Child Psychology

A psychology derived from social and historical realities that are vastly different from Nigeria's can hardly generate theory and practice that will aid our understanding of the development of the African individual. The complexity of this problem is underscored when one considers the dual nature of the sociopolitical and cultural dimensions of Nigerian society. Moghaddam and Taylor (1986) use the term *dualism* to describe the presence of two distinct economic sectors, the traditional and the modern, within the same society. They argue that each sector generates different perceptions of social reality, as well as exhibiting considerable variation with regard to access to natural, economic and institutional resources; literacy; and participation in decision making.

Members of the traditional sector are primarily rural and illiterate, and survive on subsistence or cash crop economies. In contrast, the modern sector is urban and literate, and the economic activity of its members is determined by forces in the developed world. One should note, however, that not all urban residents are part of this sector: many migrants who provide labor for the modern sector are only marginal to it, and their social and cultural referents are their traditional rural communities of origin.

The two sectors can also be distinguished on the basis of cultural affiliation. For the most part, the modern sector takes the developed world (or at least an inadequate perception of it) as its cultural reference point. Its members' values and aspirations are western-like, and they are significantly alienated from indigenous Nigerian cultures. In extreme cases, members of this sector have abandoned their indigenous languages in preference for English. The traditional sector, on the other hand, is steeped in the culture from which its members obtain their values, aspirations, meanings, and world views. The majority are monolingual, with no competence in English or any other western language. Even those who are bilingual prefer their indigenous language as a medium of communication. The predominant family structure is the extended type.

Lambo (1969) has suggested that Nigeria is in a transitional phase as it adapts to the demands of modernization. We do not share this view, and agree with Mabogunje (1982), who notes the absence of a primary characteristic of adaption: a healthy tension between traditional norms and the demands of modernization.

Applicability: Data and Interpretation

Do theories of child psychology propounded in the West have any applicability in a dual society such as Nigeria? It is our contention that they can only be appropriate for the modern sector, where the cultural orientation, family structure, and to some degree childrearing methods are modeled upon a vague perception of Western society. However, the relevance of Western theory for even this sector is highly circumspect. In spite of some crude cultural similarities, the social and historical experience of this sector is vastly different from that of occidental society, and considerable differences in intention, consequence, and meaning of childrearing behaviors are bound to exist.

In any case, fewer than ten percent of Nigerian children grow up in the modern sector. Thus, even if occidental theories do have any utility in explaining such children's thought processes or behaviors, these explanations account for only a tiny minority. Most Nigerian children, irrespective of geographical residence, grow up in traditional-sector families where the values, meanings, and attendant modes of childrearing are dictated by indigenous African cultures. The appropriateness of occidental child psychology within this context is at the very best, *minimal.* There is a lack of congruence between the socioeconomic, political and historical experience of the traditional sector and the West. More critical, however, is the difference between the occidental cultural system and indigenous African cultures which are co-terminous with the traditional sector.

Psychologists in Nigeria have been largely insensitive to this dual nature of their society and to the conflict it poses for their studies. They apply Western concepts to both the modern and traditional sectors as if they were equally valid in both contexts. This has had several consequences. First, when occidental theories of development are employed and the data from the subjects vary significantly from those obtained in the West, the variation is often interpreted as a deficit in the development of the subjects. The possibility of limitations in the theory or its lack of universality is seldom recognized or articulated. For example, studies among West African teenagers reveal a persistance of fear of supernatural forces[4] (Wilson, 1986), whereas among North American subjects such fears diminish significantly by adolescence. In the West, this diminution is associated with the growth and development of cognitive and linguistic skills, and with the differentiation between internal representation and objective reality in the determination of cause (Bauer, 1976).

The danger is that the researcher might conclude that the responses of West African adolescents reflect an undeveloped sense of cause and event and a lack of differentiation between internal and external reality, suggesting delayed or arrested development. There are, however, alternative interpretations. The contrast between internal representations and objective reality on one hand, and the link between cognitive development and separation of internal and external reality on the other, may not obtain in a social context where the supernatural is consid-

ered to be an aspect of reality and where children are being continually socialized to view it as such.

Second, understanding of the development process can be confounded because the problem is conceptualized incorrectly. For instance, the use of the mother-child dyad to analyze linguistic, cognitive, or socio-emotional development in an extended or polygynous family setting results in the isolation of a context of development that has limited significance. In fact, it creates an *artificial reality*. The mother-child dyad may not be any more important than the older sibling-child dyad, the co-wife-child dyad, or the grandmother-child dyad. There may be no one who can be designated as the primary caretaker. Furthermore, the social context of development may rarely include *any* type of dyadic formation: there may typically be more than one person interacting with the child at any given moment. Data collected and interpreted on the basis of the mother-child dyad, therefore, misrepresent the context. Any conclusions derived from such an investigation can only confound our understanding of development within the extended or polygynous family setting.

The situation delineated above suggests that we have borrowed a developmental psychology that is for the most part inappropriate for the Nigerian context. This has resulted in both incorrect assessment and inadequate interpretation of the phenomena under study.

Explanation

Explanation of development, then, still remains a critical issue for those interested in this process in the African child. Such an explanation must address two

---

[4] The items included in the supernatural category are similar to those found in imaginary or fantasy categories in fear inventories developed in the United States and Europe. The category also contains culturally relevant items, e.g., sacrifices at crossroads.

issues. The first is the process by which development takes place: i.e., characterizing those mechanisms that allow it to occur, and accounting for the emergence of qualitatively new patterns in the child's behavior and thinking (Valsiner & Benigni, 1986). Emphasis is on the *process of change*, rather than on the manifestation of static behaviors at particular ages.

Second, the explanation must consider the nature of the progression the child undergoes between birth and maturity. That is, it must describe the content of the child's behavior and the qualitative changes that occur as he or she advances in age. This information should enable us to answer the question, what should a child be expected to do or understand at a particular phase in development? The basic requirement for such an explanation is the holistic study of children as they grow up within their culture. Such an inquiry cannot have as its point of departure the comparison of Nigerian children with those of other societies. Rather, it must be the characterization of the social context and the analysis of interactions within this context. This approach implies the generation of new theories and methods with relevance for the Nigerian reality.

The Developmental Context

Generally, when differences in the developmental setting for the African and the western child are acknowledged, the primary focus has been on the cultural context (Cole, Sharp, Gay & Glick, 1971; Cole & Scribner, 1974). We recognize the importance of culture and do not wish to diminish its centrality; however, we believe that the concept of "context" must

be expanded if an adequate and comprehensive explanation is to be obtained.

We can identify several contexts or subcontexts that have impact on development. These combine to form a unitary whole, which comprises the full context in which child development occurs. Although they are interrelated, we will delineate them here in order to highlight the nature of analysis required for adequate explanation. The subcontexts afford a framework for analyzing the environment and for examining both influences on development and potential sources of discontinuity in the developmental process.

Definition and Specification of the Developmental Context

The author has adapted the construct of the subsystems of human action as propounded by King, Dixon, and Wilson (1976). King et al. argue that the human condition is comprised of four subsystems: namely, the biological, socioeconomic, cultural, and personal-dynamic. It is our contention that the first three can also be viewed as aspects of the context in which development takes place.

The *biological system* includes all aspects of the environment related to physical development, growth, and health status. At issue here are such factors as prenatal and neonatal environments, nutrition, access to safe water, and medical care. Also included are other aspects of the physical environment that are directly related to the health of children and their caretakers, such as environmental sanitation and adequate shelter.

The *socioeconomic system* is concerned, first and foremost, with the pattern by which material resources in the society are generated and appropriated. A second concern revolves around an outgrowth of this pattern: the nature of the relationship between individuals and their social institutions. Several issues are central to this context:

Who produces the wealth in the country?

Who determines how the wealth is to be used and distributed?

What is the relationship between those who produce the wealth and those who determine its distribution?

The answers to these questions reveal the economic organization of a society. They are also determinants of other aspects of social reality, including the political organization, the delivery of social services such as education, and the dispensation of justice.

Of concern here is the amount of control individuals have over their social reality — their potential for full participation in various institutions. Potential for participation is measured not merely by access to but also by the ability to assist in the determination of policy.

The socioeconomic system is conditioned by history, and conversely, it provides the scaffolding on which the cultural system evolves. Over a long period of time, major changes within it result in the modification of culture.

The *cultural system* is composed of the various configurations of values, beliefs, language, perceptions, and other referential behaviors that are conditioned by history and the socioeconomic system rather than by hereditary or biological factors. This constellation is shared by an identifiable group and provides a framework of shared meanings and intentions for all who belong. These meanings and

intentions in turn affect behavior and thought. An important aspect of this component is the way those responsible for the upbringing of children ensure that they acquire the particular shared meanings, values, and preferred behaviors of the group.

As noted above, these three subsystems can be viewed as interrelated factors which when combined constitute a full developmental context. Development of the Nigerian child can only be understood if attention is given to all three. This task is particularly formidable when one considers two features of contemporary Nigeria: the dual nature of the society, as discussed earlier, and the multicultural nature within the traditional sector. There is not one indigenous Nigerian culture: there are over four hundred! Although there are many similarities among them, there are also distinct differences, which may imply differences in the goals and procedures of the socialization process.

In the next section we will briefly examine each of the subcontexts of development identified above. We hope to pose questions that may aid the process of explanation and make suggestions regarding method. Given the fact that contextually sensitive analysis has a limited tradition in Nigeria, our discussion here is both tentative and rudimentary. Its primary value may in fact be only heuristic.

Biological Context

As noted above, information related to health status and biological functioning of both children and their caretakers is relevant here. The incidence of infant and child mortality, nutritional status, availability of medical care, and amenities such as pipe-borne water, toilet facilities, and adequate shelter all influence the way in which the daily lives of children may be structured.

On one hand, the biological context of development may be viewed as having primary significance in idiographic studies of development. For example, if a particular child in a particular family suffers from malnutrition we can make some predictions regarding the progress of this child's development based on his or her age and the length and severity of illness.

In addition, there is another sense in which the general health status of a community and the safety of the physical environment provide a framework for explaining normative development. In a region where childhood malnutrition is endemic, the growth and development of all children are likely to be affected, as are parents' expectations of their capabilities. In a community where infant and child mortality are high, various adaptations involving both belief and action are likely to evolve. The observed tendency of women to bear many children in an attempt (whether conscious or not) to offset the effects of probable child death on family size may be such an adaptation. How, then, does the constellation of large numbers of pregnancies and births coupled with the potential of child death affect the organization of daily life? This is a question that requires investigation.

Most of the data needed to construct a sketch of the biological context of development in Nigeria are available. However, there is no tradition of psychologists, demographers, and community health specialists making collaborative efforts to understand the relationship between the statistics, the environmental conditions they reflect, and the organization of the child's experiences.

Let us consider the issues of infant and child mortality, access to safe drinking water, and malnutrition. Childhood mortality rates are considered good indicators of health status and general living conditions within a community. According to the Nigerian Fertility Survey (1984), based on a representative national sample the childhood mortality rate for the period 1975-79 was 144.5 per 1000 while the infant mortality rate was 84.5 per 1000 live births. (In both age groups the survival chances of girls were better than boys.) There was a significant difference between urban and rural areas: 63.8 urban infant mortality contrasted with 88.5 in the rural sector, and 116.4 urban childhood mortality as opposed to 150.6 in rural communities. Although data are not available, the contrast between traditional and modern sectors would be even greater. The formation and development of attachment between adults and children or among various siblings must be analyzed giving full consideration to the possible effects of high childhood mortality. Caretaker-child behaviors that appear strange or illogical may be better interpreted and understood when one considers the inaccessibility of basic medical care and the repeated cases of child death in many communities.

It is estimated that only 30% of the population has access to safe drinking water on a year-round basis, from sources such as pipes, boreholes, or clean rivers. The Nigerian Fertility Survey (1984) indicates that 50.5% of the rural population report a source of well, pump, or pipe-borne water, while the figure for urban dwellers is 96.3 percent; however, there is no guarantee that a water source is functional year round, as it is not uncommon for taps and wells to stop yielding in both rural and urban areas, particularly in the dry season. Children six years and over residing in urban slums or rural villages may be expected to collect water for the family, from five in the morning until classes begin, and resuming immediately after school adjourns.

Estimates indicate that 40% of the rural population (both adults and children) are undernourished, while 25% of urban residents lack sufficient incomes to purchase adequate food. This trend has shown no improvement over the past twenty years, and in fact appears to be worsening (International Labour Office, 1981). Like most of their counterparts in other developing countries, 60% of Nigerian children under five years of age will suffer protein energy malnutrition. The results may include developmental delay and lack of resistance to infection (Durojaiye, 1976). Unless the symptoms become severe or the family participates in a maternal-child health program, the affliction may remain undetected and untreated.

Socioeconomic Context

Although available data are scanty, it is possible to sketch a reasonably realistic picture of general socioeconomic trends and to consider these factors in relationship to children.

Since the publication of the Second National Development Plan (1970-74) the Nigerian government has consistently articulated a social and economic policy that espouses egalitarianism, democracy, and equal opportunity. Despite this official policy, the most commanding feature of the domestic socioeconomic structure is inequality: unequal distribution of income, property, and wealth; unequal access to amenities and social services.

Inequality in Nigeria is multidimensional and can be identified on the basis of three interrelated dichotomies: geographical (North vs. South); sectoral (urban vs. rural); and socioeconomic (modern vs. traditional).

Based on an analysis of income distribution during the first decade after independence (1960-70) Diejomoah and Anusionwu (1981) maintain that the extent of inequality in Nigeria was moderate. Given the buoyancy of the Nigerian economy between 1970-77, one would have expected an improvement in the quality of life as well as more equitable distribution of wealth, goods, and services. Such was not the case, and the evidence from 1970 to the present suggests that inequality has significantly increased rather than diminished.

For example, although 77% of the population are rural dwellers, 50% of whom are children, the differential in per capita income between urban and rural residents rose from 2.65 in 1962-63 to 9 in 1975-76 (ILO, 1981). The gap between rich and poor has also increased in both relative and absolute terms, with the percentage of families living below the poverty line steadily increasing in both rural and urban areas, while members of the elite, particularly the military, business, and professional elite, flaunt their newly acquired wealth with ostentatious consumption.

Although education expanded rapidly with the introduction of nation-wide universal primary education in 1976-1977, literacy rates and access to education also reflect considerable inequality. Despite a significant rise in enrollment, the historical gap between the less educated northern and the more educated southern parts of the country continues. Currently no state is able to claim 100%

enrollment of six-year-olds, although some of the southern states may achieve the goal by 1990 (ILO, 1981).

Within states, the rural/urban dichotomy with regard to accessibility and quality of schools is apparent. Within urban areas, when the quality of educational institutions is correlated with the education and occupation of the students' fathers, upper-class families dominate the best quality schools while middle-class families dominate average schools. Low income families are in the minority in high and average quality schools and 6.3% of children from low income families have access to the best quality institutions. At all levels of education girls are under-represented (Diejomoah & Anusionwu, 1981).

Literacy rates are difficult to estimate. Among female respondents of the Nigerian Fertility Survey (1984) between the ages of 15 and 49, only approximately 30% were functionally literate, that is, competent to read a letter or newspaper in any language. Literacy is intimately linked with a people's capacity to participate in decision-making, particularly when power is vested in the hands of a literate minority. Access to shelter, health care, and criminal justice reflect similar inequalities.

The rise in inequality in spite of the oil boom revenue was primarily the result of improper development planning, mismanagement of the economy, and massive corruption. Evidence of this corruption has recently been brought to light by various government-sponsored investigation panels and military tribunals. Numerous politicians, high-ranking military personnel, and top civil servants have been convicted of corrupt enrichment involving millions of dollars. It is common knowledge that the Nigerian treasury has been looted by a few unscrupulous individuals, and the development of the country has been retarded tremendously.

What does this mean for children? The child's gender, the section of the country where he or she grows up, the rural or urban residence pattern, and class membership combine to produce a particular social context. A majority of Nigerian children grow up in poor families with substandard nutrition and shelter and with limited access to health care. Primary education is not automatic, meaning that realistically many children between the ages of 6 and 16 must work to insure the survival chances of their families.

In urban communities, those not in school may labor as many as 16 hours a day in environments where they are exposed to various forms of abuse, and socialized into various forms of deviant behavior (Dyorough, 1986). Girls working in cheap hotels, beer parlors, or hawking provisions on the street are often molested; boys working in motor parks or as bus conductors are often introduced to petty theft (Ewuruigwe, 1986). Children who labor to earn school fees may work four to eight hours daily in addition to their regular classroom attendance.

In addition to this objective reality, the psychologist must be sensitive to the subjective perceptions generated by the prevailing social context. There is a growing sense of "futurelessness" among children and adolescents, particularly the urban and rural poor. These youngsters have seen their prospects for development and progress thrown away by the adults who were in charge of the nation, and there is no group in whom they can place faith, politicians or military. Consequently, many express limited faith in adults, or in their personal future or the future of the nation. This view is not confined to the poor: university graduates, who are faced with massive unemployment primarily due to mismanagement, also accuse past leaders of having destroyed their futures. The extent of this phenomenon among older children and adolescents requires investigation.

In a society characterized by inequality, the exigencies of the socioeconomic reality may conflict with and take precedence over caretaker aspirations and values as articulated by the culture. In an environment where education is costly, income negligible and families large, caretakers may be forced to forego the formal education of several children to insure the continued general welfare of the family unit. Caretaker control over the child's environment and activity may be greatly diminished in conditions of inequality.

The development of morals in visibly corrupt society and the development of political attitudes and values can only be understood after consideration of the socioeconomic contest. Psychologists must carefully articulate and understand the objective and subjective realities experienced by families before they can understand the interactions within them.

The Cultural Context

Without a doubt culture is the most all encompassing aspect of the developmental context. Anthropologists concede that attempts to arrive at a universally acceptable definition of what constitutes culture have been highly problematic (Cole & Scribner, 1974). However, it is generally held that culture encompasses all the accepted and patterned behaviors of a given people as well as the attitudes, meaning, and values that underlie these behaviors and their material expression (Brown, 1963).

Culture is dynamic and may also be viewed as the adaptive response of human beings to problems generated by the environment. Perceptions of problems such as the biological and the socioeconomic systems are mediated by culture. In addition, the resolution of these problems results in modes of behavior and systems of value and belief that are incorporated into the culture as they become generally accepted.

Explanations of development based on the interactive process between child and environment are impossible without an understanding of the culture in which this takes place. This knowledge is not merely a reference point for describing the child's background; it also makes possible the interpretation of caretaker behaviors. More importantly, knowledge of the culture is instrumental to the formulation of theories, research questions, and data gathering techniques.

As we have noted above, Nigeria is a multi-ethnic, multi-cultural society; consequently, the identification of the cultural environment in which a particular child develops is a most complex task. Another difficulty is the selection of those aspects of the culture to which the psychologist needs to pay particular attention. In the course of investigating child-environment interaction processes, at some point almost every aspect of culture may be relevant. However, some features are particularly salient if a holistic study is contemplated. At a very minimum, the researcher should be sensitive to and knowledgeable about marriage customs, family structure, the philosophy of childhood, and the roles of caretakers (particularly women) within the society. We will here consider family structure and the philosophy of childhood.

Knowledge of family structure is vital, not merely for descriptive purposes. Each type of family structure has unique features, and awareness of these features, coupled with an understanding of roles, norms, and behavioral expectations, enables the researcher to more adequately hypothesize regarding the potential range of experiences each affords.

A variety of family structures can be identified in Nigeria: polygamous, monogamous, extended, nuclear, and single parent (usually female-headed) households.[5] Many extended families are polygynous, but monogamous families can also have an extended formation. Each structure (with the exception of the single-parent family) is considered normative. Residential patterns within each structure vary considerably. In polygynous settings the husband and wives may co-habitate, or the women may live in separate residences, usually in different communities. If educational opportunities are better in a particular location or if the father requires assistance in his work, it is likely that one wife may be responsible for the care and upbringing of a majority of the children, including those not her own. In extended monogamous families, all members (nuclear family, grandparents, aunts, uncles, cousins, etc.) may reside within the same compound, or the nuclear family may live together and host a succession of relatives for brief or lengthy periods of time. The bonds between such family members are very close and there is considerable reciprocity and sharing of roles.

According to the Nigerian Fertility Survey (1984), approximately 23% of Nigerian women live in polygynous households. A major factor affecting the incidence of polygyny is economics. A man who has more than one wife must be able to provide adequately for the additional women and children. The extended family structure is still dominant although its incidence is declining in urban areas.[6]

Extended family settings provide a variety of experiences that may be rare in nuclear families (Durojaiye, 1976). Multiple parenting is one of such experiences. The child has many parent-figures — natural parents, father's other wives, aunts and uncles, grandparents, and older siblings. All are equally responsible for the child's upbringing. As a result of this contact with a wide range of caretakers, children form a variety of attachments at an early age. They also have multiple encounters with a large number of adults, so are exposed to a variety of personalities and have the opportunity to observe and interact with many adults performing a wide range of tasks. Thus, social horizons are expanded very early in life.

As with all family structures, interpersonal problems such as rivalry, jealousy, or ineffective communication are a part of life in an extended household, and are likely to be especially volatile when larger numbers of individuals are involved. Many traditional cultures in Nigeria put a high premium on harmonious family re-

---

[5] There are several residential patterns associated with the polygamous and extended family structures. In this discussion we are referring to those settings where the family shares a residential unit and where childrearing functions are mutually shared by most of the adult females within the household.

[6] In the absence of the extended family, urban nuclear families are evolving various adaptions to obtain some of the benefits associated with it. Neighbors or coworkers combine to form extended networks that provide mutual support, particularly childcare. There does not appear to have been any systematic investigation of this phenomenon.

lationships. Among the Yoruba, for example, great importance is placed on solidarity, peace, and cooperation (Fadipe, 1970; Wilson, 1973).

In an effort to achieve these goals within an extended family setting, the development of loyalty to biological parents may be discouraged in preference for solidarity with the larger unit. The result is a series of behavioral expectations and prohibitions that are designed to mitigate the effects of attachment to parents. Investigators, therefore, require knowledge of the family's goals, norms, and behavioral expectations before they can determine precisely what is being observed or identify the appropriate unit of analysis.

Another aspect of culture requiring the psychologist's attention is the philosophy of childhood. This philosophy provides answers to a variety of questions that have significant import for the manner in which the child is raised.

The first question is, how does the culture perceive children? What is their essence? They may be considered a *tabula rasa*, or, as with the Yoruba, it may be believed that they come to the earth with their characters formed and a predetermined (although slightly modifiable) lot. Does a child have only one life, or are there thought to be former and future existences? What is the child's contribution to the family: economically, socially, psychologically, and spiritually? What does the family expect? What is the nature of filial responsibilities?

The second question considers what the child is to become. Every society has expectations for the type of individuals it wishes to create. Some emphasize development of the mind and body in a harmonious relationship; others stress the development of individualism, acquisitive skills, or self-fulfillment.

Third, what methods are used to effect the desired development? What is the culture's theory and techniques for guiding and modifying behavior?

Another question relates to parents. Who are the parents, and what responsibilities do they have toward the child?

Finally, what is the nature of childhood itself? When does it end? In the duration, are there particular moments of special significance?

In Nigeria, the psychologist who attempts to answer these questions will of necessity be required to utilize research methods that have been associated with anthropology. Relatively little anthropological work in Nigeria has emphasized the philosophy of childhood, so in many cases the psychologist will be required to analyze various artifacts of culture. There are many that have relevance. For instance, in spite of the fact that many indigenous languages now have written forms, there remains a high premium on orality. The oral literature of a cultural group, its proverbs, poems, praise songs, and literary divinatory corpus reveal a great deal regarding conceptions of children and childhood. Folk tales, lullabies, and riddles are equally informative. The rituals that mark rites of passage during childhood are reflective of those developmental milestones that the culture considers significant.

Unraveling a philosophy of childhood among members of the modern sector may be more problematic. This sector is alienated from the indigenous cultures it sprang from, but its image and conception of the western cultures it seeks to approximate are often distorted. In fact, no clear-cut philosophy of childhood may exist. Analysis of rites of passage, the language employed with children, and stories (both written and oral) may be useful in the attempt to articulate the philosophy that obtains in this sector.

In both sectors, attempts to specify a philosophy of childhood will be greatly aided by participant observation. Once the researcher knows who a child is, what he or she is to become, and who is responsible for this development, it is possible to identify the intentions of caretakers and to comprehend the logic of their actions.

In summary, adequate and appropriate explanation of the development of psychological processes and behaviors in the Nigerian child requires a contextually sensitive approach. Knowledge of the cultural context is central to such an approach but not identical to it. Attention must also be given to the influence of biological and socioeconomic factors.

CONCLUSION

Nigeria is a neo-colonial society that is heavily dependent on western industrialized countries for its economy. Its study and practice of psychology reflect a similar dependency: theories and methods developed in different social, cultural, and historical contexts are imported and utilized despite their questionable utility. With specific reference to psychology, this situation has resulted in inadequate and incorrect explanations of the development of the African child.

The crisis in explanation created by dependency psychology can only be resolved if the African child is studied holistically, taking interactions with the environment into account. Such an inquiry requires an understanding of the full environmental context, with emphasis on the biological, socioeconomic, and cultural factors that combine and interact to make up this context.

Explanations of development based on child-environment interaction may necessitate that psychologists collaborate with other social or health scientists. Alternatively, they may expand their methodologies to incorporate data gathering techniques utilized in anthropological research.

It is only when African children are studied on their own terms, using contextually appropriate data-gathering techniques, that we can adequately account for their development. Findings from such studies could then be utilized to formulate a theory of development that is truly universal.

REFERENCES

Anazonwu, C.O., & Ugwuegbu, D.O. (1986) Dimensions of attitudes to automobile accidents in Nigeria The views of accident victims. In E.B. Wilson (Ed)., *Psychology and Society*. Ile-Ife: Nigerian Psychological Association.

Bauer, D. (1976) An exploratory study of developmental changes in children's fears. *Journal of Child Psychology and Psychiatry, 17*, 69-74.

Bowlby, J. (1969) *Attachment and Loss*, Vol. 1, Attachment. New York: Basic Books.

Brown, I.C.(1963) *Understanding Other Cultures.* Englewood Cliffs, NJ: Prentice-Hall.

Cole, M., Sharp, D.W., Gay, J., & Glick, J. (1971). *The Cultural context of learning and thinking*. New York: Basic Books.

Cole, M., & Scribner, S. (1974) *Culture and thought*. New York: John Wiley.

Dada, M.K. (1986) *The relationship between locus of control and psychopathology*, an unpublished M.Sc. thesis. Benin, Nigeria: University of Benin.

Diejomoah, V.J., & Anusionwu, E.C. (1981) The structure of income inequality in Nigeria: A macro analysis. In Henry Bienen and V.P. Biejomaoh (Eds.), *The political economy of income distribution in Nigeria*. New York: Holmes & Meier.

Dixon, V.J., & Foster, B. (1971). *Beyond black and white: An alternate America.* New York: Little, Brown.

Durojaiye, M.O.A. (1976). *A new educational psychology.* London: Evans Bros.

Dyorough, A.E. (1986). *The problematics of child labor in Africa.* Unpublished paper presented at the First International Workshop on Child Labor in Africa. Enugu.

Ewuruigwe, F.A. (1986). *Exploitation of child labor in Choba, Port Harcourt: A political economy approach.* Unpublished paper presented at the First International Workshop on Child Labor in Africa. Enugu.

Fadipe, N.A. (1970). *The Sociology of the Yoruba.* Ibadan: Ibadan University Press.

Feshbach, N.D. (1973). Cross cultural studies of teaching styles in four year olds and their mothers. In A.D. Pick (Ed.), Minnesota Symposium on Child Psychology, vol. 7, Minneapolis: University of Minnesota Press.

Galejs, I., & D'Silva, C. (1982). Locus of control differences among Anglo-American, Latvian-American and Nigerian schoolage children. *Cross Cultural Psychology Bulletin*, 16, 3-4 (Aug-Nov).

Gilligan, C. (1982) *In a different voice.* Cambridge, Mass: Harvard University Press.

Gordon, I.J. (1969). Early childhood stimulation through parent education. Final Report, Childrens Bureau, Social and Rehabilitation Service, H.E.W., Grant No. PHS-R-306. June.

Hess, R.D., & Shipman, V.C. (1965) Early rxperience and the docialization of cognitive modes in children. *Child Development*, 34, 869-886.

International Labour Office (1981). *First things first: Meeting the basic needs of the people of Nigeria.* Addis Ababa: ILO.

King, L.M., Dixon, V.J., & Wilson, E.B. (1976) *Fanon Center restoration model, an emancipatory strategy.* Washington, D.C.: N.I.E. Grant Number NIE-R-75-0018.

Kluckhohn, F.R., & Strodtbeck, F.L. (1961). *Variations in value orientations.* Evanston, Ill.: Row, Peterson.

Kohlberg, L. (1969). Stage and sequence: The cognitive-development approach to socialization. In D.A. Goslin (Ed.), *Handbook of Socialization Theory and Research.* New York: Rand McNally.

Lambo, T.A. (1969). The child and mother-child relationships in major cultures in Africa. *Assignment Children*: 10 (June): 61-71.

Mabogunje, A.L. (1982) Profile of the social sciences in West Africa. In L.D. Stifel, R.K. Davidson, & J.S. Coleman, *Social Sciences and Public Policy in the Developing World.* Lexington, MA: Health.

Moghaddam, F.M., & Taylor, D.M. (1986) *Towards appropriate training for developing world psychologists.* Unpublished paper, Department of Psychology, McGill University, Montreal.

Nigeria (1971). *Second National Development Plan.* National Planning Office, Federal Ministry of National Planning, Lagos.

Nigeria (1984). *The Nigerian Fertility Survey 1981/82.* Lagos: National Population Bureau.

Nobels, W. (1977). *Conceptual incarceration and the study of the Afro-American Child.* Unpublished keynote address delivered at the Annual Conference of the National Black Child Development Institute. Houston.

Rotter, J.B. (1966). Generalized expectancies for internal vs. external control of reinforcement. *Psychological Monographs*, 80, 609.

Valsiner, J. (1985). Parental organization of cognitive development within the home environment. *Psychologia*, 28 (3), 131-143.

Valsiner, J., & Benigni, L. (1986). Naturalistic research & ecological thinking in the study of child development. *Developmental Review*, 6, 203-223.

Wilson, E.B. (1973). *Social control and childhood among the Yoruba.* Unpublished M.A. critique. Claremont, California: Claremont Graduate School.

Wilson, E.B. (1986). Age and sex differences in self-reported fears of Nigerian adolescents. In E.B. Wilson (Ed.), *Psychology and Society.* Ile-Ife Nigerian Psychological Association.

Chapter 3

Organization of Children's Social Development in Polygamic Families

Jaan Valsiner

Research on child development has overwhelmingly limited its focus to those cultural conditions within which the discipline has emerged. Thus, child psychologists have extensively discussed problems of social development in the occidental cultural settings of Europe and North America, which are organized around one or another religious belief system based on the heritage of Christianity. As a natural result of such cultural history, children's social development has been conceptualized assuming the monogamic form of marriage to be the rule in the children's native families.

However, in following their own culturally socialized understanding of what the "normal" family is like, child psychologists have overlooked the reality that is characteristic of different cultures around the world. According to Murdock's *World Ethnographic Sample*, only 20% of the world's cultures (that are described in the Atlas) have been (or are) strictly monogamous (Stephens, 1963, p. 33). Thus, around 80% of the world's cultures allow (although do not necessarily prescribe) one or another form of polygamy as their version of social organization of family groups. Different religious frameworks, especially Islam, have undoubtedly facilitated the acceptance and maintenance of polygamy in marriages. Historically, polygamy (mostly polygyny) has been overwhelmingly dominant all around the world. The ancient civilizations of India and China permitted it; signs of polygyny are evident in the descriptions of life in the Old Testament; and pre-Christian tribes of Europe practiced it. One of the ways in which the Christian religion set occidental societies apart from the rest of the world was by outlawing polygamy (Taylor, 1954).

It follows from the widespread nature of polygamic marriages that the social environment of many children growing up in different cultures around the world is likely providing them with a unique angle of knowledge of social relationships and experiences that differ from those of their Western counterparts. The goal of this chapter is to analyze in what ways polygamic family organization affords children opportunities for gaining socially relevant knowledge. The data on which the present discussion is based are taken from anthropological literature, which is often incomplete insofar as detailed accounts of child socialization are concerned. Anthropologists have rarely viewed the cultures they study from the perspective of child development. Their treatment of child socialization has usually had the goal of getting to know the culture, within which child socialization is but one aspect among many.

The focus in the present chapter is on the analysis of the *possible* social experiences that polygamic and monogamic marriage forms may afford to children. In order to understand this issue in general terms, a theoretical reconstruction of the developmental courses of the two kinds of families, and of the experiences of children within them, will be performed. Any theoretical reconstruction effort of this kind is an idealized picture of reality that may be adequate for some empirical examples, but probably not for many. The empirical reality is always by far more complex than any reconstruction of its selected aspects can be, as will be obvious from the few selected empirical examples that are used here to illustrate that complexity.

MARRIAGE FORMS AS CONTEXTS FOR CHILD DEVELOPMENT

The forms of social relationships between marriage partners, together with the composition of family households (e.g., extended, or joint families), set up the social structural context within which child development takes place. A child who is born into a particular family "inherits" the social environment of that family. Unless there are major changes in the family environment during the childhood years (e.g., death of a parent, divorce, addition or departure of live-in relatives), this social environment is set up in a stable, structured form from the time of birth. The child develops within that social context until he or she leaves the natal home and immerses in other social contexts. Thus, at least for the years of early childhood, the development of the child is organized by the family network of the parents' household. The time of leaving the natal home varies greatly across cultures. In Western industrial countries children usually leave it in conjunction with education, or when entering the labor force. In contrast, the practice of "child borrowing" (sending children of 3-15 years of age to live with relatives — see Cunningham, 1964) or West African child fosterage (see Isaac & Conrad, 1982) may lead to demographic situations in which by adolescence over 50% of children live in households into which they were not born. This "movement" of children between households is closely linked with the dynamics of family organization within any given culture (Goody & Goody, 1969). Different marriage forms — monogamic or polygamic — constitute the core structure to which children's upbringing is intricately tied.

POLYGAMY AND MONOGAMY

Within the layperson's knowledge in occidental cultures, unrealistic characteristics have often been attributed to polygamy. Sometimes these characteristics are mere projections of the observers' wishes; on many occasions they constitute simple superstitions, based on the normative models of thought of monogamically socialized Westerners. What, then, is polygamy?

Polygamy is plural marriage. It includes three sub-types: *polygyny* (one husband married to two or more wives), *polyandry* (one wife married to two or more husbands), and *group marriage* or *polygynandry* (two or more wives simultaneously married to two or more husbands). There exists a substantial asymmetry in the distribution of these forms: both geographically and in terms of acceptance by people in different cultures, polygyny is the statistical "norm." In contrast, polyandry and polygynandry (which can be seen as a combination of polygyny and polyandry) are present within a very specific range of cultures, mostly located on the Indian subcontinent and its neighboring regions (Jain, 1980; Majumdar, 1963; Saksena, 1962).

The three types of polygamic marriage forms are not separate classes to which a particular marriage can be easily assigned. Rather, they are *states* that a marriage may take, if the culture allows for polygynandry or polyandry aside from polygyny (and, of course, monogamy). In contrast to Western historically developed practice which prescribes only monogamy in different versions (e.g., a "strict" version allowing no divorce, or a "serial" version that allows re-marriage but in order to marry again the person has to be divorced from the former spouse), transitions between different marriage forms are more variable in the rest of the world.

In the case of the monogamous marriage form, the cultural requirement that the previous marital relationship be ended before entering another serves as the controlling factor. When that rule is non-existent, all three polygamic forms can easily develop out of the monogamic form. In that case, a husband may get married to a new wife *while retaining the previous one,* thus transforming a monogamous marriage into a polygynous one. Likewise, if an older brother is married, and his younger brother becomes an adult, he may take the role of a "co-husband," thus turning the marriage into a polyandrous one (the majority of cases of polyandry in the world are fraternal). If, say, this arrangement is not agreed to by the parties involved, the younger brother may bring another woman into the household (thus making it an extended family, with two parallel monogamous marriages). If the sexual access boundary between the two monogamous marriages becomes eliminated, the extended family becomes a case of polygynandry or group marriage. A similar transformation of a polyandrous or polygynandrous families into a monogamic form can occur. For example, if one of the wives in a two-husbands and two-wives polygynandrous marriage dies, the co-husbands (most likely brothers) are left with one wife (a case of polyandry). If the wife prefers one brother to the other, and restricts her sexual relations to him, the polyandrous marriage becomes *de facto* a monogamic marriage, plus an unmarried brother. If the latter leaves the household, and the wife and/or the remaining husband decide to bring in another woman, the marriage becomes polygynic in its form. When viewed dynamically, the marriage form of a particular case is not a stable, fixed entity, but constitutes a structural adaptation that can dynamically adjust itself to different needs (economic, social, psychological, sexual, etc.) of the family members at any given time (see Bhatt, 1980; Majumdar 1954/55, 1955). Of course, any structural transformations of the marriage form depend on the constraints set upon those within the given culture. Whereas tribes in the Himalayas may flexibly move between all four forms as needed, many historically well-known efforts within the Western cultural contexts to deviate from the monogamic traditions have been suppressed or stigmatized.

Of the three sub-types, polygyny is undoubtedly the most frequent marriage form around the world's cultures (see Clignet, 1970). Its roots go back in history beyond the beginning of the development of our species. In the sub-human animal world, heterosexual relationships are primarily polygamous in their organization. Monogamy is a rare mating system among the mammalian species in general (see Kleiman, 1984). Among most polygynous species, the mother-young unit is the primary relationship that organizes development of the offspring. From a sociobiological standpoint, polygamous relationships can be estimated to provide for superior adaptational advantages at the level of the species.

Within human cultures, polygyny's relationships with monogamy can be viewed from different angles. Very often, anthropological reports from cultures that allow polygyny report that many families lead monogamous lives. Sometimes (e.g., Westermarck, 1930) this finding is taken to demonstrate the "unusual" or "exceptional" character of polygyny as compared to monogamy — i.e., assuming that the latter is the "normal" state of organization. The Western ethnocentric basis of this estimation is obvious: since the culturally sanctioned Western monogamy is considered the desirable state of affairs, all different organizational forms of marriage are seen as aberrations.

An alternative perspective that the present author takes is the reverse: in the context of the development of individual families within a culture, *monogamic arrangements can be cases of underdeveloped polygyny,* where the full-fledged polygynic form of marriage has not emerged, for whatever reasons (e.g., economic — high brideprice, or demographic — insufficient number of marriageable women). That is, the monogamic condition that is observed alongside the accepted and valued practice of polygyny is not similar in its nature to the Western culturally prescribed norm. Demographic statistics from different Third World countries that may demonstrate high frequency of monogamic marriages may aggregate data that are of qualitatively different psychological background. There undoubtedly exist monogamous marriages where that arrangement is the form that is desired by both spouses. Alongside with those cases, there exist monogamous marriages in which the spouses are oriented towards transforming their presently monogamous arrangement into a polygynic one. Contrary to the hopes of Christian missionaries and the ethnocentric public opinion in Europe and North America, polygyny in Africa is not on its way to disappearing, although the economic changes in life conditions may make that desired marriage form more difficult to attain than was the case in the past (see Ahmed, 1986; Ekechi, 1976). Missionaries' efforts to eradicate African polygyny in the past often led to a combination of "Western" (official, monogamic) and "African" (unofficial, polygynic) marital arrangements, where behind the monogamic facade a polygynic reality was hidden (see Mann, 1983).

In Western popular understanding, "blame" for polygynization of most of the world's cultures is often directed towards Islam. It is usually overlooked that polygamic marriage forms were the rule in many cultures *before* Islam emerged as a unifying major religion (Farah, 1984). It is also not considered that the Koranic commandment about marriage is a factor that *limits* (rather than enhances) the proliferation of polygyny, setting up economic and organizational rules under which a man can marry more than one woman. The Koranic prescription is concise:

> Marry women of your choice, two, or three, or four; but if ye fear that ye shall not be able to deal justly (with them) then only one. (Khan, 1983, p. 27)

Islamic teaching sets up the criterion of just treatment of wives as the major decision-maker as to whether a monogamic or polygynic marriage form is appropriate on a particular occasion. The rules of Islamic marriage set up role expectations for both husband and wives (see a translation of Al-Ghazali's work, in Farah, 1984). The influence of Islam on marriages depends on the social organization of life in different countries, between which immense differences can be found (see Beck & Keddie, 1978). Like Judaism, Christianity, or any other religious framework, Islam has fulfilled an organizational function for guiding the human lives and marital relationships of the people who adhere to it. The patterns of everyday life of these people set other constraints upon the organization of their families.

POLYGYNY AND RESIDENCE PATTERNS

Any discussion of child socialization in polygynic families requires attention to an important factor: namely, the residence pattern of the co-wives, which can introduce substantial differences into the children's social environments. At one extreme are arrangements where the co-wives have separate and independent households (often in geographically dispersed locations) which their joint husband visits regularly for some time. This, residentially dispersed "visiting husband" arrangement may be little different, if viewed from the children's perspective, from a monogamous home environment where the father is present periodically. The children might even not know their father's other wives and children personally. This arrangement is in many ways formally parallel to the "serial" monogamy in Western industrialized cultures, where increased frequency of divorce and remarriage may create social environments for children where the mother is the sole household head, and the father is allowed limited "visiting time" by court-ordered or personal arrangements.

In contrast, the residence pattern where the co-wives live together on the same home territory (compound) and share everyday chores creates a social environment for children that substantially differs from that in monogamic families. However, the sharing of the home territory need not be absolute — in many cases it is divided into sub-units that belong to different co-wives; the care-giving functions of every wife's children may be principally retained by the biological mother; and the husband may "circulate" between the co-wives' units on an agreed-upon time-schedule (see

Goldschmidt, 1976). It is also important to bear in mind that usually the "small group" of co-wives in a polygynic marriage consists of women of different ages, which provides the opportunity for stratification of the wives' group (e.g., the "senior", most dominant wife is usually the oldest in the group). The age differences between co-wives sharing the home compound also creates the women's social network through which knowledge and skills can be learned (e.g., assuming that the younger women have less knowledge of important aspects of life — childbearing and household management — than their more senior peers). This network can also serve as the basis for forming coalitions that could *de facto* reduce the husband's leadership role in the family only to its nominal label.

At the same time, of course, such polygynic arrangements also provide more opportunities for inter-wife quarrels, in which case the husband is expected to use his diplomatic skills and power role to bring the "team" of his wives back into a state where their joint activities are run in an acceptable way. One of the major roles that Islamic teachings require from husbands in polygynous families is the skill of even-handed treatment of the wives, and reconciliation of their possible conflicts (Farah, 1984). In addition to that, the husband is required to provide all the wives (and oftentimes also their kinship groups, through brideprice) with certain material wealth. This leadership role in a potentially conflictful women's group, combined with requirements of provision, makes the role of the polygynous husband a complicated psychological task, which is quite different from the popular Western image of the harem-owner idling

under the excessive care of his wives, with his whims and wishes satisfied in an instant.

Another aspect of polygynous families that is related to residence patterns of co-wives is the movement of the wives between their husband's home compound and their original homes. In many cultures, a pregnant woman in a polygynous marriage leaves the husband's compound for the native home, gives birth in her childhood home (with the help of her mother and other female relatives), and returns to the husband only after a number of months. Alternatively, she may be subjected to elaborate pre- and post-partum sexual abstinence requirements that exclude her from sexual cohabitation for one to three years (dependent upon the length of breastfeeding, since that usually marks the length of post-partum sexual abstinence). As Ware (1983, p. 23) has indicated about West African families, a woman who marries at 16, bears six children who are born alive and one stillbirth, and becomes a widow at the age of 41 (typical for much of the region) would spend more than fifteen of her twenty-five years of married life abstaining from sexual intercourse. During the substantial abstinence periods, whether she stays with her parents or with her husband, the woman is free from the need for catering to her husband's sexual wants by the presence of other wives in the family. She need not, however, be spared of participation in the subsistence activities of the whole family, as women who bear 6-7 children also provide 60-80% of the agricultural labor on the continent of Africa (Ware, 1983, p.21). This latter issue makes it necessary to understand the economic function of polygyny.

POLYGYNY AS AN ECONOMIC AND ORGANIZATIONAL ASSET AND LIABILITY

Polygyny is closely related to the economic side of the life of the family, in respect to both its present and future economic standing. The male and female perspectives on polygyny are predictably different. From the male perspective, the ability to be married polygynously is both a sign of wealth and a means of becoming economically better off in the future. The presence of more than one wife provides more labor for the family's subsistence tasks. In addition, more wives increase the chances of having more children, thus increasing the possibility that a sufficient number will survive beyond the vulnerable first couple of years of life. Children become economically useful either directly (by performing subsistence tasks) or indirectly (by freeing adults and older siblings to perform subsistence tasks, e.g., as in the case of delegation of child-care tasks from parents to older siblings, and from older siblings to younger ones — see Ochs, 1982; Weisner and Gallimore, 1977). Having more children and more wives is a viable strategy for the husband. The Sebei saying, "A man with but one wife is a friend to the bachelor" (Goldschmidt, 1976, p. 231) illustrates the dangers inherent in the physical and economic survival conditions of the monogamous family. A man with only one wife is constantly under the risk of her dying or divorcing him, which could render the economic survival of the household under risk. Multiple wives reduce such risk of economic collapse. In the long-range perspective, having many surviving children can grant the parents (especially mothers, since most of the wives are younger than their husband and are likely to outlive him) the old-age security that can be granted only through family and kin ties in the overwhelming majority of developing countries.

The female perspective on polygynic marriage oftentimes emphasizes different advantages. If the co-wives share the family household, this provides an opportunity to share the household and agricultural workload (Ware, 1979). On the side of liabilities, such an arrangement can be potentially difficult in terms of interpersonal relationships. Themes of jealousy are often attributed to African reasoning of polygyny (see Saunders, 1978). However, jealousy between wives need not be primarily related to sharing the sexual relations of the same man. Rather, if it occurs, it constitutes rivalry that is aimed at securing economic benefits (Ware, 1979).

In cases of polygyny where co-wives have separate households, the polygynic marriage form makes it possible for the women to be engaged in their independent economic activities, farming or trading, most of the time outside the control by the husband. In contrast with traditional activities of middle-class women in Europe and North America as housewives, African (at least West African) women have been far more actively involved in independent economic activities outside the home (see Agiobu-Kemmer, 1984; Ware, 1979, 1983). Contrary to the assumptions of Western feminists whose notions of African women have at times emphasized their "suppression" by the hostile male-dominated public world, many African women themselves consider issues of "women's liberation" a curious Western pastime. Ware's survey of Yoruba women in Ibadan reveals this perspective rather dramatically:

Men are not perceived as rivals or barriers in the path of female progress because of the firm belief that a woman who works hard enough can reach top on her own, although success would come more easily if she could rely upon the cooperation rather than the rivalry of her fellow women. This optimistic, achievement-oriented view is possible despite the very limited role that women do play in the formal sector . . . because women are viewed as the equals or even superiors of men in the large informal sector. (Ware, 1979, p. 193)

On the side of male economic liabilities, the possibility of exchanging the uncertainty of single-wife marriage for the polygynous case is itself a complicated adventure that is not open for everybody because of the costs involved (e.g., bride-price). Not surprisingly, several investigators (e.g., Agiobu-Kemmer, 1984; Assael, Namboze, German & Bennett, 1972; Bennett, Saxton, & Junod, 1968; Cederblad, 1968; Goldschmidt, 1976; Leiderman & Leiderman, 1974, 1977) have discovered that at the time of their fieldwork, the socially allowed and cherished ideals of polygynous marriages were actually practiced by only a minority of people in the populations. Furthermore, the change in the economic role of children — who are turning from being an economic asset to liabilities that require economic investment, such as financial support for schooling (see Bledsoe, 1980) — is likely to affect the presence of polygynic arrangements in African cultures. Such changes in the value of children may illustrate how monogamy is a special case of polygamy, where because of economical or psychological reasons, the number of spouses in the marriage is reduced to the minimum of one wife and one husband.

CHILD DEVELOPMENT IN POLYGAMIC AND MONOGAMIC FAMILIES

Theoretical perspectives in developmental psychology have historically been limited to the ethnocentric ideas of middle-class Western cultures, presenting a particular Western view on child development as the norm, and all differences from that norm as aberrations. The representation of any single viewpoint as the norm of child development stems from the maximizing ethos that is widespread in psychologists' thinking (Valsiner, 1987, pp. 28-30). The maximizing perspective leads investigators to overlook the possibility that child development can take place along a multiplicity of pathways, each (or at least many) of which are equally adequate for arriving at the desired outcome. In order to understand the differences and similarities between monogamic and polygamic families in organizing child development, it is necessary to change our theoretical mindset from a maximizing to a "satisficing" perspective.

Satisficing in Child Socialization

Marriage forms are social devices that organize life in family units in ways that satisfy the multitude tasks of family members: immediate subsistence, extension of kinship network, reproduction, child socialization, old-age security, etc. Within the web of this multitude of tasks, child socialization goals are *guaranteed* in the majority of cases in the sense that the socialized children become sufficiently adequate members of their society. In child socialization, as in many other problem-solving tasks, *satisficing* (finding a satisfactory solution to the problem under the given circumstances — see Simon, 1957) rather than maximization of "benefit/cost" ratio is the rule. The particular socialization goals that parents have in different cultures are intricately tied to other aspects of life (immediate subsistence, old-age security), rather than being separate from them (LeVine, 1979). Therefore, any direct comparison of polygamic and monogamic family types in the sense of "which of the two is better" is theoretically alien to the satisficing perspective on child socialization. By the mere fact that *both* types of family organization are widespread suggests that they have both been proven sufficient for the task of bringing up children in particular cultural contexts. Obviously there exist differences between monogamic and polygamic families in how children become socialized, but these are simply *different routes to the same goal* — childrens' becoming sufficiently socialized adult members of the society.

Psychological Accounts of the Role of Polygamy in Socialization

Western commonsense ideas of non-monogamic family organization have had an influence on the very few empirical studies in psychology that have addressed the issue of child socialization in polygamic settings. The studies that the present author has located have all taken the maximization, rather than satisficing perspective as the basis of their approach. They have often attempted to prove that polygamic family background of children in different cultural conditions is detrimental to child development in its different aspects, or at least less optimal

than the Western ideal of child development within monogamically organized families. Not surprisingly, investigators' thinking in this respect follows along the same lines that Christian missionaries have utilized in their accounts of child development around the world.

The existing research literature on children's development in polygamic families is indeed scarce. Despite the rarity of polyandrous and polygynandrous family frameworks on the world's scene, some empirical evidence on the summary effects of these family backgrounds on children's psychological differentiation has been obtained (Bisht & Sinha, 1982). Issues of child development in polygynic families have found somewhat wider, although still insufficient, coverage. Thus, Minde (1975, p. 54) tried to demonstrate on the basis of epidemiological data that the polygynic family background of children of Buganda (in Uganda) is linked with more frequent "problem behaviors" in children (as estimated by adults), than the control condition of monogamic nuclear families. Cederblad (1968), who conducted an extensive epidemiological study in three Sudanese Arab villages near Khartoum, found that children from polygamic families were represented more frequently among a group with symptoms of nocturnal enuresis, anxiety, and phobias. Owuamanam (1984), studying adolescents in Oyo state (in Nigeria) using self-report questionnaires, found that subjects from polygamous families tended to report less positive self-concept than their peers from monogamous families. Assael, Namboze, German and Bennett (1972, p. 390) reported that among pregnant women with "mental abnormalities" (near Kampala, Uganda) the percentage of women who were co-wives was higher than in the control group. These studies have all been based on the epidemiological research strategy of quantitative comparison of samples of adults (and children) from polygamous and monogamous family backgrounds, on the basis of populational rates of some psychiatric or psychological outcome measures. The actual social interaction processes within these families were not investigated in these studies, although authors attempt to explain their results via reference to some aspects embedded in those processes (e.g., stress in the family, caused by co-wives' conflicts or half-siblings' rivalry — cf. Minde, 1975, p. 54; Owuamanam, 1984, p. 597).

More direct evidence about the differences and similarities in childrearing practices between monogamic and polygynic households comes from observational research in real-life settings. Observations of attachment behavior of Hausa infants of 6-14 months conducted by Marvin and his colleagues in Nigeria (Marvin, VanDevender, Iwanaga, LeVine & LeVine, 1977) revealed that all the infants in the sample were attached to more than one caregiver, even if the mother remained the major caretaker of basic nutritional needs of the particular infant. The polygynic and patrilocal arrangement of the family compounds created a situation where the number of familiar adult caregivers was wide in range (from 1 to 10 per compound). Adults' responsiveness to an infant crying was distributed almost equally between biological mothers and other caregivers (53% versus 47% — see Marvin et al., 1977, p. 251). Similar findings emerge from the empirical comparison of monogamic and polygynic families of the Kipsigis in Kenya — in polygynous families, biological mothers were more frequently absent from their infants, but this ab-

sence did not affect the quality of care given to the infants, since it was organized collectively within the family network (Mulder & Milton, 1985). These findings point to the adequacy of the satisficing perspective on child care — different family structures organize care given to infants and children in different ways, all of which (with the exception of few insufficiencies in the few "unusual" families, either monogamic or polygamic in structure) are sufficient for that objective.

Hypothetical Modeling of Family Development in Polygyny and Monogamy

Despite the sufficient nature of child-care arrangements in both monogamic and polygamic families, children's experiences while growing up necessarily differ in some respects. In the remaining part of this chapter, a hypothetical analysis of the differences between a monogamic and a full-fledged (four-wife) polygynic family arrangement is provided. It should be stressed that this exercise of hypothetical modeling remains schematic in its nature. The reality of family arrangements around the world probably provides for fewer differences than are emphasized below, since on many occasions even monogamic families actually constitute either extended or joint families in which co-inhabitants are related through kinship ties.

The present attempt at reconstruction of the effect of polygyny on child socialization is based on one subtype of that marriage form — the family where the co-wives of the husband *share the same home compound,* are *sedentary agriculturalists* in their subsistence basis, are *patrilineal* in their descent, and *neolocal* in their residence. In this hypothetical case, the polygynic marriage starts from its monogamic state: a young man marries a young woman from a different village, and they establish a new family compound within his village. That state may last for a few years. For example, Goldschmidt (1976) reports differences between the taking of the first wife to the second among the Sebei ranging up to 11 years. The length of the monogamic phase of polygyny largely depends upon the economic power of the husband.

The differences between monogamic and polygynic states of the family, viewed from the children's perspective, emerge when the decision is made to bring in another wife. The psychological background of this decision can be highly variable: in some cases, it is the husband's initiative and may be contested by the first wife; in others it may be initiated by the wife and accepted by the husband. Walter Goldschmidt describes that psychological background among the Sebei (interviewed in 1954) in Kenya:

> . . . women differ in their feelings about polygynous relationships; some wanting to be first or only wives, some not caring or preferring to be junior wives. Where attitudes toward co-wives were expressed, they were, by and large, more friendly than hostile. One of the women said with respect to her junior wife: "I just saw him coming with her one day, and we became friends and love one another." Another said she wanted her husband to have another wife, but they were too poor to buy one, and a third claimed she had selected her husband's second wife, for whom her husband paid more than he did for her, as the brideprice had gone up by then.

Men consider it very bad for a woman to try to prevent her husband from taking additional wives. Nevertheless, a wife has many ways of blocking a second marriage; she may tell her husband bad things about the girl (that she is lazy, her mother rude, and so on), complain to the girl about him, saying that he is sexually impotent, or she might use treachery to break up the marriage before the final ceremony, perhaps by defecating in the new wife's house so that when the husband finds the evidence he suspects his new wife of witchcraft. (Goldschmidt, 1976, p. 233)

Co-wives' relationships with one another, and their attitudes towards moving from the monogamic stage of the marriage to its polygynic stage, can be highly variable. Therefore, actual investigations of marital relationships in polygamic families may find *both* conflict and harmony in co-wives' relationships (Saunders, 1978; Ware, 1979). Such wide potential variability is expected, as both of these extremes of relationships, or transitions of a family from mutual love to hatred over time, provide children with important (albeit vastly different) social experiences. One important way in which the polygynic family group differs from its monogamic counterpart is in the number of children of the same husband that are present *together* to experience the social relationships within the family. In order to illustrate this basic difference, I constructed a simple computer program to model the marital and reproductive development of both polygynic and monogamic families in the case of the neolocal residence pattern. A result of this modeling is presented in Figure 1. The figure provides a graphic illustration of how many children could be present in the households in each consecutive year, with the marriage starting at Year 0. The model was constructed on the basis of the following assumptions: (1) the interval between births by the same mother is three years; (2) in the polygynic case, each new wife arrives in the family four years after the last one, and starts child-bearing about one year later; (3) each wife is married into the household at the same age, and has an estimated 20 years of reproductive capability ahead of her, (4) children become adults at age 16 years and leave home at that time.

As is evident in Figure 1, the number of children present in the household begins to differ exceedingly starting from Year 6. By Year 24 in the monogamic case the number of children in the household has started to decline, as the oldest children leave home — sons by establishing their own neolocal households, daughters by leaving for their husbands' households. The maximum number of children present in the household in any year was estimated to be six (Years 16-17 and 19-20). In contrast, the polygynic household reaches a peak of 20 children by Years 23-25, after which the number begins to decline slowly. The decline in the polygynic case (not shown in Figure 1) arrives at the equivalent of the maximum number of children of the monogamic case (6) by Year 39, and reaches 0 by Year 48. In contrast, the last child would have left the monogamic family by Year 35 of its development.

The data in Figure 1 illustrate the longer time-span during which the polygynic family includes children. In comparison, the last child leaves the monogamic home much earlier. However, the data in Figure 1 are somewhat unnaturally elevated because the very important consideration of *infant mortality* was not included in the model — rather, the model assumed full (100%) survival of children once they had remained alive in the first two years. Figure 2 presents the data where

this condition has been entered as a constraining condition that determines, on the basis of comparison of a random number with the given mortality rate, whether a particular hypothetical child survives beyond the first two years of life or not. The calculations that resulted in Figure 2 were based on a 50% infant mortality rate, which is a realistic estimate given the historical conditions in African countries.

Figure 2 reveals results similar to those in Figure 1, only somewhat smaller in the absolute number of children at any given year. This follows logically from the assumption that all conditions, with the exception of the two marriage forms, are equal for both monogamic and polygynic families within the same culture and physical environment. The 50% infant mortality rate affects both kinds of households *proportionally* in a similar way, but the polygynic arrangement retains its absolute superiority over the monogamic case in the number of children born, and in the number who survive.

CHILDREN'S EXPERIENCES IN POLYGYNIC AND MONOGAMIC FAMILIES

It is clear that the formal difference between monogamic and polygynic families in the number of different-age children who are members of the household is only one step towards reconstruction of the differences in the children's experiences in these households.

A summary of the contrast between areas of children's experiences in polygynic and monogamic households is presented in Table 1.

It is evident that the differences between children's experiences within the

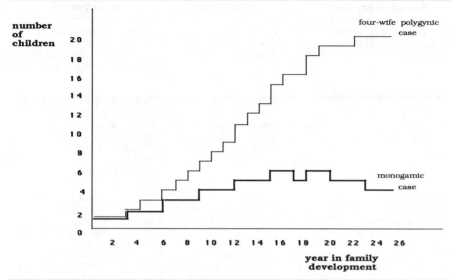

FIGURE 1

A COMPARISON OF THE NUMBER OF CHILDREN AT EVERY YEAR OF FAMILY DEVELOPMENT IN THE MONOGAMIC AND POLYGYNIC HYPOTHETICAL CASES

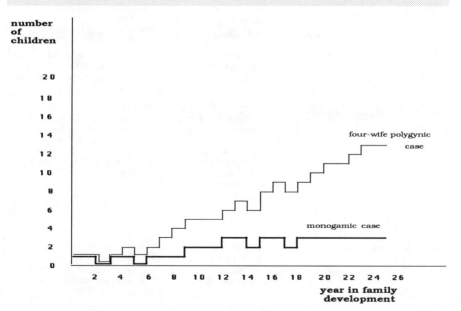

FIGURE 2

A COMPARISON OF THE NUMBER OF CHILDREN AT EVERY YEAR OF FAMILY DEVELOPMENT IN THE MONOGAMIC AND POLYGYNIC HYPOTHETICAL CASES ASSUMING OF 50% CHILD MORTALITY IN THE FIRST TWO YEARS

TABLE 1
CHILDREN'S EXPERIENCES IN POLYGYNIC AND MONOGAMIC FAMILIES

Nature of experience	Monogamy	Polygyny
1. Observation of adult-adult interaction in the family	Only husband-wife interaction can be observed	Husband-wives, and co-wives interaction can be observed in dyadic, triadic, and small group form
2. Observations of changes in the family composition	BIRTHS and DEATHS of siblings are observed less frequently than in the polygynic family	BIRTHS and DEATHS of siblings are observed more frequently than in the monogamic family. Unique observation: addition of new wives to the father's household
3. Children's possible effects on adults' relationships	Only effects on husband-wife relationships are possible (e.g., child "plays out" the father against the mother in order to attain some goal)	Less possibility of influencing father-wives relations, because of the greater distance between father and the co-wives, and lesser role of any of the children in the family system
4. Effects of adults' relationships on the child	The children are the direct observers and co-participants of father-mother relationships. Adults may use children as mediators, or scapegoats in their conflicts	Unique effect: the relations between co-wives can affect siblings' relationships. Attenuating factor: the conflicts between adults can be attenuated because of multiple wives in the family, and by separation of child/adult lives
5. Social support in case of need to cope with loss	The death of the mother leads to either one-parent family, or /and introduction of a new woman into the family. Social support available from relatives or peers	The death of the child's mother may lead to the care of the child by her co-wives. Social support in case of loss is available within the surviving family.
6. Experience with children	Less opportunity than in polygynic family (lesser number of children)	More opportunities with other children than in the monogamic family; lesser age-differences between siblings.

two family forms stem from the presence of more than one wife in the family. Basically these experiences may be divided into two categories: (1) *observational* (the children have the opportunity of observing the adults' action and interaction in particular settings), and (2) *direct participation* in family life (the children are included in some activities that are organized by the adults, which are relevant or routine for the household).

I. Observational experiences

Observation of adult-adult interaction within family. Children in both monogamic and polygynic families are observers of what goes on in their parents' relationships. In Western middle-class families, parents may try to hide certain aspects of their relationships behind the closed doors of their bedroom — only to realize that children can perceive the presence of conflict between them from some little comments, or tone of voice, that they forget to control when interacting in their child's presence. The examples used for the monogamic/polygynic comparison are based on the assumption that the living conditions of the hypothetical families do not afford architecturally created concealment of parents' relationships from the inquisitive eyes and ears of their offspring. In our examples, both in the monogamic and polygynic case any kind of interaction between the father and the mother(s) is potentially observable. The polygynic case, however, also provides children with the possibility of observing different kinds of *female* relationships within their home compound, ranging between the extremes of liking and hostility.

Addition of new members to the family. Both types of families are similar as far as the birth of children is concerned — the older siblings observe the arrival of their new brothers or sisters. In addition, the polygynic arrangement uniquely provides the children with observational experience of the arrival of new *adult* family members — the husband's new wives. This event is usually connected with architectural rearrangements (e.g., the husband may need to build a hut for the new wife), which obviously are observed and actively explored by the children. The actual arrival of the new wife enlarges the children's social interaction sphere at home. Her subdominant role is easily observed by the children, who witness everyday interaction between the co-wives about everyday matters. There is a substantial difference between the addition of a newborn child and of a new co-wife to the family. A new sibling is soon to be taken care of by the older children, whereas a new co-wife may become instrumental in directing some of the actions of the senior co-wives' children in everyday life.

Observation of peers' behavior. Both monogamic and polygynic families afford the younger siblings possibilities of observing their older siblings' behavior. However, there exist possible differences between the two types of families in how many siblings are available, and how close in age (and experience) these older siblings are to the younger ones. A look back at Figure 1 reveals that after the sixth year (and until Year 17) in the polygynic family, at least one child is born to the household every year. This creates close spacing between the ages of children of different wives, which is quite different from the monogamic case (with the exception of the birth of twins) where the birth spacing of the only wife creates larger age intervals for the siblings. The polygynic family not only has more children in the household, but each of these children can observe other children who are only slightly ahead of them in development, whereas the monogamic case does not afford such closeness in the targets of observational learning.

II. Direct participation experiences

The majority of experiences that children get in both monogamic and polygynic households in traditional cultures are direct, since all family members are involved in social happenings within the family. Therefore, a number of experiences in this category are extensions of the observational experiences, as the children are necessarily included in many issues of adults' activities and relationships.

Effects of adult-adult relationships. The polygynic family makes it possible that different kinds of relationships between co-wives have their effect on children. This is perhaps most evident in the case of rivalry between co-wives that can extend to their respective offspring. The mothers may themselves promote the rivalry between their children and those of their co-wives, or the children of different wives may simply pick it up from observing their mothers' interaction. Another way in which adults' relationships directly affect children in polygynic families is through the co-wives' possible use of children of their rivals to express their feelings. For example, the child of a rival may be made a scapegoat by her co-wife for issues that have noth-

ing to do with the child. These kinds of direct experiences for children are not possible in the monogamic family.

Experience of loss. Given the high infant mortality rate in many cultures, children in both types of families can be expected to have many opportunities to witness the death of a sibling. This experience involves both observational (seeing the sibling die) and participatory aspects (taking part in the funeral rituals). In addition, they may experience the loss of some adult family members through death or divorce of some of the co-wives (e.g., see Ardener, 1962). The difference between monogamic and polygynic families in the children's experience of loss becomes evident if we consider the *resources of social compensation* for the loss that exist within the family. In the monogamic case, the death (or divorce) of the wife brings the existence of *that* family to its end. In the case of the wife's/mother's death, the father will either marry again soon, or invite a female relative to come take care of the household and children. In either case the children face the arrival of a new woman into the household, who will immediately occupy the dominant position in household management (including overseeing children). As a result of this necessity for a new "manager," the household goes through a substantial period of uncertainty. In contrast, coping with loss in the polygynic family is supported by the presence of the social network of co-wives who can substitute for the deceased mother. The situation in both cases is more complicated when the husband dies. In many cultures, this may lead to the "inheritance" of the wives (and children) by another male relative in the husband's lineage.

Caregiving to siblings. In both types of families, older siblings act as caregivers and socializers to their younger brothers and sisters after the latter have been weaned. Most certainly this activity is under adult supervision, and in this respect the difference between monogamic and polygynic families is evident. In the latter case, there is a greater opportunity for the co-wives to delegate the overseeing-function of older siblings' caregiving from one wife to another. This frees the remaining wives for other important tasks. In contrast, the mother in the monogamic family has to accomplish both the subsistence tasks *and* overseeing of older siblings' caregiving of younger ones in parallel. Furthermore, in the polygynic family there are simply more children who can substitute for one another in taking care of younger siblings, or help the adults in their subsistence activities.

GENERAL CONCLUSIONS

Monogamic and polygamic forms of marriage set up organizational social frameworks that constitute the context within which children develop. In this chapter, it was pointed out that monogamy and polygamy are states of family organization that can change from one to another, provided that the cultural meaning system allows for such transformations. All forms of marriage that have been devised in the course of human cultural history are adaptations to the need of organizing both everyday life, and the transition from one generation to the next. All these forms are equally sufficient for bringing up children in the ecological-economic situation within which they are practiced. Within each of the forms of marriage, both interpersonal

conflict and harmony may be observed. In general terms, none of the forms is inherently more conflictful (or harmonious) than any other.

The schematic modeling of the developmental course of monogamic and polygynic families reveals a number of structural differences in children's social environments between these two forms. However, it is essential to bear in mind that it was based on a set of assumptions that represent a simplified picture of the complex variety of marriage forms in families around the world. First, it assumes that no one beyond the husband-wives-children network is living in the home compound. This assumption was necessary to demonstrate how the "pure" cases of monogamy and polygyny work from the children's perspective. However, in real life, in both monogamic and polygynic cases this assumption need not apply. Families may include close or distant relatives who share the same home compound, for a shorter or longer period of time. Furthermore, the assumed conjunction of patrilineal descent and neo-locality may be a rare case in reality, and the present model would not apply in cases where the first son continues within his father's home compound as his heir, and only other sons may establish neo-local residences when they marry. The presence of the grandparental generation in the home would alter the social strcture of the family. Finally, the greater number of children present in the poly-gynic family may be somewhat of an overestimation, given the frequent use of child-exchange between related families (e.g., a child who is capable of taking care of household tasks may be sent to relatives who need help, but have no children that age of their own). Both monogamic and polygynic families exist in the framework of inter-family relationships, where the intra-family environment that the children experience can be altered to a great extent if necessary from the perspective of the wider kinship network. Given such complexity of the reality of family life in different cultures, the present effort to model children's social experiences in monogamic and polygynic families remains mostly a heuristic device. It may perhaps alert child psychologists to the need for explanation of how child socialization is guaranteed sufficiently well by the variety of culturally structured social environments that surround and direct development.

NOTE A preliminary version of this chapter was presented at the Biennial Meeting of the Society for Research in Child Development, Toronto, April, 27, 1985.

REFERENCES

Agiobu-Kemmer, I. (1984). Cognitive and affective aspects of infant development. In H.V. Curran (Ed.), *Nigerian children: Developmental perspectives* (pp. 74-117). London: Routledge & Kegan Paul.

Ahmed, J. (1986). Polygyny and fertility differentials among the Yoruba of Western Nigeria. *Journal of Biosocial Science, 18,* 63-73.

Ardener, E. (1962). *Divorce and fertility: An African study.* London: Oxford University Press.

Assael, M.I., Namboze, J.M., German, G.A., & Bennett, F.J. (1972). Psychiatric disturbances during pregnancy in a rural group of African women. *Social Science and Medicine, 6,* 387-395.

Beck, L., & Keddie, N. (Eds.) (1978). *Women in the Muslim world.* Cambridge, MA: Harvard University Press.

Bennett, F.J., Saxton, G.A., & Junod, V. (1968). Family structure and health at Kasangati. *Social Science and Medicine, 2,* 261-282.

Bhatt, G.S. (1980). Constraints of being polyandrous-tribal: The case Jaunsar Bawar. In S.M. Dubey, P.K. Bordoloi, & B.N. Borthakur (Eds.), *Family, marriage and social change on the Indian Fringe* (pp. 59-82). New Delhi: Cosmo Publications.

Bisht, S., & Sinha, D. (1982). Family experiences and psychological differentiation. In R. Rath, H.S. Asthana, D. Sinha, & J.B.P. Sinha (Eds.), *Diversity and unity in cross-cultural psychology* (pp. 37-46). Lisse: Swets & Zeitlinger.

Bledsoe, C. (1980). The manipulation of Kpelle social fatherhood. *Ethnology, 19,* 29-45.

Cederblad, M. (1968). A child psychiatric study of Sudanese Arab children. *Acta Psychiatrica Scandinavica Supplementum, 200.*

Clignet, R. (1970). *Many wives, many powers: Authority and power in polygynous families.* Evanston: Northwestern University Press.

Cunningham, C.E. (1964). Atoni borrowing of children: An aspect of mediation. In M.E. Spiro (Ed.), *Symposium on new approaches to the study of religion* (pp. 21-37). Seattle: University of Washington Press.

Ekechi, F.K. (1976). African polygamy and Western Christian ethnocentrism. *Journal of African Studies, 3,* 329-349.

Farah, M. (1984). *Marriage and sexuality in Islam.* Salt Lake City: University of Utah Press.

Goldschmidt, W. (1976). *The culture and behavior of the Sebei.* Berkeley: University of California Press.

Goody, J., & Goody, E. (1969). The circulation of women and children in Northern Ghana. In J. Goody, *Comparative studies in kinship* (pp. 184-215). London: Routledge & Kegan Paul.

Isaac, B.L., & Conrad, S.R. (1982). Child fosterage among the Mende of Upper Bambara chiefdom, Sierra Leone: Rural-urban and occupational comparisons. *Ethnology, 21, 3,* 243-258.

Jain, Km. S.D. (1980). Woman's status in

marriage and family in a polyandrous society. In S.M. Dubey, P.K. Bordoloi, & B.N. Borthakur (Eds.), *Family, marriage and social change on the Indian fringe* (pp. 83-89). New Delhi: Cosmo Publications.

Khan, M. U. H. (1983). *Purdah and polygamy*. New Delhi: Harnam.

Kleiman, D. G. (1984). Implications of monogamy for infant social development in mammals. In M. Lewis (Ed.), *Beyond the dyad* (pp. 91-108). New York: Plenum.

Leiderman, P.H., & Leiderman, G.F. (1974). Affective and cognitive consequences of polymatric infant care in the East African Highlands. In A.D. Pick (Ed.), *Minnesota symposia on child psychology*, vol. 8 (pp. 81-110). Minneapolis: University of Minnesota Press.

Leiderman, P.H., & Leiderman, G.F. (1977). Economic change and infant care in an East African agricultural community. In P.H. Leiderman, G.F. Leiderman, & A. Rosenfeld (Eds.), *Culture and infancy: Variations in human experience* (pp. 405-438). New York: Academic Press.

LeVine, R. (1979). A cross-cultural perspective on parenting. In M.D. Fantini & R. Cardenas (Eds.), *Parenting in a multicultural society* (pp. 17-26). London: Longman.

Majumdar, D.N. (1954/55). *Family and marriage in a polyandrous society*. Eastern Anthropologist, 8,2, 85-110.

Majumdar, D.N. (1955). Demographic structure in a polyandrous village. *Eastern Anthropologist, 8, 3 &4*, 161-169.

Majumdar, D.N. (1963). *Himalayan polyandry*. Bombay: Asia Publishing House.

Mann, K. (1983). The dangers of dependence: Christian marriage among elite women in Lagos colony, 1880-1915. *Journal of African History, 24*, 37-56.

Marvin, R.S., VanDevender, T.L., Iwanaga, M.I., LeVine, S., & LeVine, R.L. (1977). Infant-caregiver attachment among the Hausa of Nigeria. In H. McGurk (Ed.), *Ecological factors in human development*

(pp. 247-259). Amsterdam: North-Holland.

Minde, K.K. (1975). Psychological problems of Ugandan school children: A controlled evaluation. *Journal of Child Psychology and Psychiatry, 16*, 49-59.

Mulder, M. B., & Milton, M. (1985). Factors affecting infant care in the Kipsigis. *Journal of Anthropological Research, 41, 3,* 231-262.

Ochs, E. (1982). Talking to children in Western Samoa. *Language and Society, 11*, 77-104.

Owuamanam, D.O. (1984). Adolescents' perception of polygamous family and its relationship to self concept. International *Journal of Psychology, 19*, 593-598.

Saksena, R.N. (1962). *Social economy of a polyandrous people*. Agra: Agra University Press.

Saunders, M.O. (1978). *Marriage and divorce in a Muslim Hausa town*. Unpublished Ph.D. Dissertation, Indiana University. Bloomington, IN.

Simon, H. (1957). *Models of man*. New York: Wiley.

Stephens, W.N. (1963). *The family in cross-cultural perspective*. New York: Holt, Rinehardt and Winston.

Taylor, G.R. (1954). *Sex in history*. New York: Ballantine Books.

Valsiner, J. (1987). *Culture and the development of children's action*. Chichester: Wiley.

Ware, H. (1979). Polygyny: Women's views in a transitional society, Nigeria 1975. *Journal of Marriage and the Family, 41,* 185-195.

Ware, H. (1983). Female and male life-cycles. In C. Oppong (Ed.), *Female and male in West Africa* (pp.6-31). London: Allen and Unwin.

Weisner, T., & Gallimore, R. (1977). My brother's keeper: Child and sibling caretaking. *Current Anthropology, 18, 2,* 169-180.

Westermarck, E. (1930). *A short history of marriage*. New York: Macmillan.

Chapter 4

Kohlberg's "Just Community" and the Development of Moral Reasoning

A Chinese Perspective

Mei-Ha Wong

INTRODUCTION

Studies of moral development have raised many questions that are at least as difficult, if not more so, than the questions they aim to resolve. This chapter is a theoretical discussion of Kohlberg's "just community" approach (Higgins, Power, & Kohlberg, 1984; Kohlberg, 1978, 1984, 1985; Kohlberg & Lickona, 1980) in moral education. Proponents of this alternative educational system argue that the moral atmosphere it creates helps to build up the sense of trust, concern, and rationality in young people that is necessary if any moral growth and action is to take place. Supportive results have been reported from various age groups. However, most proponents (e.g., Aubrey, 1980; Lickona & Paradise, 1980; Stuhr & Rundle, 1980) have been unable to relate their views clearly to the factors of internal consistency and cultural relativity. This chapter aims at analyzing both theoretical and practical problems that need to be dealt with if the approach is to prove useful in other cultural settings.

The chapter consists of three parts. First, I shall present the basic design of the just community approach; its normative orientation, practical goals, and empirical assumptions. Second, I shall point out that despite some of its insights, it is premature to claim (i) that it is the only right and good way to practice moral education, and (ii) that its original basic design should be implemented as completely as possible. I shall discuss several fundamental problems, including the interpretation of the positive results reported, the value premises, and the theory of misbehavior of the approach.[1] Applicability of the approach in Hong Kong, a predominantly Chinese society, will then be discussed to substantiate these arguments. Finally, I shall attempt

[1] I am not arguing for the relativistic nature of Kohlberg's theory - at least, that is not the focus of this chapter. People may respect individual dignity and lives without actually understanding democracy or community feelings. Also, they may pay attention to other values that are specifically important for their culture, e.g., respect toward the teacher. Practicing moral education in these cultures mean that such values have to be taken into account (Snarey, 1985).

to pinpoint some issues that have never been directly confronted. Some suggestions regarding moral education in Hong Kong will be made based on these insights. The aim is not to discuss moral education in Hong Kong in detail, but to make a theoretical conjecture of how some aspects of the just community approach may be useful for people in other cultural settings.

A REVIEW OF THE JUST COMMUNITY APPROACH

Origin

Attempts to apply Kohlberg's moral development theory to educational settings began with the hypothesis that if students were given the opportunity to discuss moral dilemmas in the classroom (Socratic discussion) and exposed to moral reasoning one stage above their own, the resulting cognitive conflict would stimulate movement toward the next stage (Power & Reimer, 1978; see Appendix I for a description of Kohlberg's moral development stages). Blatt (Blatt & Kohlberg, 1975) was the first person to apply this, and reported that junior and senior high school students who discussed hypothetical moral dilemmas in his semester-long program generally gained, on the average, one third to one half in their stages of moral reasoning. Subsequently this so-called "Blatt effect" has been successfully replicated in about a hundred different classrooms (Kohlberg, 1985). Nevertheless, the relationship between increased moral reasoning and behavior remains unclear — for instance, students in these studies were as likely to cheat in experimental tests after they had participated in the program as before. These results

suggest that Socratic discussion alone is not a sufficient means for affecting how people will act in moral conflict situations.

When a moral education program was set up in a Connecticut prison, Kohlberg and his colleagues soon discovered various shortcomings of relying solely on hypothetical moral-dilemma discussions (Kohlberg, Scharf, & Hickery, 1975; Power & Reimer, 1978). Inmates frequently described real life dilemmas experienced in prison that were at least as difficult to resolve as the ones originally devised by Kohlberg. When these dilemmas were discussed, the gap between how the group thought they should be resolved and how they actually were resolved became apparent. Some inmates admitted that they could not act in their high-stage resolutions and survive in prison society, where everyone acts according to the lowest stages of moral reasoning (either to avoid punishment or to further their own interests). Again, there was a gap between moral judgment and action. The need to create a prison environment in which inmates could learn to act according to their highest stage of reasoning led to the establishment of what is now called the "just community." Kohlberg and his colleagues eventually received permission to open a cottage in a women's prison that was run as a democratic community. Inmates and guards agreed to arrive democratically at decisions on how to govern the cottage and how to enforce the rules they made. This marked the beginning of a series of exploratory studies on the concept. Since then, just communities have been set up in some American alternative schools as small units of larger high schools. Their purpose was to allow participants to experience something different from traditional education in terms of emphasis on students' individual needs, student-teacher ratio, and interaction (Codding & Arenella, 1981). Subsequently, the approach was extended to elementary schools as well (e.g., Kohlberg & Lickona, 1980; Lickona & Paradise, 1980; Power, 1985; Stuhr & Rundle, 1980).

Nature and Design

Broadly speaking, the objective of a just community is to establish a practicable program of "manifest" moral education (as opposed to the so-called hidden curriculum) (Kohlberg, 1970) which can have an impact on moral action. Specifically, Kohlberg's approach was intended as a reaction to the inadequacies of the classic Socratic discussion approach. There are basically three elements to this intervention. First, it focuses on fostering a sense of community: trust and caring among members. Second, it tries to promote democratic governance whenever possible. For instance, except for some very basic rules in American law that must remain, rules are made up and enforced by the community members on the basis of participatory democracy. Third, in the rule-making processes, community members discuss different hypothetical and real life moral issues and dilemmas. Kohlberg (1978, 1984, 1985) argues that the process of democratic governance through communal discussion of such issues would stimulate growth of individuals' moral reasoning. At the same time, the communal concern of the members would provide a "psychologically optimal" environment for inducing moral actions.

To appreciate Kohlberg's assertions fully, it is important to have some knowledge of the normative orientations, practical goals, and empirical assumptions of this approach. In later discussion, I shall regard the normative and practical goals as a given and only challenge the empirical assumptions. Specifically, I would like to question whether the structural design of the approach is as effective and unmodifiable as its proponents claim.

Normative Orientations

Let us briefly identify the normative components in Kohlberg's approach. As his recent statements indicated (Kohlberg, 1984, 1985), the motivational and philosophical foundation for the moral content advocated in the just community approach had two sides: "rightness/justice" and "goodness" considerations. On the rightness side, Kohlberg was allegedly in the modern Kantian tradition. He saw basic agreements between his "moral musical chair," Rawls's "veil of ignorance" (1971) and Habermas's method of "discursive will formation" (1979), all of which essentially affirm the Kantian principles of liberty and equality. In Kohlberg's terms, "at the heart of these theories is the attitude or principle of universalized and generalized respect for individual human personality and autonomy enunciated by our example of a stage 6 response to the Heinz dilemma" (Kohlberg, 1985, p.36).

While the rightness side only suggests very general and abstract principles, the goodness side points to some concrete virtues. Specifically, Kohlberg acknowledged the concept of "social responsibility" as exposited by Dewey (1960), the virtue of "loyalty" as discussed by Royce (1982), and the "spirit of altruism" as explained by Durkheim (1973). Moreover, he appeared to have implicitly agreed with his predecessors that these virtues were good for civil community, for individual well-being, and for the enhancement of justice. Given these beliefs, it seems reasonable to require a moral education program to be consistent with and to facilitate the growth of these values.

Practical Goals

Besides normative requirements, Kohlberg also pointed out some practical goals for an effective moral education program. We have mentioned above that one of the fundamental limits of the Socratic discussion approach appears to be the relation of judgment to action. Research in schools and prisons has not shown clearly whether changes in the stage of moral judgment actually lead to change in moral action.

Another limit of the Socratic discussion approach is that it rules out the possibility of teaching *specific* moral values. Leaders of the discussion group are only supposed to expose members to a higher stage of reasoning without actually teaching what is right or wrong from their own point of view (Kohlberg, 1978). The teaching of specific moral content is related to the philosophical issue of indoctrination. Before introducing the just community approach, Kohlberg felt that indoctrination was invalid both philosophically and psychologically — philosophically because the value content taught was culturally and personally relative and thus a violation of the child's right, and psychologically because it could not lead to meaningful structural change in moral reasoning. However, he later changed these negative views, and stated that the concepts guiding moral education have to be partly "indoctrinative"

because moral education programs must be effective in the real world, in which individuals engage in stealing, cheating, aggression, etc.

Besides the fundamental limits of Socratic discussion, there is another practical concern underlying the just community approach — the lack of teachers' initiative and commitment to the value of moral education. Kohlberg regarded this problem as a result of the "psychologist's fallacy" (Kohlberg, 1985), meaning that psychologists tend to assume that what they view as important is also considered important by practitioners in the classroom. This became a major concern when he found that not one teacher who had participated in a research program studying the relationship of hypothetical moral dilemmas and the teaching of social studies continued to lead moral discussions when the study ended. Thus, it appeared to be a "one-way street" model — imposing what the researcher thought was important on the practitioners but not speaking enough to the needs of teachers, even though moral discussions had been shown to cause a significant moral stage change in their students.

Empirical Assumptions

Kohlberg has made the most prominent contribution toward devising a method of moral education that promises to be right, practicable, and effective. We have briefly stated the core elements of his method. Now is the time to sum up the rationales given to this design, especially the two new components added to the Socratic discussion approach — *participatory democracy* and *community*.

Several empirical propositions have been invoked to establish the desirability of participatory democracy. First, it can best protect against indoctrination, because a teacher has only one vote when the group decides on a rule or policy. Hence, it is felt to be a "right/just" method. It is also believed to be effective because it should help develop just reasoning as well as just action. Kohlberg (1985) suggested that when students form rules and disciplinary decisions for themselves, they are more likely to take responsibility for them. Also, peers would exert pressure on any discrepancies between one's public reasoning and one's actions.

Similarly, various empirical assumptions have been made in the contentions for community. Both Durkheim (1973) and Dewey (1960) argued that a sense of community should lead to respect for the group and group norms; as such it would be conducive to altruism and social responsibility. Further, Royce (1982) contended that it is a necessary condition for the development of individual psychological well-being — individuals would be motivated to participate in the community and fulfill their moral responsibilities voluntarily. Community is thus an effective method for facilitating the congruence of moral judgment and action. Collective acts of care and responsibility for the welfare of the group and its members will foster the development of a sense of justice (Kohlberg, 1985); hence community also reinforces the effect of the democratic side of the approach.

To be sure, this approach is to a large extent simply an extension of Dewey's notion of democratic community. However, it is to Kohlberg's credit that he has more fully specified both the method and the rationales, as well as systematically carried out field work that provided an empirical base for some of his ideas. As mentioned earlier, positive results have been reported by several schools.

Nevertheless, a closer scrutiny of the empirical assumptions stated above shows that they are far from well-documented. Kohlberg has cited the original thinkers who proposed these concepts and propositions, but he hardly explicitly or systematically assesses their empirical validity. In fact, even Durkheim's theory of group and society has been challenged (e.g., Lukes, 1977) despite its masterful empirical arguments. More importantly, as I shall discuss below, the positive empirical evidence needs to be interpreted more carefully before one can acknowledge the effectiveness of the just community approach.

GENERALIZABILITY OF THE POSITIVE RESULTS OF THE JUST COMMUNITY APPROACH

Proponents of the just community approach have been very enthusiastic and optimistic about it, to the extent of arguing that it should be implemented as completely as possible even in settings that are drastically different from the alternative schools in which it first became known to educators (e.g., Power, 1985, in large high schools; and Aubrey, 1980; Lickona & Paradise, 1980; and Stuhr & Rundle, 1980, in elementary schools). They tend to attribute negative findings to the incompleteness of implementation of the design: for instance, the failure to carry out democratic governance in a fifth grade class was explained as a failure of "building positive relations among kids and a sense of community in the class" (Lickona & Paradise, in press, p. 330). Thus, advocates appear ready to believe that the just community approach is the only right and good way to practice moral education. Furthermore, they hold that the design has an intrinsic long term value:

". . . even if these children had not yet worked out higher stage reasons for obeying rules — their experience still has value. They are engaged in a behavioral process of acting on their social environment in ways that open the door to the eventual development of more sophisticated social-moral reasoning. They are, in their group discussions, taking more initiative, doing more thinking, actively constructing rules instead of passively relating to them as external givens. In short, they are beginning to relate to their social world in ways that will make it easier to have the equal-to-equal, reciprocal social interactions, based on mutual respect, that ultimately stimulate structural social-moral development" (Kohlberg & Lickona, 1980, pp. 39-40).

In the next two sections, I shall show that such claims are in fact premature.

Conditions Needed for Success: What Do Positive Results Mean?

Positive results from just community studies with different age groups in both junior-high, high, and elementary schools, have been reported (e.g., Higgins et al., 1984; Kohlberg & Lickona, 1980; Power, 1985). These educational settings ranged from alternative schools (i.e., units within large public schools) to traditional classrooms, but there were certain elements in common. First, all these just communities consisted of a group of *motivated* students — their participation was entirely voluntary. In many cases, members were those who had already been extensively involved in school politics or admininstration (Wasserman & Garrod, 1983).

Second, such communities consumed a tremendous amount of resources. A large number of teachers or other administrators was required to share the tasks of teaching, guiding students through different democratic processes (e.g., discussions, debate, coordination of different meetings), individual attention, meeting with parents, working on retreats, and other community-building activities. Besides, the personnel involved had to be trained by education consultants who were familiar with the processes. Given all these requirements, the student-teacher ratio usually had to be lowered; for instance, in the "Cluster School," an alternative school in Cambridge, Massachusetts, the ratio was 10 to 1 (Wasserman & Garrod, 1983). All of this meant that schools had to spend a great deal of extra money, time, and energy.

These conditions cannot be taken for granted in settings where people are not very familiar with the approach and are dubious of its effects. The problems of unmotivated students and limited resources would have to be confronted; to make the problem worse, the amount of resources needed may be even greater with such students because they are more likely to be apathetic to community life and democratic processes. The favorable conditions under which the approach worked originally are usually not present in most schools of the United States and other countries.

Other issues have to be considered too when interpreting positive results. First, we do not really know what makes the just community approach work: all we know is that students who participated in it developed higher moral stages, and misbehaviors seemed to be more under control. It is easy to claim that all these positive effects were related to democractic governance and community solidarity; however, this is not necessarily the case. Other factors such as the community's small size (in large schools, feelings of community solidarity were emphasized by the smaller units), its flexibility in academic schedules and matters such as grading (which freed students from regular academic pressures), etc., confound the design.

Second, there are almost no data on students' behaviors outside the communities and whether their moral growth (i.e., in reasoning and courage to act according to their highest moral stage) persists after they leave. As Habermas (Kohlberg, 1985, p. 82) pointed out, "there is a degree of illusoriness in a democratic process in the classroom or alternative school which is often in contradiction to the actual authoritarian character of the broader school structure, the home or the street." How do students react to or resolve such conflicts? Would they think and act morally only when they are in the community setting? As long as these questions are not adequately dealt with, one does not really know what kind of effectiveness exists. The goals of establishing just communities are to foster growth in moral reasoning and courage, and genuine growth should mean permanent gains that would not just manifest themselves during school hours.

To summarize, the above issues raise two concerns: i) we don't know whether the just community approach will work in all social/cultural settings — the positive results reported may only be true where favorable conditions are present; and ii) we don't know exactly how useful the approach is in fostering moral growth, moral action, psychological well-being, etc. — there is no convincing empirical evidence that this development will persist outside the community. Thus, I believe it is premature to grant complete credit to the approach and as such, it would be unwise to treat its structural design as if it were an absolute, sacred dogma.

In addition to these practical drawbacks, I shall discuss two metatheoretical assumptions of the just community approach, which raise certain issues that proponents have never directly addressed.

Metatheoretical Assumptions

Value premises. For those familiar with Kohlberg's moral development theory, in many ways the just community approach is simply a natural extension. The ideal end point of development, i.e., postconventional reasoning or stages 5 and 6, is the ultimate goal of a just community, although due to the members' current moral stage the immediate goal may be lowered. Most aim at promoting conventional reasoning, i.e., stages 3 and 4. As mentioned earlier, Kohlberg is a firm believer in the Kantian principles of liberty and equality — the universalized and generalized respect for individual human personality and autonomy. As Shweder, Mahapatra, and Miller (1985) contend, the "individual" in Kohlberg's theory is essentially an abstract entity. First, individuals are regarded as autonomous entities distinct from their social identity, and each is assumed to have an intrinsic value and dignity regardless of his/her role and status. Second, differences in power, intelligence, ability, etc. are not considered relevant in evaluating a person's moral worth. Third, one is assumed to be able to make voluntary rational choices, free of constraints imposed by the society.

Such value orientation shapes the philosophy behind this form of moral education. This is why participatory democracy (one individual, one vote) is assumed to be the ideal way to run schools (although some proponents have leaned toward the implementation of representative democracy, it is considered a second-best alternative: see Power, 1985). It is also the reason why community meetings, in which members discuss and debate different moral issues/dilemmas, are given paramount attention: through engaging in rational and objective discussions and defending their own moral reasoning and principles, it is hoped that members will be able to make autonomous decisions.

Community solidarity, another backbone of the approach, is developed from Kohlberg's recent recognition of the virtue of social responsibility and the need to understand an individual's action in its social/group context (see Kohlberg, 1984, for the recent reformulation of his theory). One of Kohlberg's favorite examples of this is the My Lai massacre of the Vietnam War, in which American soldiers murdered noncombatant women and children — not because the soldiers were mentally ill, but because they were acting according to the group norms at that time. Kohlberg maintained that the collective interpretation of moral issues may (although need not) be distinguished from the individual's interpretation. It is believed that altering the moral atmosphere would facilitate individual moral actions: that is, the feelings of identification would develop into caring and concern among members, which in turn provide a supportive environment for moral growth (e.g., congruence between moral stage and moral action). Yet individual duties do not exist prior to individual rights: responsibility, loyalty, and altruism are

there to promote respect for rights and justice. In just communities, justice would mean treating everybody the same — everybody is equal, regardless of age, goals, professions, resources, etc. It is individuals who come first (the people who play the parts), not their roles or statuses (the parts to be played) (Shweder et al., 1985). However, in cultures other than mainstream American society, it remains an empirical question as to whether such value premises will be understood and practiced similarly.

Theory of misbehaviors. Kohlberg asserted that altering the moral atmosphere would facilitate moral actions; Power (1985) also considers crime and disruption in high schools as a result of a declining moral atmosphere. Such atmospheres are seen as originating from the fact that high schools are not run democratically but bureaucratically, with an emphasis on efficiency and maintenance of order. The bureaucratic structure of those schools renders coordination between different personnel difficult, while large student bodies mean that individual attention is almost impossible. Methods to combat crime and disciplinary problems, e.g., employing security guards, are designed to maintain efficient order rather than promote moral education. In the long run, Power argued, there would be a decline of culture and moral atmospheres in schools — students would become more negative and rebellious towards authorities; and more crime and disruption would result. He regarded the just community approach as the ultimate solution for this vicious cycle.

Kohlberg and his associates seem to believe that the moral atmosphere is one of, if not the most important factor accounting for school problems. They fail to put the issue into a societal and cultural context — school is not a closed system functioning on its own. Other educational policies such as curriculum design, workload, examination policies, and failure to motivate students also affect behaviors considerably, as well as social problems such as poverty, racial segregration, drugs, etc.

I shall now discuss the case of Hong Kong, a predominantly Chinese society. The objective of this analysis is to point out more concretely the theoretical problems of practicing the just community approach in a different cultural setting.

THE CASE OF HONG KONG

Some Background Information

Hong Kong is located off the southeast coast of China. It has been a British colony since 1842, but it is arranged that Britain will return Hong Kong to China in 1997. Once called "the barren island," Hong Kong has undergone significant changes in the last three decades (Parsons, 1983). Originally a small fishing community, it has become one of the world's most densely populated, urbanized, and industrialized societies. It is now the third-largest container port and third-largest gold-dealing center in the world. In addition, it is the financial capital of Asia, and exceeded only by New York and London as a banking and financial center.

Like other industrialized societies, Hong Kong has been subject to Western influences — not simply in fashions and household appliances, but also in the way people feel, think, and act. Yet some traditional Chinese values and practices still seem to have a persistent effect on residents' reasoning and behaviors (e.g., Sun, 1983).

Moral Education

In Hong Kong, order and control (especially in secondary schools, 7th to 13th grades) have long been a problem. In the early 1980s, the government published a notable report on the problems and prospects of moral education; however, it did not seem to help and the problems continue. In most schools, especially private ones, students create major disturbances in classrooms and teachers cannot even perform their basic job of transmitting knowledge (T. Cheng, 1982). The majority of classsrooms are not suitable places for individual development, yet despite concern, there is a lack of knowledge of how to implement moral education in schools (Chung, 1982). Most teachers rely on punishment, although they know it may only be effective in the short run. The general attitude is "after all, what else can we do?" There is an urgent need to implement moral education in schools. Below, I shall assess the applicability of the just community approach in Hong Kong by first examining how people there may perceive the value premises underlying the approach, and then discussing the resources that would be available for Hong Kong educators to practice moral education.

Democracy and Community: A Chinese Perspective

Democractic governance and feelings of community solidarity are considered to be backbones of the just community approach. They are means to achieve given ends, i.e., moral growth as described in Kohlberg's theory, and moral actions that are consistent with such growth. Democratic governance is also regarded as an end in itself (e.g., Mosher, 1978) — the process carries with it various role-taking opportunities and experiences that are believed to have an intrinsic long-term value, which will ultimately stimulate development in moral as well as non-moral domains. Proponents have argued that these are the only two means that are theoretically and practically sound, yet it must be noted that they can be distinguished from the main goals.

When the just community approach is practiced in another culture, it remains an empirical question as to whether it is the best means to achieve the ends, because i) these two means may be inconsistent with other belief/values systems; and ii) there may be other belief systems that closely regulate people's behaviors but are not addressed by the design. This is not the same as arguing against the tenets of Kohlberg's theory: people in other cultures may accept the values upheld in the theory but still believe in other cultural-specific values that are absent from it (Snarey, 1985). For instance, when confronted with a dilemma in which a father breaks his promise by not allowing his son to go camping, some Chinese subjects in Taiwan felt that both keeping promises (a value that is present in Kohlberg's higher stages) and filial respect (a traditional Chinese value) were important — that people should make compromises between the two and avoid situations that pose conflicts between them. The value of keeping promises is not *always* upheld; only in "important" situations. Even when filial respect has to give way to other values, it is believed

that the son should compensate his father. This type of reasoning — solving a dilemma by placing different values into different hierarchies at different times — has not been adequately addressed by Kohlberg's scheme. The upshot is that proponents of just communities must be sensitive to how people in other cultures perceive the processes of democracy and community, and whether there are other important cultural values that should be taken into account when the approach is implemented.

Democracy. The Chinese in Hong Kong are not accustomed to democracy. A few government officials are elected, yet traditionally the majority of people have not been enthusiastic about the election process (e.g., Fong, 1985). This situation has been improving recently but many feel that there is still a long way to go before most citizens, including government officials, really value democracy (Chi, 1986; Fong, 1986). In order to understand how people in Hong Kong view democracy and what might happen if the just community approach, with its strong emphasis on democracy, were implemented in schools, we have to first understand some of the traditional Chinese world-views and value systems that regulate interpersonal relationships.

The Chinese conception of humanity and the emphasis on propriety. The Chinese word for human being is pronounced the same as "jen," one of the moral virtues that Confucianism upholds. "Jen" is said to be one of the innate moral tendencies of human beings. The character for "jen" consists of the symbol for a person and the symbol for two, and has been translated as "benevolence," "love," "humanity," etc. (Dien, 1982). The Chinese "self" is defined in terms of other people through a web of reciprocal obligations (Fairbank, 1980) — an individual's identity cannot be separated from his or her social identity.

There is a strong emphasis on propriety; individuals learn to internalize social conventions and subordinate themselves to those conventions. It is believed that personal well-being as well as social stability will be maintained if people behave according to their roles and statuses in the hierarchy (Sun, 1983). Socially, the individual is supposed to have "proper relations" with others: one is supposed to cultivate and discipline oneself to fulfill the obligations that are dictated by one's position in a hierarchy. Whereas Westerners emphasize individual *rights*, Chinese emphasize individual *duties*.

Personal dignity is embedded in one's relationships with fellow humans, and determined by "right" conduct and social approval (Hsu, 1970). An individual's worth is not regarded as innate, but has to be acquired. People are assumed to have different capacities owing to different backgrounds, (e.g., education) and characteristics (e.g., age) (Fairbank, 1980). It is therefore accepted that some people should dominate others because of their status. Abuse of power is not prevented by elimination of different statuses and hierarchies (as in a democratic setting). It is generally believed that persons of higher status have a decent conscience, and will behave according to the rules of propriety or "li." If they don't, others have the right to get rid of them (politically, this would usually mean rebellion) and substitute leaders who would abide by those rules.

The Chinese conception of the individual, in contrast to Kohlberg's view and the Kantian tradition, is not one of an abstract entity. Here, roles and statuses determine one's dignity; differences in abilities are believed to be relevant in evaluating one's worth; one's behaviors are very much constrained by social identity and the related obligations it imposes. As such, it is not difficult to understand why the western conceptions of "rights" and "equality" are so foreign to the Chinese.

The teacher-student relationship. Traditionally, Chinese teachers are absolutely obeyed, respected, or even feared by their students (Munro, 1969, 1977). They are regarded as elders who are intelligent, knowledgeable, wise, and with moral integrity. This is partly because teachers are well-educated, and educated people are respected in traditional Chinese society, and also partly because of the emphasis of the subordination of lower status individuals (in this case, students) to those of higher status.

In Hong Kong, the teacher-student relationship has become more egalitarian in past decades (Chung, 1982). However, the emphases on differences of status and the subordination of lower status people still shape the expectations of many teachers. They feel that students should treat them as their elders and respect their authority — which not only includes acquiring knowledge but learning to live under discipline. They expect themselves to be able to maintain order and control in their class and would feel failure if they could not do so (Ma, 1982) (As we shall see later, maintaining order and control is not only a cultural value but has practical significance in the education system of Hong Kong.) On the other hand, learning to submit to the teacher's authority is not something new to students — they are taught to relate to their parents and other elders in the same way, although more and more are becoming reluctant to do so.

Thus, we must consider two issues. First, the Chinese conceptions of humanity and ideal society are basically different from western democratic values. This is not to say that Chinese do not respect individual dignity — as Fairbank (1980, pp. 135-136) noted, "Chinese humanism included a concern for the dignity of the individual, but from a social point of view . . . [the individual] was neither unique, immortal, nor the center of the universe." In other words, for the Chinese, respect for the individual has not translated into a quest for equal rights, but rather into a preoccupation with duties, obligations, and obedience. The exposure of Hong Kong to Western influences has gradually changed its outlook on democracy, as reflected in recent political processes. Yet it is still too early to judge the outcome of this change. And in any case, there is no reason to equate "respect for the individual" with school democracy. It is obvious that respecting students does not imply giving them the rights of teachers and administrators. Moreover, the implementation of school democracy is not just a matter of value orientation, but also involves other practical issues, e.g., the function of schooling, the structure of education system, etc. (This will be discussed in detail in another section.)

Second, the basic design of the just community seems to contradict some Chinese values. Respecting elders (including teachers) is still perceived as a virtue by the society at large. In the just community, however, teachers would have to give up their authority and decision-making power completely. This in turn leads us to the following questions:

i) are there other ways (besides a full-scale implementation of democracy) to practice moral education, and ii) whether the environment of Hong Kong schools is really conducive to moral development.

Community.   Community solidarity is another backbone of the just community. Members' concerns for one another and the community as a whole are supposed to induce moral actions that are consistent with their moral stage. At first glance, the emphasis on social responsibility, altruism, and loyalty appears to be consistent with the so-called "group-oriented" attitude of the Chinese. A more in-depth analysis, however, indicates that they are very different. The former stresses the *voluntary* nature of the affiliation (everybody is free to participate or leave the community), equality (one person one vote, treating everybody the same, etc.), and individual rights (as supposed to individual duties; the duties are there only to protect the rights). In contrast, the latter focuses on the obligatory nature of the relationship, particularistic treatment, and duties. I shall now elaborate these characteristics of the Chinese culture.

The strong social orientation of the Chinese does not imply that they are willing to sacrifice their welfare for just anyone. The groups that an individual would feel obliged to take care of are those who have blood ties (e.g., family members and relatives), emotional relationships (e.g., close friends), or instrumental relationships (e.g., colleagues, employers) with them. The individual develops a strong sense of attachment and identification with these people, and the web of relationships is characterized by the concepts of obligations and repayment of favors. Early on, one is taught that these people have done one favors, and one has to repay the favors in return.[2] Therefore one is responsible for the welfare of others in the network, anytime and anywhere. This sense of obligation reinforces the ties between group members and feelings of "togetherness" (Sun, 1983), which in turn strengthens the sense of obligation. In other words, the "repayment" never ends. All these beget a strong tendency of particularistic treatment to in-group people. Responsibilites, not rights, are the focus of the relationships. Freedom of choice is downplayed — in some cases (as with relatives), there is no choice; in other cases (as with close friends) commitment and obligations are emphasized. This type of social orientation is therefore very different from the one that the just community attempts to develop.

Given this perspective, it would be quite difficult for the Chinese to reach the ideal of the just community approach — relating to all members on the basis of communal love and concern. It is well known that the Chinese do not easily unite for a common cause, whether social or political (Hsu, 1970; Pang, 1983; Sun, 1983). This can be attributed to the tremendous amount of energy, both physical and psychological, devoted to the "in-group." Individuals feel too tied down and probably too overwhelmed to invest their attention elsewhere. Moreover, contracts and explicit regulations are simply not the rule of the game in Chinese culture.

Then, there is the issue of the processes of interaction between members of just communities, who are expected to discuss real-life moral issues in order to arrive at explicit rules governing the community. It is assumed that by engaging in this sort of Socratic dialogue, members' moral thinking is stimulated. I think the Chinese would have special difficulties in engaging in this kind of interaction. Their concern for propriety and maintaining good relationships has developed into a strong tendency to sentimentalize social interactions and take things personally even when they shouldn't. There is no strong distinction between personal and impersonal relations — people are expected to relate more or less the same to one another all the time. The debates, arguments, and discontents that often occur at just community meetings would adversely affect Chinese members' identification with the community. Furthermore, the process of rule-making would make the problem worse. Implicit norms and understandings characterize Chinese relationships, and the sacred "rules" of just communities, which are supposed to be a spiritual reminder of the nature of interactions, may actually become an obstacle to the development of genuine relationships.

Interactions Between Moral Education and Other Functions of Schools

In modern society, schools have long been given multiple functions, two of which are the transmission of knowledge and the enhancement of social mobility. For the Chinese in Hong Kong, these two functions are major motivations, which would pose a basic conflict to the just community approach to moral education. Owing to its colonial status and its uncertain political future, economic prosperity has been the main concern of both government and citizens. Since many resources are directed to the development

---

[2] Doi (1971) also talked about similar concepts in his analysis of the Japanese culture.

of economic activities, the education budget has always been tight. The percentage of government expenditure on education was only 2.5% of the GNP in 1979, as compared to 3.5% in Singapore, 6% in Japan, 7% in the U.S.A., and 9% in Sweden (S. Cheng, 1982). The student-teacher ratio in Hong Kong is also among one of the highest in the world. In secondary school (7th to 11th grade), the ratio in 1979 was 30.8:1, as compared to 26:1 in Singapore, 19.1:1 in Japan (public schools), and 18.5:1 in the U.S.A. (public schools) (Lam, Fong, & Cheung, 1982). The tight budget has resulted in a pryamid-like educational system that emphasizes efficient transmission of knowledge and effective screening mechanisms — after nine years of compulsory education (1st to 9th grade), various public exams gradually eliminate students. According to a survey done in 1981, only 1% of all elementary school students ended up in the two universities (Lam et al., 1982). Much of the attention of school administrators, teachers, and students has therefore been directed toward exams and grades.

As detailed earlier, a complete implementation of a just community is very resource-consuming, both in terms of labor and money. Teachers, administrators, and students have to spend a great deal of time and energy working out rules and policies (Power & Reimer, 1978), and as some participants soon realize, democracy takes time (Lickona & Paradise, 1980). Training sessions, evaluation meetings, planning and consultation also require a great deal of money and effort, because teachers have to be freed from some of their regular duties in order to participate in community-related activities (Wasserman & Garrod, 1983). All these mean diverting substantial resources from other school functions. It is hard to conceive of persuading the government to institute and the students to participate in this at the expense of efficient transmission of knowledge. Changing this status quo would mean shaking up the entire social fabric, which is very sensitive because of the special political context mentioned above (Lau, 1985).

Misbehaviors in School

Proponents of the just community approach in the United States focus on the declining moral atmosphere within schools as a major cause of student misbehaviors. Thus, some kind of design to improve school atmosphere is therefore desirable. This assumption is quite controversial even in the United States. In the case of Hong Kong, it is obvious that the school atmosphere is sometimes so poor that it breeds crime and discourages learning (T. Cheng, 1982; Young, 1983), and the implementation of explicit moral education is believed by some (e.g., Chung, 1982; Ma, 1982) to be an important step in dealing with delinquency problems. However, moral education does not seem to be sufficient. Many critics argue that problems of misbehaviors are multifaceted, and are products of the complex interplay between factors that have nothing to do with moral education. To cite a few: the emphasis on examinations has made learning more a pressure than an enjoyment (Szetu, 1983; Tam, 1982); the compulsory nine-year grammar school education and the unchanged curriculum have kept many unmotivated students learning something that they neither understand nor are interested in (Chow, 1983; Fong, 1983); English as the main language of instruction (this situation may change after the British government returns Hong Kong to China in 1997) makes learning even more difficult (S. Cheng, 1982; Siu, 1982); and the high student-teacher and student-counsellor ratio (in 1981, the latter ratio was 1:4000) has made individual guidance very difficult if not impossible (Yau, 1982). If moral education is indeed only one aspect of delinquency problems, one must question if the just community approach would become a priority for educators in Hong Kong.

A NEED FOR MODIFICATION: UNRESOLVED PROBLEMS AND SOME DISTINCTIONS

I have tried to pinpoint the major problems of practicing this approach to moral education in the schools of Hong Kong. I think these problems are not only relevant for other societies as well, but also bring up certain theoretical issues that have not been confronted before.

Three Unresolved Problems

Motivation. Getting the cooperation of students, teachers, and administrators was not a major problem in the original just communities, because funding was available from major research grants, and the individuals involved were very motivated to begin with. Students participated on a voluntary basis, thus the fact that some were apathetic was not important as long as there were always some active members to participate in meetings and committees. It was probably not difficult to find this enthusiastic minority, because many Americans are brought up in a society that believes in individual rights and democracy.

However, the issue becomes important in settings where the education budget is tight, teachers are busy and overworked, and students are overwhelmed by exams and schoolwork and simply lack time and energy. The world is not all hungry for just communities, but rather consists of very different people with very different goals. "Autonomy" has always been important in Kohlberg's moral development theory (1981, 1984) and thus voluntary participation is stressed. It is precisely because of this emphasis that the motivation issue deserves more attention. If the approach is meant to be useful and effective for more than an enthusiatic minority in the U.S.A., Kohlberg and his supporters owe a more explicit statement on the following problems: are there any practical strategies to motivate students and school personnel? What kind of compromises ought and need to be made to increase motivation? How would these compromises modify the basic design of the appproach?

Teachers' authority. The concern for individual autonomy and equality led Kohlberg and his associates to propose a complete implementation of democracy in the school, which means taking away practically all the teacher's authority. Discipline, order, and sometimes even grading are negotiated between and decided by members. Such emphasis has led to the worry of "teacher intimidation," i.e., even if teachers only have one vote in the decision-making processes, students may still be intimidated by them because they are the ones who give grades, write recommendations, talk to their parents on behalf of the school, etc. It is believed that taking the authority away from teachers provides a non-threatening environment that stimulates moral growth —

moral values can never be taught; moral behavior can never be coerced.

Students [in a just community] are learning, we believe, not that "I must conform to the group" but that "we are legislating norms and if we all legislate these norms we must all act upon them", i.e. the Kantian notion of autonomy (Kohlberg, 1985, p.85).

The first major function [of the just community] . . . is the creation of a setting for problem-solving or conflict-resolving moral discourse. The social structure of the discourse Habermas calls egalitiarian or symmetrical . . . An ideal speech situation involves the possibility of unlimited discussion in which moral claims can be "redeemed" or *justified* by open argumentation of a sort similar to that elaborated by moral philosophers. Such an ideal speech situation must involve not only unlimited discussion but discussion that is free from distorting influences, especially open domination and strategic or manipulative behavior. Symmetry implies that speakers have the same chance to employ regulative speech acts to recommend and forbid, to criticize etc. (Kohlberg, 1985, p. 84).

It is obviously not true that stripping the teacher of all authority is the only way to create a supportive environment for genuine moral development, for this would imply that successful moral education has never really occurred in other settings. There is no reason to think that if the teacher retains some authority, there would be no room for students to exercise their autonomy. Having autonomy is not an either-or issue. Two issues immediately follow: one empirical, one normative.

It is debatable whether more autonomy means more moral growth. While Kohlberg's theory endorses this claim, there is so far no empirical evidence to demonstrate that systematic variation of the teacher's authority would result in different rate of moral development. In fact, it is also arguable that from the society's point of view, school is an institution to prepare children to live with authority, not just to question it (Dreeben, 1967; Durkheim, 1973). Kohlberg himself seemed to realize this, as in summarizing the Durkheim and Dreeben sociological tradition he said, " . . . you cannot get rid of authority in the classroom, because you need people who can live with it in the bigger society" (Kohlberg, 1970, p. 106). He resolved the authority-autonomy dilemma by developing the just community approach — "In our society authority derives from justice, and in our society learning to live with authority should derive from and aid learning to understand and to feel justice" (Kohlberg, 1970, p. 122): which means granting students as much autonomy as they can have in the first place. However, it remains a value judgment as to whether such autonomy should be granted, especially when the decision may pose tremendous difficulties for the school to carry out other functions, e.g., transmission of knowledge.

Misbehaviors. The emphasis on the moral atmosphere in schools and its intimate relationship with moral behaviors is a major development of Kohlberg's theory in recent years. Here we see an effort to elucidate the social negotiation processes and its effect on the individual, which was never a major agenda of the theory before. In looking at the Hong Kong education system, I argue for a still broader view for how and why misbehaviors come about — that they do not necessarily relate to individual moral stages or the moral atmosphere of the schools, but to other independent factors such as curriculum, exams, and even less directly related aspects such as the use of drugs. Provided that proponents of just communities do not attribute all misbehavior problems to declining moral atmospheres or to the incomplete implementation of their processes, I think that research on just communities would provide very useful information for educators and psychologists. There are, however, two issues that need to be addressed.

First, the establishment of a just community is to provide students with a context to negotiate with others about moral dilemmas and behaviors. If an "8:00 to 3:00" attitude and behavioral change is all that results, how should the design be restructured to be more relevant for issues outside the school community? For instance, should discussions of moral issues be confined to those that are immediately relevant for the community? What issues should be given priority in meetings? How should members build up the mutual feelings of support and trust that are likely to result in communication about other moral issues outside school?

Second, if moral atmosphere is only one of the many factors that lead to misbehaviors, and if the implementation of a just community is so costly, how should educators allocate their resources? Should they choose between a full implementation of the program and other administrative changes, or should both be implemented with modifications? What kinds of modifications would be acceptable, and what parts of the design should be kept at any cost? These are practical questions that cannot be ignored if one is advocating the general usefulness of the approach. Otherwise there is risk of committing the "psychologist's fallacy"

again — believing what is important for developmental psychology research is also important to practitioners in the classrooms (Kohlberg, 1985).

There appears to be an unwillingness to more explicitly consider modifications and systematic comparison with other approaches. Such feelings may be related to a confusion of the following distinctions about the usefulness of the approach.

Five Distinctions

Necessary and sufficient vs. multiple facilitating conditions. Proponents of the just community approach feel that participatory democracy and a sense of community are necessary and sufficient conditions for inducing moral growth and action. This view, however, presupposes the validity of the empirical propositions summarized above (which as argued above are far from well documented) — e.g., what does the effectiveness that has been reported really mean? What has made it work in the past — democracy and community, or just more individual care, flexible class schedules, and special grading methods? If some of the empirical assumptions are invalid, the approach is at best one of several possible facilitating conditions for moral development.

Full-scale transformation vs. limited change. Some insist on a complete implementation of participatory democracy, claiming that anything less is insufficient to bring about the desired effects. Almost all just communities have attempted full-scale transformations that aim to democratize practically every aspect of school life. There has been no systematic attempt to empirically examine whether a more limited implementation or even other approaches would achieve similar effects. Alternatives would be especially useful for educators who have fewer resources at their disposal.

Positive vs. negative consequences. In general, any social institution has positive consequences for some values/goals, and negative consequences for others. It is apparent that proponents of just communities have overwhelmingly focused on the former and ignored the latter; for instance, the likelihood of chaos and discipline problems resulting from the implementation of participatory democracy (especially in cultures where people are dubious about democracy) and the possible interference with other functions of the school, such as the transmission of knowledge. These problems have not been confronted directly.

Possible vs. probable effects/outcomes. Idealistic and unilinear reasoning seems to be common in the literature. For example, some elementary school educators proposed that participatory democracy could be practiced with children as young as nursery schoolers, claiming that there is an intrinsic value of such practice (Lickona & Paradise, 1980). Yet the idea that it is *possible* for small children to benefit from this approach does not mean it is very probable that this outcome will occur. In the case of Hong Kong, owing to various cultural practices, values, and world-views, it is very improbable for people there to benefit from the approach without considerable modifications.

Feasible vs. optimal methods. Similar to the last point, many do not seem to distinguish what is *feasible* from what is *op-*

timal. It seems obvious that one should try to choose the most effective or efficient means for some given ends; however, those arguing for the appropriateness of this approach (e.g., Kohl-berg & Lickona, 1980; Power, 1985) only look for means that are consistent with the basic design. It seems that their goal is the preservation of the basic design, rather than the construction of an optimal design. They do not lay out the specific goals and constraints that would be required in new settings; nor assess alternative strategies. As the target groups, goals, and constraints in any new setting are quite different from the original, it is probable that the optimal designs for these settings may be very different.

The upshot of pointing out these unresolved problems and distinctions is that for various theoretical and practical reasons, the basic design of the just community approach ought to be modified. The problems that exist should be acknowledged honestly, rather than being attributed to incomplete implementation. It is high time to spell out more clearly how the approach would be useful to students and educators outside the original enthusiastic groups. This calls for a more critical examination of the underlying assumptions of the approach, a more detailed analysis of its effectiveness and efficiency, and a more realistic assessment of how it may affect other school functions. My experiences give me the impression that its advocates put all their efforts into finding ways of sticking with the basic design and working toward some ideal, rather than exploring the above possibilities.

The point is, first, that it is quite doubtful that this approach is the only ideal method of moral education, especially in cultures other than the United States, and second, working toward an ideal means that one has to make compromises along the way. How can these issues simply be swept aside?

Suggestions

I shall now attempt to make some suggestions for moral education in Hong Kong based on some of the insights of the just community approach. I hesitate to call the suggestions "modifications" because I think they differ sufficiently from the original design. The term, though, is not important. What is important is whether it is possible for people in other cultures to learn and work on the insights in a realistic way. The aim of this chapter is not to explore the characteristics of moral education in Hong Kong; therefore this section will be very brief, but I hope that it will stimulate more detailed research on moral education (of whatever approach) so that educators in all societies may someday benefit from more practical methods.

There are several elements of the just community approach that are important for any educator to bear in mind. First, moral values and behaviors cannot be coerced. *Understanding* of the rules set up by teachers and administrators would help to maintain order, and this is made possible through students' making up and enforcing rules themselves. Second, some sort of equality in status allows students to voice their grievances. Both of the above help prevent delinquency through rebellious attitudes or retaliation. Third, peer support (or conversely, pressure) is a major factor affecting adolescents' behaviors, including moral ones.

I believe that educators in Hong Kong can make use of the above insights in the following ways, even though most people there do not understand and probably would not endorse a complete implementation of democratic governance and community solidarity in schools, the education budget is tight, the student-teacher ratio is high, etc. These suggestions basically do not interfere with normal class schedules, do not involve restructuring the school organization, and are consistent with (or at least not in opposition to) the cultural values, practices, and worldviews.

The classroom as the basic unit of moral education. The classroom is the ideal place for developing concern and care. As classes seldom merge in Hong Kong schools, students spend most of the time with the same people, and it can be assumed they have some friends there whom they care about to some extent. Even though these feelings may not be strong enough to provide a supportive environment for certain moral behaviors, the fact that Chinese are very sensitive to those who interact closely with them (e.g., Sun, 1983; Hsu, 1970) would make the development of feelings of concern and identification very probable.

Rules and discipline: Learning to like it. For rules to work, students must understand them by going through the processes of making and acting upon them. However, they must first be convinced that such processes are worthwhile. There is strong evidence in studies of social interactions (Youniss, 1980) that children spontaneously develop rules and respect in play and other types of informal but structured activities. Within the context of the classroom, there are plenty of such opportunities. For instance, extracurricular activities such as field trips, ball games, singing contests, etc., allow students to negotiate with one another about their own behaviors — what they should or should not do in particular circumstances. Students would presumably be motivated to set up rules and make sure that they are obeyed if they like the activities. It is to be hoped that they would gradually learn that rules and discipline are not just punishing and controlling by nature, but are indispensable for social interactions and the enjoyment that comes with them. Because of the motivation that such activities are usually able to invoke, the relationship between extracurricular activities and moral education should be more carefully examined.

With respect to discipline in the classroom, a similar approach can apply. Because of the long syllabus and the importance attached to school work and exams, some basic rules (e.g., class attendance, attentiveness, etc.) must be set and enforced by the teacher. However, the teacher can involve students in setting up specific rules, such as the kinds of treatment toward those who abide and do not abide by the rules.

The teacher as creative leader and moderator. Because of particular cultural views, the authority of the teacher cannot be taken away completely. However, this does not necessarily mean that there is no chance for students to exercise their autonomy. In fact, this authority can be used responsibly and constructively in at least three ways: i) to creatively initiate different kinds of extracurricular activities and issues related to classroom discipline that would allow students the opportunities to learn to make up rules

and act upon them; ii) to skillfully lead the class into spontaneous discussions about different moral and discipline issues related to the rule-making processes; and iii) to tactfully moderate discussions that are becoming too negative, out-of-focus, etc.

CONCLUDING REMARKS

In this chapter, I have attempted to point out that the just community approach is not the only right and good way to practice moral education. Through examining its basic value premises, the conditions underlying its success, theories of misbehaviors, and usefulness in a non-western culture, it is clear that there are many unresolved problems. If the approach is to claim its usefulness in different cultures, these problems have to be confronted. The enthusiasm and passion of its advocates are valuable; however, I am convinced that we need more than zeal in moral education. It is hoped that this chapter will help stimulate research or theoretical thinking on different modifications, applications, and criticisms. There are many insights underlying the just community approach — we have to learn how to use them.

ACKNOWLEDGEMENTS An earlier draft of this chapter was presented at the Eighth Biennial Metting of the International Society for the Study of Behavioral Development at Tours, France, 1985. I have benefited greatly from the comments and suggestions of R. Howard, E. Myers, C. Power, J. Snarey, T. Tam, and J. Valsiner.

APPENDIX I

The Six Stages of Moral Development
(Kohlberg, 1981, pp. 409-412)

Stage 1. Punishment and Obedience

Right is obedience to rules and authority, avoiding pubishment, and not doing physical damage to people and property.

Stage 2. Instrumental Purpose and Exchange

Right is following rules when it is serving someone's immediate interests and needs and letting others do the same. Right is a fair deal, an equal exchange.

Stage 3. Interpersonal Expectations, Relationships, and Conformity

Right is living up to what is expected by people close to oneself or what people generally expect of people in one's roles. Playing a good (nice) role is important.

Stage 4. Social System and Conscience Maintenance

Right is fulfilling the actual duties to which one has agreed. Laws are to be upheld except in extreme cases where they conflict with other fixed social rights and duties. Right is also contributing to society, the group, or institution.

Stage 5. Prior Rights and Social Contract or Utility

Right is being aware that people hold a variety of values and opinions, that most values and rules are relative to one's own group but should always be upheld because they are the social contract. Some nonrelative values and rights such as life and liberty must be upheld in any society regardless of the majority opinion.

Stage 6. Universal Ethical Principles

Right is following self-chosen ethical principles. Particular laws or social agreements are usually valid because they rest on such principles. When laws violate these principles, one should act in accordance with the principles. Principles are universal principles of justice: the equality of human rights and respect for the dignity of human beings as individual persons. The reason for doing right is the belief that as a rational person, one has seen the validity of principles and has become committed to them.

Note: There is a transition stage between each of the stages.

REFERENCES

Aubrey, R. (1980). Moral development in elementary school classrooms. In R. L. Mosher (Ed.) *Moral education: A first generation of research and development* (pp. 250-264). New York: Praeger.

Blatt, M., & Kohlberg, L. (1975). The effects of classroom moral discussion upon children's level of moral udgment. *Journal of Moral Education, 4,* 129-161.

Cheng, S. (1982). An evaluation of the secondary school curriculum in Hong Kong. In C. Lam, Y. Fong & K. Cheung (Eds.), *Perspectives on Hong Kong education* (Chinese, pp. 71-80). Hong Kong: Wide Angle.

Cheng, T. (1982). Teaching in a private school for 5 years. In C. Lam, Y. Fong & K. Cheung (Eds.), *Perspectives on Hong Kong education* (Chinese, pp.137-142). Hong Kong: Wide Angle.

Chi, S. (1986). The officals in Peking do not feel at ease to give a free hand to the Hong Kong people. *The Nineties (Chinese, Hong Kong) 195*, 44-46.

Chow, N.W. (1983). An explanation of juvenile delinquency. In S. Yau (Ed.), *An inquiry of Youth Problems in Hong Kong* (Chinese, pp. 109-114). Hong Kong: Going Fine.

Chung, Y. (1982). Students-teachers relations in the eighties. In C. Lam, Y. Fong & W. Cheung (Eds.), *Perspectives on Hong Kong education* (Chinese, pp. 135-136). Hong Kong: Wide Angle.

Codding, J., & Arenella, A. (1981). Creating a 'just community': The transformation of an alternative school. *Moral Education, Forum, 6(4).*

Dewey, J. (1960). *Theory of moral life.* New York: Holt, Rinehart, & Winston.

Dien, D.S. (1982). A Chinese perspective on Kohlberg's theory of moral development. *Developmental Review, 2,* 33-341.

Dreeben, R. (1967). The contribution of schooling to the learning of norms. *Harvard Educational Review, 37,* 211-237.

Doi, T. (1971). *The anatomy of dependence.* Kondansha.

Durkheim, E. (1973). *Moral education.* New York: Free Press.

Fairbank, J.K. (1980). *The United States and China.* Cambridge, MA: Harvard University Press.

Fong, S. (1983). Moral education and juvenile delinquency. In S. Yau (Ed.), *An inquiry of youth problems in Hong Kong* (Chinese, pp. 12-136). Hong Kong: Going Fine.

Fong, S. (1985). An interview with Mr. Denis C. Bray. *The Nineties (Chinese, Hong Kong), 180,* 22-31.

Fong, S. (1986). Can democracy go a step further? *The Nineties (Chinese, Hong Kong), 195,* 47-49.

Habermas, J. (1979). *Communication and the evolution of society.* Boston: Beacon Press.

Higgins, A., Power, C., & Kohlberg, L. (1984). The relationships of moral atmosphere to judgments of responsibility. In W. Kurtines & J. Gerwitz (Eds.), *Morality, moral behavior and development* (pp. 74-106). New York: Wiley Interscience.

Hsu, F.L. (1970). *American and Chinese: Purpose and fulfillment in great civilizations.* New York: Natural History.

Kohlberg, L. (1970). The moral atmosphere of the school. In N. Overlay (Ed.). *The unstudied curriculum: Its impact on children* (pp.104-127). Association for Supervision and Curriculum Development, Washington, DC.

Kohlberg, L. (1978). Revisions in the theory and practice of moral development. In W. Damon (Ed.), *New direction for child development* (Volume 2). San Franciso: Jossey-Bass.

Kohlberg, L. (1981). *Essays on moral development, Volume One: The philosophy of moral development.* San Franciso: Harper & Row.

Kohlberg, L. (1984). *Essays on moral development, Vol.Two: The psychology of moral development.* San Franciso: Harper & Row.

Kohlberg, L. (1985). The just community approach to moral education in theory and practice. In M.W. Berkowitz & F. Osher (Eds.), *Moral education: Theory and application* (pp. 27-87). Hillsdale, NJ: Erlbaum.

Kohlberg, L. & Lickona T. (1980) Cognitive-developmental approaches to social and moral education in early education. Forthcoming in DeVries, R. & L. Kohlberg (Eds.), *Programs of early education.* New York: Longmans.

Kohlberg, L., Scharf, P., & Hickery, J. (1975). The 'just community' approach in corrections: The niantic experiment. In L. Kohlberg (Ed.), *Collected papers on moral development and moral education* (Volume 2). Cambridge, MA: Center for Moral Education, Harvard University.

Lam, C., Fong, Y. & Cheung, W. (1982). Education in Hong Kong. In C. Lam, Y. Fong & W. Cheung (Eds.), *Perspectives on Hong Kong education* (Chinese, pp. 3-9). Hong Kong: Wide Angle.

Lau, S. (1985). Political reform and political development in Hong Kong: Dilemmas and choices. *Hong Kong Economic Journal Monthly (Chinese, Hong Kong), 8 (11)*, 12-21.

Lickona, T. & Paradise, M. (1980). Democracy in elementary schools. In R.L. Mosher (Ed.), *Moral education: A first generation of research and development* (pp. 321-340). New York: Praeger.

Lukes, S. (1977). *Emile Durkheim. His life and work: A historical and critical study.* New York: Penguin.

Ma, M. (1982). Please help the teachers. In C. Lam, Y. Fong & W. Cheung (Eds.), *Perspectives on Hong Kong education* (Chinese, pp.165-166). Hong Kong: Wide Angle.

Mosher, R.L. (1978). A democratic high school: Damn it, your feet are always in the water. In N.A. Sprinthall & R.L. Mosher (Eds.), *Value development as an aim of education* (pp. 69-116). New York: Character Research.

Munro, D.J. (1969). *The concept of man in early China.* Stanford: Stanford University Press.

Munro, D.J. (1977). *The concept of man in contemporary China.* Ann Arbor: The University of Michigan Press.

Pang, M. (1983). The superiority of the Chinese. *The Seventies (Chinese, Hong Kong),160*, 62-63.

Parsons, M. (1983). Hong Kong 1983. Hong Kong: Government Information Services.

Power, C. (1985). Democratic moral education in large public high schools. In M.W. Berkowitz & F. Osher (Eds.), *Moral education: Theory and application* (pp. 219-240). Hillsdale, NJ: Erlbaum.

Power, C., & Reimer, J. (1978). Moral atmosphere: An educational bridge between moral judgment and moral action. In W. Damon (Ed.), *New direction for child development* (Volume 2). San Franciso: Jossey-Bass.

Rawls, J. (1971). *A theory of justice.* Cambridge, MA: Harvard University Press.

Royce, J. (1982). *The philosophy of Josiah Ross* (edited by J. Roth). Indianapolis: Hackett.

Shweder, R., Mahapatra, M., & Miller, J. (1985). Culture and moral development.

Forthcoming in J. Kagan (Ed.), *The emergence of moral concepts in young children.* Chicago: University of Chicago Press.

Siu, P. (1982). An evaluation of the policy of the medium of teaching in Hong Kong: Four issues and five suggestions In C. Lam, Y. Fong & W. Cheung (Eds.), *Perspectives on Hong Kong education* (Chinese, pp. 91-96). Hong Kong: Wide Angle.

Snarey, J.R. (1985). Cross-cultural universality of social-moral development: A critical review of Kohlbergian research. *Psychological Bulletin, 97*, 202-232.

Stuhr, D., & Rundle, L. (1980). Moral education in elementary schools: Unconventional methods for conventional goals. In R. L. Mosher (Ed.), *Moral education: A first generation of research and development* (pp. 237-249). New York: Praeger.

Sun, L. (1983). *The 'deep' structure of the Chinese culture.* Hong Kong: Yi Shan.

Szetu, W. (1983). Examinations, teenagers and the social trend. In S. Yau (Ed.), *An inquiry of youth problems in Hong Kong* (Chinese) (pp. 122-127). Hong Kong: Going Fine.

Tam, T. (1982). How to change the public examination system? In C. Lam, Y. Fong & W. Cheung (Eds.), *Perspectives on Hong Kong education (Chinese,* pp. 87-90). Hong Kong: Wide Angle.

Wasserman E., & Garrod A. (1983). The cluster school and its extension to the wider school. In Pring, R. (Ed.), *Personal, Social and Moral Education.* Falmer.

Yau, L. (1982). The development of counselling facilities in schools of Hong Kong. In C. Lam, Y. Fong & W. Cheung (Eds.), *Perspectives on Hong Kong education* (Chinese, pp. 123-134). Hong Kong: Wide Angle.

Young, K. (1983). Studying in a private school. In S. Yau (Ed.), *An inquiry of youth problems in Hong Kong* (pp. 22-28). Hong Kong: Going Fine.

Youniss, J. (1980). *Parents and peers in social development: A Sullivan-Piaget perspective.* Chicago: The University of Chicago Press.

Chapter 5

To Spare or Not to Spare the Rod

A Cultural-Historical View of Child Discipline

Ellen S. Peisner

INTRODUCTION

He that spareth the rod hateth his son: but he that loveth him correcteth him betimes. (Proverbs 13:24)

Throughout the history of the Western world, the issue of discipline has been of concern to theologians, philosophers, educators, psychologists, and others interested in methods of raising children. The methods they advocate to parents are clearly underlined by their beliefs about the nature of children; beliefs that have their origins in culturally and historically based societal beliefs. Many contemporary ideas about childrearing can be found in the religious, philosophical, and educational works of previous centuries. The continued interest of experts in publishing their advice demonstrates both the variety of choices available and the difficulty of choosing a consistent philosophy of childrearing. The persistence of such works testifies as well to the great importance placed on the methods used in raising children in Western society.

While these experts may be the ones who document and advocate the child rearing beliefs and practices of the times, parents are the ones who determine to what extent such beliefs and practices are actually followed. As parents generally are the primary administrators of discipline, they must decide how to incorporate beliefs about their children's capabilities and their own parental responsibilities into a philosophy and practice of discipline.

In addition, the structure of American society, both past and present, dictates that parents do not retain sole responsibility for the socialization of their children. The large portion of time children spend in school under the direct authority of a teacher means that both home and school are primary settings for discipline. This dual focus of responsibility for children's socialization entails consideration of both the parent's and the teacher's beliefs and practices, as well as the continuity of actions across the two settings.

111

DISCIPLINE FROM THE PERSPECTIVE OF DEVELOPMENTAL PSYCHOLOGY

A major tenet in the field of psychology is the importance of continuity in children's development. The assumption is that continuity in the socialization practices of various caretakers is beneficial to children's social and emotional development, while discontinuity may result in less optimal development. One purpose of socialization is to teach children which behaviors are expected in which situations. Through their own behavior and reactions, caretakers impart messages to children about their expectations for behavior in particular situations. Children therefore must infer general rules for behaving from specific disciplinary experiences. When the socialization messages are continuous with one another, the child is better able to learn these rules.

Continuity in discipline involves responding consistently to some behavior by the child across similar situations. Consistency, or inconsistency as the case may be, can be found within an individual as well as between individuals. It often may be that beliefs are more unitary than are actual practices. Inconsistencies in discipline may exist within the family itself, both between parents and within a parent across situations, as well as between the parent and the teacher. In the latter case, while some differences in disciplinary practices may be accounted for by the setting (i.e., home versus school), underlying philosophies about children and childrearing may differ as well.

The study of these three sources of continuity in discipline can help explain children's development. Through the use of discipline, caretakers guide children in controlling their behavior and modifying their ways of thinking before internal control of these processes is developed. These external control techniques serve to explicitly delineate socially and morally proper actions and thoughts. Discipline may be administered on the basis of overt behavior, or perceived underlying motivations, such as the child's intentions or traits. Its immediate purpose is to modify the child's actions or thoughts in a specific situation; in the long-run, however, its aim may be to alter perceived beliefs or personality characteristics that may influence behavior in a variety of situations.

Discipline can be either positive or negative in nature, labeled reward and punishment, respectively. Historically, this distinction has been made in the field of behavioral psychology as one type of social learning that leads to increases or decreases in the frequency of some behavior according to its consequences. This view has since been modified to allow for other factors such as thoughts, beliefs, emotions, and the nature of the relationship between agent and recipient. While such factors must be considered in the use of reward and punishment with children, the distinction nevertheless is a useful way of categorizing socialization practices on the basis of their intended purpose.

Reward refers to contingent reinforcement of thoughts or actions, such as praising, giving extra privileges, or reducing homework. The immediate purpose of reward is to show the child that certain behaviors are desired. However, it also may serve to teach the child that this behavior is special and not always expected, as expected behavior usually is not rewarded. It may be used to encourage more mature ways of acting and thinking, or the completion of unpleasant or difficult tasks. The use of reward gives the child implicit information about the caretaker's values, both in terms of the types of behaviors that are desirable and the types of rewards considered reinforcing. If a particular action or object is not considered reinforcing by the child, however, it will not be effective as a reward. That is, the intentions of a reward may be defined by the caretaker, but its effects are determined by the child.

Punishment refers to the contingent use of aversive verbal, physical, or psychological techniques, such as scolding, spanking, or isolation. It is used to show the child that certain behaviors or ways of thinking are not desired or appropriate. The child's knowledge of right and wrong and intentions underlying the misbehavior often are taken into account in the administration of punishment. The use of punishment also communicates information regarding the caretaker's beliefs about right and wrong, and about when and why various types of punishment are warranted. Just as with reward, the effectiveness of punishment is determined by whether a technique is aversive to the recipient. For example, a child who is scolded for clowning around in class may not consider this a punishment if it is the only time the teacher gives him individual attention. Additionally, the teacher's actions may further reinforce this behavior by elevating the child's status among peers, thereby serving as a potent (though unintended) reward.

While the intent of punishment is to change some characteristic the child demonstrates by the misbehavior, the purpose of reward is to maintain the displayed characteristic. In both cases, discipline serves to control behavior through the use of external techniques that can vary in form, intensity, and administrator, all of which may contribute differently to its effectiveness. Accordingly, the use of reward and punishment serves one socialization function of teaching children expected and appropriate ways of acting and thinking through the consequences of their behavior.

COGNITIVE PROCESSES AND CONTINUITY IN CHILD SOCIALIZATION

If discipline is viewed as a method by which caretakers transmit their values to children, then such socialization is influenced by both these values themselves and the consistency with which they are transmitted. As is true in any area of human cognition, internal beliefs and values can be judged only on the basis of external conduct. Thus, for children, inconsistent disciplinary actions on the part of their parents or teachers is likely to make discernment of appropriate behavior and the underlying values more difficult. Accordingly, the extent to which caretakers are guided by a consistent philosophy of childrearing may influence the continuity of their practices.

As parents and teachers are the agents of discipline, their decisions about when it is warranted will affect the continuity experienced by the child. These decisions are determined not only by the individual's underlying philosophy about childrearing, but also by his or her interpretation of the immediate situation within the framework of that philosophy. In the case of behaviors that are more easily categorized as "good" or "bad" within the framework, disciplinary actions may be more clear-cut. However, when behaviors are not so easily categorized, either because they fit less well within the framework or because of the caretaker's lack of any consistent philosophy, then discontinuity is more likely to occur. Thus, continuity is relevant not only when discipline is used, but also in deciding not to use discipline under certain circumstances. Furthermore, the nature of the philosophy itself may provide more or less endorsement of continuity itself as a value in childrearing. For example, a philosophy that advocates a highly fixed schedule for the child provides inherent sanctions for continuity, whereas one that discounts any type of scheduling precludes continuity within this realm.

It is the child's interpretation of the situation, however, that determines whether he or she will experience continuity. Regardless of the intent of discipline, the child defines caretakers' actions as punishments or rewards. While parents or teachers may think they are being consistent, if the child's interpretation of the situation differs, then the experience will be one of discontinuity. In their use of discipline, caretakers consider two aspects of each situation. One is whether the child's behavior warrants any type of disciplinary action, and the other is the similarity of the present circumstance to past situations. Thus, caretakers may choose to discipline or not to discipline in any given situation, and to be consistent or inconsistent with their past actions. The child makes similar decisions with regard to his or her expectations about the caretakers' reactions. Since every situation is to some extent unique, the interpretations of caretakers and children may not always match, thereby leading to unavoidable disconti-

nuity in children's experiences. An additional source of disagreement in interpretation is created when parents or teachers make judgments on the basis of the child's underlying motives, rather than overt consequences.

When children's interpretations match their caretakers', they more easily learn the rules for behavior. The child may still decide to disregard those rules, of course, but will expect to be disciplined contingent upon that disregard. If this expectation is not met, however, then the child may revise the inferred rules for behavior. The more discontinuity experienced, the less clear are the rules. At times, this may lead to even more discontinuity: since the child has fewer rules for behavior, there is less chance of overlap with caretakers' expectations. Over the long run, however, discontinuity may be an inevitable process for clarifying rules. As the child develops and encounters new disciplinary situations, old expectations and rules may no longer apply. However, it is through this discontinuity that the child learns to modify the rules for behavior in the process of growing up.

Furthermore, the more apparent the relationship between beliefs and practices, the easier it is to discern the general rules for behavior. The nature of development makes change inevitable on the part of the child, and caretakers often adapt their practices accordingly. This may not cause discontinuity, however, if the child is able to see the link between their beliefs and practices. Nevertheless, if the beliefs of parents and teachers do not result in similar use of discipline, the child is confronted with two different sets of expectations for behavior. These differences necessarily result in discontinuity between the adults' disciplinary actions and therefore in the child's experiences. Furthermore, parents, teachers, and children may not always behave in accord with their beliefs, creating additional discontinuity. However, the stronger caretakers' beliefs are about the importance of particular childrearing practices, the more likely they are to be consistent in following those beliefs, and the greater will be the child's experiences of continuity.

THE RELEVANCE OF INDIVIDUAL HISTORY TO DISCIPLINARY ACTION

In order to understand why parents choose one form of discipline over another in a particular situation, we must examine their beliefs about children and childrearing, and how these beliefs were formed. That is, in order to interpret present disciplinary actions, we must look at past experiences leading up to the present. At one level, the present use of discipline can be understood by reference to previous disciplinary encounters with the child in the near and distant past.

For example, if a boy accidentally breaks something by carelessly running through the house, his mother may warn him to be more careful. If a similar incident occurs again soon after, this time he may receive a stronger and presumably more effective form of discipline, such as a spanking. Thus, the parent's choice of spanking in this situation can be better understood by reference to the earlier incident. That is, a particular punishment may be administered not only on the basis of the child's behavior and parent-child interaction in previous minutes, or hours, or weeks, but also with regard to the effectiveness of specific disciplinary techniques in the past. Analysis at this level also takes into consideration the parent's recent experiences affecting emotional state, and willingness to administer a more or less severe form of punishment.

However, at a broader level of analysis we can interpret parents' present disciplinary actions by examining their general beliefs about childrearing. These beliefs are influenced by the information read on the subject, by the people sought for advice, and by the parent's own experiences both as a child and a parent. Thus, caretakers shape their roles both through direct methods of instruction and adaptation as adults, as well as through less direct methods of social learning based on their own childhood experiences.

Goodnow (1985) makes a similar distinction in describing four sources of experience that influence variation and change in parents' ideas about child socialization: interaction with children, the parent's own upbringing, other parents undergoing similar experiences, and the advice of experts. One's own upbringing is cited as the major source of ideas about parenting, while the influence of the other sources may depend upon the particular socialization situation, the strength of the particular belief, and the child's developmental progress. Goodnow argues, moreover, that parents must be predisposed toward change and/or new information must be discrepant with old beliefs. In addition, the cultural background and specific experiences of the individual mediate the effect of these four sources on parental beliefs. Every parent undergoes a unique set of events during his or her lifetime, which affects the interpretation and acceptance of information about childrearing.

A CULTURAL-HISTORICAL
VIEW OF DISCIPLINE

In addition to individual influences, there are certain commonalities of experiences and beliefs about childrearing that result from membership in a particular culture. From a historical point of view, changes in societal beliefs and structures influence parental ideas about socialization and the acceptance of changes in these ideas. These cultural ideas are intertwined with an individual's experiences in the process of creating and modifying beliefs about children. Thus, an individual's beliefs are the cul mination of his or her own social history and the broader social history of the society.

Such an approach is taken in the cultural-historical school of thought initiated by Lev Vygotsky in the 1920s (e.g., Vygotsky, 1978, 1986). The social origins of higher psychological processes, such as thinking and language, are emphasized as the mechanisms by which both cultural beliefs and individual experiences are incorporated into development. Individual development progresses to higher levels through the internalization of cultural forms of behavior. Initially, such behaviors are learned through interpersonal interactions, and then become internalized as intrapsychological processes. Thus, children develop self-control of their behavior first through the external controls imposed by parents in the form of discipline, and then through the internalization of these actions. Likewise, parents develop their beliefs about children on the basis of their interpersonal socialization experiences as children and as adults, which become internalized as their philosophy on childrearing.

Moreover, this interaction between cultural and historical factors is dialectical. That is, society influences the development of the individual, and the individual in turn influences the development of society. Furthermore, the cultural beliefs that parents and children incorporate are modified themselves by dialectical processes of change in the course of human history. Thus, through the powers of human cognition, individual beliefs are likely to change as societal acceptance of these beliefs changes.

The historical approach to child development assumes that present behavior can be understood only as an outcome of all past behavior. The cultural side of the cultural-historical approach additionally reminds us of the dialectical nature of interaction between individuals and society, so that present behavior is also the result of the extent to which cultural beliefs have been internalized. This approach entails investigation of historical processes of change at two levels, the individual parent and the wider culture, along with their reciprocal influences. Evidence can be gathered not only for the development of individuals' childrearing philosophies, but also for the development of cultural philosophies. Thus, when examining parents' socialization behavior, it is instructive to consider both the course of their own developmental history, and the historical changes in society that have interacted to produce their present beliefs and behaviors.

Mechling (1975) discusses four methods individuals use to learn about and modify childrearing customs: identification, imitation, instruction, and invention. He argues for the primacy of identification and imitation for learning the parenting role, as these are methods of "primary socialization," concerned with the establishment of values. In contrast, direct instruction (as in reading childrearing manuals) and invention or adaptation to new situations that arise in the course of parenting are considered "secondary socialization," concerned with overt behavior. He further claims that the internalized childrearing values established during the parent's own childhood are difficult to change through secondary socialization methods in adulthood; therefore, historians studying childrearing manuals cannot rely on them as evidence of actual values of the times, but only as evidence of the values of the manual writers and as a sociology of knowledge about childrearing.

While there is no doubt that childrearing literature provides evidence of the latter two forms, the cultural-historical perspective also provides the argument that it does influence parenting behavior to some extent. Since the interaction between parental values and cultural beliefs is dialectical, changes at the cultural level are likely to be reflected in changes at the individual level, and vice versa. Moreover, the development of a childrearing philosophy through "primary socialization" methods includes the incorporation of cultural as well as personal values. Once these are internalized, they are open to change through "secondary socialization" methods as they become more or less representative of current cultural beliefs. Furthermore, from the present perspective, values and behavior are not established through separate processes, but are present simultaneously in all socialization situations.

The incorporation of new cultural beliefs by reading childrearing manuals can be likened to the processes of assimilation and accommodation in Jean Piaget's theory of development (e.g., Piaget, 1983).

These complementary processes are utilized in the course of an individual's adaptation to the environment, whereby new knowledge is constructed through interactions with the external world. This knowledge is integrated with extant cognitive beliefs through the process of assimilation, and likewise, these beliefs are modified by this new knowledge in the process of accommodation. Cognitive adaptation involves both these processes in the maintenance of equilibrium.

In using childrearing manuals, parents will interpret what they read in terms of what they already believe: i.e., any change in their philosophy will be constructed by balancing the incorporation of new ideas with the modification of existing ones. Hence, the mother who reads advice discrepant with her own ideas may not be motivated to change her own behavior 180 degrees, but perhaps to modify it somewhat, so that the childrearing values she inculcates in her daughter are reflective of this advice to a much greater degree than her own values are. Thus, while experts' advice may not radically alter the behavior of the present generation of parents, perhaps it will have a greater impact on the next generation. Otherwise, if parenting behavior were primarily the result of internalizing our own parents' behavior, little change would be expected over generations. As mothers, we would be imitating our own mothers, who imitated their mothers, and so on, continuing back until the creation of humanity, or at least modern society.

Accordingly, the childrearing literature can be a valuable source for studying the concomitant processes of change in cultural and individual beliefs. As a sociology of childrearing knowledge, manuals provide a means of analysis of the societal conditions providing the impetus for their existence. Moreover, if childrearing values and behavior are viewed as the product of both cultural influences and individual experiences, then it is important to study constancy and change in both individual parents and society. To disregard half the evidence is to come up with only half the answer to how these values are established. Just as all parents in a society at a given time do not discipline their children in the same way, they will not follow experts' advice to the same degree either. However, the labeling of the manual writers as "experts" by society, and the survival and popularity of their works, suggests their representativeness of at least some cultural beliefs. If their advice were completely unacceptable to society as a whole, their works would not have been read, or published, or known. In this chapter, then, as one side of the study of contemporary American beliefs about discipline and childrearing, some evidence of historical changes in cultural patterns of discipline at home and school will be considered.

HISTORICAL VIEWS OF DISCIPLINARY PRACTICES

Examination of beliefs about children from a variety of cultural-historical periods suggests that issues of discipline have often been a key concern of educators. It seems always to have been a widely accepted understanding that children need some form of discipline at times. The assumptions underlying this idea reveal two basic beliefs about the nature of children: they are unable to control their behavior without external guidance, and such control is necessary and desirable for their functioning in society. The differences lie in the beliefs about what

types of discipline should be used and when it is warranted.

Discipline serves both an immediate function of modifying behavior, and an anticipatory function of creating a future adult armed with particular beliefs about the nature of humanity and the function of society. Therefore, the methods parents use will affect the degree to which such cultural beliefs are internalized by their children and perpetuated in society. Changes in disciplinary practices reflect changes in cultural-historical conceptions about children's abilities and needs, including their present and future roles in society.

DISCIPLINE IN ANCIENT CIVILIZATIONS: A MEANS FOR PRESERVATION OF CULTURE

Many modern Western childrearing practices can be traced back to ancient Hebrew, Greek, and Roman practices. In all of these ancient Mediterranean civilizations, children were recognized as different from adults, with their own set of special needs (Borstelmann, 1983; French, 1977). One characteristic that pervades the biblical and philosophical writings about children of these times is the necessity for discipline and control, both at home and at school. Children were seen as unformed and moldable, in both the physical and psychological spheres, yet with tendencies toward disorder or unruliness.

They also were valued as the embodiment of the future of the family and society. Consequently, childrearing methods determined the ways in which cultural beliefs and values were preserved. Discipline, therefore, was influenced both by parents' beliefs about past events that had created present society, as well as by present practices that would determine its future. In a passage from Plato's *The Laws,* which is a description of methods for creating a Utopian society written around the fourth century B.C., he acknowledged the presence of precursors to the future of society in the play of children. In a view advocating the continuity of cultural heritage, he warned that children who innovate in games disrupt the link between generations, and as adults similarly are not likely to value preserving the laws of their fathers. This view also sees children as playing an active role in their own socialization, a common theme of many modern theories of child development.

If you control the way children play, and the same children always play the same games under the same rules and in the same conditions, and get pleasure from the same toys, you will find that the conventions of adult life too are left in peace without alteration. But in fact games are always being changed and constantly modified and new ones invented, and the younger generation never enthuses over the same thing for two days running . . . they worship anyone who is always introducing some novelty or doing something unconventional . . . this fellow is the biggest menace that can ever afflict a state, because he quietly changes the character of the young by making them despise old things and value novelty. (Plato, *The Laws,* Book VII, Chapter 12, p. 283)

All legislators suppose that an alteration to children's games really is just a "game" ... which leads to no serious or genuine damage. Consequently, so far from preventing change, they feebly give it their blessing. They don't appreciate that if children introduce novelties into their games, they'll inevitably turn out to be quite different people from the previous generation; being differ-

ent, they'll demand a different kind of life, and that will then make them want new institutions and laws. (Plato, *The Laws,* Book VII, Chapter 12, p. 284)

Moreover, the particular childrearing methods parents chose were also a product of cultural beliefs and societal structure, as well as a means of preserving them. While their disciplinary practices may seem harsh by today's standards, they often were imitative of the harshness of adults' lives in those societies (Borstelmann, 1983). The relationship between parent and child was characterized as analogous to that between citizen and state, or gods and mortals. In this sense, then, discipline may have served to directly prepare the child for similar difficulties in adult life.

Ancient Hebrew Culture

The link between parent-child relationships and the perpetuation of cultural ideals underlined the practices of the ancient Hebrews, who considered education and discipline to be the job of both parents. Children often symbolized their hopes for the future, and the family was accorded central importance in the social structure. The parent-child relationship was considered akin to the relationship between God and the people of Israel: just as they were the "chosen people," and expected to obey their God's commandments, so were children seen as a special gift to their parents yet under obligation to obey them. Obedience toward both parents is required by the Fifth Commandment: "Honour thy father and thy mother" (Exodus 20:12). The need for discipline in the struggle between parents and children is reminiscent of the documented struggle between human nature and the edicts of God. Just as God was supposed to have punished those who disobeyed his word, so did parents punish their children for misbehavior. Yet God also is seen as caring and forgiving in the Jewish religion, a role that may have been paralleled by parents.

The focus on obedience, guilt, and punishment, along with forgiveness of sins, was endemic to the experiences of both adults and children. Children were characterized as willful and prone to misbehavior, and therefore in need of firm discipline. One biblical passage speaks to the importance of discipline for the welfare of the child, a theme often repeated later in history by the Puritans.

> Withhold not correction from the child: for if thou beatest him with the rod, he shall not die. Thou shalt beat him with the rod, and shalt deliver his soul from hell. (Proverbs 23:13-14)

In contrast to some other patriarchal cultures, the importance of the mother's role in the education of both sons and daughters was clearly acknowledged. According to Jewish tradition, the religious heritage of a child is determined by the mother's beliefs, rather than the father's. During the early years, children were primarily her responsibility; after about three years old, fathers then took on more responsibility for instructing their sons (Borstelmann, 1983). The first synagogues were unique as places for all ages to come to learn as well as to worship. It is not clear when separate schools began, but by A.D. 63 the High Priest ordered all boys, even orphans, to attend school, thereby relieving the burden of education from parents (Sommerville, 1982). The goal of early education, through the study

of Scripture, was obedience rather than speculation. Only those who went on to higher education, in the study of the Talmud, engaged in theological speculation. Teachers at these levels were accorded the highest status, unlike other societies of the times (Sommerville, 1982). This attests to the great importance placed on the continuity of cultural beliefs through religious education of the young. Moreover, sons were instructed always to obey the highest authority, the commandments of God, even if this required going against the teachings of their fathers (Borstelmann, 1983). Thus, the focus on obedience and punishment remained a fundamental characteristic of the socialization of children in the Hebrew culture.

Cultures of Ancient Greece

The belief in the obligation to obey a higher authority was taken to an extreme in the Greek state of Sparta, where loyalty to the state was emphasized over loyalty to the family. The methods used in training children reflected the militaristic attitudes and structure of this society. Children were given great attention, as their training determined the future security of the state. From ages 7 to 20, boys were sent to boarding schools designed to harden them physically and mentally. Flogging competitions were held to see who could endure the most without uttering a sound, with parents cheering on their sons. While this may seem like cruel torture nowadays, it was not considered punishment but rather an honor. If a boy died during such a competition without making a sound, he became a hero. Girls were given similar training to help prepare them for childbirth, as women were primarily considered breeders, and encouraged to practice eugenic methods as part of their duty to the state to produce the best children possible. Physical and mental discipline was thus a definitive cultural concept; it served the dual functions of preparing and testing loyal and hardy citizens, and accordingly was applied both to children and adults (Sommerville, 1982).

However, this militaristic attitude was not representative of ancient Athenian culture. While the importance of training mind and body was acknowledged in terms of the future of society, the value of children within the family also was emphasized. At all levels of society a couple without children were considered incomplete, lacking a link to the future (French, 1977). Much attention was devoted to the care and training of the young, and children were valued and loved in their own right. Discipline and self-control were stressed as fundamental to character formation. In *The Laws,* Plato expressed this belief in his discussion on early education:

> In the fourth, fifth, sixth and even seventh year of life, a child's character will need to be formed while he plays; we should now stop spoiling him, and resort to discipline, but not such as to humiliate him . . . discipline should not be enforced so high-handedly that they become resentful, though on the other hand we must not spoil them by letting them go uncorrected . . . (Plato, *The Laws,* Book VII, Chapter 12, p. 278)

The ancient Greeks emphasized the malleability of the child, who was seen as a *tabula rasa,* or blank slate. The purpose of discipline, therefore, was to insure proper development rather than to punish evil behavior. Accordingly, parents were advised to use more mild forms of discipline. Plutarch asked fathers not to be too harsh with their children, suggesting that just as they accept shortcomings in their friends, they should accept them in their children (French, 1977). Plato advised that the best form of training was for parents to set good examples for children in their own practices; such consistency would benefit the parents themselves as well.

> The best way to educate the younger generation (as well as yourself) is not to rebuke them but patently to practise all your life what you preach to others. (Plato, *The Laws,* Book V, Chapter 8, p. 193)

Education was a means of promoting the cultural and moral development of individuals, and by extension, of the society as a whole. In Athens, upper class boys were sent to school to receive a liberal education solely in order to become erudite, rather than to learn a trade. Furthermore, this emphasis on the pursuit of knowledge carried over into adulthood. The elements of schoolchildren's and adults' culture were continuous: books, music, poetry, and athletics (Sommerville, 1982). However, the differences between the characteristics of children and adults were clearly recognized. The cultural focus on the moral development and impressionability of children was acknowledged further by the existence of the *paidagogus,* a member of the household whose job was to insure the proper development of the child, including discipline when needed. Moreover, many of the Greek philosophers also recognized that individual and developmental differences exist among children, and suggested that education should be attuned to these (Borstelmann, 1983; French, 1977).

Culture of Ancient Rome

Many of the childrearing practices and beliefs of ancient Rome were assimilated from Greek society. Roman culture differed, however, in its belief in absolute *patria potestas,* or paternal power (Borstelmann, 1983; French, 1977). This belief was exemplified by Roman law, which allowed fathers control over the life and death of their adult children until the second century A.D., and allowed the practice of infanticide until A.D. 374. In Greece, in contrast, although infanticide was practiced, once a child was accepted into the family his or her safety was secure.

Nevertheless, the rearing and education of children was important to Roman culture. Family life was emphasized as a means for teaching children self-control and reverence for their parents. Similarly to the Greeks, the Romans maintained a *tabula rasa* view of children, emphasizing their moldability, ignorance, and unawareness, and therefore, potential corruptibility. Quintilian, a Roman educator during the first century A.D., was concerned with the importance of early character formation of the young child, whom he saw as innocent and easily molded.

> ...let us remember that no child is so tender in years as not to learn at once the distinction between right and wrong, and that he requires to be moulded with the greatest care at the age when he is still innocent of deceit and yields most readily to his instructors. For you would sooner break than bend straight those who have once become set in vicious habits. (Quintilian, *Institutio Oratoria,* Book I, Chapter 3, p. 32)

Children tended to be described in a more negative light by the Romans, who also saw them as unruly, deceitful, and angry (Borstelmann, 1983; French, 1977). Thus, discipline was considered essential to the moral and social development of such a child.

The focus of education was on the formation of good character, and parents were urged to set good examples in acknowledgement of the imitative nature and natural innocence of children. In early Roman civilization children learned by parental instruction and example, accompanying their parents from about seven years of age (French, 1977; Sommerville, 1982). However, the importance of maintaining a balance between love and discipline was stressed in many of the ancient writings.

Once Rome began building its empire, education became professionalized. Responsibility for the child's moral development thus was entrusted to the teacher, who reprised the father's role in molding the child. Quintilian acknowledged this purpose of education, and emphasized the importance of discipline and self-control for both teacher and student:

> It is not enough that he should himself show rigid self-control, he must also by the strictness of his discipline control the behaviour of the pupils who gather round him. Let him, then, above all things adopt the attitude of a parent toward his pupils and consider that he is taking the place of those who entrust their children to him . . . . He must constantly dwell upon the honourable and the good; for the more he admonishes his pupils the less he will require to punish them. He must never lose his temper, yet he will not pass over what deserves correction . . . . In correcting faults he will not be harsh and never abusive . . . (Quintilian, *Institutio Oratoria,* Book II, Chapter 2, pp. 73-74)

In practice, however, both Roman and Greek children received spankings, beatings, and whippings in the course of their education. Punishment generally was justified as showing the proper spirit in a teacher, in line with the Roman values of authority and control (Sommerville, 1982). In contrast to the prevailing cultural view of that time, Quintilian along with other writers professed a view against the use of corporal punishment. He suggested that if teachers were sensitive to the individual child, such punishment would not be necessary.

As for corporal punishment...I am altogether opposed to it, first because it is disgusting, fit only for slaves and undoubtedly an insult (as appears, if you change the age of the victim): in the next place, because a pupil whose mind so ill befits a free man's son as not to be corrected by reproof, will remain obdurate even in face of blows ...and finally because such chastisement will be quite unnecessary if there is someone ever present to supervise the boy's studies with diligence... it seems usually to happen that the carelessness of *paedogogi* is amended by the pupils being punished for doing what is wrong instead of being compelled to do what is right. (Quintilian, *Institutio Oratoria,* Book I, Chapter 3, pp. 32-33)

Discipline and control of children was a key concept in the childrearing beliefs of all three of these ancient Mediterranean civilizations. They all maintained conceptions of the child as moldable, yet susceptible to bad influences without proper guidance. The formation of good moral character formed the basis of educational theories and practices, with discipline considered a necessary element in this process. The role of parents in educating their children eventually was taken over by professional teachers, who often practiced rather harsh forms of punishment.

Although such authoritarian techniques were criticized by many educators and philosophers of the times, they may have remained in place as precursors to the harshness of adult life. Nevertheless, children were valued, both for their contributions to family life and for their role in the perpetuation of cultural beliefs. A great deal of attention, therefore, was given to the methods used in childrearing, as adults recognized the importance of children to the continuity of their civilization.

THE ROLE OF DISCIPLINE IN PURITAN BELIEFS: A STEP TOWARD MORAL SALVATION

Puritan conceptions of the child as willful yet moldable, and therefore in need of firm discipline and instruction, recall some of the ancient views. This society differed, however, in its beliefs about the contradictory doctrines of infant depravity and innocence. Rather than adopting the ancient Greek and Roman views of a *tabula rasa,* children were seen as entering the world imbued with original sin; thus, the need to break their wills through strict discipline was a prime responsibility of parenting. The conflict between rebellion and submission was a key concept in Puritan culture. In their own history, they were required to rebel against the current religious and social order of sixteenth and seventeenth century England in order to be obedient to their God.

The Puritans' fervent religious beliefs, which impelled them to seek sanctuary in the American colonies, made spiritual purity and moral salvation a major concern. As knowledge of Scripture was necessary for salvation, their main educational focus was on developing the moral character of their children through religious indoctrination. In a societal institutionalization of this belief, a Massachussetts law dated 1642 required heads of household to be sure that their children and charges were taught to read, with similar laws following in other states (Gordon, 1978). It was the parents' obligation to enforce good behavior in the family, which would provide necessary though not sufficient evidence for salvation (Beekman, 1977; Borstelmann, 1983).

Similarly to the ancient Hebrews, the Puritans maintained that the parent-child relationship replayed the relationship between God and his people. The "original sin," Adam's rebellion against God, was reiterated in the conflict between parental dictates and the child's will. The basis of the Puritan cause was obedience to the will of God; accordingly, all social relationships were defined in terms of a dominant-subordinate structure, which presupposes conflict. The Puritans also believed that an individual's first allegiance was to God, not to parents, as did the ancient Hebrews. In practice, however, religious submission could be taught only through parental authority.

The parental role consisted of two obligations: instruction and discipline (Beekman, 1977; Borstelmann, 1983; Demos, 1971; Sommerville, 1978). The child was born both ignorant and sinful, but with proper guidance could acquire knowledge and self-control. However, knowledge alone was no guarantee of appropriate behavior; parental instruction and example were not sufficient for socialization. Firm discipline also was necessary in order to overcome the child's will and insure behavior in accord with reason rather than nature.

Puritan childrearing manuals discouraged harsh treatment, for just as obedience to God must be offered freely, so should obedience to parents (Borstelmann, 1983; Sommerville, 1978). The purpose of discipline was moral guidance. Goodness had to be instilled from without, rather than drawn out from within. Children were taught to revere their parents, and to fear loss of parental love for not meeting their expectations. Parents were cautioned not to allow their affection for their children to place them on equal ground. They were told to set good examples for their children in the important early years of life, and not to encourage naughty behavior for their own amusement, as such behavior would later require severe methods to dislodge the bad habits. Consistent and thoughtful discipline, which would be less harsh in the long run, was urged. If admonishment was sufficient, then it was preferred to physical punishment: beatings, whippings, or spankings were to be used only as a last resort, in the face of the cardinal sins of stubbornness and disobedience. "Shaming" was considered the most useful disciplinary technique in accord with the moral purpose of punishment. Children were taught to feel ashamed of their faults, a method that requires an internal moral sensibility, in line with the belief that obedience should be offered freely.

As in ancient civilizations, the form of punishment was consistent with that of adult life, and therefore, may have served as preparation for such. Adult crimes also were frequently punished through public shaming methods, such as the stocks, branding, or badges of infamy, where the shame of punishment was often stronger than the pain (Demos, 1971). The principal evil was the concealment of sin, and even defendants sentenced to death were exhorted to confess in order to protect the morality of the community (Hoffer &

Hull, 1984). As the agent of immediate social control, this placed a great deal of responsibility on parents, especially the father, to maintain surveillance over the household to prevent sinful behavior (Flaherty, 1972).

As a social reform movement, the Puritans may have been sensitive to the need to preserve their beliefs through the primacy of the family and the church with regard to the state. Thus, obedience was required first by the family, then by the church, and finally, when these failed, by the legal system. Even then, the responsibility for discipline frequently was delegated to the family. For example, children brought to court in colonial New England often were sentenced to punishment by their parents, or could be released if the father testified that he had already punished them at home (Flaherty, 1972). By maintaining the family as the agent of discipline, the intimate relationship between parent and child may have made punishment more effective. Not only would children bring public shame upon themselves by a transgression, but they also would disappoint their parents who must punish them. The family context would provide continuity in the method and meaning of the punishment in accord with the child's history. However, this was also likely to result in differences between families in the practice of discipline, making punishment less standardized than when carried out by the legal system.

As a dissenting social movement, the Puritans were aware of the need to strengthen their power through their offspring, and therefore devoted great attention to them in order to assure the continuity of their beliefs. It may be that childrearing becomes an even greater concern when parents are seeking to change the prevailing cultural beliefs, rather than to maintain them. Clearly, the great concern of reform movements for perpetuating their ideas by influencing subsequent generations was followed by the Puritans. As the first English social reform movement, they attempted to change not only the Church of England, but the entire character of national life. Failing to achieve this directly, they attempted to influence society from the "bottom up," through their childrearing manuals and children's stories (Sommerville, 1978; Stone, 1979). The Puritans issued the bulk of the childrearing advice in the seventeenth and eighteenth centuries, as a means of insuring that their beliefs were put into practice appropriately. They also were the first English authors to write books exclusively for children, and showed an apt appreciation of their special communication needs. As in their parenting manuals, they hoped to create a strong moral base through their stories, which would provide the power to challenge the prevailing social authority.

These stories were usually about pious children who met early deaths. The reasons for such stories were twofold: first, they may have evoked sympathy for their cause by showing children as the victims of persecution, and second, it was safer than writing about living children who could later discredit the cause. Furthermore, the abundance of such works does not seem so shocking when consideration is given to mortality rates of the times, which made such experiences commonplace (Sommerville, 1978). By creating these works, the Puritans also were acknowledging the moral and intellectual autonomy of children. Children were viewed as having the ability to choose the course of their actions, although not necessarily the knowledge or self-control to choose the proper path; therefore, parents had the responsibility to guide them through instruction and discipline.

While the idea of infant depravity formed the basis of their childrearing beliefs, there is no evidence that the Puritans were any harsher than other parents of that era (Borstelmann, 1983; Pollock, 1983; Sommerville, 1978). Conversely, the concept of infant depravity may have served to induce sympathy for the child, as the parent was held responsible for overcoming this natural state (Sommerville, 1978). As is true in any culture, parents varied in their disciplinary practices; some relied heavily on physical methods, while others used only psychological ones. Teachers also varied in their practices: while corporal punishment was common at school, not every child experienced it, nor did every parent agree with its use. Both at home and at school, it was believed that discipline should be applied with consideration of the particular child and his or her traits, temperament, and past behavioral history. Moreover, evidence from diaries and autobiographies suggests that there was no clear link between religious beliefs and the types of discipline used. What may have mattered was the parents' beliefs about the purpose of discipline in a given situation, the effectiveness of various techniques in achieving this end, their view of the parental and tutorial roles, and their beliefs about their child (Pollock, 1983).

A cultural-historical explanation suggests that Puritans' interpretations of how to best achieve authority over their children varied according to their individual experiences. However, the consistencies among them regarding their beliefs about the nature of children and the purpose of parenting is also coincident with a cultural-historical interpretation. Even parents who may have been ambivalent about using authoritarian disciplinary methods were bound by their cultural beliefs to do so; by not punishing their child when disobedient, they were risking his or her eternal damnation. Thus, Puritan practices must be interpreted in light of their cultural beliefs. Their emphasis on child discipline showed their concern not only for their society's future, but also for their children's future — their beliefs dictated that the best way to show their love and concern for their children was through insuring their moral salvation. The purpose of discipline was to create a rational and moral being from an ignorant and willful one. This goal necessitated a significant investment of time and effort on the part of the parents, which was likely to occur only if there were concomitant feelings of care and love.

LOCKE: THE RATIONAL CHILD

John Locke, the son of English Puritan parents, wrote what became one of the most influential childrearing manuals in England, France, and America during the first half of the eighteenth century. Some evidence of Puritan ideology is present in his work *Some Thoughts Concerning Education* (1693/1899), as expected from the cultural-historical viewpoint. However, his manual was not intended as a guide to Puritan beliefs about childrearing, as he was opposed to the cornerstone concept of an evil child whose will must be broken. Similarly to the ancient Greek and Roman views, Locke professed the belief that the child was born as a *tabula rasa,* or blank slate; hence, development could be molded entirely through experience. He advocated a toughening program for children, such as making them wear leaky shoes in wet weather and light clothing during the winter, believing that such training would build endurance. Adopting the philosophy of "sound mind and sound body," he lauded the Spartans as models.

However, harsh discipline by parents or teachers was not encouraged, as Locke believed that this would break children's spirits as well as their wills, and thereby cause them to lose all interest in learning and achieving. The importance of raising children so that they desire to work to their full capacity, as expressed by the Protestant work ethic, is still an American ideal. Locke supported this belief in his views on discipline, encouraging the development of energetic and industrious, rather than passive and low-achieving, children.

> ... For I am very apt to think, that great Severity of Punishment does but very little Good, nay, great Harm in Education; and I believe it will be found that . . . those Children who have been most chastis'd, seldom make the best Men. (Locke, 1693/1899, p. 29)

> ... if the Mind be curb'd, and humbled too much in Children; if their Spirits be abas'd and broken much, by too strict an Hand over them, they lose all their Vigour and Industry . . . (Locke, 1693/1899, p. 30)

Locke encouraged parents to appeal to the rational side of children in their discipline, as this would be more effective than relying on physical punishments and rewards. He viewed the latter as training children to increase their desires for bodily pleasures, which he considered the basis of all evil behavior. Moreover, physical punishment might teach children merely to avoid externally caused pain rather than to develop internal control of their own behavior. Instead, if from the beginning parents relied on reason in guiding their children, they would encourage the development of their natural propensity for rational self-discipline, which would lead to a productive life. Self-discipline at all ages is a guiding theme of the Protestant work ethic; accordingly, Locke believed that children should be taught that rewards and punishments are determined by their behavior, just as in adult life.

> But if you take away the Rod on one Hand, and these little Encouragements which they are taken with, on the other, how then (will you say) shall Children be govern'd? Remove Hope and Fear, and there is an End of all Discipline. I grant that Good and Evil, Reward and Punishment, are the only Motives to a Rational Creature: These are the Spur and Reins whereby all Mankind are set on Work, and guided, and therefore they are to be made use of to Children too. For I advise their Parents and Governors always to carry this in their Minds, that Children are to be treated as rational Creatures. (Locke, 1693/1899, p. 33)

Fulfilling the Protestant work ethic requires a rational individual who is governed by internal rather than external control. In acknowledgement of developing this internal control, Locke believed that praise and shame were the most effective forms of discipline, the primary techniques advocated by Puritan ideology as well. In order to strengthen their effects, he suggested that they be coupled with the presentation or withdrawal of desired objects. By so doing, children would learn that material things, along with the love of others, were earned by good behavior, while bad behavior led to material and psychological neglect. Such techniques promote the development of an internal sense of discipline, i.e., that the child can control events by controlling his or her behavior.

> ... those that are commended and in Esteem for doing well, will necessarily be belov'd and cherish'd by every Body, and have all other good Things as a Consequence of it; and on the other Side, when any one by Miscarriage falls into Disesteem, and cares not to preserve his Credit, he will unavoidably fall under Neglect and Contempt; and in that State, the Want of whatever might satisfy or delight him will follow (Locke, 1693/1899, p. 35).

Locke urged strict control over children from the beginning, so that no bad habits of will would be instituted. Parents were told to retain authority and power over their children through fear and awe in the earlier years, and through love and friendship later. By establishing an early pattern of obedience to authority, it would come to be expected; giving in to the young child who does not understand the reasons for saying no meant that harsher methods would later be required.

> He that is not us'd to submit his Will to the Reason of others *when* he is *young,* will scarce hearken to submit to his own Reason when he is of an Age to make Use of it. (Locke, 1693/1899, p. 23)

By maintaining a pattern of submission to a reasonable authority from an early age, children would then incorporate the abilities of reason and good judgment in their own development.

Physical punishment was deemed necessary at times during the younger years in order to establish a pattern of authority over children before they were capable of evaluating their own behavior. However, once this had been effected, then praise and shame should comprise the necessary techniques of discipline. Overall, Locke emphasized a balance between authority and affection, tempered by reason. While he advocated strict control, it was a means for the child to internalize qualities of self-discipline and reason, rather than to overcome an evil nature. Early education was considered to have a lasting effect, therefore parents should be consistent, yet moderate, in their practices. Above all, Locke believed that the capacity for rational thought was inherent in children as well as adults, and should be the guiding theme of socialization practices. He provided the premier modern argument for the power of nurture over nature, rekindling an ancient debate that continues today.

ROUSSEAU: PROTECTING THE CHILD OF NATURE

A more controversial plan for childrearing was proposed by the eighteenth century philosopher Jean-Jacques Rousseau, who disputed the prevailing view that the task of parents is to create an obedient child from an unruly creature. Although his ideas were not followed by American parents as closely as Locke's during this time, he articulated the ensuing view of an innocent child whose development was directed by the power of nature, acknowledged during the nineteenth and twentieth centuries. In his book *Emile, or Education* (1762/1914), Rousseau took issue with Locke's idea of the rational child, believing that the capacity for reasoning does not develop until about twelve years of age.

If the infant sprang at one bound from its mother's breast to the age of reason, the present type of education would be quite suitable, but its natural growth calls for quite different training. The mind should be left undisturbed until its faculties have developed . . . (Rousseau, 1762/1914, p. 57)

Rousseau formulated his ideal plan for childrearing based on an innocent and amoral child. Punishment for wrong behavior, therefore, made no sense, an idea that was the antithesis of the prevailing Puritan view of infant depravity.

Before the age of reason we do good or ill without knowing it, and there is no morality in our actions . . . (Rousseau, 1762/1914, p. 34)

Give your scholar no verbal lessons; he should be taught by experience alone; never punish him, for he does not know what it is to do wrong . . . Wholly unmoral in his actions, he can do nothing morally wrong, and he deserves neither punishment nor reproof. (Rousseau, 1762/1914, p. 56)

If a child broke some object, for example, he blamed the parent for leaving it within reach of the child, who should not be punished for the parent's own carelessness.

Rousseau proposed the idea that nature is inherently good, while societal conditions create evil. The child, although guided by impulses, was innocent. Any evil behaviors or traits were learned from the environment.

Let us lay it down as an incontrovertible rule that the first impulses of nature are always right; there is no original sin in the human heart, the how and why of the entrance of every vice can be traced. (Rousseau, 1762/1914, p. 56)

He believed that children's innocent nature could be harmed by outside influences; thus, it was incumbent upon parents and teachers to provide proper guidance for their charges, who knew no better. However, this guidance consisted of strict control to guard against the child learning bad habits from others, rather than teaching moral precepts.

The only habit the child should be allowed to contract is that of having no habits . . . (Rousseau, 1762/1914, p. 30)

Therefore the education of the earliest years should be merely negative. It consists, not in teaching virtue or truth, but in preserving the heart from vice and from the spirit of error. (Rousseau, 1762/1914, p. 57)

With such training, children would then be open to learning from reason and understanding once they were capable. Development was seen as a naturally unfolding process, with the young child's actions motivated by an innocent curiosity about the world. Children should be unrestrained in their exploration of the world. If a child became hurt while playing, for example, this served as a lesson of nature in bearing pain and developing courage.

Rousseau believed that children learned best through their own experiences. While they were to be given liberty to actively fulfill their natural curiosity, this was not to become power over the parent: parents should be firm with their young children, who were motivated solely by their impulses. Unreasonable demands or unnecessary wants should not be met. In the natural order of the world, children would learn that they were weak, while the authority was strong. Parents must however be careful not to demand unnatural behaviors merely for social convention.

Fathers and teachers who want to make the child, not a child but a man of learning, think it never too soon to scold, correct, reprove, threaten, bribe, teach, and reason. Do better than they; be reasonable, and do not reason with your pupil . . . (Rousseau, 1762/1914, p. 58)

The job of parents was to guide their children in order to prevent harmful influences of society from leading them awry, while moral education and proper punishment would be received through nature. Formal education would begin around 12 years of age, when children's natural motivation impelled them to seek more learning. Rousseau acknowledged both the natural innocence of children and the active role they play in their own development. While similar ideas had been expressed hundreds of years earlier by writers such as Plato and Quintilian, Rousseau was unique among his contemporaries in their proposal. Furthermore, his belief in allowing the natural forces inherent in development to proceed unimpeded, a true advocate for the nature side of the age-old nature-nurture controversy, provided a radical new view of the task of parenting.

DISCIPLINE IN AMERICA IN THE NINETEENTH CENTURY: ISSUES OF CONSISTENCY

In contrast to earlier works on childrearing, manuals published in America during the nineteenth century were concerned with the mother's role in raising her children, as fathers now spent more time working outside the home. While most of the earlier American ideas about childrearing were imported from England, as expected in an immigrant nation, the first substantial body of American literature appeared by the 1830s (Borstelmann, 1983; Sunley, 1955). Rapid changes in the character of family life brought about by industrialization and urbanization created concern about the best ways to prepare children for a new and uncertain future. As their children would determine the subsequent course of society, parents were responsible for the growth and development of the nation through their childrearing methods. Thus, these broad societal changes affected the cultural philosophies about childrearing adopted by individual parents; here, the dialectical interaction between individuals and society is evident. As the needs of society regarding its future workers changed, so did the views about preparing them.

Three different views of the nature of children and corresponding methods of child training could be discerned. One view retained Puritan tones, emphasizing the evil nature of the child and the importance of discipline for proper moral development. It was the mother's responsibility to keep herself "morally pure" in order to provide a good example. Character formation occurred during the first six years of life, and mothers were seen as devoted to this purpose, even to the neglect of their husbands and older children. Firm and consistent rather than harsh discipline was suggested, the goal being the complete obedience and submission of the child requisite for moral salvation (Beekman, 1977; Borstelmann, 1983; Rodgers, 1980; Sunley, 1955). Around the beginning of the century, middle-class mothers began forming Maternal Associations, meeting to discuss methods of achieving such control over their children. These groups also published magazines about childrearing, exhorting mothers to fulfill their duty by breaking their child's will, which they thought often was not successfully accomplished. Mothers were viewed as reluctant to punish their children, thereby providing them with inconsistent moral training. However, this was considered a result of their inexperience in such matters, while fathers were being neglectful of their disciplinary duties (Borstelmann, 1983; Kett, 1977; Rodgers, 1980; Sunley, 1955).

The influences of Locke's and Rousseau's ideas were evident in a second view, whose key concept was hardening the child in the manner proposed by Locke. Children were seen as possessing a tendency toward evil behavior, but in the tradition of Rousseau, this was believed to result from exposure to the dangers inherent in society rather than from an innate depravity. The need for establishing parental authority and strict obedience still was stressed as fundamental to good character formation, but this view lacked the religious orientation of the Puritan literature (Beekman, 1977; Borstelmann, 1983; Sunley, 1955).

A third view first appeared in the literature of this time, advocating gentle treatment of the child. Although less widespread than the Puritan orientation, it was influential, growing in power over the century. The child was considered simply ignorant of right, rather than compelled toward wrong. Therefore, the task of parents was to lead their children along the proper path, rather than to force them into submission. Consistency and firmness in discipline, administered with understanding and justice, were advocated. Punishment and reward were dispensed on the basis of children's motives in their actions. The use of encouragement and reward was highly regarded, while the common techniques of physi-

cal punishment and shaming were repudiated. Maternal love was given high praise, in contrast to other views that discouraged parents from showing too much affection (Borstelmann, 1983; Rodgers, 1980; Sunley, 1955).

Consistency in discipline was a prevalent theme among all these childrearing philosophies. Many of the problems related to the rapid social changes occurring during this time were attributed to inconsistent training by parents and teachers. A prevalent belief was that all children were equally "perfectable" with proper diligence on the part of parents. Therefore, if a child turned out badly, it was due to poor training rather than an inherent depravity. The importance of the environment in establishing proper habits was stressed: consistent training would result in a highly developed internal moral code. In a rapidly changing society, such an internalized moral sense was necessary for the maintenance of social order. Rather than focusing solely on the individual child's moral salvation, systematic discipline was considered essential to the future cohesiveness of American society.

Consistency was also a concern since mothers were now the primary disciplinarians. It may be that it is easier to be consistent when the parent-child relationship is more distant than when interacting frequently with the child as the primary caretaker. Consequently, mothers tended to be more lenient and less willing to administer punishment even when necessary. Even parents subscribing to the Puritan view of "breaking the child's will" would be impulsively indulgent at times, counteracting the effects of strict obedience training. However, firmness in discipline did not necessitate harsh methods. Corporal punishment was advocated only as a last resort, and usually was the primary childrearing task of fathers. A similar trend was found in the school system, where corporal punishment was commonly used throughout the first half of the century when the teachers mainly were men, but decreased in use by the 1860s as teaching became the domain of women (Rodgers, 1980; Sunley, 1955).

Children experienced another form of inconsistency in disciplinary practices at school with the use of mixed-age classrooms prior to the 1830s. They read lessons individually during most of the day, and spent only a small amount of time reciting at the front of the classroom under the direct scrutiny of the teacher. With the installation of age-segregated schooling, children now were more directly supervised, and consequently received more consistent discipline (Rodgers, 1980).

The themes contained in children's stories also changed as society changed. Earlier, moralistic Puritan themes of obedience and restraint characterized children's literature, but by the second half of the century, heroism was the predominant theme (Borstelmann, 1983; Rodgers, 1980). This created another source of inconsistency in socialization, as the methods of parents and teachers did not always match these themes. Thus, children received contradictory messages from those parents and teachers who tended toward strict discipline, self-restraint, and systematic methods, in comparison to literary models who emphasized heroism, impulsiveness, and spontaneous love.

As the century wore on, the basic Puritan values that had characterized much of American society until this point came into increasing conflict with the new ideals of independence, individualism, and self-

sufficiency. Accordingly, many of the old beliefs were modified: while obedience and moral development still were a central concern, the methods became less authoritarian as the child came to be viewed as more innocent. Parents were urged to set good examples and to encourage their children, rather than to control and dominate them. Widespread social changes made discrepancies between parental practices, educational methods, and children's literary models inevitable. Although these forces of socialization were changing in line with the new needs of the society, this often meant that individual children were presented with contradictory expectations. While the older, more authoritarian methods may have created an orderliness for individuals in the midst of widespread social upheaval, they also were less suited to meeting the future needs of society. Hence, the dialectical nature of the interaction between these systems made change predictable, but also made consistency unlikely.

DISCIPLINE IN AMERICA IN THE TWENTIETH CENTURY: THE INFLUENCE OF SCIENTIFIC BELIEFS

Toward the end of the nineteenth century much of the advice to mothers was becoming more permissive, in line with the "gentle treatment" method and the new American values. The view in general could be characterized as "mother knows best," whether mother believed in breaking her child's will or gently guiding her child along the proper path. Around the beginning of the twentieth century childrearing manuals became stricter in tone once again, emphasizing the early formation of good habits and character. Strict scheduling and systematic care for infants was the focus of most manuals at this time (Vincent, 1951; Weiss, 1978; Wolfenstein, 1955). However, this strictness was not conceived of as a moral obligation so much as a medical recommendation. As the moral authoritarianism of Puritan beliefs was losing its sway with the American middle class, the rational authoritarianism of medical experts was taking its place (Newson & Newson, 1974). The view was changing to "experts know best," a good deal of which is still evident today.

A new source for childrearing information also became available in America around this time in the form of scientific studies of children (Borstelmann, 1983; Schlossman, 1976). As the field of behavioral science grew, the justifications underlying advice shifted from a moral stance to a scientific one. From the mothers' points of view, they may have felt as obliged to follow the new experts' medical and scientific advice as they had to adhere to church doctrine in the past. However, the reasons underlying their practices now were based on the health and welfare of their children, rather than on their moral salvation.

The strictness advocated in childrearing manuals coincided with the rise of the behaviorism movement in the scientific community. Behaviorism in its strongest form proposed a blank-slate model of the child, leaving development completely under the control of the environment. Such a view necessitated a firm and watchful mother to insure that only proper habits were learned, much in the tradition of Locke. In addition, however, remnants of Puritanism could be seen in descriptions of the child as endowed with a tendency toward bad habits that required

strict discipline on the mother's part (Vincent, 1951; Weiss, 1978; Wolfenstein, 1955). This approach has been characterized as the era of the "goodness morality," when the mother's role was to insure the development of a moral and well-behaved child by her vigilant practices (Wolfenstein, 1955). However, the concern was less with moral salvation than with mental hygiene. Just as the medical experts were stressing the necessity of regular habits for proper physical development, they applied the same reasoning to moral and emotional development. By couching their advice in familiar moralistic authoritarian tones, mothers may have been more prepared to accept the word of these new experts as authority (Newson & Newson, 1974).

The development of the Parent-Teacher Association (P.T.A.) in 1897, originally called the National Congress of Mothers, provided another outlet for disseminating the advice of experts. The original purpose of the P.T.A. was parent education, in the form of advancing the current scientific beliefs about children to mothers. Yet the continued influence of the moralism surrounding childrearing could be seen in the function of this organization in its early years. During the first two decades there was a religious component concerned primarily with social reform — middle-class mothers considered it their moral duty to educate the lower-class about the best ways to raise their children. Thus, while parent education was deemed important for all, the views were constructed by middle-class mothers and passed on to lower-class mothers (Schlossman, 1976).

The nature of parent education by the P.T.A. changed during the postwar era, focusing mainly on instructing middle-class mothers and their preschool children. The goal was to raise a deferential, socially conformist, emotionally controlled child by relying on the scientific principles of habit formation derived from behavioral psychology. Nursery schools also became more popular during this time as a place to teach middle-class children correct habits and their mothers correct parenting. The concern was for the child's social and emotional growth, not the cognitive growth that has been stressed in recent years. The scientific theories of Watson, Freud, Dewey, and Gesell were adapted to show the importance of early experience and the power of parents in shaping their child's behavior (Schlossman, 1976). Thus, scientific principles were becoming the guiding force in parent education by the early part of the twentieth century.

Around the 1940s, a shift was evident in the childrearing manuals toward greater concern with psychological welfare. The child was conceived of as more cooperative and self-regulating; hence, a more permissive schedule was advocated. The rebellious and evil-hearted child of the Puritans had become cooperative and innocent by the middle of this century. The mother's job likewise had changed; no longer concerned with vigilantly guarding her offspring's moral character, she now was expected to promote her child's cognitive growth and happiness in all their interactions (Newson & Newson, 1974; Vincent, 1951; Weiss, 1978; Wolfenstein, 1955). The emphasis had shifted to a "fun morality"; it was the mother's obligation to make life enjoyable, rather than morally pure, for her baby and herself (Wolfenstein, 1955). While mothers still were responsible for their children's and society's future, producing well-adjusted and intelligent children now was seen as the best way to

fulfill obligations to both. Rather than reducing the mother's duties, this more permissive view of childrearing may have expanded them, as now she was also responsible for her child's cognitive and emotional growth in her socialization practices (Newson & Newson, 1974; Weiss, 1978; Wolfenstein, 1955).

Two corresponding movements in the field of child development that supported this new outlook also occurred during this time. The normative studies of motor and mental development conducted at the newly developed child welfare institutes provided scientific data on child development and family processes. However, changes in popular childrearing advice often reflect changes in middle-class thought and current theories on education and personality development, rather than new evidence based on recent empirical data (Vincent, 1951). The second relevant scientific movement was the translation of psychoanalytic theory into social learning theory terms (e.g. Dollard, Miller, Doob, Mowrer & Sears, 1939). Mothers now could be told what kind of influence specific parenting techniques, such as reward and punishment, would have on their children's personality development.

Much of this permissive view has remained in place during the ensuing years of the twentieth century. One of its best known proponents is Benjamin Spock. The gist of his advice on discipline has changed little over the years from his first book *(The Common Sense Book of Baby and Child Care, 1946)* to more recent versions *(Baby and Child Care, 1977)*. The first edition told parents not to give too many reasons to small children as this will only confuse them, a modification of the legacy of Rousseau. They were told to be firm and friendly with their children, in order to train them to get along with others. This point was expanded in the later edition as the cornerstone of parents' socialization practices.

> The everyday job of the parent, then, is to keep the child on the right track by means of firmness . . . . You come to punishment (if you use it at all) once in a while when your system of firmness breaks down. (Spock, 1977, p. 373)

> In both editions, punishment was emphasized as necessary at times, but not as a primary teaching method as was often the case in the past. [Punishment] is never the main element in discipline — it's only a vigorous additional reminder that the parents feel strongly about what they say. (Spock, 1977, p. 372)

Spock also reassured parents that even physical punishment was acceptable occasionally, as long as it accomplished the goal of changing children's behavior without making them defiant or breaking their spirits. He suggested that it might be better to spank a child occasionally in anger and get it over with than to remain disapproving or guilt-inducing, a view that contrasts greatly with Puritan ideas.

A focus of more recent editions was the emphasis on creating a loving atmosphere within the family as a method of discipline that would cause children to be loving and cooperative in return.

> The main source of good discipline is growing up in a loving family — being loved and learning to love in return. We want to be kind and cooperative (most of the time) because we like people and want them to like us. (Spock, 1977, p. 372)

While the fun morality emphasis of the mid-century has remained to a great ex-tent, it has been expanded to include affection and love as primary tools of discipline. Although the idea of using love with discipline often was included in historic accounts of childrearing, it was not seen as a replacement for punishment. This last view requires an innocent child, rather than one who is swayed toward evil; such an outlook seems to have gained popular acceptance only recently.

While discipline is still a major concern in childrearing, it has become more of a management issue than a moral one. The question seems to be how should discipline be used so that children learn what is expected of them, and then learn to expect it of themselves. The importance of consistent parental practices has remained a major focus, although now this is seen as crucial for learning to get along with others rather than for personal moral salvation. As long as the American ideals of independence, individualism, and self-sufficiency are retained, there will be conflicts between authority and freedom in raising children. The dialectical nature of the interaction between cultural heritage and individual experiences insures that no single ideal solution exists for every family. However, by understanding the roots of our cultural philosophies, it is possible to better understand our own behavior.

CONCLUSIONS: A CULTURAL-HISTORICAL EXPLANATION OF CONTINUITY IN DISCIPLINE

Both continuities and discontinuities in child socialization are evident from a cultural-historical perspective on discipline. These can be traced from one generation to the next, or, for a given child, from one situation to the next. While parents aim for continuity in their disciplinary practices and in the beliefs they inculcate in their children, in reality some discontinuities are inevitable. Both children and societies are constantly developing and changing, making absolute consistency in practices or views impossible. However, it is through the continuities in beliefs that parents perpetuate an aspect of themselves — their values — through their children. The existence of many historical continuities in beliefs about discipline in American society indicates the importance given to preserving childrearing values in the process of cultural transmission.

In present-day American society, the influence of many past cultural values is evident. For example, the Protestant work ethic followed by the Puritans and evident in the writings of John Locke continues to guide socialization efforts. Training children to achieve as much as possible has long been a goal of both parents and teachers; in line with the cultural-historical viewpoint, however, this ethic has been modified to fit with newer ideals. Achievement is valued more for personal gain than for community contribution or moral obligation. This ethic is apparent in popular slogans such as the American army's "Be all that you can be," and in the dilemma faced by the modern woman over how to have it all — career, family, and happiness. In accord with the "fun morality" emphasis of the latter half of this century, the problem that parents and educators face is how to raise a child who enjoys working hard and striving to achieve. By retaining these contradictory ideals, individuals today are confronted with the conflict of how to combine work and fun in all their activities, as both are omnipresent cultural values. Seemingly the only resolution to

this dilemma is to attempt to make all work fun and all fun work, a solution that is unlikely to satisfy either value in practice.

The idea that children's experiences should prepare them for similar experiences as adults has been a continuous socialization theme throughout history. While particular forms of training haved changed as society's needs changed, the major focus of discipline has paralleled cultural values and social structure. For example, the Spartans trained their children in military preparedness, the Hebrews and the Puritans emphasized moral obedience, and the neo-behaviorists of the twentieth century focused on habit formation. In all cases, disciplinary philosophies were based on fundamental cultural experiences. In a society such as the Puritans', for example, the principles of religious reformation on which it was founded guided the experiences of all its members, both adults and children. The socialization experiences of children have anticipated their future adult life, whether that life was one of militaristic austerity, religious authoritarianism, or goal-oriented achievement.

Based on their own experiences with subordinate roles as adults, parents may apply similar reasoning to their beliefs about children. Across cultures, the parent-child relationship often has been a recapitulation of the governing authority-adult relationships inherent in the society. Such relationships provide a long-term continuity of experience from childhood to adulthood. For the Hebrews and the Puritans, for example, the parent-child relationship was analogous to the relationship between their God and his people. In their societies, allegiance ultimately was owed to God as the highest governing authority. As the ones in direct control, however, parents were placed in the same position with regard to their children. Accordingly, many of the same conflicts between rebellion and submission experienced by adults in relation to authority also were experienced by children in relation to their parents. Hence, a continuity existed between adult experiences within the culture and parental philosophies about children.

As children mature, however, the authorities governing their behavior change from primarily external to primarily internal. Therefore, a common theme across various cultural philosphies has been the importance of teaching children to develop self-control, a prerequisite for maintaining an orderly society. Accordingly, during the various historical periods examined, experts encouraged parents to set good examples since children assimilate parental behavior in their moral development. In most of these societies, the behavior of young children was highly controlled by their parents. This external control often was rather strong and wide-reaching, especially during the early years of life; the underlying idea was to provide a good foundation for developing self-control through clearly imparted moral principles. The purpose of socialization was for children to internalize parental discipline, so that they could become self-disciplined.

As the capacity for internal control of behavior increases, the external controls within society become fewer and less direct, although not necessarily less demanding. Adults are usually responsible for their own conduct in accord with societal principles, insofar as legal or religious authorities have little direct control over their behavior from day to day. As adults, individuals more often are free to follow their own guidelines for

behavior without threat of external punishment. They do what is right because they want to, not because they are afraid of being punished by others. For example, children who are raised in the religious traditions of their parents are often obligated to follow their customs. Once they are adults, however, they may choose to disregard this heritage in their own practices. Yet if they attend a religious service in the tradition of their parents' beliefs, they will still respect its customs, even if these are different from their own. This action is derived from an internal moral sense that respect for others' beliefs is right, rather than from fear of external censure by some authority. In order to be prepared for adult life, children therefore must develop this internal sense of right and wrong.

The awareness that discipline provides a means for children to internalize parental beliefs about right and wrong underlies many of the disciplinary techniques that have been used. For instance, "shaming," advocated as the punishment of choice by the Puritans and John Locke, promoted the development of an internal sense of guilt over doing the "wrong" thing. It may be that as children internalize parental discipline, they achieve greater continuity in their experiences. When the shame is external the child is punished only if caught, but when the shame becomes internal, the child feels guilt even if no one discovers the transgression. Self-discipline, then, may provide greater continuity in the consequences of behavior than external discipline.

The idea of self-discipline has been incorporated in the religious beliefs in an omnipresent God who has knowledge of all sins, and individuals who have the freedom to choose their acts. Such ideas were fundamental to the beliefs of the Puritans, who thought that the goal of socialization was to create an individual who freely chose to obey God. This belief creates an external reason for experiencing the internalized feelings of shame and guilt over wrongdoing. Not only has the individual chosen to act against his or her own principles, but in so doing also has chosen to act against the commandments of God, and even if no one else discovers the transgression, both the individual and God will know it was committed. Therefore, such experiences of self-discipline involve moral censure of a dual nature, for transgressing against one's principles and against God.

This pattern of change from external to internal control coincides with Kohlberg's theory of moral development (e.g., Kohlberg, 1984). At the earliest, pre-conventional stages, children judge the morality of an act externally, on the basis of its consequences. A more internalized form of control is apparent at the conventional level, where morality is determined by the rules of society. While such beliefs require internalization of social standards, these standards are still determined by external forces. It is not until the postconventional level that judgments are made from a personal set of internal standards. In accord with the cultural-historical view, these standards are formed from the interaction between cultural beliefs and individual experiences. The process of moral development consists of moving from externally derived judgments to internally based principles. By internalizing the disciplinary actions and beliefs of parents, children form the basis for their own moral standards.

Such a view contains an implicit assumption that children play an active role in their own development. As they inter-

nalize the standards and beliefs of their parents and society, they form their own philosophies about morality. Socialization involves the incorporation of cultural principles relevant to adult life, but these ideas are always interpreted and modified with respect to the individual's own experiences. Thus, in the process of developing an internalized sense of control, children modify the beliefs underlying the external controls imposed upon them by caretakers. Therefore, over the course of history within a culture, each succeeding generation will develop a set of beliefs that retain many similarities to those of the preceding generation, but also contain some changes in line with the unique circumstances of their lives.

The awareness throughout history that the way parents raise their children will determine the future of the society acknowledges the power of children to modify cultural beliefs. As discussed, Plato pointed out long ago that if children are not taught to value preserving the culture, then they are likely to change its ways. Therefore, not only are the values parents teach their children important, but so is the way in which they are internalized. The more consistent parents are in training their children, the more likely that their values will be preserved. Consistency in discipline has been a major concern in the works of all these different cultural and historical periods. While perfect consistency is an ideal that fits various childrearing philosophies, it may be stressed because it is never a reality. Parents and teachers are not omniscient, and therefore cannot be completely consistent in their use of discipline. Some incidents may not be punished because they are not known about, while others may be inappropriately punished because of incomplete knowledge.

Children also change and develop, making consistency on the part of caretakers, as well as from the child's point of view, rather difficult. Discipline is necessarily a bidirectional process; children influence their parents' and teachers' disciplinary conduct toward them, which in turn affects the continuity of disciplinary practices. In addition to their general beliefs about socialization, caretakers also must consider the particular child and past interactions in making decisions about discipline. The practice of discipline involves accommodating one's beliefs to the child and the circumstances, and assimilating changes in those beliefs on the basis of such experiences. Therefore, at any given period, the actual practices of individual parents and teachers will vary, involving a balance between cultural beliefs, personal values, and children's individual characteristics. Although their beliefs may advocate continuity, it may not always exist in practice when dialectical interactions are involved.

During the various historical periods examined, discrepancies often existed between parents' and teachers' practices. Such discontinuity is an inherent aspect of any changing cultural system, since individual practices and societal values will not always mesh. In general, the school system tends to be representative of mainstream cultural values. The greater constraints placed on teachers' conduct and the more explicit rules for children's behavior at school make the experience of continuity within this setting more likely than across home and school. Parents often have more freedom than teachers to impose personal beliefs on cultural norms; consequently, children are likely to experience some degree of discontinuity between home and school. However, the closer parents' practices are to cultural models of discipline, the greater will be the child's experience of continuity across both settings; therefore, the easier it will be to internalize clear standards for behavior.

Consequently, discontinuity is an expected part of socialization in any cultural-historical setting. Children's development, adults' fallibility, and the multiple agents of socialization within a society all contribute to the child's experiences of discontinuity. Not only may parents and teachers adhere to differing views and practices, but the advice of experts and the literature children read provide additional ideas about values and beliefs. These different sources may reflect variations on common cultural themes, or may contain ideas opposed to the cultural mainstream. Such discontinuity provides a catalyst for changes in the cultural beliefs of the succeeding generation in the dialectical interaction between individuals and society.

Discontinuity, then, is an inherent aspect of the growth and development of individuals as well as cultures. Not only may children and parents disagree in their expectations, but so may parents disagree with the predominant cultural beliefs. This absence of consistency provides the motivating force for change. Historical changes in cultural beliefs about childrearing reflect broader changes in the structure and values of society. While beliefs about the nature of children and the obligations of parents have changed, the belief that the methods used to raise children will determine the future of society has remained. The desire to preserve one's beliefs unaltered seems to be a universal value, though an impossible achievement within a dialectical system. Because children's internalizations of parental beliefs determine the continuity of cultural beliefs, consistency on the part of parents has been stressed as a means for cultural preservation. Thus, a common theme of different philosophies has been the need for continuity in discipline, since it is through consistent practices parents can best impart a clear set of values to their children.

By tracing historical changes in cultural beliefs, areas of continuity and discontinuity in childrearing philosophies across generations are made apparent. While there have been many changes up to the present time, many values still have been preserved. The continued relevance of the ideas of educators and philosophers from past centuries speaks to this point. The cultural-historical view suggests that our philosophies about childrearing are derived not only from our own experiences, but also from the history of our society. The search for continuity is relevant, therefore, in terms of both individual development and cultural beliefs.

The nature of individuals and society makes change an inherent aspect of history, while simultaneously providing avenues of continuity from one generation to the next. If the continuity of cultural values were not important, there would be little concern about how children are raised. As people in all societies believe in the importance of their values, so must they believe in the importance of their children for maintaining those values. Just as the past provides a key for understanding the present, the present is the key to the future. By understanding our past history we can appreciate the influence of our present values, as it is through these values we influence the future of succeeding generations.

REFERENCES

Beekman, D. (1977). *The mechanical baby: A popular history of the theory and practice of child raising*. New York: New American Library.

Borstelmann, L. J. (1983). Children before psychology: Ideas about children from antiquity to the late 1800s. In P. H. Mussen (Ed.), *Handbook of child psychology: Volume 1. History, theory, and methods* (pp. 1-40). New York: John Wiley & Sons.

Demos, J. (1971). Developmental perspectives on the history of childhood. *Journal of Interdisciplinary History, 2,* 315-327.

Dollard, J., Miller, N. E., Doob, L. W., Mowrer, O. H., & Sears, R. R. (1939). *Frustration and aggression*. New Haven, CT: Yale University Press.

Flaherty, D. H. (1972). *Privacy in colonial New England.* Charlottesville, VA: University of Virginia Press.

French, V. (1977). History of the child's influence: Ancient Mediterranean civilizations. In R. Q. Bell & L. V. Harper (Eds.), *Child effects on adults* (pp. 3-29). Hillsdale, NJ: Erlbaum.

Goodnow, J. J. (1985). Change and variation in ideas about childhood and parenting. In I. Sigel (Ed.), *Parental belief systems* (pp. 235-270). Hillsdale, NJ: Lawrence Erlbaum.

Gordon, M. (1978). *The American family: Past, present and future*. New York: Random House.

Hoffer, P. C., & Hull, N. E. H. (1984). *Murdering mothers: Infanticide in England and New England,*1558-1803. New York: New York University Press.

The Holy Bible (King James Version). New York: Harper & Brothers.

Kett, J. F. (1977). *Rites of passage: Adolescence in America 1790 to the present.* New York: Basic Books.

Kohlberg, L. (1984). *Essays on moral development: Volume 2. The psychology of moral development.* San Francisco: Harper & Row.

Locke, J. (1673/1899). *Some thoughts concerning education.* Cambridge: Cambridge University Press.

Mechling, J. (1975). Advice to historians on advice to mothers. *Journal of Social History, 9,* 44-63.

Newson, J. & Newson, E. (1974). Cultural aspects of childrearing in the English-speaking world. In M. P. M. Richards (Ed.), *The integration of a child into a social world* (pp. 53-82). Cambridge, England: University Press.

Piaget, J. (1983). Piaget's theory. In P. H. Mussen (Ed.), *Handbook of child psychology: Volume 1. History, theory, and methods* (pp. 103-128). New York: John Wiley & Sons.

Plato (1970). *The laws* (Translated by T. J. Saunders). Harmondsworth, England: Penguin Books.

Pollock, L. (1983). *Forgotten children: Parent-child relations from 1500-1900.* Cambridge: Cambridge University Press.

Quintilian (1966). *Quintilian on education* (Institutio Oratoria translated by W. M. Smail). Richmond, VA: William Byrd Press.

Rodgers, D. T. (1980). Socializing middle-class children: Institutions, fables, and work values in nineteenth-century America. *Journal of Social History, 13,* 354-367.

Rousseau, J. J. (1762/1914). *Emile, or on education* (Translated by B. Foxley). New York: Basic Books.

Schlossman, S. (1976). Before Home Start: Notes toward a history of parent education in America, 1897-1929. *Harvard Educational Review, 46,* 436-467.

Sommerville, C. J. (1978). English Puritans and children: A social-cultural explanation. *The Journal of Psychohistory, 6,* 113-137.

Sommerville, C. J. (1982). *The rise and fall of childhood.* Beverly Hills: Sage Publications.

Spock, B. (1946). *The common sense book of baby and child care.* New York: Duell, Sloan & Pearce.

Spock, B. (1977). *Baby and child care.* New York: Simon & Schuster.

Stone, L. (1979). *The family, sex and marriage in England 1500-1800.* New York: Harper & Row.

Sunley, R. (1955). Early nineteenth-century American literature on child rearing. In M. Mead & M. Wolfenstein (Eds.), *Childhood in contemporary cultures* (pp. 150-167). Chicago: University of Chicago Press.

Vincent, C. E. (1951). Trends in infant care ideas. *Child Development, 22,* 199-209.

Vygotsky, L. S. (1978). *Mind in society.* Cambridge: Harvard University Press.

Vygotsky, L. S. (1986). *Thought and language.* Cambridge: Massachusetts Institute of Technology.

Weiss, N. (1978). The mother-child dyad revisited: Perceptions of mothers and children in twentieth century child-rearing manuals. *Journal of Social Issues, 34,* 29-45.

Wolfenstein, M. (1955). Fun morality: An analysis of recent American child-training literature. In M. Mead & M. Wolfenstein (Eds.), *Childhood in contemporary cultures* (pp. 168-178). Chicago: University of Chicago Press.

Part Two:

Interdependence Between Culture and Child Development

Introduction

Part Two of this book focuses on the ways in which culture and child development are intricately linked, through adult-child interaction and through the reasoning processes of both parents and children. Chapter 6 takes the reader to view cross-cultural differences in adult-infant interaction in three major cultures within one country (Malaysia). While this study is an example of cross-cultural research (in the sense of *comparing* different cultures), it transcends that framework in favor of a culture-inclusive perspective. The authors emphasize the fact that *culture arranges the physical settings* within which the developing child interacts with adults, which facilitates the development of particular social relationships, and in turn leads to generalized understanding of social relationships within the given culture.

Chapter 7 considers the interaction processes through which culturally expected patterns of conduct emerge in childhood. Social courtesies exist in all cultures, and in vastly variable versions. This chapter presents data about how American toddlers begin to wave or say "bye-bye" to departing visitors. This particular way of organizing departure settings may be highly culture-specific, but the cultural framing of the social demands on children to behave in an appropriate way may be general to relevant behavior settings across cultures.

Within a given culture, individuals cannot escape its demands during their childhood years. Chapter 8 brings to the reader observations from a remote rural area in Nepal, where adolescent girls and young women are strictly socialized to accept their gender roles. That socialization also specifies the ways in which individuals can express their personal dissatisfactions with their social roles — through singing, rather than through directly talking about these feelings in public. The psychological function of singing as a cultural means of expression and interaction points out the value of using folklore as viable research material in developmental psychology. Despite the high relevance of children's learning (and being taught) to sing, dance, and tell stories, there is hardly any serious investigation conducted by developmental psychologists on the psychological use of these expression media, even in Western cultures.

Finally, Chapter 9 illustrates the ways in which *parental* thinking about child socialization issues depends on the culture. The research site — New Zealand — is a highly suitable location for such demonstration, given the immigrant status of both the Western (British) and Samoan inhabitants. The sociocentric focus of the reasoning of Samoan informants about both moral issues and childrearing tasks is clearly in contrast to the principle- and self-oriented perspective that New Zealanders of European origin were observed to display.

The contributions to Part Two share the common theme of substantive interdependence of culture and the ways in which child development is organized. In both parental reasoning and acting, cultural meanings dominate. The developing child is confronted with redundant expectancies for culture-appropriate conduct that are pervasive in the surroundings. Even though one need not fulfill these expectations on *every* occasion, eventually one will meet them, since there is no option left to act differently. Redundant encoding of social expectations into different life situations guarantees that culture's main socialization goals will be achieved, at least in the majority of cases. That is, the culture becomes internalized by the developing child through imposing expectations for acting in some, rather than other, ways in a given situation.

Chapter 6

Features of Infant Social Interaction in Three Cultures in Malaysia

Robert H. Woodson and Elizette da Costa

CONCEPTUAL CONTEXT OF THE RESEARCH

Cultures are distinct and persistent. Attempts to explain these features have given direction to cultural anthropology since its inception. One type of anthropological explanation is particularly relevant in the context of cross-cultural comparisons of the infant's social world. The "culture and personality" school views the characteristics typical of a society's adults as products of their childhood experiences (LeVine, 1982). Through adult caretakers, a culture shapes an essentially passive and culturally mute infant into a form that is appropriate and typical. Since this process of socialization (or acculturation) includes the acquisition of the culture-typical caretaking system, the process is central to the continuation of the culture.

This perspective on the role of culture examines goals, attitudes, beliefs, and intentions regarding children and child-rearing. It consequently diverts attention away from discrete, observable behavior, particularly that of the infant on whom socialization operates. When behavior is mentioned, it is typically the caretaker's and is usually interpreted in light of the above-noted internal factors. If infant behavior is mentioned, it tends to be cited as evidence of the progress of socialization.

While the socialization perspective is as important in the discipline of child development as it is in anthropology, an alternative perspective has arisen in this field that is receiving increasing attention in the cross-cultural literature. This alternative draws its primary theme from Bowlby's (1969) characterization of the infant-caretaker relationship as a *reciprocal phenomenon,* created and maintained by both members of the dyad. Bowlby's emphasis on reciprocity in social ontogeny echoed Bell's (1968) observation concerning the bidirectional nature of socialization, with infant-to-caretaker effects no less likely or influential than the reverse. The recognition of the developing child's contribution to social ontogeny was also facilitated by the constructivist account of cognitive development elaborated by Piaget (1970). Finally, Sameroff and Chandler (1975) drew attention to the way in which the mutual effects of individual and environment (i.e., transactions) not only constitute but also regulate ontogeny.

Together with the introduction of ethological concepts and methods to the study of human ontogeny (Blurton Jones, 1972), the paradigmatic shift that was embodied in the recognition of the reciprocal nature of social development prompted a methodological shift. Any account of social development would be incomplete without documenting the infant's contribution. How best could this contribution be described? One can hardly interrogate an infant with regard to the internal, cognitive, and occasionally unconscious factors on which socialization research focused. However, there is always the infant's overt behavior. Furthermore, any direct experience that the infant has of its caretaker's attempts at socialization occurs through the caretaker's overt behavior. With the concern of anthropologists and psychologists over the distinction between individuals' behavior and their own or others' accounts of that behavior (Harris, 1968), the shifting zeitgeist on social ontogeny prompted an intense focus on discrete, observable, overt behavior.

The research on which this chapter is based has adopted and applied this focus. Its fundamental concern is the overt behavior of infants and caretakers from different cultures. In focusing on overt behavior, we ally ourselves with those who believe that behavior has received too little attention in the cross-cultural study of human ontogeny. Of course, we do not mean to imply that childrearing is devoid of interesting, important "internal" phenomena.

THE CONTEXT OF THE CURRENT REPORT

There are two direct ways in which a culture frames the social interactions of its infants. First of all, it arranges the physical setting in which those interactions occur. This is a point too easily ignored. For instance, in some cultures child and parents sleep together and in others the child sleeps alone — a difference with likely consequences for the amount and kind of infant-parent (and parent-parent) interaction during the hours of darkness (Caudill & Weinstein, 1969; LeVine, 1970). Furniture is another cultural marker with clear consequences for infant-caretaker interaction: the one-year-old in a typical American home who tries to climb onto the lap of someone seated in a chair faces a more daunting task than does the Ganda infant who, owing to the absence of furniture, finds potential interactive partners literally at its own level (Ainsworth, 1967).

Cultures also frame infants' behavioral interactions through their organization of the social environment. In role assignments, economic activities, and residence patterns, a culture effectively selects those individuals with whom an infant may interact. Consider the different social experiences of the infant reared at home by the mother in an isolated nuclear family, the one tended by the various caretakers of an extended family, and the one carried by its mother as she joins other women and children in gardening or gathering trips (Chavez & Martinez, 1979; DeVore & Konner, 1974).

Clearly, knowing an infant's culture allows one to predict with some accuracy various features of that infant's behavioral interactions. However, other influences also merit recognition. Of such factors, the present report considers three: the infant's maturational status, the identity of its partner in a particular interaction, and the caretaking context in which the interaction occurs.

Whether the effects of such factors on infant social interaction are specific to a given culture or comparable across cultures is a central issue in what Leiderman, Tulkin, and Rosenfeld (1977) term the comparative study of infant development. Where a factor's effect differs from one culture to another, we witness the flexibility available to (and exploited by) human caretaking systems. Where its effect is the same in otherwise diverse cultures, we glimpse the limits that these systems must observe.

Documenting the similarities and differences among groups is the basis of the classical comparative approach. In zoological comparisons, groups are composed of individuals from different taxonomic categories. There is, however, no reason to assume that the logic or power of the comparative approach is weakened when applied to cultural group membership. The approach simply requires a balanced perspective on similarity and difference — neither is more important or more sought after than the other. In cross-cultural research this is often not the case: some workers emphasize the culturally unique, while others stress what diverse societies share. A balanced approach recognizes that the universal and the unique together form the complementary sets of information that are essential to any truly general account of social ontogeny.

In order to realize an even-handed treatment of the culturally unique and the culturally universal, an observational study such as this needs to select its behavioral measures with care. In the case of infant social interaction, a strong candidate for the title "universal" is the set of attachment behaviors (Bowlby, 1969) which reflects the activity of a species-typical system regulating the infant's proximity to others. The high levels of physical contact reported in non-western cultures (Ainsworth, 1977; Caudill & Weinstein, 1969; Dixon, Tronick, Keefer, & Brazelton, 1981; Konner, 1977; Munroe & Munroe, 1971) suggest that measures of physical contact may well capture a culturally unique feature of social interaction.

Hence, this report examines the effects of culture, infant mobility, interactive partner, and context of interaction on infant-other physical contact and proximity regulation. It asks two basic questions: (1) How does culture compare to other factors in terms of its ability to capture and explain variation in infant social interaction? and (2) to what extent are the effects of those other factors dependent upon or independent of culture?

CULTURAL CONTEXT OF THE RESEARCH

The nation of Malaysia is composed of the former British colony of Malaya (now referred to as west Malaysia), and the island territories of Sabah and Sarawak (collectively called east Malaysia). The research reported here was conducted in a rural area of west Malaysia, extending approximately 60 square miles around a small market town south of the federal capital of Kuala Lumpur. Its primary economic activities are the private agriculture of rubber, rice, and local fruit, the corporate estate-based agriculture of rubber and palm oil, and the distribution, exchange, and marketing of agricultural products.

The attraction of Malaysia for the cross-cultural researcher is quite simple. The country contains three substantial and quite distinct cultures: the Malay, the Chinese, and the (Indian) Tamil. Except for parts of the peninsula's east coast, it is relatively easy in west Malaysia to locate families from each culture living close by one another. Although it is of at least two generations' duration, this proximity has hardly diminished the linguistic, religious, economic, and ecological distinctions among the three cultures. The following discussion highlights some of these distinctions.

Malays are Moslems who speak Bahasa Melayu, a language similar to that spoken in ethnically close Indonesia. Families derive income from the sale of raw agricultural products, typically rice, latex, or fruit grown on family-owned plots located some distance from the market town. At least some of these plots stand adjacent to the house, which is typically a wooden structure resting above ground on concrete or heavy wooden pilings. Within the house, areas for cooking, bathing, eating, and receiving guests are physically separate. Infants are usually seen by guests (such as our observation team) in a relatively small, minimally furnished sitting room whose wooden floor is covered with soft rattan mats.

The home is occupied by a nuclear family of parents and offspring, and is usually adjacent to the homes of three to six related families, thus forming a small settlement. The maternal grandmother traditionally moves in for four to eight weeks following a birth, and her stay is the only period of the infant's first year during which an adult alternate caretaker is consistently present. Siblings also assume caretaking responsibilities from time to time, but their availability (as is the case with the other cultures) is limited by school attendance. Mothers work the family's agricultural plots, those with infants tending to limit each day's endeavor to a few hours in the plots nearest the home. No Malay woman in our research sample was employed outside of the home.

The Chinese in this region are primarily second-generation descendants of Cantonese-speaking people of the Buddhist faith. Chinese families derive income primarily from the production, processing, and distribution of latex or rice grown on land owned by or leased to a family or a group of related households. Women supplement the family income by contracting their labor to agricultural estates during certain times of the year. Those with young infants, however, usually do not do so. Houses are situated in or near the town and its market facilities, often some distance from the agricultural plots. They are typically substantial edifices of brick and wood with a concrete foundation and enclosing concrete floors. A characteristic feature and the virtual hub of the home is a relatively large, furnished room with a bare floor in which food is prepared and consumed and where agricultural products are processed and stored. This room always includes at least one fireplace or stove, which is easily accessible to a mobile infant.

The nuclear family living alone is rare among this population; more often, the household includes a family extended vertically through three generations and horizontally through first cousins. The Chinese infant's waking hours are consequently spent in a large, busy area peopled by adult, adolescent, and child relatives who live under a single roof as an extended family.

Tamils in Malaysia are usually first-generation descendants of Tamil-speaking Hindus from either the south Indian state of Tamil Nadu or Sri Lanka. With the exception of one town-dwelling shopkeeper's family, the Tamil families in this study lived on large corporate agricultural estates, deriving their income from contract labor. The living quarters provided by the estate are cinder-block row houses called "labor lines," arranged to form highly dense residential settlements. These are small homes — most could fit inside a Chinese house's multipurpose room. Cooking and bathing facilities are kept outside, with the fireplace typically located on a concrete apron extending from the rear of the house.

The Tamil home is usually occupied by a nuclear family, although an elderly relative is sometimes included in the household. The large majority of women work at least part-time tending the estate's trees, usually starting at sunrise and ending before noon. A typical visit to a Tamil home finds the mother, having returned from work, tending the fire and preparing food outside of the house, within which the infant can be found. Infants under a year of age are rarely encountered outside the house, and then always in someone's arms.

The preceding descriptions fairly summarize the physical, social, and economic circumstances of the three main cultures found in the rural areas of Malaysia. The extent to which these circumstances frame the patterns of interaction in which infants of each culture are enmeshed is a central issue in our discussion.

THE STUDY

Sample

The research reported here involved 39 infants and their families: 12 Chinese, 12 Malay, and 15 Tamil. The Tamil group included seven male and eight female infants, while the other groups contained equal numbers of each sex. With the exception of one first-born Tamil infant, all of the infants had at least one sibling living at home.

Each family was contacted through the local government-run clinic that provided basic health services, including prenatal care, midwifery, and pediatric follow-up. The midwife who had provided antenatal care to the mother accompanied the researchers on the initial visit to each family. This individual's cooperation was invaluable, since the mother's trust of her reduced the family's initial suspicion of the research. Only two families refused to participate in the study. All infants were recruited for the study before reaching two months of age.

Procedure

A female interpreter of the same culture as the family accompanied the authors on home visits every four to five weeks until the infant's first birthday. These visits were unannounced, took place during daylight hours, and lasted approximately 90 minutes. The first third of the visit was devoted to casual conversation through the interpreter, with observations of behavior beginning after this initial "settling in" period.

Using the behavior catalog developed for a set of cross-cultural studies (Chisholm,1983;Wolkind,Hall & Pawlby,

1977) and described in Blurton Jones and Woodson (1979), the observer would write down, in shorthand, a running commentary on the infant's behavior and interaction with others. An earphone attached to an electronic timer signaled the lapse of each 15 seconds, at which point the observer began a new line of commentary. Each author observed the infant for 30 minutes during each visit, unless the infant fell asleep. Simultaneous observations by both authors were performed from time to time to check reliability. The raw observations were coded and transcribed for computer-analysis on return from the field. The data for the analyses reported here come from the more than 110 hours of detailed observation.

Measures

The following measures were extracted for analysis. Interobserver agreement values, calculated by dividing agreements by the sum of agreements and disagreements and multiplying the result by 100, appear after each description.

Location of infant: Coded each 15 seconds as being in either physical contact, not in physical contact but in the mother's sight, or neither in physical contact nor in the mother's sight. (93%)

Occurrence of contact: All instances of a bout of physical contact with one individual's arms (at least partly encompassing and/or supporting the other's body) excluding those instances occurring in the context of feeding, cleaning, or dressing the infant. (98%)

Duration of contact: The length of a bout of holding (to the nearest 15 seconds). (92%)

Situation after contact: The end of each bout of contact, coded as leaving the infant either confined or free to move about the physical environment. (98%)

Infant terminate/initiate contact: Contact was judged to be infant-initiated if the child clung to, reached both arms up to, or clambered onto another person prior to the start of a bout of contact. It was judged to be infant-terminated if the child leaned or pushed away from the holder's body prior to being placed down, or crawled out of the holder's lap or arms. (83%)

Proximity change: An "approach" was attributed to the individual whose loco-motion was initially if not ultimately responsible for increased proximity to another. Hence, if the infant moved toward an individual while or immediately after looking at them, the resulting increase in proximity was considered an infant approach even if the child stopped short of establishing contact. Similarly, a "leave" was attributed to that individual whose locomotion was initially responsible for *decreased* proximity to another. (84%)

Context of holding: A hold was considered to have occurred in the context of consoling if contact began during or not later than 30 seconds after the end of crying. Play holds were those not meeting these criteria and not occurring in the context of cleaning, dressing, or feeding. (88%)

Vocalize-with-look: A vocalization that occurred while the infant is looking at an individual. (75%)

Analyses

The between subjects factor in these analyses was culture (three levels: Chinese, Malay, and Tamil). Within subjects factors included (as appropriate): interactive partner (mother vs. alternate caretaker), context of interaction (play vs. console), and infant maturational status. This last factor divided the observations into those occurring before and after the infant began to crawl, according to McGraw's (1945) criteria. Crawling was first observed at an average of 7.3 months. Thus, this last factor distinguished the period of relative immobility from that of effective mobility.

Results

Before considering the detailed behavioral content of our observations, it is useful to describe their composition in broad terms. What were infants and their caretakers doing when observed, where were they in relation to one another, and what factors affected these aspects of the observation?

Approximately 20% of the average observation of the younger, less mobile infant was taken up by standard caretaking interactions — feeding, cleaning, and dressing (Table 1). This figure fell to approximately 11% as the babies matured. This effect of maturational status (F [1,36] =16.70, p < .001) was partly a consequence of our observation protocol: since we began an observation only if the infant was awake and discontinued

if it fell asleep, and since younger infants generally sleep more, standard care- taking sequences tended to be concentrated in the earlier observational sessions.

Where were the infants and their caretakers during our observations? Awake infants were virtually never left alone with the observer. The mother's location when the child was awake and not requiring standard caretaking was influenced by both maturational status and culture (Table 2). In all cultures, mothers were absent from the room for a larger proportion of the earlier observations (F[1,36]=15.02, p < .001). Increased maternal presence thus accompanied increased infant mobility. However, Tamil mothers spent a greater proportion of all observation periods out of their infants' sight than did either the Chinese or Malays (F[2,36]=17.04, p < .001). The layout of the Tamil home, particularly its outdoor cooking apron, likely accounted for this tendency. In addition, it is worth noting that because of the small size of the home, a Tamil mother could be out of sight yet actually closer to her infant than the typical Malay or Chinese mother.

As noted earlier, extensive physical contact is often reported in studies of non-western infants. The families observed in Malaysia proved no exception. When awake, infants were in physical contact with someone for over half of an

TABLE 1
EXTENT OF STANDARD CARETAKING
(Percentage of Observation Time) *

	Chinese	Malay	Tamil
Maturational status			
Premobile	19.6 (3.2)	19.2 (2.5)	21.8 (4.1)
Mobile	10.7 (2.8)	13.5 (3.3)	10.1 (3.0)

* In all tables, the mean is followed by the standard error.

TABLE 2
EXTENT OF MOTHER ABSENCES
(Percentage of Noncaretaking Observation Time)

	Chinese	Malay	Tamil
Maturational Status			
Premobile	16.2 (5.0)	13.4 (2.3)	40.0 (3.1)
Mobile	15.0 (4.3)	5.4 (1.3)	23.1 (4.0)

TABLE 3
EXTENT OF PHYSICAL CONTACT
(Percentage of Noncaretaking Observation Time)

	Chinese	Malay	Tamil
Maturational Status			
Premobile	56.9 (6.7)	53.4 (6.8)	51.7 (4.8)
Mobile	26.5 (5.5)	34.3 (6.5)	34.6 (5.4)

TABLE 4 A
ADULTS PRESENT AT OBSERVATION
(Percentage of Observations)

	Chinese	Malay	Tamil
Maturational Status			
Premobile	71.5 (8.0)	45.2 (8.5)	72.3 (6.7)
Mobile	58.3 (12.2)	30.5 (9.6)	56.9(8.8)

TABLE 4 B
AVERAGE NUMBER OF CHILDREN AT OBSERVATION

	Chinese	Malay	Tamil
Maturational Status			
Premobile	3.5 (0.5)	2.6 (0.4)	2.5 (0.6)
Mobile	4.2 (0.7)	1.6 (0.4)	2.0 (0.3)

TABLE 5
FREQUENCY OF HOLDING
(HOLDS PER HOUR)

	Chinese	Malay	Tamil
Maturational Status: Premobile			
Mother	2.8 (0.7)	5.2 (0.7)	4.8 (1.1)
Other	1.4 (0.3)	1.5 (0.3)	1.9 (0.3)
Maturational Status: Mobile			
Mother	6.8 (1.2)	14.0 (1.7)	12.6 (2.4)
Other	4.2 (0.9)	4.3 (1.2)	5.4 (1.8)

average session during our early observations, and for approximately a third of the session during later observations (Table 3). This effect of maturational status on physical contact ($F[1,36]= 31.26$, $p < .001$) occurred across all cultures.

Physical contact. While interactions in each culture involved comparable proportions of physical contact, were the cultures similar in terms of who the infant's partner was in that contact? Social organization varied in two particularly relevant features of our observational record. As Table 4a shows, the cultures differed in terms of the percentage of observations at which an adult (in addition to the mother) was present ($F [2,36] =4.59, p < .025$). (The decreased availability of adults during the later observations was also a significant change ($F[1,36]= 5.05, p < .05$).) As seen in Table 4b, culture also influenced the number of children school-aged or older who were present at the average observation ($F[2,36]= 5.12, p < .01$). These children and extra adults formed a pool of potential alternate caretakers in each culture. Malays differed from Chinese and Tamils in having extra adults present less often, while the Chinese differed from Malays and Tamils in having more chil-

dren present. Since physical contact is so fundamental and (to western eyes) so distinctive a feature of caretaker-infant interaction among these cultures, the contribution of alternate caretakers to physical contact deserved special scrutiny.

Analyses indicated that, despite cultural differences in the availability of alternate caretakers, mothers held their infants more often than did others ($F[1,36]=41.62, p < .001$) (Table 5). This pattern held for each culture and was independent of maturational status. Thus, although alternate caretakers accounted for a substantial portion of physical contact experiences, it was the mother who partnered the infant most of the time. Did this maternal preeminence in physical contact apply to both consoling and playful bouts of holding? One might expect that the mother would be the recognized "consoler" of the infant whereas other individuals would be acceptable "playmates," but no evidence of such a pattern could be found. In all cultures, mothers held more often and for longer bouts regardless of the context.

Maturational status was related to both the frequency and the duration of holding (Table 6). When younger and less mobile, infants were held less often

TABLE 6
DURATION OF MOTHER'S HOLDS
(Minutes per Hold)

	Chinese	Malay	Tamil
Maturational Status			
Premobile	8.7 (1.7)	5.3 (1.0)	6.2 (1.8)
Mobile	1.8 (0.5)	1.6 (0.4)	1.7 (0.4)

TABLE 7
FLOOR FREEDOM FOLLOWING HOLDING
(Percentage of Holds)

	Chinese	Malay	Tamil
Maturational Status			
Premobile	31.1 (10.2)	75.6 (8.7)	53.2 (5.6)
Mobile	65.4 (6.4)	89.3 (3.6)	79.3 (7.4)

TABLE 8
INITIATION AND TERMINATION OF PHYSICAL CONTACT BY INFANT
(Percentage of Holds)

	Chinese	Malay	Tamil
Initiate	3.9 (2.1)	22.8 (4.8)	6.7 (2.5)
Terminate	6.0 (2.8)	32.4 (7.9)	13.5 (3.6)

TABLE 9
PROXIMITY CHANGES ATTRIBUTABLE TO INFANT
(Percentage of Changes)

	Chinese	Malay	Tamil
Approach			
Mother	25.2 (5.2)	53.0 (7.3)	34.8 (6.0)
Other	17.0 (3.9)	48.2 (7.8)	44.9 (7.9)
Leave			
Mother	37.5 (9.0)	76.1 (6.6)	47.0 (6.4)
Other	5.8 (2.5)	8.6 (4.2)	23.0 (8.0)

(F[1,36]=53.11, p < .001) but for longer periods (F[1,36]=35.59, p <.001). As they matured and achieved mobility, they were involved in more frequent but briefer holds. An interaction was also found between maturational status and partner in physical contact, with the increase in frequency especially pronounced with the mother (F[1,36]=9.63, p < .01).

Proximity regulation. In general, physical contact in all cultures was quite comparable. More diversity occurred at the other extreme: infant-caretaker separation. As noted earlier, Tamil infants were more often observed out of the sight of their mothers than either the Chinese or Malays. Regardless of culture, however, all babies were more often left unattended when younger and less mobile. These broad features of proximity regulation are embroidered by the analyses that follow.

A central tenet of the attachment formulation is that the infant-caretaker relationship is the joint creation of both members — attachments are bidirectional in origin and maintenance. The infant's contribution includes the various "attachment" behaviors through which proximity to the attachment figure is influenced. In younger infants, behaviors such as clinging and crying are prominent, while with the advent of mobility, the child's opportunity to influence proximity is increased. In order to investigate how proximity is regulated, we decided to examine what happens after a bout of holding — whether the infant is left confined or free to move about.

When older and more mobile, infants of all cultures were less often placed after being held into a cot, playpen, chair, etc. (F[1,36]=18.71, p < .001) (Table 7), with Malay infants being confined least of all

(F [2,36]= 10.05, p <.001).

Ainsworth (1967) used the phrase "floor freedom" to describe the situation presented to the unconfined infant. The ramifications of these consistent cultural differences in the amount of floor freedom became clear with the advent of locomotion. Of the three groups, Malay infants played the most active role in determining proximity, initiating and terminating a higher percentage of holds (F[2,36]=10.18, p < .001) (Table8) and being more often responsible for approaching and leaving their interactive partners (F[2,36]= 7.27, p < .01) (Table 9). Hence, cultural differences in the infant's contribution to both physical contact and proximity regulation paralleled cultural differences in its freedom to move through the physical environment.

The greater floor freedom afforded Malay infants may have contributed to another striking cultural difference: the specificity with which infants initiated physical contact (Table 10). Malay infants were more likely to direct contact initiation to their mothers than to other individuals, while the reverse was true of Chinese and Tamils (F[2,36]=7.93, p < .001). Since fewer alternate caretakers were available to Malay infants, their apparent preference for the mother as a contact partner needs to be interpreted with caution. The appropriate experiment would give infants of all cultures equal access to both the mother and to alternate caretakers. Differential responses under such a condition would be evidence of a preference for a particular interactive partner. Such an experiment is, of course, not possible.

However, we can compare the initiation of contact with another behavior that Malay infants were observed to do more

TABLE 10
INFANT INITIATIONS OF HOLDS DIRECTED TO MOTHER
(Percentage of Total Initiations)

	Chinese	Malay	Tamil
Initiate	16.4 (9.3)	75.5 (10.4)	39.2 (12.1)

TABLE 11
INFANT VOCALIZATION-WITH-LOOKING DIRECTED TO MOTHER
(Percentage of Instances)

	Chinese	Malay	Tamil
Maturational Status			
Premobile	43.4 (6.4)	53.2 (6.0)	49.6 (6.5)
Mobile	51.2 (5.3)	52.5 (4.6)	39.1 (5.4)

frequently: vocalize-with-look (Table 11). Unlike the initiation of physical contact, no group differences existed for this behavior. Given that it was deployed under the same conditions of access to the mother and alternate caretakers, it is tempting to conclude that in their initiations of physical contact Malay infants did in fact express a clear and specific preference for their mothers. The lack of a comparable preference among the Chinese and Tamil infants may at this point only be noted — the data do not permit any attempt at explanation.

The floor freedom afforded infants was not the only factor that influenced proximity regulation. Regardless of culture, infants accounted for a larger proportion of proximity changes with the mother than with alternate caretakers (F[1,36]=25.14, p < .001). In addition, while they were more likely to leave than to approach their mothers, they were more likely to approach than to leave other people (F[1,36]= 41.50, p < .001). Thus, with regard to the maintenance of infant-mother proximity, mothers played a relatively more active role, whereas the babies played the more active role with regard to others. In addition, the infant's contribution to proximity regulation vis-à-vis the mother was the reverse of that vis-à-vis alternate caretakers.

DISCUSSION

Our initial questions concerned the magnitude of cultural influences on infant social interaction, and the extent to which other influences on this interaction depended upon culture. The results show that culture is indeed a frequent influence on basic aspects of physical contact and proximity regulation. However, culture's influence is not notably greater than that of other factors. In addition, in no analysis did the effects of factors such as maturational status, interactive partner, and interactive context depend upon culture.

The Chinese, Malay, and Tamil infants observed in this study differed markedly from one another both in terms of the physical environment of their homes and the social organization of their families. These correlates of culture helped to illuminate several of the differences found.

Differences in floor freedom, for instance, seemed clearly linked to the immediate ecology of crawling and the social context in which crawling occurred. Both Chinese and Tamil babies spent their waking hours in rooms with bare, hard, and cold concrete floors — hardly an optimal surface for infant locomotion. The Chinese home also included easily accessible fires and a relatively large number of people, especially children. The Tamil infant, on the other hand, was often out of its mother's sight. Thus, although for different reasons, the relative lack of floor freedom afforded Chinese and Tamil infants seems an appropriate, even necessary "fit" to the complex of social and ecological factors that characterize the two cultures' homes.

The substantial floor freedom available to the Malay infant seems an equally appropriate fit to that culture's social and ecological factors. The relative lack of adult or child alternate caretakers in the typical Malay home meant that the caretaker would likely be the mother herself, while the paucity of children at the typical Malay observation insured that the infant left free to crawl about would not be trampled under childish feet. The soft rattan mats covering its wooden floor, its minimal furnishings, and its living room quality made this setting particularly safe and congenial for crawling. In short, extensive floor freedom fit the social and ecological features of the Malay home.

The fit described in the preceding paragraphs is one of the more obvious but most difficult-to-document qualities of a culture. It is a phenomenon that cross-cultural investigators have often described and discussed (Ainsworth, 1967; Munroe & Munroe, 1971). Given the multiple factors involved in this fit, it is tempting to nominate one or another as that to which the remaining factors adapt. In the cross-cultural study of infancy, for instance, the economic demands upon the family (Leiderman & Leiderman, 1977) and the behavioral characteristics of a culture's infants (Chisholm, 1983) have both been nominated as the factor around which the caretaking system is organized.

We can question the assumption that a culture's caretaking system forms itself around and remains stable with respect to some constant factor. A more organismic and dynamic perspective seems more apt. Just as no culture — "primitive" or "modern" — is a static entity, no caretaking system is a fossilized integration of factors. A continuing culture testifies to the existence of social structures that protect and nurture the young. Yet the culture uses those structures not only for nurturing but also for its economic activities. In a strictly functional sense, no culture persists except through the co-adaptation of all of those features on which it relies and by which it is typified. Hence, it should not be suprising to find either that social, ecological, and behavioral factors form a distinctive fit in a particular culture, or that the pattern of this fit is as much the product of one as any factor. Indeed, it is something of a surprise to find that a particular factor has the same association with features of social interaction in different cultures.

Such resemblances were plentiful in the analyses reported here: in no instance did the factor of culture interact with the other factors that also influenced features of social interaction. How are we to interpret the absence of interactions of culture with infant maturational status, interactive partner, and context of interaction? What does it mean to find that such factors not only strongly influence social interaction, but also exert their influence independent of culture?

The effects of infant maturational status may reflect the accommodations that all caretaking systems must make. While cultural practices may affect the child's rate of physical or motor development (Leiderman et al., 1973), the scope of such influence is clearly limited by intrinsic factors (Gesell, 1946). Short of depriving its infants, a culture can do little to prevent them from growing larger, becoming motorically more competent, and displaying the curiosity characteristic of the young (Bruner, 1972). The only option open to the caretaking system would seem to be to adjust itself to such maturational changes. For this reason, the older, more mobile infant would be expected to have greater locomotion opportunities, with a consequently greater role in determining proximity, than would the younger, less mobile infant regardless of culture.

While the culturally stable effects of maturational status may admit a straightforward interpretation, the situation seems less clear with respect to factors such as interactive partner and context of interaction. Maturation of motor competence seems beyond the effective control of culture. These other factors seem much more open to cultural determination. As LeVine (1977) notes, while all cultures can expect their infants to become motorically competent with age, each culture may adopt radically different practices regarding the encouragement of infant locomotion and exploration depending upon factors such as the proximity of open fires, steep stairwells, or valuable breakables. As already discussed, the relatively quieter and safer arrangement of the Malay living quarters seemed clearly to go hand in hand with the Malay infant's greater floor freedom. How can this obvious variation among cultures in the management of infant motor activity be reconciled with the culturally stable patterns regarding the context of infant-other physical contact or the infant's role in proximity regulation?

A partial answer to the question begins to emerge as we step back from specific behaviors and consider the general function of a caretaking system. What must such a system accomplish? It must, of course, insure the survival of the young. One requirement for survival is the maintenance of the young's physical well-being, a requirement that all caretaking systems strive to meet. Yet physical welfare is not sufficient, for ours is not a species that leaves an individual to fend for itself at the end of childhood. A culture must also make its young part of itself, since culture is, to borrow Dawkins' (1976) phrase, the individual's survival machine. A caretaking system must therefore insure the acculturation of the young to insure their survival, as well as that of the culture.

The acculturated individual observes culturally specified roles — those patterns of behavior that are deemed appropriate for particular individuals interacting in particular settings. While they often differ in terms of the precise nature of these expectations, all cultures have such expectations. Failure to acquire and observe this social code leaves one culturally mute, just as failure to acquire a language's syntax leaves one linguistically mute.

Since there appears to be no genotypic basis for informing members that these roles exist, such information must be gleaned from experience. Hence, a basic requirement of a caretaking system is to provide the immature individual with experience in the sort of partner- and context-dependent, reciprocal patterns of interaction that are characteristic of human social intercourse. Cultures may thus be relatively free to determine such things as how much control the infant exercises over contact and proximity regulation. However, they may at the same time be constrained to expose the infant to the sorts of roles (i.e., initiator-responder, leader-follower) assumed in interaction with different interactive partners in different contexts, because fluency in this aspect of the interactive language is a prerequisite for life in social settings.

Although the preceding may help to explain the context-dependent nature of certain interactions involving infants, there remains the issue of the infant's interactive partner. Why are the differences between mothers and alternate caretakers so stable across cultures? An answer may lie in the way that humans utilize existing and manage new social relationships.

The human pattern is not to establish an initial relationship in ontogeny which is then replicated, reproduced, extended, or generalized in subsequent relationships. The fundamental insight of the relational attachment formulation (Sroufe, 1985) is that the initial, focused relationship facilitates and complements but does not specify subsequent relationships. Consider the use of the attachment figure as a secure base for exploration (Ainsworth et al., 1978). The function of the secure base is not to enable the infant to establish yet more secure bases; instead, it supports exploratory and affiliative forays that may well be novel, challenging, or otherwise stress-inducing for the infant. It is thus in the very nature of the attachment relationship for infants to be more likely to leave than approach their mothers than alternate caretakers. A primary attachment relationship, typically with the biological mother, is a universal feature of human ontogeny. As proximity maintenance and physical contact are basic indices of attachment, then culturally stable differences on such indices between the primary attachment figure and the infant's other interactive partners should be anticipated.

ACKNOWLEDGEMENTS The authors wish to thank the Ministry of Health, Malaysia for its assistance. This research was made possible by a grant from the Harry Frank Guggenheim Foundation.

REFERENCES

Ainsworth, M. (1967). *Infancy in Uganda.* Baltimore: Johns Hopkins University Press.

Ainsworth, M. (1977). Infant development and mother-infant interaction among Ganda and American families. In P. Leiderman, S. Tulkin, & A. Rosenfeld (Eds.), *Culture and infancy: Variations in the human experience.* New York: Academic Press.

Ainsworth, M., Blehar, M., Waters, E., & Wall, S. (1978). *Patterns of attachment.* Hillsdale, NJ: Erlbaum.

Bell, R. (1968). A reinterpretation of the direction of effects in studies of socialization. *Psychological Review, 75,* 81-85.

Blurton Jones, N. (1972). *Ethological studies of child behaviour.* London:Cambridge University Press.

Blurton Jones, N., & Woodson, R. (1979). Describing behavior: The ethologist's perspective. In M. Lamb, S. Soumi, & G. Stephenson (Eds.), *Social interaction analysis: Methodological issues.* Madison: University of Wisconsin Press.

Bowlby, J. (1969). *Attachment and loss, Volume I: Attachment.* New York: Basic.

Bruner, J. (1972). The nature and uses of immaturity. *American Psychologist, 27,* 687-708.

Caudill, W., & Weinstein, H. (1969). Maternal care and infant behavior in Japan and America. *Psychiatry, 32,* 12-43.

Chavez, A., & Martinez, C. (1979). Behavioral effects of undernutrition and food supplementation. In J. Brozek (Ed.), *Behavioral effects of energy and protein deficits.* Washington: Government Printing Office.

Chisholm, J. (1983). *Navajo infancy.* New York: Aldine.

Dawkins, R. (1976). *The selfish gene.* London: Oxford University Press.

DeVore, I., & Konner, M. (1974). Infancy in hunter-gatherer life. In N. White (Ed.), *Ethology and psychiatry.* Toronto: University of Toronto Press.

Dixon, S., Tronick, E., Keefer, C., & Brazelton, T. (1981). Mother-infant interaction among the Gusi' of Kenya. In T. Field, A. Sostek, P. Vietze, & P. Leiderman (Eds.), *Culture and early interactions.* Hillsdale, NJ: Erlbaum.

Gesell, A. (1946). The ontogenesis of infant behavior. In L. Carmichael (Ed.), *Manual of child psychology.* New York: Wiley.

Harris, M. (1968). *The rise of anthropological theory: A history of theories of culture.* New York: Crowell.

Konner, M. (1977). Infancy among the Kalahar' Desert San. In P. Leiderman, S. Tulkin, & A. Rosenfeld (Eds.), *Culture and infancy: Variations in the human experience. New York: Academic Press.*

Leiderman, P., Babu, B., Kagia, J., Kraemer, H., & Leiderman, G. (1973). African infant precocity and some social influences during the first year. *Nature, 242,* 247-249.

Leiderman, P., & Leiderman, G. (1977). Economic change and infant care in an east African agricultural community. In P. Leiderman, S. Tulkin, & A. Rosenfeld (Eds.), *Culture and infancy: Variations in the human experience.* New York: Academic Press.

Leiderman, P., Tulkin, S., & Rosenfeld, A. (1977). Overview of cultural influences in infancy. In P. Leiderman, S. Tulkin, & A. Rosenfeld (Eds.), *Culture and infancy: Variations in the human experience.* New York: Academic Press.

LeVine, R. (1970). Cross-cultural study in child psychology. In P. Mussen (Ed.), *Carmichael's manual of child psychology.* New York: Wiley.

LeVine, R. (1977). Child rearing as a cultural adaptation. In P. Leiderman, S. Tulkin, & A. Rosenfeld (Eds.), *Culture and infancy: Variations in the human experience.* New York: Academic Press.

LeVine, R. (1982). *Culture, behavior, and personality.* New York: Aldine.

McGraw, M. (1945). *The neuromuscular maturation of the human infant.* New York: Columbia University Press.

Munroe, R., & Munroe, R. (1971). Household density and infant care in an east African society. *Journal of Social Psychology, 83,* 3-13.

Piaget, J. (1970). Piaget's theory. In P. Mussen (Ed.), *Carmichael's manual of child psychology.* New York: Wiley.

Sameroff, A. & Chandler, J. (1975). Caretaking and the continuum of reproductive casualty. In F. Horowitz (Ed.), *Review of child development research, Volume 4.* Chicago: University of Chicago Press.

Wolkind, S., Hall, F., & Pawlby, S. (1977). Individual differences in mothering behavior: A combined epidemiological and observational approach. In P. Graham (Ed.), *Epidemiological approaches in child psychiatry.* London: Academic Press.

Chapter 7

Socialization of American Toddlers for Social Courtesy

Jaan Valsiner and Paula E. Hill

INTRODUCTION

Human beings are polite animals. Rules of polite conduct are both the product and the mediator of cultural history. These rules are constructed in collective action within society. Children construct their understanding of polite conduct in the course of their childhood years, using adult models in innovative ways, in conjunction with their personal experiences. In this respect, polite conduct is a product of cultural ontogeny. Once established, personal understanding of courtesy regulates social interaction, and it is also usable for maintaining or changing interpersonal relationships.

Through polite action, individuals in any culture can accomplish a great variety of tasks. All issues of politeness in interaction are embedded in the web of the given culture by systemic and often-times implicit linkages (see Appadurai, 1985). This chapter is devoted to the study of the beginning of socialization for polite conduct in the contemporary American middle-class subculture. We

will demonstrate how children, during their second year of life, are directed by adults to act in accordance with social expectations in departure situations. We are interested in the developmental processes that guide children from the beginning of saying or waving "bye-bye," to adults' mastery of concluding interaction episodes.

ADULT ORGANIZATION OF CONVERSATIONAL CLOSINGS

The phenomenon that we are analyzing here from a developmental perspective belongs to the general category of "conversational closings"—processes by which an ongoing interaction process is brought to an end. Despite its everyday relevance, the issue of conversational closings (as well as openings) has rarely been studied even among adults (see Schegloff, 1968; Schegloff & Sacks, 1973); thus, the lack of its study in child psychology is not surprising. Children are often described as "egocentric" in their interaction with others — a description that probably is partially derived from their lack of adult-like interaction habits. Hence it is easy to believe that their ways of closing or opening interaction episodes is either "egocentric" or lacks any organization.

In adult conversations, closings take a variety of forms in everyday life. However, their basic (minimally necessary) structure involves only two turns:

Turn I (pre-closing):

Partner A: "O.K.," or "I'll let you go back to [whatever appropriate]," etc.
Partner B: "O.K.," or " It was nice to talk to you," etc.

Turn II (final closing):

Partner A: "Bye-bye," or "Take care," or "See you later," etc.
Partner B: "Bye," or "You too," or "See you," etc.

(See also Schegloff & Sacks, 1973, p. 309 and p. 317.)

The function of the pre-closing statements in this minimal sequence of closing is to prepare the partner for the speaker's intention of terminating the conversation. If the partner goes along and signals similar intent (or at least agreement), the closing process can proceed to its final turn. However, both partners have the option of changing their strategy at both turns. Thus, B can introduce a new topic of conversation at turn I (thus undermining A's intended course of action), and if A accepts that, the conversation may continue. Likewise, A can change his or her mind at turn II, and instead of moving to the final closing

(which was prepared by the pre-closing, suggested by A and accepted by B), may suddenly introduce a new topic (e.g., "By the way, how about . . ."), thus forcing B either into another pre-closing statement (e.g., B: "Yes, but let's discuss it later, I need to go now"), or to accepting the new topic.

In the structure of real-life conversations, the pre-closing phase may be extended in length, and cover a number of turns. At each turn, the interactants can either move closer to the final closing, or introduce new content material that keeps the conversation going. In face-to-face interaction, the negotiation of partners in both the pre-closing and final closing phases involves multiple communication channels. Non-verbal and verbal elocutionary means of interaction are used in parallel with the verbal messages. Changes in body posture may add emphasis to an interactant's verbal pre-closing efforts. Furthermore, many statements made by the partners while closing a conversation carry a primarily elocutionary function, as words are used in their non-literal meaning (e.g., "see you later," or "take care" in American English discourse).

The developing child is faced with a complicated task — to learn to negotiate the closing of a conversation in the "adult" way (including the phases of pre-closing and final closing), and to establish the use of non-literal meanings of statements that are used in the context of closings. In the present chapter, this issue is addressed within an individual-socioecological frame of reference (see Valsiner, 1987), which requires a qualitative analysis of the empirical phenomena in respect to the coordination of actions of the child and the caregiver within the given context.

THEORETICAL FOUNDATIONS
OF THE STUDY

Developmental research is unique in its interest in phenomena that are in the process of their formation when they are studied. A child psychologist doing developmental research is investigating the process of emergence of a psychological function, or at least a part thereof. All of the higher psychological functions of human beings emerge in some social context, and children are either directly (through instruction, guidance, or facilitation) or indirectly (by living in culturally structured environments) assisted by the culture in their development. The present study is rooted in the first author's theoretical system (Valsiner, 1987a) involving the mutually related functioning of three "zones," the existences of which are theoretically posited.

The Zone of Free Movement (ZFM) specifies the structure of the environment that is functionally available to the developing child at a given time. Its boundaries are set through negotiations with the caregivers, and are dynamically altered as the child develops or moves to an environment with a different physical structure. ZFM is originally a delimiter of the child's actions. While it limits those actions, its structure becomes internalized by the child. Once the child's experience becomes internalized, ZFMs are being set up by the child (or adult) in his/her reasoning and affective processes (see also Peisner, this volume). The concept of ZFM is borrowed from Kurt Lewin's field theory, with slight modifications.

The Zone of Promoted Action (ZPA) is a set of activities, objects, or areas that constitute the child's environment, within which actions are facilitated by "social others." The activities that make up ZPA are non-binding: the child is encouraged, coerced, and facilitated to perform them, but non-compliance with these social suggestions has no repercussions. As the activities that are involved in ZPA promote development, the child internalizes the social expectancies communicated through them. Through internalization, knowledge is gained about the expected way of acting in a given kind of setting (Winegar, 1987; Winegar, Camden, & Matthews, 1987). That knowledge, once internalized, can be voluntarily evoked by the child to guide actions and thinking. For instance, an adolescent who "cuts" another in everyday exchanges of social courtesy knows very well how he or she is expected to act, but decides *not* to act appropriately (cf. Elkind, 1980). The developing child turns acquired social interaction skills from the object of acquisition into a means for attaining other goals. ZPA is a concept that covers the emergence of future goal-oriented acting and reasoning.

The Zone of Proximal Development (ZPD) is a concept originated by Vygotsky, which has become rather widely (and variably) used in contemporary child psychology (see Rogoff & Wertsch, 1984; Valsiner, 1985, 1987b). In its present use, ZPD captures those psychological functions that at any given moment in child development are in the process of turning from the realm of the possible to that of the actual, with the help of other people. The child's learning within ZPD involves performing actions that are not yet available in individual action, but which can be accomplished with assistance from others. In general, it is the ZFM-ZPA-ZPD complex that constitutes the description of the *process* by which child development takes place.

THE STRUCTURE OF LEARNING TO WAVE "BYE-BYE"

The particular phenomenon under study here — the development of standard actions of courtesy towards departing visitors — is eminently suitable for explanation in terms of the ZFM-ZPA-ZPD complex. For many toddlers, as we will see, saying and/or waving "bye-bye" is not yet an action that they would undertake on their own initiative. Thus, toddlerhood is the time when we are likely to find that function beginning to develop. In this respect, the "bye-bye" can be found to be within the ZPDs of particular toddlers. Particular settings in which they learn to display it involve both the adults' purposeful narrowing of the boundaries of the ZFM (e.g., the parent picks the toddler up and orients towards the departing visitor), and active efforts to make the child say and/or wave "bye-bye" (actions within a ZPA). At first, the child does not succumb to the social pressure/suggestion from the adults that exists within ZPA. With development, a delayed response to such pressure may begin, which results in the child's saying or waving "bye-bye" *after* a departing adult has left. Many parents claim to have observed this phenomenon, and often refer to it, as if to apologize to the visitors for their children's noncompliance at the "right" time.

The departing visitor is another actor who helps to create the ZPA, by also trying to get the toddler to display "bye-bye." When viewed on a time scale, the setting of departure involves two-sides coordinated efforts on the part of the adults (see Figure 1).

In Figure 1, a generalized temporal structure of a departure setting is de-

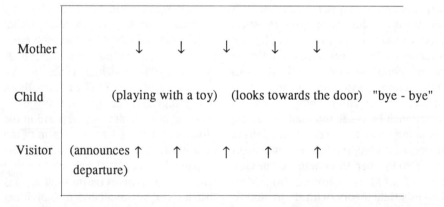

FIGURE 1
A GENERAL TIME - STRUCTURE OF THE DEPARTURE EVENT

Note: Vertical arrows denote time moments when either of the adults (mother or visitor) communicate to the child the demand for displaying "bye-bye". In this general example, the child complies with the demands, albeit *after* the visitor has left.

picted. The setting is initiated by the visitor's declared intention to leave. It is immediately followed by efforts by the mother and the visitor (taking turns) to get the child (who happens to be involved in individual play with a toy) to display departure-appropriate conduct. The sudden intense "bombardment" (time moments 1-9) of the child with the adults' demands gradually leads to the child's abandonment of the toy, and to visual orientation towards the door through which the visitor is leaving (time 9). The social pressure finally succeeds (time 10), but by then the visitor has already left.

Figure 1 represents a general time-structure of the departure setting. Individual instances of this type of setting obviously involve high variation from one instance to another. The variable parts of the general structure involve both adults' actions and those of the child. For example, a particular departing visitor may elect not to urge the child to wave "bye-bye," thereby reducing the generation of that pressure exclusively to the mother. Likewise, the mother may decide to abstain from demanding this, while the visitor may be active. The child may at times be very much involved in an ongoing individual activity, and therefore resist all demands of either or both adults, however intense those may be. At other times, the visitor may announce the decision to leave while playing with the child, thus facilitating the turn in the child's orientation from joint play to the departure event. Finally, the structure of the environment in which the departure event takes place sets up the context. For example, an architectural space where the visitor has to cover a long distance in the child's full view will necessarily increase the time within which the efforts to get the child to display "bye-bye" can suc-

ceed. In contrast, if the visitor can depart from the child's view very quickly (short distance to the door), little time is allotted to the adults' social pressure on the child to lead to the expected outcome on time.

Notwithstanding the variability across occasions and environments, children within a given culture master the social skills of displaying culturally required courtesies to leave-takers. In the adult, these skills are mastered to the extent of automaticity, which still allows for flexibility in regulating the interaction process. Developmentally, there are many trajectories that lead to this same adult outcome. However, all these life courses of children's learning of social courtesy are embedded within the culture's meaning system, which sets up the need and means for such learning. The model for the structure of interaction in departure situation that we have described is valid *only* in those cultural contexts where (a) it is believed that toddlers are acceptable interaction partners for adults, and (b) the teaching-learning process pertaining to appropriate social courtesies is believed to be best started at such an early age as toddlerhood. These criteria may be willingly accepted by the majority of European or North-American middle-class families. Our model may therefore be limited to the cultural settings that are set up on the basis of these beliefs. In contrast, in cultural environments where adults believe that young children deserve little attention as equal interaction partners, departure situations like those described in this chapter need not occur. All human conduct, and its socialization in ontogeny, is culture-inclusive in its nature: observable human conduct is intricately tied to a system of cultural beliefs, superstitions, and habits that constitute the context of that conduct.

THE EMPIRICAL STUDY

The present study constituted a part of an investigation of toddlers' stranger-contacting strategies that is described in detail elsewhere (Hill & Valsiner, 1987). In this chapter, we analyze the ways in which the leave-taking process is organized in different families, and how it develops in the course of the second year of life. We rely on descriptions of individual cases as definitive data, and treat summary results for the sample as a background for those.

Subjects and Procedure

A list of potential subjects was first obtained by examining the birth records of a middle-sized (100,000 inhabitants) town in North Carolina. Criteria for being selected as a potential participant in the study included a lack of perinatal complications, no older siblings, and a minimum of 12 years of schooling (i.e., secondary education) of both parents. Parents of the subjects were initially contacted by telephone, at which time the study was briefly described, and a preliminary home interview was scheduled. Eighteen families participated in the study, 9 with male and 9 with female children. All children were first-borns, and had no younger siblings.

Participating families were visited in their homes in the course of the child's second year of life. The procedure at each visit was the following (see also Hill & Valsiner, 1987):

1. *Base observation.* Experimenter 1 (E1) — in most cases the second author— entered the home carrying video equipment, was greeted briefly by the mother, and started to videotape continu-ously all the conduct of the child. (The parent had been previously instructed to re-direct the child's attention away from E1, if the child became interested in her.) The base observation period lasted at least 5 minutes.

I. *Presence of a stranger.* This episode began when a "visitor" (E2), who would be unknown to both child and parent, arrived. The parent, often with the child, would go to open the door for E2 while E1 continued to videotape the child's conduct. After a mutual introduction E2 would be invited in, and would converse with the parent for some minutes while remaining open to any possible contact-making overtures by the child. If the child did make such efforts, E2 would enter into play; if no efforts were made, E2 would try to engage the child in joint action. Either way, length of Episode II ranged from 6 to 20 minutes in length.

III. *Departure episode.* At some appropriate moment E2 would declare an intention to leave, thus setting the stage for the departure ritual. This involved saying good-bye to both the child and the parent, being escorted towards the exit by both of them, and then leaving. E1 would continue to videotape the child's conduct for another 5-10 minutes after E2's departure.

Different persons (males and females; all college students except for one) served as E2's. Thus, the same child encountered different persons in the role of E2 as the study continued over the year.

Altogether, 48 episodes of leavetaking were videotaped. Five children were observed longitudinally on four occasions, four children on three occasions, seven twice, and two only once. About half (25 out of 48) of these observations were done on subjects between 12 and 16 months of age, while the rest were from 17 to 25 months of age.

General Distribution of "Bye-byes" Within the Sample

Out of the 48 observed departure settings, the target children were observed to display vocal, gestural, or combined vocal-gestural "bye-byes" on 28 occasions. None was observed on 18 occasions, and in two instances it was impossible to observe the conduct in full as the child was temporarily out of the camera's view. Out of the 28 documented responses, 15 involved combinations of gestural (arm- and/or handwaving) and vocal forms, ten were only gestural, and three only vocal. Twelve out the 28 occasions involved repetition, both before or after the departure of E2. Delayed responses (i.e., no action while the visitor was still present but soon after) were observed only on three occasions, but there were many cases of repetition of "on-time" responses after the departure of E2.

The issue of developmental changes could be studied in the 16 families who were visited repeatedly. Six subjects were observed to develop from no display of "bye-bye" to displaying it appropriately; five subjects displayed it on all home visits; and four were never observed to do it at all, despite active efforts by the parent and the visitor. One child was displayed appropriate conduct at the first visit, but not in the second.

These data illustrate rather large inter-individual differences in toddlers' readiness to display culturally expected departure conduct under adults' demands. High variability within any sample (or population) is not surprising, since child development is necessarily an open-systems process with multi-trajectory life courses. Our sample data indicate that we had selected an appropriate age range for the study of the departure phenomenon, since for some children in the sample the development of "bye-byes" was emerging at the time. The individual case descriptions that follow provide evidence about children who fall into three categories: (1) those for whom leavetaking conduct was absent; (2) those for whom it was observed emerging during our study; and (3) those who consistently displayed it during the study.

Examples of No Success in Adults' Promotion Efforts

Four children were never observed to display "bye-bye" in any form. However, the ways in which *adults* tried to trigger this behavior is worthy of documentation. The following case involves two observation sessions at 12-13 months of age. (In all transcripts reported from here on, the time marker reported refers to minutes and seconds starting from the point in time at which the visitor announces the intention to leave.)

Session 1 (at 12 months). Before the beginning of the departure setting, the visitor (female) sits in an armchair, while the child (male) toddles around the room. The mother is kneeling on the floor, and encourages the child to contact the visitor. When she mentions the visitor's coat, the child moves away from the adults, smiling. The mother comments that he is going to get his stroller. The child returns to the visitor (while she is starting to put on her coat), and grabs her dress.

0.00:
VISITOR: announces departure.
MOTHER: Can you say bye-bye? (CHILD is toddling away from MOTHER and VISITOR)
VISITOR (to C): I go bye-bye now.
0.08:
VISITOR: I have to go bye-bye now, Jonathan.
VISITOR waves hand towards CHILD, asks: Can you wave bye-bye?
CHILD toddles away to the front door
MOTHER (explains to VISITOR): He used to wave bye-bye when he was real little, but not now.
VISITOR: (referring to CHILD's going to the door): He's got the idea.
MOTHER: (continues describing her and her husband's observations of CHILD's behavior).

0.30:
MOTHER picks up the CHILD saying, "come here to me," and sets the CHILD so that he faces the departing VISITOR.
MOTHER: Say bye-bye!
MOTHER: Can you say bye-bye? Say bye-bye.
VISITOR waves her right hand towards CHILD
MOTHER (to VISITOR): We're working on it.

0.39:
MOTHER tells VISITOR about her observations about CHILD's arm-waving (on occasions involving babysitters and herself)

0.48:
VISITOR waves her right hand towards CHILD again.

0.53:
VISITOR waves again and says: Can you say it? Say bye-bye!

MOTHER: Say "ba!"
VISITOR waves again.

MOTHER: Say "ba!"
VISITOR (waves again): Bye-bye.

1.01:
MOTHER: Say "ba! ba! ba!"
VISITOR (waves again): Bye-bye!
1.07:
MOTHER takes CHILD's right arm into her own right hand, and waves it towards VISITOR.
VISITOR waves her right hand towards CHILD at the same time.

1.10:
MOTHER releases CHILD's right arm, CHILD continues up/down arm movements, then stops.

1.12:
CHILD again makes ballistic up/down shaking movements with right arm like before by himself (the "bye-bye" status of this gesture here remains questionable).

1.15:
VISITOR says courtesies to the MOTHER, prepares for leaving.

1.20:
VISITOR: Bye-bye!

1.24:
MOTHER: Bye!

1.25:
VISITOR leaves

1.26:
MOTHER: Bye-bye (holding CHILD on her right arm). She is going away. She is leaving.
MOTHER: Do you want to go down and play with your toys? (lowers CHILD onto floor).

1.38:
CHILD toddles around. MOTHER and CHILD begin to play on the floor (end at 2.00).

In this session, the mother is observed to try to assist the child to say or wave "bye-bye" by providing a simplified vocal model ("Ba!" at 0.50-1.01), and assists the child by waving his arm for him. The performing of some relevant parts of action for the child by the adult, when the child is still considered to be incapable of handling them, is a general feature of social canalization of children's actions. It constitutes a case of joint action within the ZPD.

Session 2 (at age 13 months 5 days). In the beginning, the female visitor sits on the sofa. The child is standing in front of it, looking at a book on the coffee table. The mother sits at the end of the coffee table, showing the book to the child.

0.00:
VISITOR announces departure.
MOTHER: Do you want to see her to the door, Jonathan?
(takes CHILD by hands, and moves to follow the departing VISITOR. What do you say — bye-bye?

0.08:
MOTHER releases CHILD's hands in a couple of steps. CHILD continues to follow the VISITOR to the door.
VISITOR: Bye-bye, bye-bye, Jonathan!
VISITOR: Say bye-bye!

0.16:
VISITOR (at the door) bends down towards the CHILD and waves her right hand.
CHILD moves past the VISITOR to the glass door and looks outside
VISITOR makes a comment about CHILD's liking what is outside.
MOTHER pulls CHILD back from the door by armpits, and unlocks it.
CHILD fusses.

0.28:
VISITOR (opens door): Bye-bye, Jonathan!

MOTHER: Can you say bye-bye? Wave bye-bye, Jonathan! Wave bye-bye!
VISITOR: (waving to CHILD) Bye-bye!
0.32:
VISITOR leaves.
MOTHER: Say bye-bye!
CHILD gets away from MOTHER's holding, goes to the door and tries to push it open. No success.
MOTHER comes and locks the door
CHILD fusses, pushes on the door.

0.44:
MOTHER picks CHILD up, and tries to calm him. CHILD fusses

1.00:
MOTHER puts CHILD down on floor to play. CHILD cries, is not consoled by being shown different toys.

It is noteworthy that despite all the efforts displayed by the adults, the child is not observed to comply to the demands. The adults, acting in accordance with their expectations, create the structured departure setting that involves communicating demands to the child. The child is expected to become receptive to these demands eventually but the process is acknowledged to take a while; hence the acceptance by the adults of his non-responsiveness.

The Emergency of Appropriate Conduct

The next case involves the emergence of a child's display of "bye-bye" within the age range of 13-17 months. The child (a boy named Cas) was observed on four occasions.

Session 1 (at 13 months 24 days). Prior to the beginning of the departure episode, the child was involved in individual play with objects, occasionally involving the visitor (male) in play.

0.00:
CHILD takes an object and gives to the VISITOR, then goes over to the sofa and plays with an object there. The VISITOR announces his intention to leave.

0.01:
VISITOR: Bye-bye, Cas!
MOTHER: Cas, can you say bye-bye?
VISITOR: Bye-bye! I had fun playing with you.
MOTHER: Can you say bye-bye? Say bye-bye, Sammy has to go.
VISITOR: Bye-bye! Bye-bye!

0.10:
CHILD stands at the sofa, playing with object, looking in the direction of adults.

0.16:
MOTHER: Say bye-bye!
VISITOR: Bye-bye!
MOTHER: Say bye-bye, Cas!
CHILD toddles over to the MOTHER (MOTHER explains to the VISITOR: He wants to go out.)

0.26:
MOTHER picks the child up, holds facing the VISITOR who is standing in the doorway.
MOTHER: You say bye-bye? Can you say bye-bye?
VISITOR: Bye-bye!
MOTHER: Bye-bye!
VISITOR: Bye-bye!
MOTHER: Bye-bye!
VISITOR: Bye-bye! I'll see you later.
MOTHER: Bye-bye!
VISITOR (mostly to the MOTHER): Bye-bye.
MOTHER (mostly to the VISITOR): Bye-bye.
VISITOR leaves.

0.44:
MOTHER takes child back to the living room area, tries to put him down. The CHILD fusses and does not want to get down. MOTHER picks him up again.

1.05:
MOTHER: Sammy had to go home
CHILD fusses again when MOTHER tries to put him down.

1.38:
MOTHER succeeds in putting the CHILD down with the help of showing him a toy, which he grabs and moves away from MOTHER to play with.

This session provides a good illustration of the *intensity* of social demands that both the parent and the visitor subject the child to, as soon as their interaction becomes defined as a departure setting. In one nine-second period (0.01-0.10) Cas was "bombarded" with demands for "bye-bye" six times, followed by another intense bout (nine demands over the 18-second period of 0.26-0.44). Nevertheless, no form of action by the child that even came close to an approximation of an appropriate goodbye (i.e., vocal expression, or hand/arm/finger waving in the direction of the departing visitor) was observed.

Session 2 (at 14 months 2 days). Prior to departure the visitor is sitting with the child on the floor, while the mother is on a sofa facing them. The child plays with toys on the floor, occasionally exchanging them with the visitor.

0.00:
VISITOR announces her departure.
MOTHER pulls the CHILD up from floor, orients towards VISITOR.

MOTHER: Cas, can you say bye-bye? She has to go.

CHILD stands, holding a toy shovel in hand.

VISITOR: Nice meeting you.

MOTHER Nice meeting you too. (to CHILD): Say bye-bye! Bye-bye!

0.08:

The phone rings. MOTHER leaves the CHILD and goes to the phone.

0.12:

VISITOR (to CHILD): Bye!
VISITOR: Bye!
VISITOR: Bye, Cas!
VISITOR: Bye.
VISITOR: Bye-bye!
VISITOR: Bye-bye!
VISITOR: Bye-bye.
VISITOR: Say bye-bye, Cas!
VISITOR: Say bye-bye, Cas! Bye-bye.

CHILD looks in the direction of VISITOR during all the time as VISITOR repeats the "bye-byes" 9 times, but does not respond.

0.33:

MOTHER (returning): Say bye-bye!
VISITOR: Bye-bye!
MOTHER: Say bye-bye!

CHILD waves the shovel that he is holding in his hand.

VISITOR: Is that bye-bye?
MOTHER: That was close.
VISITOR (to MOTHER): Bye-bye, see you later.
MOTHER (to VISITOR): Bye-bye.
VISITOR leaves.

0.43:

CHILD manipulates shovel, then drops it. Moves to wave right arm, first briefly (at 0.54), then longer (0.55-0.56).

MOTHER: It's too late. She's left (encourages him to wave bye-bye). CHILD raises his right arm and waves it in the direction of the door (during 0.59-1.04). Then toddles around, falls, MOTHER adjusts him, and he goes to play with toys on floor.

In Session 2 we observe an intensity of demands that is comparable to the pattern of Session 1. In a 30-second period (0.12-0.42), the child was exposed to two adults' requests for "bye-bye" 12 times. Due to circumstances (the telephone call), it was the visitor who happened to be the major agent in this effort. Interestingly, the social pressure here resulted in an ambiguous arm-waving (with the shovel) that both adults were unwilling to interpret as a full-fledged farewell gesture. However, *after* the visitor left, the child initiated a display of arm waving towards the door (at 0.54 and 0.55-0.56). After the mother further encouraged him, the pattern was repeated. This session illustrates the presence of delayed action in a toddler's socialization of situation-bound forms of social conduct.

Session 3 (at 17 months 18 days). Prior to the beginning of the departure setting, the CHILD is kneeling on the floor, facing the adults (who are sitting, facing him).

0.00:

VISITOR announces her departure.

MOTHER: Cas, Penny has to go, can you say bye-bye?

MOTHER: Can you say bye-bye, she has to go.

VISITOR: Bye-bye!
MOTHER: Bye-bye!

CHILD vocalizes, then raises right arm briefly and holds it up in the adults' direction (at 0.08).

0.08:

CHILD looks briefly at E1.

MOTHER: No, Paula is not leaving yet, Penny's going.

0.14:

MOTHER: Say bye-bye!
VISITOR: Bye!

MOTHER: Say bye-bye! You're going to wait until she leaves.
VISITOR: Bye-bye, nice meeting you.

0.24:
VISITOR leaves.

0.24:
CHILD vocalizes to MOTHER, who talks to him. CHILD continues sitting on the floor and manipulating a toy (until 1.00).

In the third session, we could observe a very brief arm waving by the child, after brief (but intense) pressure from the adults (four demands in a 7-second period). However, subsequent efforts to get him to repeat the action failed. The child was also not seen to display a goodbye after the visitor's departure (contrary to the mother's prediction).

Session 4 (at 17 months 28 days). This session follows an episode of the mother and child playing hide-and-seek in the kitchen. The mother retrieves him and directs him to go back into the living room where the visitor (male) is sitting in an armchair. The child toddles towards the visitor and stops in front of him.

0.00:
VISITOR: I have to go now. (Waves to CHILD with his right hand) Bye-bye.
CHILD vocalizes briefly.
VISITOR: I have to go now.
MOTHER: Can you say bye-bye, Cas? Jaan has to go. Say bye-bye!

0.11:
CHILD holds right arm towards adults at his waist level, moves fingers and vocalizes.

0.12:
MOTHER explains aspects of CHILD's behavior to VISITOR.

CHILD toddles away from adults to the sofa.
MOTHER: Say bye-bye, bye-bye!
VISITOR: Bye-bye!

0.22:
CHILD raises right arm, waves briefly towards adults and vocalizes "bye-bye." Then turns around (away from adults) towards the sofa, then around again (facing the adults again).
MOTHER: Say bye-bye; say bye-bye!

0.26:
VISITOR thanks MOTHER for meeting him.
VISITOR: Bye-bye! (to CHILD)

0.33:
CHILD briefly raises right arm towards the VISITOR, then lets it fall to his side, and moves fingers.
MOTHER (to VISITOR): Good night!
VISITOR: Good night.

0.39:
CHILD raises right arm towards VISITOR, and waves, toddling forward towards the VISITOR.

0.42:
VISITOR leaves.

0.43:
MOTHER (to CHILD): What are you going to do now? Will you ride your bicycle?
CHILD toddles away from the door, sits on tricycle, then falls and starts to cry (end at 1.00).

In Session 4, the child's display of the "bye-bye" was observed to occur repeatedly and with relatively little social pressure exerted by the adults. It is interesting to note that the visitor followed the adult convention of a pre-closing statement that he directed towards the child rather than the mother, who repeated it in her speech oriented towards the child. The mother had been observed to use a pre-closure statement in a similar manner in Sessions 3 and 1 as well. This illustrates the socialization of the child towards the use of not only the final "marker" of departure, but also its preceding, prep-aratory phase.

Longitudinal Transformation of "Bye-Byes" in Toddlerhood

Some children in our sample could be triggered to act appropriately on all occasions that we videotaped. The *form* of their response could nevertheless be seen to undergo development, as the case of Jennifer shows.

Session 1 (at 14 months 14 days). Before the beginning of the departure setting, the child is sitting on the floor among many toys. The visitor (female) is also on the floor, about a 2-meter distance away.

0.00:
VISITOR: (taking a soft toy dog and moving it towards CHILD): I have to go, Jen. I've got to have to go.
MOTHER: Can you say bye-bye?
CHILD (looking at VISITOR) "Ba-bye"
VISITOR: (rises) Bye-bye. I have to go (moves across the floor, carefully navigating between toys). To MOTHER: It was nice meeting you.
MOTHER: It was nice meeting you. Hope to see you again.
CHILD starts creeping in the direction of departing VISITOR.
MOTHER: Bye! Jen, say bye-bye!

0.11:
CHILD continues creeping towards the departing VISITOR.
MOTHER (to VISITOR): She'll say bye-bye here, or out in the hallway.

CHILD: *"Ba bye"*!
MOTHER laughs.

0.22:
VISITOR leaves.
MOTHER talks to CHILD about VISITOR's departure.
CHILD is on floor, on all fours, inactive.

0.37:
CHILD waves left arm, and vocalizes "bye-bye" towards the door from which VISITOR had exited (until 0.40). MOTHER claps hands and laughs.

0.42:
CHILD goes back to playing with toys (end at 1.00)

In the case of Jennifer, display of adequate conduct is evident from this session onwards. The action is repetitive (vocalization twice, while the visitor was still in the child's visual field), and takes alternative forms (vocalizing only, and vocalizing in conjunction with arm-waving). However, as we will see in the subsequent sessions, the form and time locus of Jennifer's "bye-byes" develop over the 3-month period that our observations cover.

Session 2 (at 14 months 21 days). In the beginning, the child is again on the floor surrounded by toys. The mother and the visitor (male) are talking, sitting on chairs and facing the child. Child manipulates toys.

0.00:
VISITOR: I had fun today, Jenny. Thank you for showing me your toys. I am going bye. (chats with MOTHER)

0.04:
VISITOR: Bye-bye, Jenny! Bye-bye!
VISITOR: I'm leaving, bye-bye!

MOTHER: Say bye-bye!
VISITOR: Say bye-bye now, I am leaving.
Good bye!

0.14:
CHILD (looks towards VISITOR): *Bye-bye.*
MOTHER (comments): There you go. A little delayed, but ... (goes to open door to corridor)
CHILD creeps out into the corridor ahead of adults, vocalizing *"ba-bye"* four times.

0.24:
The adults follow CHILD into corridor.
CHILD climbs two steps up the stairs, looks back towards adults.
VISITOR: Bye-bye.
MOTHER: Say bye-bye!
VISITOR: Bye-bye; bye, bye.

0.37:
CHILD waves right arm briefly towards the VISITOR.
VISITOR leaves through front door (from corridor), saying to MOTHER: See you later.
MOTHER picks the CHILD up from the stairs and carries her back into living room, puts her down among toys.

0.49:
CHILD sits, proceeds to play with toys.
Vocalizes "bye-bye" to herself repeatedly at 1.04-1.08 and 1.14 (end at 1.20).

0.07:
No action. MOTHER and VISITOR chat (until 0.14).

0.14:
VISITOR stands up and moves towards the door, CHILD follows her with gaze.
MOTHER: Can you say bye-bye?
VISITOR: Can you say bye-bye, Jenny? I've got to go. Bye-bye, Jenny. Bye!
MOTHER: Say bye-bye!

0.20:
CHILD watches departing VISITOR, while sitting on sofa.
VISITOR: Bye-bye, Jenny!

0.28:
CHILD: Bye.
VISITOR leaves.
MOTHER: That's the girl, say bye-bye when the person is here.

0.34:
MOTHER: Are you ready for a nap?

0.38:
CHILD: Bye-bye.
MOTHER: Bye-bye. Ready for a nap?
CHILD rubs her eye with her fist.

0.44:
MOTHER talks to CHILD, who moves around on the sofa. (End at 1.00).

Session 3 (at 17 months 15 days). This session started with the child and the visitor (female) sitting on the sofa. The child has the visitor's sunglasses, attempts to put them on. The visitor announces her departure.

0.00:
MOTHER: She has to go bye-bye. She needs her glasses.
VISITOR takes her sunglasses away from CHILD.

Session 4 (at 17 months 20 days). In the beginning, the child is on the sofa, with some toys. The visitor (male) is sitting on a chair near the sofa.

0.00:
VISITOR announces his departure.
MOTHER: It was nice meeting you.

0.04:
VISITOR (to CHILD): Bye-bye!
CHILD sits on sofa and manipulates a toy.

0.07:

MOTHER: Jenny, are you going to say good-bye?

0.08:

CHILD: Bye-bye! (continues to play with teddy bear)
VISITOR: Good-bye.
VISITOR: Good-bye! I have to go.
MOTHER talks about the CHILD to the VISITOR.
VISITOR (standing up and moving away): I guess one "bye" was enough.
VISITOR: Good-bye!
MOTHER: Can you say bye-bye again?

0.24:

CHILD (looking at the departing VISITOR): Bye-bye! (continues to manipulate teddy bear).

0.27:

MOTHER: Can you wave? Wave bye-bye!
CHILD (Keeping right hand at the level of the sofa) *first* waves fingers, then raises the arm and waves the arm.

0.34:

VISITOR and MOTHER exchange courtesies.

0.42:

VISITOR: Bye-bye. *(leaves)*
MOTHER (to CHILD): It was nice of you to say bye-bye to him. You said it at the right time.

0.52:

CHILD continues to sit on sofa, vocalizes (end at 1.00).

By session 4, we can observe that Jennifer's saying and waving "bye-bye" has become immediate. It promptly follows the mother's effort to trigger it, *but without abandoning the ongoing activity*. The mother's appreciation of the child's saying "bye-bye" to the visitor *at the*

right time elaborates the goals of socialization that parents in this family had been working towards (compare also with Session 3, time 0.28-0.34).

GENERAL DISCUSSION

The developing child becomes integrated into a culture through a lengthy process of being included in different interaction settings. Adults structure these settings in accordance with their socialization objectives. The process of socialization that takes place can be described through a system of zone-concepts that denote adults' selective exclusion of the child's action opportunities from the given setting (ZFM), as well as specification of socially expected ways of acting (ZPA), and the mapping of these on the children's capabilities that occur in collectively coordinated settings (ZPD).

In order to enhance the chances that a given toddler will be guided towards appropriate ways of acting in departure situations, the caregiver limits the child's choices of action to facing the departing visitor, and away from distracting objects (ZFM). While keeping the child in the setting, the caregiver and the departing visitor subject the child to social demands for setting-appropriate conduct (ZPA). Given the time-compressed nature of the setting, the rate at which such demands are communicated to the child is usually high, with a bombardment of demands for saying and waving "bye-bye." Despite high variability from one occasion to another, the basic process structure of all departure situations approximates the picture that was provided in Figure 1. Depending on environmental circumstances, the demands can be organized in "bouts," rather than distributed evenly over time. Often, the bouts of demands are located within particular environmental loci; for example, the first bout may occur immediately after the visitor's announcement of intention to depart, followed by a pause (as the interactants' move to the front door), which is followed by a second high-intensity bout as the visitor leaves. After the departure the caregiver may continue to demand *delayed* "bye-byes" from the child — evidence in favor of the presence of longer-term socialization goals (see also Kindermann & Valsiner, this volume).

Development of social courtesy skills is an important objective for child socialization. Different cultural systems include different forms of social courtesy from adults, and guide children towards the mastery of these skills by various trajectories.

The example analyzed here is highly culture-specific in its form. For example, in cultures where toddlers are not viewed as "serious" interaction partners for adults, there may be no incentive to spend effort on getting young children to say or perform appropriate leavetaking actions. However, the culture-specific content of our present empirical example illustrates the culture-inclusiveness of any socialization process. Any particular child socialization system is embedded in the given culture, and by virtue of such embeddedness can be sufficiently effective even if the methods it utilizes are far from maximum efficiency. The cultural environment that developing children share with adults, older siblings, and peers makes socialization a long-term undertaking with very little risk, as viewed from the perspective of the culture. As long as a given cultural environment has no competitors for its control over child development, it can be expected that its

children will become skillful and knowledgeable participants within it. The whole of childhood is the time course during which this expectation is put into practice. Within that time frame, the "deficiencies" of any particular age period, or lack of acquisition of cultural expectations in a particular area of knowledge, can be compensated for by other experiences at later ages. Child socialization involves high levels of redundancy, where culturally important objectives can be reached through multiple routes. Psychologists' efforts to separate that socialization from its cultural context and to study it as if it were an independent system may generate extensive empirical data, but little understanding of the reality.

REFERENCES

Appadurai, A. (1985). Gratitude as a social mode in South India. *Ethos, 13,* 3, 236-245.

Elkind, D. (1980). Strategic interactions in early adolescence. In J. Adelson (Ed.), *Handbook of adolescent psychology.* New York: Wiley.

Hill, P.E., & Valsiner, J. (1987). Getting to know strangers: Toddlers' construction of relationships. In J. Valsiner (Ed.), *Child development within culturally structured environments.* Vol. 1. *Parental cognition and adult-child interaction.* Norwood, N.J.: Ablex (in press).

Rogoff, B., & Wertsch, J. (Eds) (1984). Children's learning in the "zone of proximal development." *New Directions for Child Development,* No. 23.

Schegloff, E.A. (1968). Sequencing in conversational openings. *American Anthropologist, 70,* 1075-1095.

Schegloff, E.A., & Sacks, H. (1973). Opening up closings. *Semiotica, 8,* 289-327.

Valsiner, J. (1985). Theoretical issues of child development and the problem of accident prevention. In T. Garling & J. Valsiner (Eds.),*Children within environments: Toward a psychology of accident prevention* (pp. 13-36). New York: Plenum.

Valsiner, J. (1987a). *Culture and the development of children's action.* Chichester: Wiley.

Valsiner, J. (1987b). *Developmental psychology in USSR*. Brighton: Harvester Press.

Winegar, L.T. (1987). *Children's construction of conventional procedures with teachers and peers*. Paper presented at the Biennial Meeting of the Society for Research in Child Development, Baltimore, April.

Winegar, L.T., Camden, J.A., & Matthews, M.E. (1987). *Preschool snacktime interaction*. Paper presented at the 8th Annual Ethnography in Education Research Forum, Philadelphia, March.

Chapter 8

The Socialization of Gender Identity

Observations From Nepal[1]

Debra Skinner

INTRODUCTION

In Nepal, children are born into a hierarchical Hindu caste society, and begin learning their place at a very young age. They learn that they are embedded in and defined by kinship and community ties, and that they are obligated to fulfill many social and ritual duties. Most significantly, they learn their caste and gender, both fundamental identities that pervade social interactions and perceptions of oneself and others throughout life.

Children in the Nepali hill village of Naudada[2] are present in nearly every context of village life. Parents assume that their children learn primarily through imitation and observation what they need to know in order to become competent members of their society. The development of children is compared to the ripening of a piece of fruit: both mature naturally with the passing of time. What a little girl does not understand at age four, she will understand at age six because her "wisdom ripens" as she gets older.

Most anthropologists and psychologists have tended to view child development in a somewhat different and more complex way. Both disciplines have contributed to the study of how children in any culture acquire knowledge of their own and others' social identities and the world in which these identities are relevant. However, psychologists stress the devel-

[1]This chapter briefly summarizes some aspects of Nepali children's understanding of themselves and their social world. For a fuller description and detailed argument about the progress and development of these understandings, see Skinner (in preparation). Although any flaws in this chapter are entirely my own, I wish to thank Dorothy Holland and Jaan Valsiner for providing very helpful critiques of this chapter and for providing guidance in my research, G.B. Adhikari for his skillful translations of the songs, and Harihar Bhattarai for sharing with me his immense knowledge of Nepali history and culture. I also wish to acknowledge the Fulbright-Hays Act and the Graduate School of North Carolina for funding my fieldwork in Nepal. Finally, I appreciate the help given to me in the field by Save the Children Federation, USA, and the South-East Consortium for International Development.

[2]All place and person names have been replaced with pseudonyms.

opmental stages of social cognition, but do not traditionally examine this process as it occurs within a culturally structured environment, nor study how it relates to the body of shared cultural knowledge already present in the society. In contrast, anthropologists have mostly stressed the cultural context of learning and the cognitive organization of cultural knowledge, but not the transformations or reorganizations that occur in the development of an individual's understanding of his or her social world.

This study on the socialization framework for girls' acquisition of gender identity is an attempt to integrate an anthropological approach with the neo-Vygotskian perspective in developmental psychology, in an examination of how culturally structured events and mediating devices function in an individual's understanding of her identity.

In Naudada, girls form and transform their notions of themselves and their knowledge of the wider social and moral universe in which their identities have meaning as they increasingly participate with enculturated others in spheres of everyday and ritual activities. From these interactions, they distill, construct and reconstruct, and internalize meanings pertaining to gender that are culturally shared (Rogoff, 1982; Vygotsky, 1978). Such meanings are embedded in natural discourse and in social interactions as well as in ritual events and culturally canonized genres such as songs. These genres not only present information about gender identities and roles, but also function as mediating devices, which aid the girl in organizing her thoughts and feelings concerning her gender identity. After providing some general background information about life in Naudada, I will discuss the specific operation of these culturally orchestrated events and genres in girls' acquisition of gender identity.

My research was carried out in Naudada Panchayat (a *panchayat* is a small administrative unit) located in the southern half of Gorkha District in the Himalayan kingdom of Nepal. It is an area typical of the middle hills region of this country. People live in hamlets of four to seventy houses which are scattered along ridges or in river valleys. Although the caste system has been officially abolished by the Constitution of Nepal, twelve named castes/ethnic groups are represented among the 4,376 people who live in Naudada.

Of these twelve hierarchically ranked endogamous groups, the Bahun and the Chetri are considered to be highest. Together these two castes own most of the best land and wield much of the political power. Other castes follow their traditional occupations of leatherworking, tailoring, or blacksmithing, but virtually all households are also involved in agriculture. Although there are important economic and ritual ties between families of different castes, for the most part members of only one caste live in each hamlet. Spatial separations between hamlets reflect the restrictions placed on caste interactions in certain social and ritual contexts. For example, the so-called untouchable or impure castes from whom higher castes will not accept water or cooked food live in hamlets set apart from those of the higher castes.

For 90% of the population, farming is the primary source of livelihood. Rice, maize, wheat, millet, and a small variety of vegetable species are grown on narrow terraces carved from steep hillsides. To survive in this land, which is food deficient and where people must labor from before sunrise until after sunset, children begin to learn at a young age the skills involved in maintaining a day-to-day existence. The most common saying in Naudada is, "If you don't work, you don't eat." This is a harsh reality for many hill families, as is the high death and illness rate among children. Because of the reality of infant and child mortality, the physical survival of the child and protection from forces that can harm m it are paramount family concerns in the first few years of the child's life.

In Naudada, as in other communities of Nepal, the household unit cooperates in domestic and economic efforts. A typical unit is the joint family, which is patrilineal and patrilocal. A son will live with his wife and children in his father's house. If he leaves the father's house he usually builds a separate dwelling nearby, and lives in a nuclear family until his own sons marry.

A few of the households are polygynous, with the husband's two wives either sharing the same house or living close together in separate dwellings. Children of one wife call the co-wife "mother" and are cared for by her as well as by their biological mother.

Daughters provide much of the labor for domestic and agricultural tasks, and are often the main caretakers of younger siblings. At the time of marriage they leave their natal homes to live with their husband in his village, which is often many hours' walk away.

Naudadans share the language of Nepali and the religion of Hinduism. Respect and worship of gods, elders, and ancestors is a part of and inseparable from everyday life, as is following the practices and moral tenets espoused by the Hindu religion.

This is a brief description of the cultural milieu of Naudada in which children develop. I will now discuss more specifically the content and process of girls' acquisition of identity.

THE EXPECTED LIFE-PATH FOR FEMALES

Observations of child socialization practices and children's activities in a wide range of settings in both high and low caste hamlets in Naudada reveal that girls begin to learn gender-related information practically from birth. If role-playing may be taken as an indication of sex identification, it is evident that children as young as three are aware of and display the conduct that define one as being male or female. For instance, three-year-old boys and girls play side by side, but pursue different activities. Boys play with toy cars and pretend to make roads or sacrifice buffalo — all male tasks. The girls pretend to mother their cloth dolls and imitate the work they see other women doing, such as cooking, winnowing rice, and washing pots.

When little girls do attempt something that is marked as a male activity, they often learn through an "episodic event" (see Jahoda, 1982) that they are different in some fundamental way from boys. A dramatic example of one such episodic event occurred when six-year-old Sita was in the field where her older brother was plowing. As he steered the oxen by her, she reached out playfully and touched the plow, an act that for females is a great transgression. Immediately, her brother began to hit and rebuke her. Her father and other brothers ran from the house to join in the scolding and beating, and her father told her it was a sin for a female to touch a plow and threatened to beat her severely if she ever touched it again. After this event, Sita cried and trembled for hours. When I asked her several weeks later about the incident, she remembered it well, repeating the words of her father and promising never again to touch the plow. Although Sita did not understand the wider moral universe in which her act was defined as a sin, she did learn in a dramatic way that because she was female she was restricted from acts that her brothers could freely perform.

As Sita grows older, she will acquire a vast body of gender-related knowledge that she could not learn solely in early childhood. This knowledge relates to an expected life-path for females — to the set of roles girls and women are expected to play during their lives. These roles are envisioned as part of a taken-for-granted world that cognitively organizes cultural knowledge in a manner similar to what Holland describes as a "cultural model." As such, the cultural model provides the background for girls' understandings of gender roles and expectations.

The expected life-path for females in Hindu society has been described in rich detail by several authors whose findings are very similar to my own observations in Naudada (e.g., Bennett, 1976, 1983; Das, 1979; Stone, 1978). The right-hand column of Table 1 briefly outlines this presumed path and the relevant identities and expectations at each stage.

In this taken-for-granted world as women in Naudada understand it, the prototypical female begins life as an obedient and hard-working daughter and sister. Before puberty, she is described as pure and sacred, compared to a goddess, and in the context of certain rituals worshipped by her male kin. With the onset of puberty, she changes from pure and

nonsexual to polluting and sexual. Males must be protected from the danger of her polluting menstrual blood, and her family must control her sexuality by restraints on her interactions with non-related males.

It is expected that girls will be married soon after puberty. In marriage, sexuality can be channeled to its legitimate end — the production of sons for the lineage. After marriage, the prototypical woman is a faithful and devoted wife and an obedient, respectful, and industrious daughter-in-law. With the birth of children, especially sons, she acquires what some have described as the central identity of her life: woman as childbearer (Stone, 1978). She becomes a more integral member of the household. Upon the death of her husband's parents and the marriage of her own sons, she attains a higher status and more control through her position as mother-in-law, directing the lives of her daughters-in-law. The ideal is that she never becomes a widow: if she is lucky, she will die before her husband.

Those females who deviate from this prototypical life-path are labeled and evaluated as aberrant or problematic in some way for this "simplified world" (see Holland & Skinner, 1987, for an example similar to this in U.S. society). These include women who are lazy and disrespectful, women who cannot bear children, adulteresses, widows, and women whose fate (*karma*) is so unlucky that they are considered to bring misfortune to their families.

Women in Naudada are evaluated against this taken-for-granted world of the female life course. "Bad women" are those who are evil, greedy, adulterous, sinful, lazy, dishonest, or quarrelsome. "Good women" are those who do not manifest these bad qualities and inappro-

TABLE 1
EXPECTED LIFE PATH FOR A FEMALE

Approximate Age	Life-cycle Ritual or Other Event	Transition/ Relevant Identities
6 days	*chaitom*	fate written on infant's forehead
11 days	*nuharan* naming ceremony	infant assumes patriline of father/ becomes sister and daughter
6 months	*pasne* rice-feeding	infant enters social world, the sphere of purity/pollution by eating rice which is both sustenance and symbol
6 years	*dat satne* eruption of adult teeth	correlates with stricter separation of girls from boys and greater responsibilities for work and moral behavior
15-18	*lukne* seclusion at menarche	changes from prepubescent girl to a sexually mature teenage girl
15-24	*biha* marriage	girl leaves natal home to become a wife and daughter-in-law/becomes a member of husband's lineage
17-25	childbirth	girl becomes woman and mother/ channels her sexuality into its proper course of promulgating the patriline by bearing sons
42-48	menopause	cessation of sexual activity/becomes a mother-in-law, grandmother, old woman
45+	death	cessation of social ties in this world

priate conduct, but instead labor without ceasing for the benefit of their household. Good women never talk unnecessarily or wander around the village to malinger, gossip, or flirt.

This knowledge of the expectations and values of the expected life-path is what a girl must learn in order to understand how she will be evaluated in her culture. She also comes to use this knowledge to organize her own thoughts and feelings about herself. In Naudadan society, girls are aided in these cognitive tasks by certain culturally constructed events and devices, which I will now describe.

THE SOCIALIZATION FRAMEWORK FOR IDENTITY ACQUISITION

Everyday Interactions and Gender Terminology

Several researchers have documented the importance of everyday events for the child's acquisition of cultural knowledge (e.g., Rogoff & Lave, 1984; Valsiner, 1987). This knowledge may be implicit in the cues given in social interactions, or it may be explicitly stated, or it may be embedded as moral injunctions, evaluations, justifications, and explanations (e.g., Much & Shweder, 1978).

One important means by which girls come to think about themselves and others is through learning the specialized vocabulary of gender-marked terms. In Nepal, as in the West, there are literally hundreds of terms for gender types (Holland & Skinner, 1987). People use these words in everyday conversation to describe and evaluate themselves and each other; to scold and insult or to praise and commend. This vocabulary represents an important means by which one organizes one's understanding of gender identity, as well as learns about the world in which these terms have meaning. For example, when a girl who has acquired this information hears a woman referred to as an *aputri* (roughly glossed as one who cannot bear children) or a *nathi* (one exhibiting "loose" behavior), she interprets these terms against the taken-for-granted model that she has learned. Females are expected to go through life as both fecund *and* chaste. Thus, the *aputri* is an aberration to be pitied and scorned: she is thought to have been a great sinner in a past life, otherwise she would not have earned the unlucky fate of being barren in this one. The *nathi* is an aberration from the faithful and devoted wife whose sexuality is legitimized only as it is controlled by the husband and directed toward the production of children. She is a troublesome type, as she may draw a man's affection away from his legitimate wife to her, and may in fact end up as a co-wife — a relationship that women rarely view positively.

A neophyte to Naudadan culture— whether a young child or an anthropologist —hears these labels in context, and not only comes to learn the simple definitions of the terms (e.g., an *aputri* is a barren woman) but also to understand the taken-for-granted and culturally shared world in which these types exist (see Holland & Valsiner, in press). The neophyte comes to understand why an *aputri* has the characteristics that she does and why she arouses such negative feelings.

Ritual Events

Another culturally structured means of learning gender identity is through life-cycle rituals and other events that mark transitions females go through during life. Some of these are listed in the middle column of Table 1.

These first three rituals do not mark the child specifically for gender, but do serve to establish her identity to others as a member of a particular caste and lineage. From birth she is a daughter to her parents and a sister to her siblings, two identities that are emphasized by those around her from an early age. There are no life-cycle rituals in early and middle childhood: however, there are events such as the eruption of adult teeth, which is correlated to increased responsibility; stricter separation of girls from boys; and different expectations for the two sexes.

The life-cycle rituals of *lukne* and *biha* which occur in adolescence are the most important for presenting information on cultural expectations and for marking the transition from a prepubescent girl to a sexual one (a *taruni*). The first of these is *lukne*, which occurs at the time of first menstruation. At *lukne* the girl is secluded in a neighbor's house for a period of 12 to 21 days. During this seclusion, she must not see the faces of her fathers or brothers. She must not even see her own house. In this manner, she learns in a very dramatic way that her femaleness has a dangerous and polluting quality, which others must be protected from and which sets her apart from males.

This physical transition from prepubescent child to sexually mature teenager brings about changes in the girl's own perception of herself and her relationship to others. Girls often say they dread the approach of menarche because it means that they will soon be married and sent far away from their home and the friends of their youth. They often report that when they go home after the ceremony, they feel very strange. They become shy around their father, brothers, and other males. One woman in the village told me that after *lukne*, she became so shy and afraid of being teased about her ripening sexuality that she dropped out of school in order to avoid facing the village boys.

Marriage brings about a dramatic shift in a woman's life, with her identities as a daughter and sister becoming overshadowed by the identities of wife and daughter-in-law. Marriage rituals clearly mark these changes in status. The bride is physically removed from her natal home, and her submission to her husband and in-laws is symbolically enacted. For instance, during one part of the wedding ceremony she moves from the right side of the groom to his left side — a more inferior position. She also bows to him, touching his feet with her forehead. During the final marriage rituals, which take place at the groom's home, she eats food from her husband's plate — food he has touched and made polluted. The bride also shows her respect to the mother-in-law by drinking the water that she has used to wash her mother-in-law's feet (see Bennett, 1983, for a detailed description of these and other rituals).

These various rituals are important in at least two ways for identity acquisition. The first important function is the presentation of identities in the ritual event. Rituals dramatize and bring to the fore the valued and salient identities of a society. These symbolic enactments of the identities represent and reinforce the content and affect of the identities for all participants and observers.

Even before girls go through many of these age-related rituals, they are onlookers, observing and over time learning the symbolism of the identities presented and the moral categories that shape these identities (Schwartz & Merton, 1968). In such a way, the ritual process instructs not only the initiate, but also the younger onlookers who will later go through the ceremony themselves.

Life-cycle rituals also are significant for the initiate as they mark the passage from one status to another. After assuming a new role, the initiate is free to express the knowledge she may have formerly learned as an onlooker. Even a very young girl may be aware of some of the stereotypes and expectations associated with certain roles that can come later in life, but until she passes through the ritual that marks her entering a new role, such as teenager or daughter-in-law, she never has the opportunity to consolidate her knowledge by describing it or acting out the required behavior. When she does begin to act as a member of the new social category, she begins to experience her own and others' evaluations of her acts, and she may encounter information and emotions that have not been present for her before. She starts to form some view of herself in this category, and of her being and acting in that role. However, she may not fully internalize the identity for some time in the sense of becoming emotionally attached to it. She comes only slowly to think about and evaluate herself in terms of it.

Internalization is a more gradual process that does not necessarily occur for some time after taking on a new role. There can be struggles in becoming emotionally attached to an identity or integrating it with other notions of the self (Holland et al., in preparation). An example of this process is a girl's acquisition of the identity of daughter-in-law. Even a very young girl in Naudada knows some of the behavior expected from a daughter-in-law because often she lives with her older brother's wife, or she hears older girls who return for a visit after marriage tell of their problems. However, knowing about the role she will have to assume does not always prepare her for the emotions she will feel in it. For instance, Shanta, a young woman of eight-een who had been married for six months, told me that she was having trouble adjusting to being a daughter-in-law. She described how her freedom was much more restricted in her husband's home; how she could not talk with many of her neighbors because her mother-in-law was on unfriendly terms with them; and could not go to the bazaar area because to do so would make others think she was a "loose woman." Shanta said that in her mind she still thought of herself as a daughter and a sister. She loved her natal family and cried when she remembered the younger brothers and sisters she had to leave. Instead of being able to take care of her own mother and siblings as she desired, she had to work for "strangers" — her in-laws. Although Shanta had a notion of herself in the role of daughter-in-law and was concerned as to how others judged her as one, she had not yet fully integrated or reconciled that part of her life. She was still conscious of it as an identity that did not fit her self-conceptions.

Other Mediating Devices for Identity Acquisition

Besides the specialized gender vocabulary and the gender-related ritual events, there are additional cultural devices that aid girls in internalizing or organizing their thoughts and emotions concerning their identity. Folktales, Hindu epics, myths, "sadness stories" told by women, and songs include descriptions of types of women and the pathos of the roles associated with their lives. Here, I will examine songs as an example of such a mediating device.

Women sing many different types of songs for different occasions. They sing songs about love, about their hardships, about their sadnesses. They often sing these alone as they tend their goats on the hillsides or work in the forest or fields, or they join together with other women to sing during rituals and festive occasions. What most of these songs have in common is that they portray the lives and problems of females in their various roles as wives and daughters, sisters, and daughters-in-law. The songs not only include information about the identities associated with these roles, but also contain the affective sentiments — the emotions experienced as part of the identity.

In the everyday life of the village, emotional outpourings are rare. Girls talk only to their closest friends, if anyone, about their feelings, fears, and anxieties. They have been taught that they should not express anger or say bad things against their families. In this situation, songs are a means whereby they can express their emotions to themselves about the difficulties and ambiguities of their roles in life, and perhaps control their emotions in some sense. One example of a song being used to control emotion occurred when a woman from Naudada came to my village house and asked to sing a song into my tape recorder. It was a sad song in which she regretted past acts against her mother. She lamented that she was never able to atone for these acts because she had had to leave her natal home. When she finished the song, she explained to me that she had poured her sadness into the song and that she often sings out her "heart's unpleasantness" in order to feel

less sad. I also observed her teaching this song to her fifteen-year-old daughter and her friends because she wanted them to understand her feelings. In this case and in others, it was through song that women communicated their feelings to themselves and to younger girls.

A similar incident happened when I asked Tika, a girl of fifteen, to tell her life story. Tika responded that she was too shy to talk about these things with me, but that she could express herself in song. She sang the following:

Parents have earned a little money,
but my life will be spent cutting grass and wood only.
Daughters are married off, crossing nine mountains,
but the sons are kept at home.
Mother, am I not your daughter, am I not your daughter?
Brothers are given wealth and property, but nothing is given to me.
Am I not your daughter?

What Tika is telling me here is the way she understands herself and her life. Later on as she became less shy and came to trust that I would never repeat our conversations to the other villagers, she came to express some of the same thoughts and resentments that otherwise she could only express in song. She told me how she resented being a girl and feared the time she would have to "cross nine mountains" to live with her husband's family, far away from the family and friends of her natal village. She laments a theme that is common among females, and one that they perceive at a very young age — the preferential treatment given to sons, who will stay with the parents.

These types of songs become ritualized in the annual Tij festival, a time when women ritually fast and bathe to absolve themselves of any sins they have committed due to the dangers and impurity connected with menstruation. As part of Tij, they join together to compose and perform songs, singing and dancing before the whole village. These songs carry a wealth of information about different women's roles as well as the emotional tones associated with them. Girls increasingly participate in the Tij ceremony with older women, who teach them how to compose and perform the songs. It could be argued that these songs come to function as mediating devices that the girls internalize to organize their understanding of the pathos of their roles.

The first excerpt from a Tij song reflects Tika's theme about the sorrows awaiting a daughter:

> She is decorated by combing the hair,
> and putting the vermillion in her hair.
> She should have to marry and go to an unknown place,
> it is her fate.
> Going to a strange place, being a solitary bird
> I have to pass the days of my life being sad...
> It is better for a daughter to die than to live.

When the bride takes the red vermillion powder from her husband and wears it in the part of her hair as a symbol of her marriage, she is also symbolizing the unknown fate that awaits her. She anticipates this future life as being very hard and lonely. The following song details some of these fears:

> Crossing the mountains and the hills
> I have to go to my husband's home.
> The mother-in-law scolds me, showing the stick in her hand
> The respect of my heart, how to show it?
> When I greet her touching her feet

> When I cut the grass and make the bundles
> She throws it away, blaming me that the grass is too little.
> On rainy days also, I have to prepare the rice
> It's my duty to call her *bajyai*.

The new bride must labor for the mother-in-law, but her work is never sufficient or good enough to satisfy the older woman who threatens to beat her. Yet she must hide her feelings and show her defence, addressing the in-law by the respectful term, *bajyai* (grandmother).

One final excerpt from a Tij song serves to present the difficulties and fears that many women experience as wives:

> Waiting in the kitchen, the rice becomes cool
> Waiting for the husband the night is almost gone
> How much rotten alcohol is there in Thakali's hotel
> He came with a stick at midnight
> If we suggest "Do not take wine,"
> He threatens to bring a co-wife
> The new wife will give the wine and pleasure instead of me
> and she will give orders, and bring the water to wash his feet.

As this song indicates, marriage is an uncertain fate. A woman's husband might be a drunkard who will beat her and spend all of his money drinking and gambling away the family property in the local "hotel" or tea room. There is also the threat that he could choose to marry a second wife who will take away not only his affection but also scarce resources. A woman who loses the support of her husband finds life very difficult, as oftentimes she must struggle on her own to feed herself and her children.

Other researchers who have recorded women's songs in India have recognized similar themes in them. Jacobsen (1975) examined folksongs sung by women and found the same themes of resentment and sorrow that are evident in the songs presented here. Also, Narayan (1986) has examined a particular type of wedding song, the *suhag*, as reflecting aspects of the experience that comes with the transition to marriage. She states that these songs function as a model for women, encoding values and orientations surrounding their roles, and that they also function as a socially sanctioned outlet for emotions in a society where inner states should not be discussed except in the most circumscribed situations. In a similar way, folksongs and Tij songs of Naudada provide a way of mediating and organizing the emotions and experience of the identities associated with womanhood. Through group interaction with other females and enacting the group's experiential sense of identity during Tij, young girls over time encode the emotional and expressive symbols of the experiences shared by the older women.

SUMMARY

In this chapter I have described several culturally structured events and devices available to Nepali girls for understanding themselves and their female identity. I have focused here on the culture's presentation of gender, not individual girls' actual absorption of this knowledge. However, I do suggest that these presentations are internalized: in the Naudadan situation, girls come to define themselves and others in terms of culturally specified social categories labeled by a specialized gender terminology. Through observing

and participating in life-cycle rituals, girls dramatically experience the salient identities of their society and the life-path they are expected to follow, and through the creation and performance of songs, they are provided with a means to organize their emotions about these gender roles. (For a description and analysis of further data on the patterns of development of gender knowledge, see Skinner, in preparation.) It is hoped that this study of a culture so different from the Western one in which most development theories have originated will illuminate the role of mediating devices in knowledge acquisition, and suggest possibilities for further research on the development of social cognition.

REFERENCES

Bennett, L. (1976). Sex and motherhood among Brahmins and Chhetris of East-Central Nepal. *Contributions to Nepalese Studies, 3*, 1-52.

Bennett, L. (1983). *Dangerous wives and sacred sisters: Social and symbolic roles of high-caste women in Nepal.* New York: Columbia University Press.

Das, V. (1979). Reflections on the social construction of adulthood. In S. Kakar (Ed.), *Identity and adulthood.* Oxford: Oxford University Press.

Holland, D., Cain, C., Prillaman, R., & Skinner, D. (In preparation). *Learning identities: The cultural formation of self.*

Holland, D., & Skinner, D. (1987). Prestige and intimacy: The cultural models behind Americans' talk about gender types. In D. Holland & N. Quinn (Eds.), *Cultural models in language and thought.* Cambridge: Cambridge University Press.

Holland, D., & Valsiner, J. (forthcoming). Cognition, symbols and Vygotsky's developmental psychology. *Ethos.*

Jakobson, D. (1975).Songs of social distance: Women's music in Central India. *Journal of South Asian literature, 11*, 45-59.

Jahoda, G. (1982). *Psychology and anthropology*. London: Academic Press.

Much, N., & Shweder, R. (1978). Speaking of rules: The analysis of culture in the breach. *New Directions for Child Development, 2,* 19-39.

Narayan, K. (1986). Birds on a branch: Girlfriends and wedding songs in Kangra.*Ethos, 14, 47-75.*

Rogoff, B. (1982). Integrating context and cognitive development. In M.E. Lamb & A.L. Brown (Eds.), *Advances in developmental psychology, v. 2*. Hillsdale, NJ: LEA.

Rogoff, B., & Lave, J. (1984). *Everyday cognition.* Cambridge: Cambridge University Press.

Schwartz, G., & Merton, D. (1968). Social identity and expressive symbols: The meaning of an initiation ritual. *American Anthropologist, 70,* 1117-1131.

Skinner, D. (in preparation). *Nepali children's understanding of themselves and their social world.* The University of North Carolina, Ph.D. dissertation.

Stone, L. (1978). Cultural repercussions of childlessness and low fertility in Nepal. *Contributions to Nepalese studies, 5,* 7-36.

Valsiner, J. (1987). *Culture and the development of children's action: A cultural-historical theory of developmental psychology.* Chichester: John Wiley & Sons.

Vygotsky, L. (1978). *Mind in society: The development of higher psychological functions.* Cambridge, MA: Harvard University Press.

Chapter 9

Socialization for Moral Reasoning

Maternal Strategies of Samoans and Europeans in New Zealand

Barbara Van Steenburgh Reid

INTRODUCTION

In this chapter, I look at the contextual usage of childrearing principles on the part of women of differing cultural backgrounds (Samoan immigrants and New Zealanders of European background) and demonstrate linkages between the cognitive domains of moral reasoning and parenting practices that presumably occur on the basis of higher level principles and values. These principles and values are applied to some extent to both of the above domains. Ultimately, I would contend that they are grounded in the social, political, and economic structures of a given society (see Peisner, this volume).

Embedded in cultural differences in the transmission of moral standards is the issue of gender. Gilligan's (1979, 1982) research on moral reasoning in the United States has demonstrated that there are important differences in how men and women approach moral dilemmas. Such differences are further related to socialization factors, such as those that Cho-

dorow (1974, 1978) describes, and to the underlying structures of a given society. These structures are based on such dimensions of social relations as the public versus domestic distinction proposed by Rosaldo (1974), and the modes of production described by Sacks (1979), as well as to gender constructs held on the cultural level of shared knowledge, as described by Ortner and Whitehead (1981) and by Sanday (1981). Political, economic, family and personal spheres are in part structured by gender constructs in all societies (Whitehead & Reid, forthcoming).

The chapter will begin by discussing relevant theories of parenting and moral reasoning, and provide some details of the historical and cultural background on the two ethnic groups that participated in the study: New Zealanders of either Samoan or European descent. It will then present the results of a research project in which data were obtained on the topics of moral reasoning and disciplinary techniques, including philosophies and goals held by parents. I will demonstrate the interconnections between societal structures, culturally appropriate standards of morality, and the socialization of children for moral reasoning by use of structural analysis and parents' statements.

THEORY

Two strands of anthropological theory are united in this endeavor. First, at the micro-societal level, it is important to look at the socialization of children within environmental or developmental niches (Harkness & Super, 1983; Reid & Valsiner, 1986; Valsiner, 1983), in order to have a more direct view of the process of the reproduction of moral standards. Second, at the macro-societal level, it is important to look both at structural differences within and between each of the two ethnic groups that relate to moral reasoning, including gender differences (Chodorow, 1974; Gilligan, 1979, 1982; Ortner, 1984; Sacks, 1979; Silverman, 1979).

It is a basic premise of this chapter that in their disciplinary activities, parents will communicate moral standards both directly and indirectly — that is, intentionally and unintentionally. This is borne out by work done by the author in collaboration with a developmental psychologist (Reid & Valsiner, 1986), in a study of American parents' theories. Here, it was found that parents believe that their disciplinary actions serve to teach their children right from wrong, and that such moral training is a conscious goal. Differences in severity of punishment convey moral statements about the relative rightness or wrongness of behavior, and contextual variation in disciplinary techniques conveys the parents' sense of what constitutes appropriate and inappropriate behavior in a variety of social settings.

At the level of individual social interaction, the child may be said to be socialized to a set of contexts or environments (Harkness & Super, 1983), which are culturally mediated "through providing meanings for different objects and events for humans, and by narrowing down the multitude of potential ways for acting in the environment to the ones about which members of the culture share some experience, superstitions or knowledge" (Valsiner, 1983, p. 6). Valsiner's paper is directly applicable to this investigation, as it allows us to account for the cultural differences seen in childrearing methods and philosophies by reference to differences in shared cultural knowledge. The socialization of the child for moral reasoning becomes a process by which contextual knowledge about appropriate behavior is channeled through the mediation of the cultural meanings that parents use to interpret each social context.

To ascertain what these cultural meanings are at the group level, I have adopted a cognitive-structural approach, which involves determining the cognitive contrasts that structure the moral domain for each group. To determine these contrasts I look at both the differences that hold true between the two sexes within each ethnic group, and at those that hold true between the two ethnic groups themselves. Such contrasts reveal the nature of the underlying social bases of moral orientations, and how the social structure connects with the moral domain.

This approach is inspired by a number of theoretical sources, including Gilligan (1979, 1982, 1986), Kohlberg (1981), Levi-Strauss (1967), Ortner (1984), Sacks (1979), and Shweder and Bourne (1984). Gilligan's research demonstrates the strength of using a method that contrasts the moral reasoning of women (her own subjects) with that of men (both her own subjects and those whom Kohlberg had previously found to exemplify a stage sequence of moral development). Looking at Gilligan's and Kohlberg's schemas simultaneously allows us to map a system of contrasting principles, or "binary oppositions," to use Levi-Strauss's terminology, which apply to American culture — at least as far as moral reasoning is concerned. Ortner has suggested that recent anthropological theory focuses on relations of structural inequality and difference. Of course, to obtain a more complete and adequate picture of the cognitive domain, it is also necessary to look at what principles men and women of a given culture share with regard to morality, and to further contrast these shared principles with those shared by both sexes of the other culture.

Gilligan's studies showed that American women think in terms of a cluster of interrelated principles when resolving moral dilemmas (such as whether a woman should have an abortion, or whether a man should steal a drug to save his dying wife). Chief among these principles are the attitudes of caring and feeling responsible for those close to oneself. Women try to think of realistic means for solving personal problems, which will be amenable to all concerned. By contrast, Gilligan found that, in general, American men think more in terms of rights and justice, with less emphasis on realistic solutions than on abstract problem solving such as would be appropriate for solving a mathematical or logical problem that requires no reference to broader social consequences. Women, on the other hand, are extremely attuned to just such consequences of their moral actions.

It should be noted that in her more recent work Gilligan (1986) has proposed that in the years of early adulthood members of each sex to some extent integrate into their moral repertoire some of the principles that are more predominant among the opposite sex in adolescence.

This theory is based, according to Gilligan, on Chodorow's neo-Freudian theory of socialization, the process of which is as follows: most children have as primary caretakers their mothers; the relationship of mothers to daughters differs however from that with their sons. Daughters maintain a connectedness to their mother emotionally, and are able to learn adult roles by direct observation of her daily activities; but boys must separate from her emotionally in order to attain their correct gender identity. They do so by a negative process of rejecting the feminine qualities that they see in their mothers, and attempting to suppress these qualities in themselves. Boys must also learn the adult male role in an abstracted manner, by imagining their fathers' daily work roles, as fathers are not present in the child's environment during the bulk of the waking hours, nor is childrearing a primary role of men in American society. As a result, girls develop a proclivity for attachment or connection, while boys develop an opposing tendency for separation. These are the major principles that come to structure the psyches of the two sexes, as a result of having been internalized during interpersonal contacts of infancy and early childhood.

Both Gilligan and Chodorow have questioned whether their theories would hold up for non-Western societies, where child care may take place in less isolated settings than in the American or European nuclear family home, and where sex role expectations and gender constructs familiar to Westerners may not completely apply.

Sacks' (1979) theory supports just such a cross-cultural distinction. According to Sacks, mode of production affects gender constructs. In certain non-Western cultures, such as traditional Samoan society, the mode of production could be termed "kin-corporate," in contrast to our own modern, industrialized type of production system. In many kin-corporate societies a distinction is made between two categories of women, sisters and wives, which results in a fundamentally different gender system from the one that prevails in the Euro-American situation, where the husband-wife relationship predominates. In kin corporate societies the brother-sister relationship serves as one fundamental structuring principle between the sexes, and is more important than it is in Western cultures.

The husband-wife relationship in modern Western societies entails an ideological separation of men's and women's activities into the spheres of the public and domestic respectively, as Rosaldo (1974) pointed out. However, in other sociocultural systems there may be differing underlying dimensions to male-female relationships, as I will demonstrate to be the case for traditional Samoan culture. Here, I would contend, there is less of an oppositional system based on public vs. domestic domains, than a complementary structuring based on the fundamental conceptual groupings of the sexes into the "village of men" and "village of women". Furthermore, the European system of opposing the individual against society yields here to the holistic concept of the unity of the individual with society. This conceptualization should, however, be viewed as obtaining at the theoretical and ideological levels, for Samoan women are dominated in many contexts by Samoan men, as would be true within the European system.

Samoan complementarity is based on another underlying distinction that has been proposed to obtain between Western and other societies: the sociocentric vs. egocentric difference in social orientation proposed by Shweder and Bourne (1984). Samoan culture can be considered sociocentric in orientation, and European culture egocentric. Sociocentric societies view the individual in relation to the group and see any action as situated within a web of interconnected relationships, while egocentric societies view the individual as an autonomous actor in relation to the social world. The group's well-being is the goal of a sociocentric society, while egocentric systems operate by individual advancement and personal gratification. As will be demonstrated by the data, this distinction has serious effects on how mothers socialize their children for moral reasoning.

The next section will provide some relevant background information on the histories and cultures of Samoans and Europeans in New Zealand. Such a background is necessary if we are to correctly interpret the cultural meanings involved in transmission of moral standards by parents of each ethnic group. In the final sections I will describe the study and its results and discuss the interconnections found between culture, parenting, and the transmission of moral values.

HISTORY

History of Samoa

The history of Western Samoa up to the mid-nineteenth century is known mainly from oral tradition, one excellent account of which is Brother Fred Henry's document (1979). The other major source of information on pre-European Samoa comes from archeological surveys. Based on such surveys, it is believed that Western Polynesia and Fiji were first peopled around 1300 B.C. by migrants of Asian ancestry (Bellwood, 1979). Davidson (1974, 1979) has found that by 2,000 years ago the foundations of the later settlement pattern were present. Among the archeological structures found are house platforms, star mounds, terraces, raised structures, and god houses.

Several historical benchmarks stand out during the last millenium. Legend has it that the Tongans invaded Samoa in A.D. 950 and occupied the land until their defeat and expulsion in 1250. In 1550 Queen Salamasina became one of the few individuals ever to attain control over the four most important "chiefly" titles, attaining the status of *Tafa'ifa*, a highly sought-after honor. John Williams arrived on his mission to Samoa for the London Missionary Society (LMS) in 1830, and between 1830 and 1870 Christianity became firmly established in Samoa. The LMS (also called the Congregational Christian Church) was quickly followed by the other present-day Christian denominations: the Methodists, Catholics, Mormons and Seventh Day Adventists. Today, virtually all Samoans belong to one or another of the Christian churches.

By 1870 there were three Western powers that were politically and economically active in the Samoan Islands: Germany, Great Britain, and the U.S.A. By 1900 their consuls had come to an impasse, and finally negotiated an agreement by which the island would be divided, with Western Samoa going to Germany and Eastern Samoa to the U.S.A. Great Britain withdrew in return for uncontested claim to colonize other areas (Field, 1984), Tonga being a principal acquisition. At the behest of Great Britain, New Zealand took over administration of Western Samoa from Germany at the beginning of World War I, and continued its control after the war under a League of Nations mandate. In 1962, Western Samoa, after years of agitation and petitioning, became the first nation in the Pacific to achieve decolonization and regain self-government.

Samoan immigration to New Zealand. Fairbairn (1961) has described the early trends in Samoan migration to New Zealand, which began during the late 1800s. In 1921 there were only 164 Western Samoan-born individuals residing in New Zealand; by 1956 there were almost 3,000. The major trend during the post-war period was a shift in the composition of those migrating away from those of mixed race (*afakasis*) toward full-blooded Samoans. More up-to-date figures on migration are given by Macpherson (1984) who reports census figures from 1956 to 1981. Currently, the population of Samoans in New Zealand is estimated to number about 55,000.

Traditional Samoan culture remains of great importance in New Zealand, but immigrant life varies from life in Samoa in a number of ways. First, the *matai* (chiefly) system has become primarily honorary, because matais lack the land-based power they would have in Samoa. New Zealand Samoans work exclusively in the wage labor economy, not under the direction of extended family matais. Second, given the diminished role of the matai system, the churches play a more prominent role in the immigrant community, serving as centers of Samoan culture and language, and are extremely active in maintaining the *fa'aSamoa* (Samoan way of life) as a viable cultural system (Pitt & Macpherson, 1974).

Different levels of commitment to Samoan tradition are important in what has by now become a diverse Samoan community (Ngan-Woo, 1985). Macpherson (1984) outlined three types of environments in which children of Samoan immigrants are socialized. These should be looked at as "ideal types," varying along a continuum of the degree to which a highly traditional Samoan way of life is encouraged or rejected. In one environment, parents deliberately promote Samoan values and institutions including the language, church and extended family. In the second type, they present Samoan and European values as alternatives, which can be used according to context. In the third case, they deliberately promote European values and institutions. This source of cultural variation could be assumed to have important implications for the socialization of Samoan children to moral reasoning.

History of Europeans in New Zealand

Although explorers Abel Tasman and James Cook had visited New Zealand in 1642 and 1769, respectively, it was not until the 1790s that regular visits by sealers, whalers, and traders commenced. Prior to that time the land was inhabited continuously only by the indigenous population of Maoris, who began to arrive in A.D. 800, traveling by voyaging canoes from other parts of Polynesia. Christian missionaries started to come in 1814, and from the 1830s onward permanent European settlement began. In 1840, to protect their growing economic interests in the region, the British government decided to annex New Zeland.

There were three major economic spheres to settler society: 1) a rural, farm-oriented sphere, 2) an urban, business-oriented sphere, and 3) a frontier society of gold fields and logging camps. As Houston (1970) points out, industrialization became prominent in New Zealand somewhat later than in Europe and North America, which he believes prevented the formation of a large, white, urban working class. When large-scale industrialization did come about it was concurrent with the movement of Maoris into the cities and the immigration of Samoans and other Pacific Islanders into the country, migrations encouraged by the New Zealand government to fill the increased need for manual labor. This has given rise to what sociologist Macpherson (1977) has called an eth-class situation, meaning that Polynesian ethnicity has become largely synonymous with working-class status, while the middle and upper classes are predominantly European.

Much of New Zealand law was codified during the Victorian era, and this influence continues to be felt to some extent. The early twentieth century was a time when the British population continued to grow and New Zealand found an identity as a rather isolated dominion of the British empire. But in more recent times New Zealand has found itself concerned with developing an independent identity, first due to the reduction of New Zealand imports by the British consequent to their membership in the European Common Market, and second, due to internal unrest centering on Maori rights and on New Zealand's relations with

South Africa. Most recently, New Zealand history appears to have entered a new phase that supports this independent identity, built largely around Labour Prime Minister David Lange's anti-nuclear policies. Lange's election in 1984 and re-election in 1987 attests to the popularity of the Nuclear Free Zone and other of his policies.

CULTURAL CONTRASTS

In this section I will outline and contrast the features of Samoan and European cultures most relevant to moral reasoning and socialization. The structural principles examined include: stratification systems, gender systems, modes of production, family types, religious beliefs and psychological orientations. The contrast between Samoan and European forms of these aspects of culture are shown in Table 1. The interrelationships between spheres of life based on these features is also discussed.

Samoan Culture

Anthropologists distinguish between three types of social stratification: 1) Egalitarian, usual for small scale hunter-gatherer societies that make minimal hierarchical distinctions between individuals; 2) Rank, usual for chiefdoms wherein subsistence is based on horticulture and domesticated animals, scale is at the permanent village level, and in which people attain social status vis-à-vis one another according to a complex system of ranking whereby each individual is placed on a scale from higher to lower according to relevant principles of ranking for the given group; and 3) Class, usual for large scale, urbanized societies, whose members produce food agriculturally and other products industrially, and in which differentials in wealth and pedigree place groups of people into strata having differential power vis-à-vis one another.

Samoan society is stratified by rank, while New Zealand society is class stratified (Bedggood, 1980; Ortner, 1981; Shore,

TABLE 1
CONTRASTIVE FEATURES OF SAMOAN AND EUROPEAN CULTURES

	Samoan	European
Stratification	Rank	Class
Gender System	Brother/sister Husband/wife	Husband/wife
Mode of Prod.	Kin-corporate	Industrial-capitalist
Religion	Authoritative Christianity	Nominal Christianity
Psychological Orientations	Sociocentric/ familistic	Egocentric/ individualistic

1982). This has serious implications for moral development and socialization because sources of authority, support, status, and esteem vary for these systems. In Samoan culture, rank is one of the primary organizing mechanisms motivating cultural processes, as the works of Samoan-born novelist Albert Wendt (1973, 1977, 1984) well testify. In this system of ranking, chiefs outrank non-chiefs, and in Samoa today 95% of chiefly titles are held by men; because some titles are imbued with higher status than others, some chiefs outrank others. Wives of chiefs, in a paralleling structure, outrank wives of non-chiefs; however, in the Samoan system, there is an additional status determiner of rank for women, and this lies in their role as sisters (Schoeffel, 1979). Sisters outrank brothers, so even chiefs are outranked, symbolically at least, by their sisters, older sisters being most highly esteemed. Sacks (1979) has hypothesized that this sisterly power is common for societies having kin-corporate modes of production, the Samoan version of which is described below. But as wives, Samoan women lose the purity which they embodied before marriage in the sisterly role and thereby have their sisterly rank diluted to some extent; wives are subordinate to husbands in the marital relationship (Shore, 1982). In a more practical sense, however, sisters retain certain powers over brothers, such as the power to curse them and their offspring, and the power of veto during consensus deliberation in the matter of succession to chiefly titles (Keesing & Keesing, 1956; Shore, 1982). The gender system therefore intersects with the ranking system to produce a situation in which for some contexts, marriage for example, men outrank women by virtue of the role, while in other contexts, sibling relation-

ship being primary, sisters outrank brothers. Age is also a relevant principle of ranking, and while today virtually all older men attain chiefly status, giving them an edge over older women, mothers would outrank both their brothers and also their offspring, including sons, providing another status vehicle for women.

In the economic sphere, Samoan society is still by and large operated in the kin-corporate mode, whereby extended families hold 80% of the land (non-saleable by law), which they farm as plantations. The work of men, which is for the most part the heavy agricultural work, is directed by chiefs, who do not do manual labor, while the work of women is directed by wives of chiefs and is most notable for the production of fine mats, a ceremonial item (Shore, 1981; Schoeffel, 1979). Women are also responsible for most domestic chores, directing children in these tasks. As Shore also pointed out, men's work is symbolically heavy and dirty, while women's work is symbolically light and clean. Although women's work is geographically or spatially more confined than that of men, being carried out in the household and village center while men have a larger geographic scope, taking in bush areas and deep sea fishing, women's work is of economic value and not merely decorative as Shore suggests, because prior to European contact and the introduction of a cash economy, and to some extent today also, wealth, prestige and value attach to the possession of family fine mats.

The gender system of Samoan culture is organized less on a domestic-public opposition, although this is recognized, than on the complementary and parallel structures of the "village of men" and "village of women," as described by Schoeffel:

Samoan villages were conceptually divided into a "village of ladies" (*nu'u o tama'ita'i*) and a "village of gentlemen" (*nu'u o ali'i*). This male-female division of village derived from the separate and complementary roles of sister and brother, rather than that of husband and wife. It was not based on public life opposed to domestic life, but rather on a division of moral and secular spheres of authority. Samoan women had two clearly defined and contrasting statuses. As sisters and co-descendants, they were entitled to independent status and rank from that of their husbands.

Sisters ranked higher than their brothers, but wives were subordinate to their husbands, and their husbands' sisters (p. 3).

A dichotomous organization of gender, based on this conceptual distinction, is still in operation in Samoan culture today. Each village is divided into women's and men's organizations. For men, the Council of Chiefs controls the work of males; untitled men belong to the *'aumaga,* who do the work assigned by chiefs as based on the concept of *tautua,* or service. The chiefs' council (*fono*) enacts and enforces village regulations (Shore, 1982). Schoeffel (1979) points out, however, that since European contact and the Christian emphasis on monogamous marriage which has strengthened the husband-wife relationship, and the introduction of a cash economy into Samoa, there has been an additional element of ideology that recognizes European gender contrasts, so that in a recent Samoan census the vast majority of women stated that they considered themselves to be "housewives," even though they continued to fulfill economically valuable roles within their villages.

In both economic and political spheres of life the extended family remains the family form that structures kinship in Samoa. As mentioned, families elect matai by consensus, and so each family is represented politically at the village level; work is also organized by the family unit, as matai supervise the work of men, while their wives supervise the work of women. In modern times, one change that has affected the work of women is the expanded education system. School may take up the time that children would previously have spent helping their mothers with domestic work and caring for younger siblings, which increases the amount of domestic work that must be done by the women themselves (Thomas & Simi, 1983). Nardi (1983), however, reports that children still do a considerable amount of work after school hours. In a study done on the Polynesian island of Niue, Frankovich (1974) found that even very young children assumed caretaking roles, and that a great deal of independent activity was the norm for children.

Although a raging controversy has been generated around whether Samoan parents treat their children gently or harshly (Freeman, 1983; Mead, 1961), it is agreed by most observers that the values of obedience and respect for elders serve to structure Samoan childrearing practices (Gerber, 1975). This emphasis on obedience is in keeping with a pattern of childrearing that LeVine (1974) has described as correlated with societies that rely heavily on the work of children. But it is probably also related to the acceptance of Christian teachings in a sometimes rather literal sense, and the enjoinments of the Bible to "honor thy mother and father," and to teach children moral standards at a young age, both of which are followed by most Samoan parents.

The religious sphere, however, is separated from the political, as pastors generally do not hold matai titles, and therefore may not attain power in two spheres. As 99% of Samoans profess the Christian religion, and as most attend services regularly, the word of the clergy becomes an important source of moral authority. Here again, men attain power that women cannot hold, as all pastors in Samoa are male. (In New Zealand, however, at least one Samoan woman has received a clergical post and degree.)

The psychological orientations of Samoans that are most relevant to moral thought are the predominantly sociocentric and familistic frames of reference. The former has been identified by Shweder and Bourne for non-Western societies where relationships between societal members are the predominant focus psychologically, and the webs of networks among society's members are considered when moral decisions are made. Samoan culture, however, could also be termed familistic, since one's primary unit of loyalty is ultimately the extended family unit, although some Samoan families in New Zealand have a more nuclear family focus. This and other elements of Samoan culture offer sharp contrast to the European culture in New Zealand, as will be shown below.

Samoans in New Zealand of course maintain a traditional outlook only to a greater or lesser extent depending on the individual involved; however, these facets of Samoan culture do serve to structure the moral thought of informants in the study reported to some extent, as all informants were born and most of them raised in the Western Samoan context.

European Culture in New Zealand

New Zealand society is stratified into social classes along the lines of other Euro-American cultures. There is some debate as to whether New Zealand is becoming increasingly class-differentiated or whether it has in fact been well class structured from its inception (Bedggood, 1980), but it is generally agreed that there is visible class distinction in New Zealand today. How does class society differ from rank society? In class societies there is a larger wealth discrepancy between societal members, some of whom are occupationally, educationally, and financially identified as upper class, middle class, or working class (lower class) individuals. In New Zealand, however, the actuality of class has been hidden to some extent by an ideology of egalitarianism dating to its pioneer beginnings (as far as Europeans are concerned, that is). Unlike rank society, each family unit is not represented in the political power structure (a democratically elected, universal suffrage system), nor does each family unit hold in common possession some piece of the aristocratic status in the form of a title, such as Samoans possess through the matai system. Additionally, this industrial mode of production also has implications for gender, as there is in class societies no distinction symbolically in the ranking of sisters versus wives. While there is some tendency for men to "marry down" in class societies, and for women to "marry up," class itself and the power positions in society going along with it are actually the major determinants of status. Therefore a situation arises in which the disadvantages to women are not mitigated by additional status sources such as kinship and age. Men simply dominate women, except where class intervenes. The hierarchical situation produced is one in which men of every class are considered superior to women of the same class, but in which women of the upper classes attain superiority over men of lower classes. Age is not highly relevant in the scheme of things; however, in New Zealand there is a tendency to devalue those individuals in the older age categories, both male and female.

This is in turn related to a family system that is nuclear rather than extended, and an economic system that is industrial capitalist rather than kin-corporate, and to a political system that does not give political power to elder members of families. The power of the older members of society over the younger is downgraded in such a system.

James (1982) and Houston (1970) have both commented on the extreme nuclearity of the New Zealand family, which they trace to the pioneer history of the country. But as James notes, the differences between the cultures are lessening somewhat as more and more New Zealand Europeans are native born, producing increasing numbers of three-generation families, and as Polynesians in New Zealand become more urbanized, producing more nuclear family situations and experiences with a wage economy. The difference between the Samoan and the European family types that is important here is the strong emphasis of the former on brother-sister relationships, and of the latter on husband-wife relationships.

In the economic sphere, the nuclear family is the unit of consumption for Europeans. Under industrial-capitalism, the male frequently assumes the "breadwinner" role while the female is the "homemaker." In both Samoan and European societies the children are primarily reared by women. However, Samoan extended families allow for care of children by close relatives — even siblings are caretakers for younger children — while the European system dictates that the role of biological mother includes practically exclusive responsibility for all childrearing activities. Here again, the European system is undergoing change. At one time, the most popular program for preschool children was the Playcentre, in which each mother was required to stay at each session with her own child, but this program is losing out in preference for the kindergarten programs, where mothers may leave children with a professional staff for a few hours each day.

Childrearing in New Zealand has been comprehensively studied by James and Jane Ritchie (1970, 1978, 1981). In their most recent work on the subject entitled *Spare the Rod* the Ritchies contend, based on their research with parents of young children, that European parents inculcate violence in their children — and ultimately in society — through the use of excessive physical punishment, a practice deriving from religiosity and the desire for social conformity. This form of punishment is further legitimated by the use of strapping as a disciplinary measure in schools. The Ritchies' earlier studies revealed that Polynesians used physical punishment to an even greater extent than did Europeans. In later studies, however, it was found that the percentage of European mothers never using physical punishment increased from 1 to 10 per cent, but 55% used such punishment weekly or even more frequently, up from 35% found 15 years earlier.

Among Polynesians in New Zealand, the folk wisdom on the matter of corporal punishment is that traditional Samoan childrearing is oriented toward obedience enforced by physical punishment. Ngan-woo (1985) proposed that in the New Zealand context some Samoan parents have adopted less physically punitive disciplinary methods, which are viewed as a shift to a European pattern. Informants interviewed for this study seemed to conform to a belief in this folk theory of ethnicity and childrearing. European informants did not profess a belief in severe punishment to the extent that the Ritchies have suggested, but it remains to be determined whether this is due to regional differences in the samples (Wellington vs. Auckland), culture change, or differences in research methods. Likewise, Samoan parents were less punitive than might be expected based on their own ideology.

Another major difference in economics and gender has to do with the structuring of the workplace. When European women do work for wages, their work is almost certainly directed by male supervisors and executives, as no paralleling structure exists for them such as Samoans have instituted in the form of the "village of women." Of course, the same situation would hold true for Samoan women working in the wage sector in New Zealand, as the matai system does not extend to this context.

This leads to another interconnected distinction in terms of psychological orientations. Based on the nuclear family and individual advancement, the European population is oriented egocentrically and individualistically rather than sociocentrically and familistically. An interesting parallel to Chodorow's American work has been found in research done by Barrington and Gray (1981) and Gray (1983) in their interviews with New Zealand women and men entitled *The Smith Women* and *The Jones Men,* respectively. These studies revealed a connectedness in women's psyches by which they focused their attention on their roles as

mothers and integrated other aspects of their lives such as marriage, extended family, community, and other commitments around this central focus, while men exemplified a type of disconnectedness, seeing the various roles of their lives as separated and unintegrated from one another, frequently unable to present their lives as one coherent whole. Bell's (1985) survey of New Zealand women was interesting in that she found that many respondents felt that the women's movement there had improved the lot of women as a group, but that their own lives had not substantially changed in the process.

Religion in New Zealand is also less important as a factor in moral reasoning for Europeans than it would be to Samoans, and secular morality assumes a higher importance: the source of moral decision-making resides in each individual, rather than in the extended family or community, to whom Samoans might seek recourse when contemplating a moral decision. European New Zealanders do have Christian morality ingrained in their moral thought, but this is often on a seemingly unconscious level, while Samoans are quite explicit in their belief in and reliance on such principles.

THE EMPIRICAL INVESTIGATION

Background

Field work was carried out in urban Auckland, New Zealand, from December 1984 through January 1986. During this time period informants were interviewed on two separate topics, moral reasoning and parenting. (The questionnaires used are presented in Appendices A and B, respectively.) The goals of these studies were first, to examine parenting strategies, theories and philosophies and compare them to previous research (Reid & Valsiner, 1986), and second, to carry out a cultural analysis of moral orientations related to gender and ethnicity.

Sample

For the moral reasoning component of the study there were 155 informants (Samoans N=82, Europeans N=73), and for the childrearing component there were 86 (Samoans N=32, Europeans N=52, Other N=2). The sample described here, for the purposes of interconnecting the two domains, consists of a smaller subunit (N=18) comprising those women who answered both questionnaires (Samoan N=9, European N=9).

When deciding whom to contact for these interviews, several factors were taken into consideration. First, in order to balance the sample, interviews were conducted in several different suburbs of Auckland chosen to provide socioeconomic variability. Second, there was an attempt to obtain religious variability, deemed especially important for the Samoan sample where religion is such an important element in moral reasoning.

Procedure

Interviews were carried out in two sessions, one for each questionnaire. These interviews were done in a variety of settings; in homes, kindergartens, playcentres and workplaces. Some parents were interviewed in more than one setting. The Europeans and some of the Samoans were interviewed by the pres-

ent author alone, while other interviews included a Samoan research assistant. If they so wished, Samoans were interviewed in their own language with the help of interpreters. All interviews were tape-recorded, and where possible informants read the questions from typed cards (the Samoan-language interviewees were all asked the questions verbally).

Analysis

The answers to each question were coded according to the categories that were most used by informants. A structural analysis was carried out to provide contrasts based on gender and ethnicity, and to reveal the underlying dimensions that structure moral domains for each ethnic group. Parenting questions were qualitatively analyzed in order to assess how moral principles translated to the parenting domain. Contextual analysis of answers revealed important sociocultural differences. The results of these analytic techniques are reported below.

Results

Moral reasoning results are presented first, then parenting techniques are analyzed and related to the cultural factors that emerged from the moral reasoning data. Tables 2 and 3 depict gender differences within the Samoan and European cultures respectively (based on the entire moral reasoning sample); Table 4 gives the group level cultural differences found to be most important in contrasting Samoan and European moral thought; and Table 5 shows the categories frequently used by members of both groups.

Looking at Tables 2 and 3, it can be

TABLE 2 CONTRASTIVE CATEGORIES OF MORAL REASONING OF SAMOAN MEN & WOMEN	
Men	**Women**
Connection	Relationship
Survival	Fear
Principles	Fairness, justice
Life goals	Intentions

TABLE 3 CONTRASTIVE CATEGORIES OF MORAL REASONING OF EUROPEAN MEN & WOMEN	
Men	**Women**
Fairness,	Family
justice	Personal
	Fear
	Respect
	Authority
	Public vs. private

seen that the most salient result of the moral reasoning research with regard to gender is that the contrasts between the sexes differ for Samoans and Europeans. For the former, the dimensions of contrast between men's and women's answers is not based on opposition, but on a relationship of a subset of a category to to the category as a whole, for example the category "principles" used by Samoan men is a more general level category than that of "fairness and justice" used by Samoan women, which exemplifies two specific types of principles.

Similarly, "fear," used by Samoan women, is a rather pervasive type of emotion that could be transferred across contexts, while "survival," used by Samoan men, is but one type of situation that might engender fear. Therefore, it seems that for some situations the male sphere encompasses the female, while the reverse is true for others. What seems emphatically the case, however, is that the male-female difference for Samoans does not have a built-in reference to a distinction between public vs. domestic domains, such as is found for the European group. The European sample answers moral dilemmas in a manner much closer to that which Gilligan found to be true for Americans: the male concern for fairness and justice is one that is consid-

ered appropriate to the public sphere, while the female concentration on family and personal concerns is more suited to the domestic sphere. In fact, the Samoan sample directly reverses Gilligan's male and female orientations, as Samoan men emphasize connection, while Samoan women emphasize fairness and justice, shown in Table 3. Only the category of fear is shared by women of both ethnic groups, in contrast to the moral reasoning of men of their own ethnicity, probably due to the greater physical vulnerability of women in both societies.

Turning to Table 4, there are numerous elements of contrast between the two cultural groups, perhaps the most important of which is the emphasis by Samoans of both sexes on religious principles as applied to moral dilemmas, in contrast to the European emphasis on secularity when solving moral dilemmas. Going along with this distinction are Samoan emphases on guilt, blame, and authority, contrasted with European regard for individual choice and freedom. Europeans placed greater worth on individual rights, while Samoans were more interested in hierarchy, as descriptions of the authority structures of these two societies might lead us to predict. In those cases where Samoans chose to step outside of their traditions, they often prefaced their statements with the comment "in my personal opinion."

Overall, the preferred Samoan categories reflect the sociocentric outlook of Samoan culture, while the European answers reflect an egocentric outlook. Religion is practiced as a group effort, while secular morality is more individualistic. Other preferred categories for Samoans including authority, hierarchy, and government are group-oriented principles, while Europeans used such individually oriented categories as principles, individual choice, freedom and rights, categories that also reflect the ideology of a supposedly egalitarian democracy.

Samoans do use individual level categories, but not the ones utilized by Europeans, preferring instead to speak about personal feelings, values and beliefs, intentions, guilt, and blame. The European group level principles also differ from those used by Samoans, and relate to

exploitation, balance of claims, violence, and communication. These differences in cultural use of categories signify culturally approved or disapproved themes of discourse with regard to morality. For example, although several moral dilemmas dealt with incidences of violence or possible violence, this was not a congenial area for discussion for most Samoans; but Europeans often gave elaborate descriptions of violent situations in their answers.

Table 5 presents those categories that informants of both genders and both cultural groups used to a great degree, and which could be said to be shared as primary concerns by all.

What is important here is how these principles are translated in terms of parental disciplinary techniques and philosophies. In order to demonstrate this clearly, I will concentrate on the interviews of four women, two Samoan and two European, whose moral reasoning interviews represented the sample of their group as a whole. First I will compare several answers given by these women on moral dilemmas, and analyze them in terms of the categories used, and then I will provide a comparative look at how these mothers approached disciplinary situations. Finally, I will provide a discussion of how the two domains are inter-

TABLE 4
CONTRASTIVE CATEGORIES
OF MORAL REASONING
OF SAMOANS AND EUROPEANS

Samoans	Europeans
Religion	Secular morality
Authority	Age factors
Hierarchy	Individual choice and freedom
Government	Rights
Values and beliefs	Principles
Personal	Communication
Guilt and blame	Exploitation
	Violence
	Balance of claims

TABLE 5
CATEGORIES OF MORAL REASONING
USED BY BOTH
SAMOANS AND EUROPEANS

Care
Consequences
Context
Separation
Economic factors

linked and how cultural differences affect different socialization methods, as the child is socialized according to the moral standards of the culture.

In-depth analysis of four informants' statements on morality and parenting will illustrate the cultural bases of both domains. Anthropology, unlike psychology, deals with culture as a group level phenomenon. These four informants were chosen because they exemplify well the most frequently used justifications or rationales of their ethnic group. Interestingly, these women gave responses on their parenting interviews that were highly congruent with their moral reasoning statements. The entire range of diversity within each cultural group is not shown by this particular analysis, however.

All four informants were in the 30- to 40-year-old range. Both Samoans were Samoan-born and both Europeans New Zealand-born. All were married and their husbands were employed in professional level occupations. One Samoan (#118) and one European (#62) had received post-high school education, and both of these women were employed part-time and were mothers of girls. The other Samoan (#81) and other European (#47) were both high school graduates, both were housewives at the time of the interview, and both were mothers of boys. All of the women were employed full-time before and/or after marriage.

Turning now to the data, the informants' moral statements will first be given and analyzed followed by a discussion of parenting techniques and of the interconnections between the two domains and their cultural bases.

The first statements relate to a question about a situation in which a 19-year-old university student becomes pregnant and considers having an abortion.

Samoans

Informant #81: Doesn't she have any family in New Zealand to help her? INT: I never really thought about that. 81: It's very difficult for me to answer that. As a minister's wife it's very difficult for me to answer that question about having an abortion. I'd rather have the baby. It's the life that God gives. It's like a gift and it's bad. INT: So you think it's bad for her to do that? 81: What if we put it on the one side that she has got some relations here, or we put it on the other side that she doesn't have any relations here. That she's on by her own. If she's on by her own, and she's sick, then that's up to her. It's up to what the person feels.

Informant #118: It's a good question and a hard one too. But I think in this case, as far as I know, I disagree with taking an abortion. INT: Why? For religious reasons? 118: It's not only religious reasons, but I've learned and I've read a lot about this. There's always a feeling that when you took abortion you have that feeling that you are not doing the right thing. It's not the actual feeling, but personally you are still feeling that there is something wrong in your life. That you shouldn't do whatever has been done. And you won't be happy then. It's just the same as the sound is still ringing in your ears or in your heart. That you lost somebody or that something is wrong. If you give birth to that child she or he will become a great assistance to you in the future. And then you learn from that. It's not good to have an abortion.

Europeans

Informant #47: Well, I personally wouldn't have an abortion because I would rather go through it and adopt the child, but for somebody else, in fact I have a friend of mine some years ago, she found she was pregnant, and this girlfriend — I advised her to have an abortion. For the simple reason that this girl wants to finish her studies, and she doesn't want to marry, which I think is fair enough. Sometimes if they marry because of the baby, like they used to do in the old times, that is just not — if you are resenting that child the whole time, I sometimes think it does have some effect on the child when it's born. You know it's very difficult. She's got her own soul-searching, and she has to live with her conscience. If she had it, she's got to live with that all her life, and likewise a person who actually has a child and has it adopted out. They've got to live with that as well. You know, I think if you feel you're making somebody else happy — there's people to adopt the child.

Informant #62: Oh, for sure, for sure. INT: Why is that? 62: Well, because she's selfish at the moment which I think is a normal thing. She's number one, and I think she's at the hub of her career and if she has a child now she will hold it against the child forever and I think it's wrong. Because the baby gets a bad start. And I think that's wrong. That's a bit cruel. I don't really get off with abortion, but I think she can go ahead and have the child and have it adopted out, and then go ahead and do her final year later, but as she's thinking along the lines of abortion and talking out the rights and wrongs, I think she must think it's okay, anyway. You know. Otherwise if you don't agree with abortion you don't even contemplate it. You just go straight for adoption and then change your course. So she's contemplated it, therefore she agrees with it. Personally, I would not have an abortion because I think you've been irresponsible enough to get pregnant, you know, so you deal with it in a more responsible manner. I would feel cruel that I had the privilege to conceive and that I was able to conceive a child and there are millions of people I know who can't have them. I think that would just be my subtle way of showing some form of responsibility.

These statements clearly reveal two facets of the differences between the moral standards of Europeans and Samoans. First, differences in categorical usage, such as those shown in Tables 2 through 4, are quite clearly in evidence. But perhaps more importantly, the underlying basis for the differences between the two groups' moral reasoning seems to lie in the difference between a sociocentric focus versus an egocentric one. The similarities, of course, center on feelings or emotions as the determinant of choice rather than the abstract logic which men often apply to this situation, which is necessarily outside their own personal life experience.

In answer to this moral question, one Samoan, #81, mentions both religion and the sociocentric principle that the decision is only up to the young woman if she is without family support. The other Samoan, #118, first mentions the personal feeling of guilt that she believes accompanies abortion, but ends with a statement that is highly sociocentric, that the child will be helpful to the mother in the future. Turning to the Europeans, a sharp contrast can be seen. Both informants see abortion as a more viable possibility, although both also qualify this with a statement that they personally would not take this course of action. Neither mentions religion, concentrating instead on secular moral standards. The egocentric nature of European thinking is well stated by Informant #62, who mentions the legitimacy of the student's "selfishness," and goes on to say that if the student feels abortion is possible, then by her own standards of morality it must be an option she could live with. The individual's choice is seen as more important than a standard societal norm. But the Europeans' answers are not entirely egocentric, as these informants state a personal preference for an adoption solution, considering the feelings of childless members of society. In balance however, their point of view is more individualistic because they take the right of the woman to decide on an individualistic basis as a given. Here it should be pointed out that dualistic characterizations of cultures in regard to psychological orientations cannot be supported if such dualisms or oppositions are considered mutually exclusive. In fact, both Samoan and European cultures include sociocentric and egocentric thought, but it is the emphasis on one or the other as a predominating cultural theme or value that is referred to here.

The second moral dilemma to be discussed involves a situation where a young man who doesn't get along with his boss must decide whether to leave his present job for one with a better working relationship but lower pay.

Samoans

Informant #81: It's hard to work in a job when you don't get along with your boss. But the other job offers him less, but he will have a good relationship with the others. I think that would be the best thing. To have a good relationship. INT: So he should change? 81: Yeah, he should, before he fights with the boss and gets into trouble. More trouble than before. I think that would be all right.

Informant #118: As I learned, that whatever you've done if your heart doesn't feel happy about it everything will be awful to you. But happiness is a good medicine. You can earn a lot of money, but if you don't feel happy, that's not good for you. On the other side, if he changes his job he can come to this situation again, where he doesn't get along, and then what will he do? But there are some other ways that he can solve the problem before he changes his job. He can talk to that person whom he doesn't like, or the relationship isn't too good, and then I think that it will solve the problem. Afterwards he can have the same job and the same amount and then he will feel happy too.

Europeans

Informant #47: Yes. I would take less pay with better work relationships because if you are not happy in your job as time goes on mentally I think it breaks you down. And if you're in the environment, it comes home to your home, and if you're not happy in your work, you're not happy in your home, so it kind of snowballs. And I think it affects your family, your life, your children. He is a young man, it doesn't say if he's got children. But you know, you become bitter and twisted if you're not happy in your job. To me that's a step forward. No, I think it's better to take less pay because there's no reason why given time, if you work well, that you can't better yourself and get on better. If you're not happy in your job it's just terrible.

Informant #62: No, I think change your job. Money's not everything. I mean we've done that. We did that when my husband left a higher paying job in Australia and came back to much lower salary. And that's why we did it. Because the guy that he worked for thought he owned my husband's brain and thought that my husband's brain was on tap 24 hours a day. And we felt it was really cruel in the end. It was just draining us. We were quite happy to come home to half the amount of money and to have the freedom. You know, it's happiness if you can go home from work and be relaxed in preference to being tense and grumpy.

The second dilemma, taking place in the work environment, also elicits a sociocentric/egocentric distinction. Both Samoan informants focus on the relationship between the employer and the worker, as much as on the personal happiness of the individual, although informant #118 notes that mending the relationship may be the best way for the young man to attain happiness. Both Europeans are more concerned with the personal satisfaction of the individual and his family than with the work relationship. Put another way, the European women are more focused on the way a man's work situation affects his home life, as this is their own major sphere of activity.

The final moral dilemma that I will use to illustrate cultural differences is a societal level dilemma dealing with the proposed passage through the New Zealand Parliament of a bill that would legalize male homosexuality (which, incidentally, was passed in the summer of 1986).

Samoans

Informant #81: No, don't do it. I don't want to see that homosexual law passed. INT: Why? 81: They should stop it because it's not very religious. INT: For religious reasons it shouldn't be allowed? 81: Yeah.

Informant #118: I disapprove of it. INT: Why? 118: If you think about our children, we don't want our kids to be involved in this type of thing. This kind of life. And if we say yes, then we can't get out of it. Especially our children also. But if we take the law, then that will protect us from being involved in it. INT: Is that based on religious reasons? 118: Not only on religion, but the way of living . . . . We've got no right to say no to the punishment or whatever the law has been given to everyone, that's it.

Europeans

Informant #47: I think the law should be passed, that yes, they can, but at the moment the age is 16. I don't agree with 16, I think it should be 18. That's the age where they can virtually come and go as they please, so I think if it's good for a female to get married at age 18, I think it would be justified if a male wants to too. I think it should become law, because it has been going on, behind closed doors. I don't think it's going to make any difference to me personally, but for the people who are bisexual and are still living in a married life — I think it just takes away the actual fear that if they are caught their names are going to be dragged through court . . . . They're human beings, and they do work normal jobs, lawyers, accountants, doctors, if they want to do it why discriminate. And I think you will find the ones, that if they are caught playing with little boys, but what is the difference between a man playing with a little boy and a father playing with his daughter? It's hard to prove it. A lot of mothers don't want to drag it through the court. It's dreadful really. It's certainly been a big issue. A lot of people are against it. But they have their rights.

Informant #62: Well, I really think there's nothing wrong with homosexuality. And I think to legalize it, well it's really normal. I don't think that homosexuality is abnormal, so I think why should they have to hide behind closed doors if they want to walk down the street holding hands, I think fine, go ahead. I think the age is important, and I think age should be higher up than 16. I think that you can easily convince a boy at that age that it's okay, and he may not be ready for it. I think it might given them a chance to see if they're heterosexual first, before they start being bonded into a homosexual relationship. You now, just simply by ignorance and naiveté. So I think that maybe 18 to 20 is a possibility. Eighteen would be the minimum, but 20 would be better probably, because you don't find out overnight you're homosexual. I mean how many females do you have to take out before you decide you don't like them. You know. I also think it would contain AIDS much better too if it was legalized. INT: Because? 62: Because a man that's married isn't going to divorce when it's easier to have the cover of a marriage. And then this guy is making love to his wife plus his boyfriend; I mean who the hell's he spreading it onto? It's definitely being passed around like that, and I think if it comes out into the open people are much more free to speak.

This third issue also demonstrates cultural differences between these two pairs of women. Samoan informant #81 simply states a very common Samoan answer to this question: that it's wrong for religious reasons. Notice that in informant #118's statement, although she seems to be stating a personal opinion, she speaks "we" not wanting this for "our" children, apparently voicing what she takes to be an answer acceptable to "we Samoans." The European women, once again, take a more individualistic approach. #47 notes that while many other Europeans oppose the bill, she is in favor of it, but cites one of the predominating European categories — an age consideration — in stating her one objection. She ends by stating that the rights of homosexuals are important, and that she feels their influence on society as a whole, or on children, is not necessarily more negative than that of heterosexual men. The other European echoes this concern about the age question and also cites the openness of the practice of homosexuality as preferable to having it concealed. This would differ from a Samoan point of view, according to which matters of sexuality, including

both abortion and homosexuality, would be secretive activities when they do occur. She's also concerned about the spread of disease as a result of the necessity to conceal homosexuality. Unlike the Samoans, she deals with the issue in the terminology of Western psychology, stating that she doesn't believe that homosexuality is "abnormal." Samoans who raise this issue usually relate the "abnormality" of homosexuality to religious principles, saying that God made man and woman to be together and produce a family. They show less concern with individual abnormality than with a group standard of morality.

While the sociocentric/egocentric contrast appears to be well demonstrated by these examples, and generalized by both ethnic groups across contexts (being used to some extent on personal, work-related, and socio-political issues), the major concern of this chapter is to look at how moral standards may be generalized to the domain of parenting. The following statements should illustrate that just such a generalization does take place.

The first disciplinary problem to be discussed is a situation in which one child has hit another in the process of trying to retrieve a toy snatched by the second child in a playgroup setting.

Samoans

Informant #81: No, I would tell my child go to give that toy to the other child yourself and be a nice boy. Just give him a pat on the back.

Informant #118: Tell him to take it back to the child who is the owner of this and I would talk to the parents too, to apologize. I taught him not to hit.

Europeans

Informant #47: I'd say "you don't snatch, and you don't hit." You say "please can I have my toy back." I don't think I would say anything to the other parent.

Informant #62: Stop the situation. Whoever got it first deserves it. Both children are at fault. The person who is playing with it is to continue with it.

Here the cultural contrasts are apparent again. The Samoan women, concerned with maintaining good relationships with others, a reflection of the sociocentric point of view, encourage the child to return the toy to the other child. The Europeans, on the other hand, taking an egocentric point of view, encourage the child to determine ownership of the toy; one mother by teaching her child how to get the toy back, the other by invoking a rule applying to its ownership. In the second situation, it can be seen that Informant #62 also tries to rely on rules to resolve the problem.

The second situation takes place in a supermarket, where a child has staged a temper tantrum in response to being refused a requested purchase.

Samoans

Informant #81: Calm him down. I wouldn't buy it. It might spoil him.

Informant #118: I always took my little kid to the shops and when she wants something she just touches it. When she wants it and I can't afford to buy it for her I always explain why I can't buy that toy or whatever that time. And when she understands she'll say "Okay mom, try next time."

Europeans

Informant #47: Well, I must admit I have given my son a hiding. I just make him sit there and try to get through what I have to and if not I leave until we're both in a better frame of mind, then finish my shopping. I don't give in to him. That's it.

Informant #62: If you're going to make a rule you've got to stick to it. So if I said no, the child couldn't have the item, I'd remove my child from the situation; go out until the child's calmed down and then come back, or else just ignore it and carry on. I mean you've got to go every week.

Here again, the Samoans attempt to resolve the problem through interaction with the child, preserving their social relationship focus and maintaining a high degree of connection, while the Europeans take somewhat more drastic measures; use of physical force or removing the child from the situation, measures that the Samoans seem to feel they would not need to resort to in this situation.

The final situation involves the misbehavior of a child at home. While visitors are present, the child comes into the room and picks up a valuable object, which the mother takes away, upon which the child hits her.

Samoans

Informant #81: It's difficult because the Samoan way is to hit back, but under the circumstances I would make him sit down next to me and just stay there. Otherwise he might do something worse and I would be embarrassed.

Informant #118: It's natural; when you talk to each other the kids run and ask you a question. I always excuse myself from who is talking to me and try to attend to the child and explain, and then she'll understand and be happy and stop doing it. She'll say "I'm sorry." I don't want them to be ashamed.

Europeans

Informant #47: Pick him up and put him straight into his room. Usually once he's finished crying he'll come back out and his tone of voice drops down and he'll say "I've finished" and it doesn't always work out, but we have to learn to respect other people's things. Yesterday he picked that up and it's not very valuable but I smacked his fingers. We don't go to other people's homes and pick things up. If you don't teach them at home how can they know when they go out.

Informant #62: She'll do things solely to get my attention. I'll stop my conversation and then she'll be off to something else. I'll go "Oh you revolting child." I'd explain and she'd probably storm off on her feet.

Once again, the Samoans show an orientation toward social relationships, preferring not to embarrass the child in front of visitors, and also maintain connectedness, which the Europeans do not attempt. In particular, Informant #47 sends her son to his room, and she shows the egocentrically oriented concern over people's property, rather than with the relationship between people itself. Informant #62 doesn't consider the embarrassment to her daughter that might result from calling her a "revolting child." Informant #81 shows the same concern over the escalation of the problem that she stated in her answer to an earlier moral dilemma, involving an employee who didn't get along with his boss.

The final section on parenting consists of excerpts from philosophic statements. In their statements about general methods and philosophies about parenting, the informants provided interesting contrasts that seem to be statements of two different types of parenting styles within each ethnic group. The following statements are condensed from the philosophy section of each parent's questionnaire.

Samoans

Informant #81: I don't use any praise or rewards. INT: Why not? 81: I don't want to praise them because that might spoil them. My mother praised me. So to encourage them more to learn the Bible, that's all we can do. If you know anything is wrong, or they're going to do this and it's wrong, then tell them not to do that. That would be all right.

Informant #118: First of all, they must grow up to be obedient. If you want your child to be good, as I've learned, you always praise them. Because you can't afford to give them all the rewards every time. But in general, you must praise them, talk nicely to them, because I'm not working and I'm a mother at home, and I always try to do something that is natural and easy for the future. Being a good parent is not easy, because the kids learn from the parents what they're going to do in the future, when they grow up. Being a good parent is you make yourself good, and not to talk or shout or do something that would frighten the kids at home. But behave yourself if you want them to be good too. Because what you give to them, that's what they'll give to you in the future.

Europeans

Informant #47: Sometimes you can go on and on and you can raise your voice and the child will still keep on. So sometimes a quick smack on the bottom will just stop them from what they're doing. I suppose I look back on families that I feel have been successful at bringing up their own children. You bring your children up to be acceptable to other people, to make them acceptable to other people in society. There are times when you take them out and you want them to be good, but you can't expect them to be perfect 100% of the time.

Informant #62: I just want her to be able to decide for herself what's right and what's wrong. I was told what was right and what was wrong. I didn't know the difference . . I just like it to flow, you know. I prefer just to be there, but let them develop at their own pace. And so we've just given them what we think is discipline to a point and then just let them have a lot of freedom. And we have a very strong belief in our house that if something's really bugging the kids, just take them away from it, just divert them.

The consistency between individuals' styles of moral reasoning and their parenting strategies are evident when parenting statements are compared with the moral responses. This is true both for individuals, and at the group level where informants transfer principles that are drawn from the culture and important to themselves, from one domain to the other. And the parenting methods also reflect the sociocentric/egocentric distinction, probably to a greater degree than can be seen in the philosophy statements themselves.

Here certain themes do stand out. One Samoan expresses an orientation toward religion in her parenting philosophy, while the other thinks in terms of the traditional Samoan concern over obedience. The Europeans, on the other hand, express a different set of concerns. One woman has a quite individualistic orientation, suitable to a society centered on secular morality, which is the goal of having the

child decide for herself what's right and what's wrong. The other woman, much stricter in her methods and orientation, wants her child to be acceptable to society, but rather than teaching religion or obedience she models herself after others whom she thinks of as successful parents.

These philosophic statements do reflect cultural concerns of each society, as well as the particular elements in that society that these individual mothers have come to see as most important. Informant #81, for example, has a religious orientation within the Samoan culture, being a minister's wife, mentioning religion in her opinions on abortion and homosexuality, and again in her philosophic statement. Her goal for her child is that he grow up to be a minister. Another cultural theme running throughout her statements is that conflict should be avoided by preventing escalation of a potentially troublesome situation. The other Samoan contrasts in that she has a much more secular orientation. In her answers to both the abortion and homosexuality questions, she explicitly rejects religious grounds as being her justification for her opposition to these practices, looking to the future consequences of these activities. Her concern over what her children will eventually give back to her, as expressed in her philosophy statement, reflects in her answer on abortion: that the child will be of help in the future, a quite traditional Samoan point of view. Her goals for her children are that they get good educations and become employed at whatever level their capabilities allow for, but preferably in clean, professional jobs. Even with this disparity, it is clear that both Samoans share a sociocentric orientation, as evidenced by their concern over preserving interpersonal relationships in a variety of situations.

The two Europeans also contrast with one another, most clearly on their philosophic statements. Once again they represent differing emphases from within their culture. Informant #47 is concerned that her child become an acceptable member of society; however, certain of her other answers reveal that there is an egocentric basis behind this, shown by her earlier moral statement on how to get on better in one's job, and her later parenting statement with regard to how the child should get its toy back in a socially acceptable manner. Her long-term goal for her son is that he attain self-confidence so that he can feel good about himself. Informant #62 shows a much more straightforward individualist bent in most of her statements, although this is somewhat modified by her concern over regulating situations through rules. Many of her moral statements reflect a concern over the individual's choice in arriving at major life decisions, such as abortion or homosexuality, related quite directly to her philosophic statement about wanting her child to be able to arrive at a self-chosen morality. This may seem inconsistent with her use of rules, but actually if she applies a rule she can avoid being an authority figure personally. Her goals for her children are consistent with her other statements, as she says: "So many people dream for their kids, and there's no way I can dream for my kids. They have their own dreams and we'll help them get there."

CONCLUDING REMARKS

The foregoing data illustrate well two points: 1) A connection between the domains of moral reasoning and parenting methods can be demonstrated, and cultural differences in the structuring of one domain are generalized to the other. 2) Children's social environments are mediated by the cultural meanings by which parents define situations. Parents' moral conceptualizations, parenting methods, conscious philosophies and goals for their children are maintained with consistency between these separate facets. In the Samoan case this is by a sociocentric orientation toward life revealed throughout, which contrasts starkly with the European parents' more egocentric orientation. It should be noted that not all parents exemplify these connections as clearly as do these particular four informants, but upon further analysis of these data it should be possible to construct a complex model of more general cultural linkages between morality and parenting, especially between sociocentric/egocentric orientations as they transfer to both domains. Socialization for moral reasoning can clearly be shown to be affected by these most basic cognitive orientations for Samoans and Europeans in New Zealand.

ACKNOWLEDGEMENTS Gratitude is expressed to the following people for their help on this project: first, the two research assistants who helped to collect data, and whose work proved invaluable to the project, Mr. Iosefa Tesese and Ms Taulima Ierome. I would also like to thank Joyce Ramsey of the Auckland Kindergarten Association for helping me to contact informants, and the kindergarten and play-centre programs and parents who cooperated in the study. At the University of Auckland, I received helpful comments on my research from Cluny Macpherson, Claudia Bell and Charles Crothers, all of the Sociology Department. Many thanks to Marija Frankovich Algie for discussing Polynesian childrearing with me. Jaan Valsiner provided useful comments and suggestions on earlier drafts of this paper, as did the editor at C.J. Hogrefe Publishers. Fieldwork was funded by the Duke-UNC Women's Studies Research Center, a Pogue Off-Campus Dissertation Research Fellowship from the University of North Carolina at Chapel Hill, and a travel grant from the Office of International Studies, UNC-CH.

1. An unmarried university student considers abortion.

2. The Heinz Dilemma: A man whose wife has a rare type of cancer considers stealing an expensive drug to save her life.

3. A young man who does not get along with his boss considers accepting a lower paying job to attain better work relationships.

4. A forty-year-old mother of six considers abortion.

5. A Samoan family living in New Zealand is criticized on a trip to Samoa for loss of Samoan traditions.

6. An onlooker witnesses an act of aggression in a public place.

7. A factory foreman must decide how to handle a complaint of sexual harassment involving a good friend.

8. Should New Zealand be a Nuclear Free Zone?

9. Should the New Zealand rugby team go on tour to South Africa?

10. Should Parliament pass the Homosexual Law Reform Bill?

A. BACKGROUND INFORMATION

B. DISCIPLINARY SITUATIONS

1. If your child refused to take an unpleasant tasting medicine, what would you do?

2. At a playgroup which you are attending with other parents and their children, a child snatches the toy your child is playing with. To retrieve the toy, your child hits the other child and takes it back. What would you do?

3. While shopping at a supermarket your child requests that you buy an item. Whey you refuse, the child has a tantrum and throws him/herself onto the floor as crowds of onlookers gather. What would you do?

4. You have an appointment in the morning, but your child refuses to dress. How would you handle the situation?

5. While entertaining visitors, your child enters the room and picks up a valuable object which you do not want him/her to touch. When you take the object from the child's hand the child responds by hitting you. What would you do? Would you do the same thing if visitors were not present?

6. While you are driving the car, your child starts to make distracting noises. What would you do?

7. What is the bedtime deadline for your child? Do you believe in enforcement of a bedtime deadline? Do you have any type of bedtime "routine"?

C. PARENTING PHILOSOPHY

1. What are your long term goals for your child's development?

2. Do you think there is a wider range of opportunities for male children in New Zealand than for females?

3. Could you describe what type of child your child is?

4. What are your usual disciplinary methods?

5. What do you do on a day to day basis to encourage good behavior?

6. What sources of information have you used with regard to parenting? (Plunket nurse, pediatrician, family, friends, books, courses or workshops?)

7. How would you describe your overall, general philosophy of child rearing?

8. How much discipline of your child would you say is done by you and how much by your spouse?

REFERENCES

Barrington, R., & Gray, A. (1981). *The Smith women: One hundred New Zealand women talk about their lives.* Wellington, N.Z.: A.H. & A.W. Reed.

Bedggood, D. (1980). *Rich and poor in New Zealand.* Auckland, N.Z.: George Allen & Unwin.

Bell, C. (1985). *Women and change: A study of New Zealand women.* Wellington, N.Z.: The National Council of Women of New Zealand.

Bellwood, P.S. (1979). The Oceanic Context. In J.D. Jennings (Ed.), *The prehistory of Polynesia.* Cambridge: Harvard University Press.

Chodorow, N. (1974). Family Structure and Feminine Personality. In M.Z. Rosaldo and L. Lamphere (Eds.), *Woman, culture and society* (pp. 43-66). Stanford: Stanford University Press.

Chodorow, N. (1978). *The reproduction of mothering: Psychoanalysis and the sociology of gender.* Berkeley: University of California Press.

Davidson, J.M. (1974). Samoan structural remains and settlement patterns. In R.C. Green and J.M. Davidson (Eds.), *Archaeology in western Samoa*, Vol. II (pp. 155-162). Auckland, N.Z.: Auckland Institute and Museum.

Davidson, J.M. (1979). The Polynesian Foundation. In W.H. Oliver with B.R. Williams (Eds.), *The Oxford history of New Zealand* (pp. 3-27). Wellington, N.Z.: Oxford University Press.

Fairbairn, I. (1961). Samoan Migration to New Zealand. *Journal of the Polynesian Society, 70,* 18-30.

Field, M.J. (1984). Mau: *Samoa's struggle against New Zealand oppression.* Wellington, N.Z.: A.H. & A.W. Reed, Ltd.

Frankovich, M.K. (1974). *Child rearing on Niue: An ethnopsychological analysis of aspects relevant to the goals and acquisition of a contemporary western education.* Unpublished Master's Thesis, University of Waikato.

Freeman, D. (1983). *Margaret Mead and Samoa: The making and unmaking of an anthropological myth.* Cambridge: Harvard University Press.

Gerber, E.R. (1975). *The cultural patterning of emotions in Samoa.* Ph.D. Dissertation. San Diego: University of California.

Gilligan, C. (1979).*Women's place in man's life cycle.*Harvard Educational Rev., 49 (4).

Gilligan, C. (1982). *In a different voice.* Cambridge: Harvard University Press.

Gilligan, C. (1986). *On in a different voice: An interdisciplinary forum.* Signs, 11 (2), 304-333.

Gray, A. (1983). *The Jones men: One hundred New Zealand men talk about their lives.* Wellington, N.Z.: A.H. & A.W. Reed, Ltd.

Harkness, S. & Super, C.M. (1983). The cultural construction of child development: A framework for the socialization of affect. *Ethos, 11,* 221-231.

Henry, Brother F. (1979). *History of Samoa.* Apia: Commercial Printers.

Houston, S. (1970). The New Zealand family: Its antecedents and origins. In S. Houston (Ed.), *Marriage and the family in New Zealand* (pp. 21-40). Wellington, N.Z.: Sweet and Maxwell.

James, B. (1982). Family. In P. Spoonley, D. Pearson and I. Shirley (Eds.), *New Zealand sociological perspectives* (pp. 39-57). Palmerston North, N.Z.: Dunmore Press.

Keesing, F.M., & Keesing, M. (1956). *Elite communication in Samoa.* Palo Alto: Stanford University Press.

Kohlberg, L. (1981). *Essays on moral development, Vol. I: The philosophy of moral development.* San Francisco: Harper & Row.

Levi-Strauss, C. (1967). *Structural anthropology.* Garden City: Doubleday.

LeVine, R.A. (1974). *Parental goals: A cross-cultural view.* Teachers College Record, 76(2):226-239.

Macpherson, C. (1977). Polynesians in New Zealand: An emerging eth-class? In D. Pitt (Ed.), *Social class in New Zealand* (pp. 97-112). Auckland, N. Z.: Longman Paul.

Macpherson, C. (1984). On the future of Samoan ethnicity in New Zealand. In P. Spoonley, C. Macpherson, D. Pearson, and C. Sedgwick (Eds.), *Tauiwi: Racism and ethnicity in New Zealand* (pp. 107-127). Palmerston North, N.Z.: Dunmore Press.

Mead, M. (1961). *Coming of age in Samoa.* New York: Morrow.

Nardi, B.A. (1983). Goals in reproductive decision making. *American Ethnologist, 10(4),* 697-714.

Ngan-Woo, F.E. (1985). *Fa'a Samoa, the world of Samoans.* Auckland, N.Z.: Office of the Race Relations Conciliator.

Ortner, S. B. (1981). Gender and sexuality in hierarchical societies. In S.B. Ortner and H. Whitehead (Eds.), *Sexual meanings: The cultural construction of gender and sexuality* (pp. 359-409). Cambridge: Cambridge University Press.

Ortner, S. B. (1984). Theory in anthropology since the sixties. *Comparative Study of Society and History,* 126-163.

Ortner, S.B. & Whitehead, H. (1981). Introduction: Accounting for sexual meanings. In S.B. Ortner and H. Whitehead (Eds.), *Sexual meanings: The cultural construction of gender and sexuality* (pp. 1-27). Cambridge: Cambridge University Press.

Pitt, D., & Macpherson, C. (1974). *Emerging pluralism.* Auckland, N.Z.: Longman Paul.

Reid, B.V., & Valsiner, J. (1986). Consistency, praise and love: Folk theories of American parents. *Ethos, 14(3),* 282-304.

Ritchie, J., & Ritchie, J. (1970). *Child Rearing Patterns in New Zealand.* Wellington, N.Z.: A.H. & A.W. Reed.

Ritchie, J., & Ritchie, J. (1978). *Growing up in New Zealand.* Sydney: George Allen & Unwin.

Ritchie, J. & Ritchie, J. (1981). *Spare the rod.* Sydney: George Allen & Unwin.

Rosaldo, M.Z. (1974). Woman, culture and society: A theoretical overview. In M.Z. Rosaldo and L.Lamphere (Eds.), *Woman, culture and society* (pp. 17-42). Stanford: Stanford University Press.

Sacks, K. (1979). *Sisters and wives.* Urbana, Ill.: University of Illinois Press.

Sanday, P.R. (1981) *Female power and male dominance.* Cambridge: Cambridge University Press.

Schoeffel, P. (1979). The ladies' row of thatch: Women and rural development in Western Samoa. *Pacific Perspective 8(2),* 1-11.

Shore, B. (1981). Sexuality and gender in Samoa: Conceptions and missed conceptions. In S.B. Ortner and H. Whitehead (Eds.), *Sexual meanings: The cultural construction of gender and sexuality* (pp. 192-215). Cambridge: Cambridge University Press.

Shore, B. (1982). *Sala'ilua: A Samoan mystery.* New York: Columbia University Press.

Shweder, R., & Bourne, E.J. (1984). Does the concept of the person vary cross-culturally? In R. A. Shweder and R. A. LeVine (Eds.), *Culture theory: Essays on mind, self, and emotion* (pp. 158-199). Cambridge: Cambridge University Press.

Silverman, M. (1979). Gender and separations in precolonial Banaban and Gilbertese societies. In S. Barnett and M.G. Silverman (Eds.), *Ideology and everyday life* (pp. 85-165). Ann Arbor: University of Michigan Press.

Thomas, P., & Simi, N. (1983). The new Samoan businesswoman. *Pacific Perspective, 11(2),* 5-12.

Valsiner, J. (1983). *A developing child in a developing culture: A relativistic synthesis.*

Paper presented at the 26th Annual Meeting of the African Studies Association.

Wendt, A. (1973). *Sons for the return home.* Auckland, N.Z.: Longman Paul.

Wendt, A. (1977). *Pouliuli.* Honolulu: University of Hawaii Press.

Wendt, A. (1984). *The Banyan.* Garden City: Doubleday.

Whitehead, T.L., & Reid, B.V. (forthcoming). Introduction. In T. L. Whitehead and B. V. Reid (Eds.) *Gender Constructs and Social Issues.*

Part Three:

Culture and Social-Cognitive Development

Introduction

From the perspective of culture-inclusive developmental psychology, all cognitive development is necessarily social in its nature, and all social development has its cognitive foundation (in the form of internalized experience, as emphasized by Lev Vygotsky in the 1920s). Contributions to Part Three look at specific knowledge domains for which social experiences of children are relevant. In Chapter 10, developmental "precocity" of Hong Kong (as compared to U.S.) schoolchildren's understanding of banking operations is demonstrated, and linked with the availability of information about economics (earlier experience with banks and the study of economics in school curricula). An interesting feature of this culture-inclusive investigation involves the question of interpenetration of kinship/friendship and business relationships in case of children's reasoning about shop profits. Schoolchildren in Hong Kong integrated a business ethos with the traditional Chinese emphasis on interpersonal relationships, in their reasoning about shopkeepers' decision-making.

Chapter 11 adds further information about the development of children's economic reasoning in conjunction with their environments. It constitutes a study of how Italian children understand the origins of goods. Children in this study were from two environments that provided differential access to knowledge about production of goods: in a rural village they could observe many aspects of agricultural production first-hand, whereas in an industrial town such knowledge was limited, since most goods come in through distribution networks and their actual production is hidden from children's experience. The reasoning about goods was found to reflect these differential experiences, similarly to the Chinese case (Chapter 10).

Finally, Chapter 12 leads the reader to the informal context of a small community in Morocco, in a study of adolescents' formal-operational reasoning. A case history approach is used to present data about both the successes and difficulties of administering cognitive probes in contexts where the knowledge base of subjects differs from that of Europeans or North Americans. It is pointed out that the *goals* of subjects should be taken into account when their cognitive processes are studied, as goals are necessarily personal constructions based on a person's relationships with his or her culturally organized life environments.

In sum, Part Three outlines *experiential relativity* of children's cognitive processes. Experiences in different cultural and economic environments differ as the contexts differ; in this respect, then, research on children's social cognition would benefit from an explicitly culture-inclusive methodological perspective. Traditional research on cognitive development, however, has largely overlooked this direction.

Chapter 10

Children's Acquisition
of Economic Knowledge

Understanding Banking in Hong Kong and the USA

Mei-Ha Wong

Compared to other areas of social development such as moral judgment, political socialization, person perception, role taking, or the understanding of intentionality, the study of economic socialization and the understanding of economic institutions is relatively underdeveloped (e.g., Damon, 1978; Stacey, 1982). Interest in the development of cognitive representation of property, business, money, and possessions, evident in pre-1939 literature on psychology, has only recently been renewed (Stacey, 1982). Most of the studies, according to Stacey, can be broadly classified into four areas: money (its functions, transactions, savings, and economic relationships dictated by its production and exchange), possessions (understanding of private ownership and property, development of related affect such as feelings of control, efficacy, social competence, self-esteem, ambitions, regulation of social relationships, etc.), social differentiation and inequality (perceptions of inequality, recognition, legitimation and perpetuation of social differences and the existing economy,

etc.) and socioeconomic understanding (development of knowledge about the operations and functions of different socioeconomic institutions, economic socialization, etc.).

This chapter focuses on the development of understanding of bank and shop profits. It also examines how such knowledge affects the decision-making process of children if they are to become economic actors; in this case, shopkeepers. One concern of this chapter is to emphasise how differences in the social environment may account for differential development in socioeconomic understanding. Maturity of intellectual functioning is not enough for grasping the complexity of the economic world. As most economic operations (e.g., bank transactions) cannot be directly observed, children have to acquire relevant information from their social environment. Therefore, the nature and demands of the environment strongly influence the trajectory and pace of development of socioeconomic understanding. Comparisons of different environments may bring out one of the most intriguing aspects of socioeconomic development: the interplay between cognitive maturity and social factors. Another concern is the attempt to assess the effect of cognitive differentiation of norms in the personal (e.g., reciprocity, fairness) and impersonal/business spheres. Both Furth (1980) and Jahoda (1981) have suggested that the ability to distinguish between transactions in these two spheres is critical in the development of economic knowledge.

Research on the development of understanding of shop profit usually includes knowledge of the functions of money, wage systems, supply and demand of goods, etc. On the other hand, knowledge of banking operations and bank profit is a relatively new and until recently, unexplored area. Almost all studies have a tendency to posit universal stages that children from different social backgrounds have to go through, and downplay if not ignore differences in trajectories and pace of development. Considering that researchers' interest is to relate Piagetian cognitive theory to the sphere of socioeconomic reasoning, it is not difficult to understand this universalistic emphasis. However, merely focusing on similarities is at best an incomplete representation of the reality, and at worst, is discarding interesting and meaningful questions in the area of economic knowledge. As we shall see, this may be the reason why many important issues have been left unexplored.

Development of Understanding of Banks

Efforts to reveal the development of children's understanding of banks began with Jahoda's study (1981), who was interested in the developmental sequence of knowledge of well-defined economic systems. Two theoretical issues underlie this concern. As with his research on shop profit, Jahoda regards such economic systems as fundamentally similar to physical systems in traditional Piagetian research, in that some underlying principles are involved that have to be grasped. But unlike physical processes, most economic processes cannot be directly observed, e.g., how the bank pays interest and makes a profit. To construct a correct representation of economic reality, Jahoda believes that children have to acquire relevant information from their social environment and pull together those different bits of information themselves. This view is similar to those of Furth (1978) and Turiel (1978). The latter has suggested that the nature of individual-environment interactions determines the path of development to a large extent. Another factor that Jahoda regards as important is children's ability to distinguish between the personal and the impersonal sphere, which has also been mentioned by Furth. Equality and reciprocity may characterize interpersonal transactions, but are quite irrelevant in economic transactions.

Jahoda interviewed 96 Scottish children from three age groups, with mean ages of 11 years 7 months, 13 years 10 months, and 15 years 10 month. He purposefully designed his interview in a way that would allow him to examine possible individual-environment interactions. Thus, both working class and middle class children were included in his sample. Also, he attempted to assess the impact of the interview itself on the subjects' thinking by inducing cognitive conflicts. After the subjects answered questions about deposit and loan interest, they were asked to explain how the bank obtained money to pay interest, employees' salaries, etc. Then they were asked to answer the same questions on interest rates again, and interviewers would remind them of their initial responses. Jahoda interpreted their responses to ascertain how far an incomplete separation of the personal and societal spheres would create difficulties in understanding a bank's operations.

Based on these responses, Jahoda postulated a series of stages that children have to go through in order to develop a mature understanding of banks. At first, children have no knowledge of interest; they simply state that one always gets back or pays back the same amount. Then they begin to understand deposit interest only; they realize an investor gets back more, but continue to think that a borrower pays back the same. Later, they understand both deposit and loan interest but think that the rate for the former is higher than the latter; then, they believe that both are more or less the same. Finally, they correctly estimate that the rate for loan interest is higher than deposit interest but cannot give an adequate explanation as to why this is so. At the highest stage, children are able to explain that the difference between the two interest rates is in relation to bank profit.

The results indicated that no significant differences existed between middle and working class subjects before the study, although the former were slightly more advanced in the youngest group. However, middle class subjects seemed to obtain more positive impact from the study, i.e., they gave more correct answers about interest rates after being exposed to the "cognitive conflict" questions. The differences were especially sharp at the youngest age level and declined in older age groups. Moreover, the percentage of middle class subjects using economic terms (e.g., "investment", "shares") in their answers was higher than that of the working class group. Jahoda attributed the difference to the "differential exposure to relevant information and/or differential interest in such topics" (Jahoda, 1981, p.71). However, he did not specify clearly how and why these processes may take place.

With respect to children's ability to distinguish between the personal and societal spheres, Jahoda agreed with Furth (1980) in that a failure to recognize that the latter is not governed by interpersonal norms (e.g., fairness and reciprocity) prevents some subjects from understanding the operations of banks (e.g., one must pay back more than one borrows).

Ng's (1983) study of children's knowledge of banks seems to confirm Jahoda's findings. There were two major goals to his study. First, he aimed at assessing the generality of Jahoda's stages in other cultural settings. Second, he wanted to test the effect of what he called "cognitive constrasts" (by asking half of his subjects questions that contrasted a real bank with a piggy bank) and "cognitive conflicts" (by adopting Jahoda's questions and asking subjects to explain how banks obtain money to pay interest and employees). He interviewed 96 subjects in Hong Kong. All subjects were male and predominantly middle class. There were four age groups in the sample: first grade (aged 6-7 years), third grade (aged 8-9), fifth grade (aged 10-11), and seventh grade (aged 12-13).

His findings were largely consistent with those of Jahoda, except that he proposed two additional stages — in the "funny idea" stage, the children believed that the return on a deposit/loan is less than the initial sum, and in the "loan interest" stage, they only understood the meaning of loan interest. The cognitive contrast effect had a weak impact on performance. Recognizing the difference between a piggy bank and a real bank was a necessary but not sufficient condition for understanding banking operations. On the other hand, Ng observed that the contrast between borrowing money from a friend and from a bank did not have much cognitive impact on subjects. Some mentioned that they were required to pay interest to their friends. Ng suggested that this probably indicated "the encroachment on the personal sphere by an economic norm of the impersonal sphere" (Ng, 1983, p.220), which might be quite common in a highly commercial society such as Hong Kong. He thinks that psychologists have placed too much emphasis on the cognitive differentiation between knowledge about personal and impersonal norms.

In fact, the former are not usually distinguished from the latter in real life. For instance, a shopkeeper may sell something at a discount rate to a friend, hoping to maintain the buyer both as a friend and a customer. This is especially salient in societies where it is believed that the impersonal and personal spheres should not be strictly separated, and particularism (treating people differently based on one's own preferences rather than on general rules) should always be upheld. The point is: interpersonal knowledge does not necessarily impair children's ability to understand economic concepts. One needs both in order to survive in the so-called impersonal business world.

Perhaps the most interesting finding is that Ng's Hong Kong subjects demonstrated a more advanced knowledge of banks than did Jahoda's Scottish middle class subjects. Ng suggested that such differences were closely related to the business ethos of Hong Kong society, and contended that the pattern of economic socialization and the social demands confronting children might be quite different in the two societies. However, he has not specified clearly the characteristics of Hong Kong environment and its unique demands. Moreover, his subjects were all middle class male children enrolled at a relatively prestigious school that is well known for the precocious academic achievement of its students. One wonders if this advanced performance would also be seen in lower class children, who constitute the majority of the population.

Development of Understanding of Shop Profit

Strauss (1952) interviewed 66 middle class American children, aged 4.5 to 11 years, on 71 questions related to the meaning of money, wages, and shop profit. He categorized their responses into nine stages. In stage I, money is merely associated with buying and its value is assumed to depend on its size (i.e., bigger coins buy more). The exchange between the shopkeeper and the customer is thought of as a ritual. In stages II to IV, the value of money, the customer's obligation to pay, and the shopkeeper's motive to earn money are correctly understood. In stages V to VII, the fact that the shopkeeper uses customers' money to buy more goods is comprehended. Not until stages VIII and IX is the concept of profit correctly discerned. The median age at which subjects understood shop profit was 10 years 7 months. No sex differences were reported.

Danziger (1954) also employed the interview method. His subjects were 41 Australian children, aged 5 to 8 years, from blue-collar, white-collar, and small-business families. They were asked questions on numerous topics such as the purpose of money, relationships of employers and employees, buying and selling, etc. He suggested that there are two stages for the understanding of money and the roles of the "boss." Danziger's stage I roughly corresponds to Strauss's stages I to IV, and his stage II to Strauss's stages VI and VII. In this study, no subjects less than 8 years old reached stage II, similar to Strauss's findings.

The work of Furth and his colleagues (Furth, 1978, 1980; Furth, Baur, & Smith, 1976) represents a major effort to study children's conceptions of society within the Piagetian framework. Through examining knowledge of different social roles and institutions, including economic ones, Furth hoped to reinterpret and modify Piaget's theory so as to make it more relevant for social understanding. He interviewed 195 children, aged 5 to 11, in three different locations in southern England: a small village, a small town, and a larger town of over 20,000. A free interview technique similar to Piaget's clinical interview was employed to obtain information on social institutions such as money and shop business, societal roles, and images of community and government.

Four stages of societal understanding were proposed, which are to a large extent similar to those of Danziger (1954). In stage I (personalistic elaborations and absence of interpretive system), children do not recognize the functions of money. Money is believed to be freely available and money transactions are perceived as simply a ritual. Children of stage II (understanding of first-order societal functions) regard money as simply a special instrument of exchange. In transactions, they observe but generally ignore the shopkeeper's payment for goods, or do not clearly relate it to the customer's payment. Approaching stage III (part-system in conflict), their interpretations begin to go beyond observations; the shopkeeper's payment for goods is acknowledged and believed to be derived from customers' payment, yet they do not take into account how different systems are coordinated and therefore cannot grasp the concept of profit. Not until stage IV (a concrete-systematic framework) do they understand the basic mechanism of monetary transactions: that the shopkeeper buys for less and sells for more, and the profit obtained is necessary to run the shop. Only 2% of subjects at age 9 reached stage IV, compared to 18% at age 10 and 36% at age 11. No gender or social class differences were reported.

Jahoda (1979) also investigated knowledge of buying and selling in 120 Scottish working class children aged 6 to 12, using role play techniques and semi-instructed interviews. The youngest subjects had some knowledge about the wage system (i.e., selling one's labor), but failed to understand that shopkeepers had to pay for the goods they sold. When the shopkeeper's costs were acknowledged, children believed that goods were bought and sold at the same price; thus, buying and selling were perceived as two unconnected systems. From age 10 onwards, there was an increasing awareness of the "profit" notion; buying and selling were considered as two integrated systems. Again, no sex differences were apparent. These findings were interpreted in a Piagetian framework. Jahoda sees basic similarities between typical Piagetian tasks and understanding of economic transactions — both require children to "construct" knowledge themselves, integrating different bits of information from their observation and inferring the unobserved.

Ng (1983) employed a structured interview method to examine understanding of shop profit in 96 Hong Kong boys, aged 6 to 13. While he reportedly adopted a more stringent criterion than Jahoda's, the percentage of children of different ages understanding the profit concept was roughly the same in the two samples. Yet Ng's subjects attained a more advanced understanding earlier than subjects in other countries: American (Strauss, 1952), Australian (Danziger, 1954), English (Furth, 1978), and Malaysian Chinese (Tan & Stacey, 1981). As stated earlier, Ng attributed the precocious knowledge of Hong Kong children to the high level of economic socialization and consumer activities, and the business ethos of the society. Nevertheless, he has not developed his interpretation in detail.

Some Unanswered Questions

All in all, there are three issues that need to be dealt with in the research of understanding of shop and bank profit and economic knowledge in general. First, as both Stacey (1982) and Jahoda (1981) suggested, researchers should pay more attention to the impact of the social environment on children's understanding of economic concepts. Furth (1978) noted that many operations and transactions in the economic system cannot be observed directly and must be learned from others, who constitute the environment. If this is the case, one cannot understand exactly

how children obtain and develop such knowledge without also studying the characteristics or peculiarities of their environment. Simply introducing social class or culture as design factors, reporting statistical results, or acknowledging the effects of the social environment is not enough. Thus far, no researchers has done a systematic analysis on the interaction between the environment and the individual. For instance, how do the social and cultural environments structure subjective reality, impose demands, dictate attention patterns, and develop different values and aspirations of the individual? More careful analyses on social, cultural, and gender differences are necessary in order to delineate the complex interaction between the complementary roles of intellectual maturity and environment in development.

Second, it is suggested above that a preoccupation with norms in the "personal sphere" need not impair knowledge in the "impersonal sphere" because both are needed in economic/business decisions. In societies like Hong Kong, owing to some cultural values such as particularistic treatment, people are not eager to distinguish between the two. The ability to make this distinction may not be as critical to the development of economic knowledge as has been suggested.

Third, none of the existing studies actually deal with children's decision-making processes in the economic sphere — how they may make use of knowledge on certain business-related decisions (see also Stacey, 1982). More research is needed to help us to answer important questions such as: What does this knowledge mean to children? Are there other aspects that individuals would consider in making decisions? If so, what are they?

THE EXPERIMENTAL STUDY

The present study, then, had two objectives. The first was to explore the possible impact of different cultural and social environments on the development of economic knowledge. Second, I studied how children's knowledge of operations in the impersonal/economic sphere might be affected by their preoccupations with norms in the personal sphere, through examining their decision-making processes — how does their knowledge affects their decisions? What other factors do they consider? In this study, I asked subjects to imagine themselves as shopkeepers and asked them different questions about how and why they would set up prices for different customers.

A total of 264 children were individually interviewed (see Table 1). They were selected from three places: a small town in Hong Kong, a rural town in the U.S.A., and an university town in the U.S.A. There were 116 children (aged 6-15) in the first group, the majority from working class families. The second group contained 48 children (aged 8-13), predominantly from lower middle class or lower class families, with most of their parents farmers or unskilled workers. One hundred children (aged 6-15) were in the third group, mostly from middle or upper middle class families with many of the parents being university professors, doctors, or other professionals.

Content of the Interview

There were three sets of questions — bank interest and bank profit, shop profit, and differential treatment of customers. The first two sets of questions were taken from the studies carried out by Jahoda

(1981) and Ng (1983). American students were only asked to answer the first set of questions.

The questions on banks were designed to detect subjects' understanding of deposit interest, loan interest, and how the bank obtains profit by setting up different interest rates. Either Hong Kong or U.S. dollars were referred to, depending on the samples; the exchange rate was H.K. $6 to U.S. $1 at the time.

1. ("Warm-up" question) If you put your pocket money savings of $50 into a box at home and do not use it, how much will be in the box after one year?

2. If I open a saving account in a bank and put $100 in it, how much do you think will be in it after one year: $100? More than $100? Less than $100?

3. What would the exact amount be? Why?

4. Do you know how the bank would use my $100?

5. If the bank gives me back less than $100, why would people still put their money there? If it gives back $100 exactly, how could it obtain money to pay its rent and pay the people who work there? If it gives back more than $100, where does it get the extra money?

6. ("Warm-up" question) If a child borrows $5 from a friend, how much should be returned after one year?

7. If I borrow $100 from the bank, how much should I return after one year: $100? More than $100? Less than $100?

8. What would the exact amount be? Why?

The questions on shop profit were designed to examine subjects' knowledge of buying and selling prices and how shopkeepers earn their living by buying for less and selling for more:

TABLE 1
AGE AND DISTRIBUTION OF MALE AND FEMALE SUBJECTS INTERVIEWED

grade/ age	Hong Kong Lower Class		U. S. Lower Class		U. S. Middle Class	
	M	F	M	F	M	F
1st (6-7)	12	10			10	10
3rd (8-9)	11	12	8	10	10	10
5th (10-11)	12	12	5	12	10	10
7th (12-13)	12	11	5	8	10	10
9th (14-15)	13	11			10	10
Total	50	50	60	56	18	30

1. ("Warm up" questions) Have you been to a toy store before? What kinds of toys do you like?

2. If a toy costs $10, how much money should you pay if you want two? (This is to make sure that the subject understands that $10 is the selling price.)

3. How much do you think the shopkeeper paid for the toy? $10? More than $10? Less than $10? Why?

4. Imagine you are a shopkeeper. You spend $60 for a toy. If a customer wants to buy it, what will you ask for it? $60? More than $60? Less than $60? Why?

Finally, the questions on differential treatment of customers were aimed at studying subjects' decison-making processes by involving them in a hypothetical situation: they were asked to imagine themselves as a shopkeeper and in a position to set up prices for their goods:

1. Would you lower the prices of your goods to some customers?

2. If yes, who would those customers be? Why?

3. Would you lower your prices for your:

a. family?
b. other relatives?
c. close friends (including neighbors or classmates)?
d. acquaintances?
e. people who are introduced to you by any of the above? Why?

The Interview Session

All interviews took place within schools and were tape-recorded. Six interviewers worked with the Hong Kong sample and two with each of the American samples (the investigator participated in all).

The interviewers would begin by introducing themselves. They then showed the subjects the tape recorder and asked if they would mind being recorded. (This procedure was omitted for Hong Kong subjects, whose responses were immediately written down by the interviewers.)

Subjects were assured of the confidentiality of their responses, that their responses would not affect their grades, and that they had the right to terminate the interview if they felt uncomfortable. Finally, they were encouraged to be truthful in their responses, e.g., telling the interviewers that they did not know the answer if this was so. A friendly atmosphere was maintained throughout, and subjects were generally cooperative and responsive. Each interview lasted twenty to thirty minutes.

Coding

Responses were transcribed and coded according to criteria described below. Separate coding schemes were adopted for questions on banking operations, shop profit, and differential treatment of customers. Twenty transcripts from each group of subjects were coded by two independent coders so as to establish inter-rater reliability. The reliability ranged from 95% to 100%.

Responses to questions on banks were coded on a seven-point scale similar to the one used by Jahoda (1981) and Ng (1983). A score of 1 indicated that the subject had no concept of interest.

TABLE 2
UNDERSTANDING OF BANKS:
RESPONSES AND SCORING

Response	Score
No interest concept	1
Deposit interest only	2
Loan interest only	3
Deposit interest > loan interest	4
Deposit interest = loan interest	5
Deposit interest < loan interest (no understanding of profit)	6
Deposit interest < loan interest (understanding of profit)	7

TABLE 3
UNDERSTANDING OF SHOP PROFIT:
RESPONSES AND SCORING

Responses	Score
Higher buying price & lower selling price	0
Lower buying price & higher selling price	2

A score of 2 meant that only deposit interest was understood, and 3, only loan interest.

All other combinations were coded as 1 (Past research by Jahoda and Ng showed that children generally begin to understand deposit interest before loan interest.) A score of 4 meant that the subject understood both deposit and loan interest but said that the former was greater than the latter; 5 was assigned when they were said to be equal; and 6 implied a correct understanding that deposit interest rates are greater than loan interest rates. However, these subjects could not explain *why* that would be the case. A score of 7 indicated the ability to relate the concept of bank profit to explain why loan rates are necessarily greater than deposit rates. Table 2 summarizes this scoring system.

Questions on shop profit were again coded according to Ng's (1983) scheme. A score of 0 was given when the subject suggested a buying price that was higher than the selling price. Subjects who thought the selling price was higher than the buying price were assigned a score of 2, indicating a concept of profit. All other combinations were scored as 1 (Table 3).

Finally, questions on differential treatment of buyers were categorized according to the types of customers described.

RESULTS

Understanding of Banks

For all three groups of subjects (Hong Kong, American lower class, and American middle class), the mean scores from each grade showed a monotonic increase in the knowledge about the concepts of interest and bank profit (see Tables 4, 5, 6). Analysis of variance using grade and sex as factors showed that only the grade effect was significant (Hong Kong: $F[4,106]=36.08$, $p<.001$; American lower class: $F[2,42]=9.13$, $p<.01$; American middle class: $F[4,90]=29.76$, $p<.001$). With age, children gradually began to understand different kinds of interest and how the bank makes profit out of different rates for deposits and loans. Neither a main effect of gender nor an interaction (gender x age) effect was observed.

A comparison between the Hong Kong sample and the U.S. lower class sample indicated the precocity of the former. For each grades, the means of the two samples were significantly different (third grade: $F[1,39]=4.75$, $p<.05$; fifth grade: $F[1,39]=16.42$, $p<.001$; seventh grade: $F[1,34]=8.35$, $p<.01$). The difference was not as dramatic between the U.S. middle class sample and the H.K. group. H.K. subjects only performed significantly better in the seventh ($F[1,41]=4.08$, $p=.05$) and ninth grades ($F[1,42]=10.12$, $p<.01$). A comparison between the U.S. lower class and middle class sample did not demonstrate a dramatic difference between these two either. A significant difference was only found in the fifth grade ($F[1,35]=6.95$, $p<.05$).

The responses to question 4 (do you know how the bank would use my $100?) showed some interesting patterns. Hong Kong subjects seemed to have more ideas about how the bank makes use of people's money, and more readily referred to economic terms when necessary. For the subjects who either understood deposit interest or both deposit and loan interest, more Hong Kong subjects (50%) than American subjects (6.5% middle class, 1% lower class) mentioned different ways of how the bank could make profits besides giving loans (e.g., investment, bonds, shares, opening up new branches). More American subjects (25.8% middle class and 65% lower class as compared to 13.9% of H.K. subjects) said they did not have any idea.

For those subjects who did not fully understand how banks make a profit, question 5 (why would people put money in the bank if they lost money by doing so? Or, how does the bank get money to pay its rent and employees? Or, how does the bank get its extra money?) seemed to be very difficult to comprehend. Yet many of them were able to overcome the difficulty by speaking of ideas such as:

"The bank has money in its safe and takes it out whenever it's time to pay rent and salaries." (first grade, H.K. male)

"The bank gets money from the government to pay rent and salaries." (first grade, H.K. female)

"The manager of the bank must be rich!" (third grade, U.S. female)

"The bank gets money from people who put money in it, so it always has extra money to pay interest." (third grade, U.S. male)

"The bank can give people interest because it keeps printing money whenever it needs it." (third grade, H.K. female)

"One should pay the bank for storing money there because saving money in the bank will prevent them from being robbed." (third grade, H.K. female)

"The bank probably gets money from Washington and from people's taxes." (fifth grade, U.S. female)

TABLE 4
NUMBER OF H.K. LOWER CLASS SUBJECTS
UNDERSTANDING BANKING OPERATIONS

Grade	1st		3rd		5th		7th		9th	
	M	F	M	F	M	F	M	F	M	F
Score										
1	8	7	3	8	1	3	0	0	0	0
2	2	1	4	0	2	1	2	1	0	1
3	1	1	1	0	0	1	0	0	0	0
4	0	0	1	2	1	1	0	1	0	0
5	1	1	1	0	6	1	0	1	1	0
6	0	0	0	1	1	4	2	2	0	0
7	0	0	1	1	1	1	8	6	12	10
Mean	1.67	1.70	2.73	2.42	4.33	4.00	6.00	5.91	6.85	6.55
S. D.	1.23	1.34	1.90	2.23	1.78	2.30	1.91	1.64	0.56	1.51
Grade Mean	1.68		2.57		4.17		5.96		6.71	
Grade S.D.	1.25		2.04		2.01		1.75		1.08	

TABLE 5
NUMBER OF U.S. LOWER CLASS SUBJECTS
UNDERSTANDING BANKING OPERATIONS

Grade	3rd		5th		7th	
	M	F	M	F	M	F
Score						
1	5	8	4	7	1	3
2	1	2	1	2	1	0
3	1	0	0	1	1	0
4	1	0	0	0	0	0
5	1	0	0	1	0	2
6	0	0	0	1	1	2
7	0	0	0	0	1	1
Mean	1.75	1.20	1.20	2.08	3.80	4.00
S. D.	1.17	0.42	0.45	1.73	2.59	2.56
Grade Mean	1.45		1.82		3.92	
Grade S.D.	0.86		1.51		2.47	

TABLE 6
NUMBER OF U.S. MIDDLE CLASS SUBJECTS
UNDERSTANDING BANKING OPERATIONS

Grade	1st		3rd		5th		7th		9th	
	M	F	M	F	M	F	M	F	M	F
Score										
1	9	9	4	8	0	3	0	1	0	1
2	0	1	4	1	4	2	2	0	1	0
3	1	0	0	0	3	0	0	2	0	0
4	0	0	1	1	1	1	1	0	2	1
5	0	0	1	0	1	2	2	5	2	3
6	0	0	0	0	1	2	1	1	1	2
7	0	0	0	0	0	0	4	1	4	3
Mean	1.20	1.10	2.10	1.40	3.20	3.30	5.20	4.50	5.40	5.30
S.D.	0.63	0.32	1.37	0.97	1.40	2.11	1.99	1.72	1.71	1.83
Grade Mean	1.15		1.75		3.25		4.85		5.35	
Grade S.D.	0.49		1.21		1.74		1.84		1.73	

Understanding of Shop Profit

Only Hong Kong subjects were given these questions. Their understanding of shop profit showed a montonic increase with age (see Table 7). Two-way analysis of variance with age and sex as fac-tors showed a main effect of age ($F[4,105]=27.57, p<.001$). Three children in the first grade (14.3%), already showed a complete understanding of profit. The percentage of those who understood it increased to 47.8% in the third grade, 87.5% in the fifth grade, and 100% in both the seventh and ninth grades.

Differential treatment of customers. Again, only H.K. subjects were given this set of questions. The majority (first grade: 80%, third grade: 86.4%, fifth grade: 79.2%, seventh grade: 87%, ninth grade: 78.3%) responded positively when asked whether they would lower their prices to some customers, yet the type of customers they spontaneously referred to appeared to be different across grades. The number of subjects who mentioned that they would lower their prices for humanitarian reasons was very similar across grades (see Table 8), and chi-square tests revealed that age differences were not significant. The most frequent responses in this category were the physically or mentally handicapped, the poor, the elderly, and young children. Subjects did not seem ready to explain why they would do so; many seemed to expect the interviewers to understand why they responded as they did and restated their answers, or simply said that those people needed help. Chi-square tests did not

TABLE 7
NUMBER OF H.K. LOWER CLASS SUBJECTS UNDERSTANDING SHOP PROFIT

Grade	1st		3rd		5th		7th		9th	
	M	**F**	**M**	**F**	**M**	**F**	**M**	**F**	**M**	**F**
Score										
0	4	0	1	1	0	0	0	0	0	0
1	7	7	4	6	1	2	0	0	0	0
2	1	2	6	5	11	10	12	11	13	11
Missing	0	1	0	0	0	0	0	0	0	0
Mean	0.75	1.70	2.73	2.42	4.33	4.00	6.00	5.91	6.85	6.55
S.D.	1.23	1.34	1.90	2.23	1.78	2.30	1.91	1.64	0.56	1.51
Grade Mean	0.95		1.39		1.88		2.00		2.00	
Grade S.D.	0.59		0.66		0.34		0.00		0.00	

indicate any significant sex differences in these responses.

On the other hand, there was a significant difference across age on the frequencies of mentioning utilitarian reasons, X^2 (4)= 19.18, p<.001. Virtually no subjects in the first and third grades gave such reasons, while older subjects expressed such concerns frequently. Below are some of the most typical responses:

"I would lower my price to those who have been doing business with me for a long time because they usually buy a lot." (fifth grade, male)

"I probably would try to lower my price or simply launch a sale to attract new customers from time to time, like having an anniversary sale or something." (seventh grade, male)

"The price for those who buy lots will be lower. I'll end up earning lots anyway. . it's much better than selling less at a higher price." (seventh grade, female)

"If somebody comes in and truly wants to buy a particular good but does not have enough money, I would lower the price for them. Otherwise they would just go to an-

other shop." (seventh grade, male)

"I would lower the price when I want to get rid of the stock." (ninth grade, male)

"If there comes a time when I do not have much business I think I'll have to lower the price." (ninth grade, female)

As shown, these children's answers were not that different from what one would learn in an introductory business course in college. In fact, it appears that most subjects had an appropriate idea of how money is earned.

Compared to the humanitarian and the utilitarian categories, relatively more subjects spontaneously referred to the familiarity factor. The most frequently mentioned reduced-rate customers were family members, relatives and close friends. Chi-square analyses did not show any significant difference across age. When subjects were asked specifically whether they would lower the prices for such people, chi-square analyses again did not indicate any notable difference across different age groups — older subjects were as likely as younger ones to

TABLE 8
NUMBER OF H.K. SUBJECTS WILLING TO LOWER PRICES
FOR CUSTOMERS AND WHY

Grade	1st		3rd		5th		7th		9th	
	M	F	M	F	M	F	M	F	M	F
Humanitarian	2	4	4	4	2	3	2	2	0	3
total	6		8		5		4		3	
Utilitarian	0	0	0	0	2	0	3	2	6	3
total	0		0		2		5		9	
Familiarity	5	3	4	6	9	9	8	5	9	1
total	8		10		18		13		10	

TABLE 9
NUMBER OF H.K. SUBJECTS WILLING TO LOWER PRICES
FOR PEOPLE THEY KNOW

Grade	1st		3rd		5th		7th		9th	
	M	F	M	F	M	F	M	F	M	F
Family (1)	10	10	11	12	12	12	11	11	12	10
total	20		23		24		22		22	
Relatives (2)	10	10	11	11	10	10	11	9	12	8
total	20		22		20		20		20	
Good Friends (3)	10	9	10	10	9	11	6	10	13	9
total	19		20		20		16		22	
Acquaintance (4)	4	1	3	4	1	6	6	5	5	2
total	5		7		7		11		7	
Introduced by (1)	9	6	10	11	10	9	10	9	9	9
total	15		21		19		19		18	
Introduced by (2)	9	5	9	11	6	8	10	7	9	7
total	14		20		14		17		16	
Introduced by (3)	9	5	7	9	6	5	9	7	9	8
total	14		16		11		16		17	
Introduced by (4)	2	1	3	4	1	3	4	4	4	2
total	3		7		4		8		6	

say they would give discounts to such people (see Table 9). No gender differences were observed.

Two issues are worth noting. First, while familiarity was certainly an important factor for all, older subjects seemed to have more business-related considerations, some quite sophisticated. Some typical responses of different age groups:

"I don't know..." (first grade, female)

"Well, my family lives in the same place with me." (first grade, male)

"Because they care about me." (first grade, female)

". . . because they're my relatives and friends. They deserve it." (third grade, male)

"My family and friends are not bad people. So I know the people they know will not be bad either." (third grade, male)

"...I know them well." (third grade, female)

"Because they bought me toys and food in the Chinese New Year." (fifth grade, female)

"Well, maybe I'll lower the price once or twice . . . I'll give them a 10% discount. But I can't do that all the time, or I won't earn enough money." (fifth grade, male)

"I'll give them a 25% discount. Of course my family will get the lowest price but they cannot just take the toy because I bought it." (fifth grade, female)

"I don't think I should take my relatives' money but can't just give them the stuff because I spend a lot of money on them. Lowering the price is the only alternative." (fifth grade, male)

"They know me well, and who knows, they may be able to help me later." (fifth grade, male; seventh grade, male)

"I'll lower the price a little bit...I don't think I'll lose much anyway. Of course it will depend on whether they can help me in the future and what kinds of goods they want — I 'll adjust the price according to that." (seventh grade, female)

"Lowering the price to your friends would usually bring along more business. They'll come again later." (seventh grade, female)

"I'll keep the prices low for those people who are introduced to me by my close friends. After I've done that for several times and establish a better relationship, they'll trust me and feel like they want to come back to me. I can charge them more then." (seventh grade, male)

"Well, I would lower the prices for my friends, especially those who are shopkeepers themselves. I'll need their help sooner or later." (ninth grade, male)

"If my close friends don't ask, I'll just charge the same price. I'll lower the price only if they ask me to. Whether I'll cut the prices for people they introduced depends on how many things they want to get from the shop. If they buy a lot, I certainly will adjust the price, but not if they just want a few." (ninth grade, male)

The final issue concerns the distinction between the personal and the impersonal economic spheres. When talking about the reasons why they would treat familiar people differently, subjects usually referred to reasons that would only be relevant in the personal sphere. For instance,

" . . . otherwise we won't be friends anymore." (third grade, male)

"They have helped me before. I'd want to maintain a good relationship with them." (fifth grade, female)

"I want to make them feel like we are close to one another." (fifth grade, male)

"If I don't lower the price for the people they introduced, they'll lose face." (seventh grade, male)

"I don't want to make a lot of money from doing business with them...we like one another ." (seventh grade, male)

"My family has the best relationship with me. I don't want to earn much money from them." (seventh grade, female)

"I'll have to do business anyway. Though I'll have to lower the price if I do business with them, I know that I won't break the relationship." (ninth grade, male)

To these subjects, concerns in the personal sphere were as important as, if not more important than, the other business-related considerations. Relationships in the personal sphere shaped their behaviors in the economic sphere. Most subjects said they would not treat mere acquaintances in a preferential manner, nor the people they introduced (see Table 9). This was true across all age groups. When asked for their reasons, they just said that they were not familiar with those people and therefore had no reason to treat them differently. In such situations, money would be the only relevant consideration.

DISCUSSION

This section focuses on two issues. First, I shall concentrate on the analysis of the precocious performance of Hong Kong children compared to children in other countries of similar social background. The unique sociocultural factors that constitute the processes of economic socialization in Hong Kong will be considered in an attempt to bring out the factors that are underlie such differences. Second, I shall examine the relationship between knowledge in the personal and impersonal/economic spheres, and shall argue against the idea that the former necessarily impairs the development of the latter. I believe that the two are usually complementary, and only sometimes mutually exclusive in business-related decisions. How relevant one's personal norms are in the impersonal sphere depends largely on the pattern of social relationships that are constrained and ordered by the culture. I shall substantiate my argument by interpreting the findings of differential treatment in the context of Chinese cultural values. In short, the first part of the discussion deals with the results of knowledge of banking operations and shop profit, while the second part considers the findings of differential treatment of customers.

Role of Social Environment in the Development of Economic Knowledge

The results of this study indicate that there is indeed a strong age-developmental effect in the comprehension of banking operations and shop profit. Given these results and the findings of other research in this area, one could conclude that the age-developmental effect of economic comprehension is rather robust — it is observed across different cultures and social classes. Furthermore, children appear to develop their knowledge in more or less the same sequences that researchers have proposed (e.g., Danziger, 1954; Furth, 1980). Despite these similarities, however, differences on the *rate* of development between different countries (Ng, 1983) have been reported. I have included all these factors in the present study, and I will attempt to systematically analyze why such differences come about.

The precocious performance of Hong Kong children. The strongest difference on the understanding of banking operations found in this study was between the Hong Kong and the American lower class children. Within the same grade, the former performed significantly better.

However, a comparison between the Hong Kong and the American middle class children did not show such a dramatic difference — Hong Kong students were only significantly better in the seventh and ninth grades. When our American middle class sample is compared to Ng's Hong Kong middle class subjects, the differences become more pronounced. Except in the first grade where the differences were marginal, Hong Kong children again show more advanced understanding than Americans of comparable age (first grade: t [11.89]=1.54,[1] p=.075, one-tailed;[2] third grade: t [30]=2.39, p<.01, one-tailed; fifth grade: t [30]=3.8, p<.001, one-tailed; seventh grade: t [26.17]=3.62,[3] p<.001, one-tailed). A comparison of Jahoda's Scottish sample to our Hong Kong subjects of similar socioeconomic status again confirmed the relatively advanced understanding of Hong Kong children: the percentages of Scottish working class subjects who attained stage 7 of knowledge on banks unaided were 0% (mean age=11 years 7 months), 18.8% (mean age=13 years 10 months), and 18.8% (mean age= 15 years 10 months). The corresponding figures in our sample are 8.4% (mean age=11 years), 60.9% (mean age=13 years), and 91.7% (mean age=15 years). Ng's middle class subjects also had higher scores than Scottish subjects of similar social background (Ng, 1983).

Hong Kong children's understanding of shop profit in the present study did not

differ significantly from Ng's findings. The age at which our subjects first grasped the concept was younger than children in other studies. 14.3% of first graders (6-8 years old) and 47.8% of third graders (9-10 years old) showed this understanding. The corresponding figures in other studies were 0% and 9.9% (Furth, 1980), and 5.8% for third graders (Jahoda, 1982).

What accounts for this exceptional maturity of Hong Kong children? A close scrutiny of the social environment suggests some clues to this question. Below, I shall discuss two characteristics of the environment that are most relevant for our purposes — the business ethos and the education system. (Refer to Chapter 4 for information on the historical background of Hong Kong.)

The subjective reality: The emotional value of money. Owing to the special political status of Hong Kong (a colony of the British Government, Hong Kong will be returned to the Communist China in 1997), economic prosperity provides the most important incentive for the British Government, the overseas investors, and the local people to stay. Most people there do not see much that they can do to control their future (King, 1981) other than earning as much money as possible. The popular philosophy is that "one's money means a visa to another country" (Chan, 1986). Therefore, people tend to attach much emotional value to money because it means security and control of their lives. So the result is a "money crazy" attitude — working as much as one can; the more overtime, the better. In any case, such an attitude is consistent with traditional Chinese values.

In short, given the importance of money and economic prosperity to the system as a whole and to individuals, one would

---

1. A separate variance estimate is used because the variances of the two groups are not homogeneous.

2. A one-tailed test was used because past research showed that Hong Kong children have more advanced understanding of banking than children in other cultures (Ng, 1983). It was expected that results here would be similar to past findings.

3. Same as 1.

expect to observe such attitudes being transmitted in the socialization process (T. Parsons, 1966). Numerous studies indeed show that children internalize the importance of money as well as the means to obtain more at an early age (e.g., Chow, 1983; Y.L. Lee, 1983). It is quite possible that adults' attitudes toward money are passed on, and is therefore not difficult to understand why the Hong Kong children in our study appeared to have more ideas of how the bank makes use of deposits than did children of other cultures, and were more likely to refer to economic terms in their responses.

The objective reality: The banking industry. Children in Hong Kong are exposed to an environment that would easily induce their curiosity and consciousness of banks. The banking industry there has developed rapidly since the economic recession in the mid-1970s (M. Parsons, 1983), and it is very common to find a bank every one or two blocks. People used to make fun of this phenomenon by saying that "there are more banks than food stores nowadays." Banks are part of children's objective reality, and it would be rare if a school-age child in Hong Kong had never seen a bank. Besides, the intense competition has provided favorable conditions for people to have savings accounts. As frugality is also considered a Chinese virtue, it is quite common for parents to teach their children to save their money. Many banks attract children by providing attractive piggy banks when they open a savings account, and simplifying the deposit procedures by counting their money for them. All they have to do is to take their piggy banks back from time to time.

What we observe in the case of Hong Kong is that both the subjective and objective realities of children are shaped by the economic structure of the society. The business ethos, the high level of consumer activities, the emotional values of money, traditional values, the visibility of banks, and the possibility of direct dealing with banks themselves all seem to impose special demands to grasp economic concepts at an early age, and facilitate the development of understanding of banks and economic knowledge in general.

The education system. For years, education in Hong Kong was the privilege of a minority. Not until the mid-1970s did the government began to practice its Nine-Years-Compulsory-Education Plan, which provides free or subsidized education to all students. After the ninth grade education is no longer a universal right: then, students have to take two public examinations (in addition to numerous exams they take in schools) which determine whether they can continue. Next there is the School Certificate Examination to be taken after grade eleven, and the entrance examinations to Hong Kong's two universities. These examinations serve as an effective screening mechanism: a 1981 survey showed that only 6% of all primary students entered 12th grade, which is a preparation for university education, and only 1% actually ended up in university (Lam, Fong, & Cheung, 1982). Such educational policies, although long criticized, are very difficult to change because they serve to provide a less-educated labor force for the economy. Besides, higher education for everybody is too expensive for a government that wants to mobilize as many resources for economic development as possible.

Given the scarcity of higher education

opportunities, the competition is intense. As well, the traditional Chinese values on education and academic achievement strengthen it. Due to this intense competition, the curriculum is changed every few years (so that exams can be made more difficult and have greater discriminating power). Thus, Hong Kong students have a more advanced curriculum than Americans: for instance, the arithmetical concepts of percentage and interest rates are first introduced in the fifth grade compared to the sixth or seventh grade in the U.S. In addition, these problems are not just passively learned in class: since they are covered on the public examinations, students probably spend a great deal of time doing related practice exercises (Szetu, 1982). So, while American children spend their time after school watching cartoons or playing football, Hong Kong children, whether they like it or not, are spending it learning decimal points and interest rates.

Cognitive Differentiation Between Personal and Impersonal Spheres

Jahoda (1981) and Furth (1978) maintained that children's preoccupation with the norms of the personal sphere (e.g., fairness and reciprocity) , prevent them from understanding operations in the economic/business sphere. However, as mentioned earlier, Ng (1983) did not find such cognitive differentiation very important for his Hong Kong subjects. The present study on differential treatment of customers revealed that while children become more economically oriented as they mature (having more sophisticated ideas on how to make money), they do not tend to distinguish between operations in the personal and business spheres.

When deciding whether they would lower the prices of goods, they do not just consider business-related factors (i.e., profit) but also personal relationships. Moreover, a few children in both societies mentioned that when they borrowed money from their friends, they were required to pay interest. Interestingly, some maintained that one should pay interest to one's friends but not necessarily to the bank. All these seem to imply that the effects of cognitive differentiation between the personal and business spheres may not be as important as previously suggested. In fact, it is doubtful whether individuals always distinguish knowledge of these two spheres. Below, I shall elaborate my argument with reference to the case of Hong Kong children.

The overlapping of personal and impersonal/business transactions in Hong Kong. Our results suggest that Hong Kong children do not regard the two spheres as separate: they consider personal norms in business-related decisions, and economic norms in personal interactions. In order to understand why, one has to take into account cultural as well as economic factors. Let us first examine the encroachment of personal norms into the impersonal sphere. The Chinese culture has been described as having a strong group-orientation, as opposed to the West's individual orientation (e.g., Hsu, 1970; Sun, 1983). The individual is supposed to support the existing social order by maintaining proper relationships with others, especially the "in-group," which includes those with blood ties, those with whom one has much interaction, such as close friends, and those who have good relationships with one's family, relatives, and close friends. There is a sense of obligation to repay the favors to the in-group, and the result is that individuals feel obliged to give special treatment to such people, even in situations where they are not supposed to. Special treatment increases the group identity, which in turn intensifies the sense of obligation. This special structure of social relationships appears to have affected the decisions of Hong Kong children in the present study — subjects readily referred to interpersonal considerations such as "make them feel close to me," "maintaining a good relationship with," "save them face" etc., in their answers.

Conversely, probably because of the business ethos of the society, economic considerations are becoming increasingly acceptable in the personal sphere. This can be witnessed in some of the subjects' responses — they said they would not let their family, relatives or close friends have their goods for free, only at a lower price. As one subject said "I can't just give them the stuff, because I spent a lot of money on it." Economic considerations are more prominent when dealing with mere acquaintances; the majority of subjects said they probably would not lower prices for such people. The fact that some children mentioned that they paid interest when they borrowed from friends also shows a close relationship between personal and impersonal norms. *The personal and impersonal spheres: A false dichotomy.* The above analysis shows that the distinction of the personal and impersonal spheres may not be a crucial factor in children's grasping of different economic concepts in Hong Kong. In fact, I suspect that this factor may not be very important in other societies either. First, it is increasingly acceptable nowadays to include economic considerations in the personal sphere. Sec-

ond, interactions in the impersonal/business sphere are not only governed by financial factors but also by interpersonal norms and relationships. The degree to which considerations in these two spheres are interdependent of course depends on the cultural and economic situations of a particular society, but the differences between the two are not as great as have been believed.

I agree with Jahoda that a preoccupation with personal norms may hinder children's understanding of economic concepts. However, I believe that it is the rigid application of knowledge rather than the distinction between personal and impersonal norms that forestalls economic understanding. Besides, children who mentioned paying loan interest to friends did not necessarily understand that banks also require such interest. Just as they have to learn to deal with friends who deliberately hurt their feelings (e.g., those who do not act according to reciprocity principles), they also have to learn that economic transactions are governed by principles different from those of interpersonal interactions. In other words, they have to avoid overgeneralizing their knowledge from one situation to another. The ability to apply proper knowledge flexibly in different situations appears to be a more critical factor in the development of economic understanding than the cognitive differentiation between personal and impersonal norms.

CONCLUDING REMARKS

This chapter discusses the crucial role of the sociocultural environment in the development of economic knowledge. I have attempted to elucidate the processes through which the economic, educational, political, and cultural factors are constantly structuring children's minds. Without considering the significance of a prosperous economy, the business ethos, the emotional values of money, the pyramid-like education system, and traditional values, we would not understand the precocious performance of Hong Kong children in the comprehension of economic concepts. Nor would we be able to know why and how children apply their economic knowledge in business-related decisions without also taking into consideration the cultural value of particularistic treatment. My analysis, while it appears to be culturally specific, brings out some general implications: first, the relevance of non-economic factors (e.g., education, family socialization, cultural values) in the understanding of economic development, and second, that knowledge of personal and impersonal spheres are necessarily interdependent, and the cognitive differentiation between them in the understanding of economic concepts may not be as important as has been suggested.

This chapter also points to a more general issue: development always takes place in culturally-structured contexts. We cannot meaningfully talk about the former without invoking the latter. Most of the "facts" in developmental psychology come from studies that were done in Western industrialized countries. We will not know which are the facts and which are the artifacts until we are willing to be skeptical about these facts' validity, and understand child development in cultures other than Western ones. This chapter is an attempt toward that direction, and I hope that more research and serious thinking will be done along similar lines.

ACKNOWLEDGEMENTS I want to express my gratitude to R. Cairns, S. Ng, and T. Ting for their help in planning the study. I thank B. Cairns, K. Chan, Y. Chan, S. Lee, T. Tam, K. Winslow, and Y. Wu for their help in collecting the data. I have benefited greatly from comments and suggestions of R. Cairns, D. Messinger, M. Myers, P. Ornstein, and J. Valsiner.

REFERENCES

Chan, K. (1986). China and Hong Kong: An individual choice. *The Nineties (Chinese, Hong Kong), 200*, 70-72.

Chow, M. (1983). The girl next door. In S. Yau (Ed.), *An inquiry of the youth problems in Hong Kong* (pp.17-21). Hong Kong: Going Fine.

Damon, W. (1978). *Social cognition* (New direction for child development, Volume 1). San Franciso: Jossey-Bass.

Danziger, K. (1954). Children's earliest conceptions of economic relationships (Australia). *Journal of Social Psychology, 47*, 231-240.

Furth, H.G. (1978). Young children's understanding of society. In H. McGurk (Ed.), *Issues in childhood social development* (pp. 228-256). London: Methuen.

Furth, H.G. (1980). *The world of grown-ups: Children's concepts of society.* New York: Elsevier.

Furth, H.G., Baur, M. & Smith, J.E. (1976). Children's conception of social institutions: A Piagetian framework. *Human Development, 19*, 351-374.

Hsu, F.L. (1970). *Americans and Chinese: Purpose and fulfillment in great civilizations.* New York: Natural History.

Jahoda, G. (1979). The construction of economic reality by some Glaswegian children. *European Journal of Social Psychology, 9*, 115-127.

Jahoda, G. (1981). The development of thinking about economic institutions: The bank. *Cahiers De Psychologie Cognitive, 1*, 55-73.

King, A.Y. (1981). The political culture of Kwun Tong: A Chinese Community in Hong Kong. In A.Y. King & R. Lee (Eds.), *Social life and development in Hong Kong*. Hong Kong: The Chinese University Press

Lam, C., Fong, Y. & Cheung, K. (1982). Education in Hong Kong. In C. Lam, Y. Fong & K. Cheung (Eds.), *Perspectives on Hong. Kong Education* (pp. 3-9). Hong Kong: Wide Angle.

Lee, Y.L. (1983). An interview with the rioters. In S. Yau (Ed.), *An inquiry of the youth problems in Hong Kong* (pp. 17-21). Hong Kong: Going Fine.

Ng, S. (1983). Children's ideas about the bank and the shop profit: Developmental stages and the influence of cognitive contrasts and conflict. *Journal of Economic Psychology, 4*, 209-221.

Parsons, M. (1983). *Hong Kong 1983*. Hong Kong: Government Information Services.

Parsons, T. (1966). *The Social System*. New York: Free Press.

Stacey, B.G. (1982). Economic socialization in pre-adult years. *British Journal of Social Psychology, 21*, 159-173.

Strauss, A.L. (1952). The development and transformation of monetary meaning in the child. *American Sociological Review, 17*, 275-284.

Sun, L. (1983). *The 'deep structure' of the Chinese culture*. Hong Kong: Yi Shan.

Szetu, W. (1983). Examinations, teenagers and the social trend. In S. Yau (Ed.), *An inquiry of youth problems in Hong Kong* (pp.122-127). Hong Kong, Going Fine.

Tan, H.R. & Stacey, B.G. (1981). The understanding of socioeconomic concepts in Malaysian Chinese school children. *Child Study Journal, 11*, 33-49.

Turiel, E. (1978). The development of concepts of social structure: Social convention. In J. Glick and K.A. Clarke-Stewart (Eds.), *The development of social understanding* (pp. 25-107). New York: Gardner.

Chapter 11

Environmental Differences in Understanding Production and Distribution

Anna Emilia Berti and Anna Silvia Bombi

Paolo, a boy of five, comes home from school very excited: on his way home he saw some children selling comics at makeshift stalls and wants to do the same. "Can you give me some money?" he asks his mother. "I want to go and buy some comics at the newsstand; I want to set up a stall myself. With the money I earn I can at last buy myself a new football." Cases such as these bring the adult into contact with the "economic reasoning" of children, which is characterized by peculiar ideas. Paolo, for instance, was sure he would earn more than he spent, even though he would be selling the comics at the same price that he paid for them at the newsstand.

Until a few years ago, any adult who was made curious by these ideas and wished to gain further insight into them would have found nothing on this topic in the psychological literature; very few investigations had in fact been carried out on the subject, and those that had were comparatively unknown (Danziger, 1958; Strauss, 1952, 1954). The interest in children's knowledge of economic institutions and of social institutions in general is quite recent. It arose only after social cognition established itself as a field of inquiry as a result of the rapid expansion of research in more traditional topics, such as moral judgment and interpersonal perception.

The "state of the art" obviously differs depending on whether we are dealing with recently established fields or those of longer-standing tradition. For instance, while work has progressed beyond the collection of descriptive data in the research on moral judgment, and is now focused on explaining development mechanisms by comparing several different theories, in the field of the study of children's economic or political conceptions the first step was to pinpoint the existence of conceptions peculiar to different ages (for economics see the review by Stacey, 1982; for politics see Connell, 1971). That stage can be defined as an "explorative" and "speculative" one in which the various authors have merely established tentative links of the research with several theories of development

247

(particularly with various aspects of Piagetian theory).

Only recently has empirical research been performed in order to verify these theoretical propositions. These studies are characterized by two main trends. A number of authors have made cross-cultural comparisons in which some of the early investigations have been repeated in different countries (Hong Kwan & Stacey, 1981; Jahoda, 1983; Jahoda & Woerdenbagch, 1982). Others, occasionally critical of the cognitive-developmental approach that was characteristic of the early studies, have tended to identify differences in children's conceptions that can be related to their social class (Connell, 1977; Emler & Dickinson, 1985; Goldstein & Oldham, 1979; Leahy, 1981, 1983). In both cases, the main problem is the role played by the environment in the formation and transformation of economic conceptions, i.e., whether this role is secondary to the general improvement in the child's ability or a vital one not only affecting the rate of development but also giving rise to peculiar conceptions in particular groups of subjects.

The data collected thus far point to the existence of both similarities and differences in the economic conceptions of children living in different environments. For instance, the idea that shopkeepers sell goods at the same price that they paid for them has been found (although at different ages and with different frequencies) in all research on small-scale buying and selling carried out in various parts of the world (Berti & Bombi, 1981; Furth, 1980; Hong Kwan & Stacey, 1981; Jahoda, 1979, 1983; Strauss, 1952, 1954). Another universal conception found among preschoolers of different countries and social classes is that money can easily be earned without working. For instance, children believe that banks are willing to give you money without conditions, or that shopkeepers will generously give you "change" that may be greater than what you paid for the goods (Berti & Bombi, 1981; Burris, 1983; Duveen & Shields, 1984; Furth, 1980; Jahoda, 1979; Leiser, 1983; Strauss, 1952, 1954). Finally, the idea that the various forms in which work is remunerated are based on principles of equity (i.e., on the assumption that the remuneration is proportional to the time or effort involved in the work) is found in children from all social classes, particularly between 8 and 11 years of age (Berti & Bombi, 1981; Connell, 1977; Leahy, 1983). In most cases, the order of succession of certain kinds of knowledge appears to be independent of the environment. Thus, in all research on the remuneration of work, the idea of "easy money" precedes the construction of a connection between money and work; this connection, initially undefined, is subsequently based on the above-mentioned principles of equity. The idea that the seller makes a profit by increasing the retail price with respect to the wholesale price is acquired only after the children have succeeded in differentiating the retail price to the wholesale price, even though they believe these two prices to be the same.

On closer examination, however, the range of children's ideas concerning the economic world is seen to be quite varied. There seem to be four main types of dissimilarities between children from different ethnic and socioeconomic backgrounds, as is evidenced by the following examples.

a) Existence of totally dissimilar ideas. According to a study by Emler and Dickinson (1985), middle-class children maintain that there is a large disparity between a doctor's fees and a street-cleaner's wages. In contrast, working-class children, while likewise admitting the existence of such disparities, are less accurate in quantitifying them, always underestimating the inequalities.

b) Varying frequencies of the same ideas. Often the differences between classes are not so clear-cut and are revealed in a tendency to prefer a particular type of response, without however excluding other types. Another example taken from Emler and Dickinson (1985) shows how working-class children are much more inclined than middle-class children to accept the idea that everyone could be paid the same wage; however, both groups included individuals whose opinions clashed with that of the majority.

c) Unequal rate of acquisition of a concept. In a comparative study of northern European and African children, Jahoda (1979, 1983) pointed out that the latter were quicker to appreciate how the retailer makes a profit; also Italian children, especially middle- and upper-middle class (Berti & De Beni, 1986) have been found to be more precocious than their Scottish and Dutch peers (interviewed by Jahoda) or their English peers (interviewed by Furth, 1980).

d) "Peculiar versions" of basically similar ideas. Many children, particularly preschoolers, have a view of economics that could be labeled "finalistic" (Piaget, 1926). However, this view is made up of various specific contents, which depend on the children's actual experiences. Thus, Scottish children whose families were receiving social security contributions used this source of money to explain how shopkeepers can survive even by selling their goods at cost price (Jahoda, 1979). Italian middle-class children often expressed the idea that money can easily be obtained from banks, while working-class children claimed that the factory is where anyone (workers and others) can get money (Berti & Bombi, 1981).

The differences illustrated so far lend themselves to various interpretations. The fact that some conceptions are to be found exclusively or preferentially in certain environments (cases a and b) indicates that the development of economic ideas is not independent of the availability of particular information (if not actually determined by this information) rather than to structural modification of the child's intelligence. This information can consist both of facts observable by the child, and of ideas shared by the adults with whom the child is in contact and deliberately or accidentally transmitted by them. Second, the particular information that is available interacts with children's growing cognitive abilities so that, in some environments, the acquisition of certain conceptions is speeded up (case c) or there is a certain tendency for one particular version rather than another to occur (case d).

In the light of recent research, it seems that the environment has a role to play in the development of economic conceptions. However, the strategies with which such research has been carried out do not, in our opinion, allow any of the interpretations set out above to be verified and, above all, do not allow any detailed examination to be made of the processes mediating the influence of the environment. In several studies (Hong Kwan & Stacey, 1981; Jahoda, 1983) comparisons have been made between cultures in which numerous parameters differ, and therefore it is impossible to ascertain which are relevant with regard to different rates of development that have so far been revealed. Furthermore, comparative studies of individuals from the same country or locality who differ only in their social class (Goldstein & Oldham, 1979; Leahy, 1981, 1983) do not always take into account the overlap between the groups that is caused by having access to shared information. For example, television is a source of economic information that is not confined to the members of any given social class; this type of information has been called "free-floating" (Connell, 1977) and, to the extent to which it is relevant to a particular form of knowledge, it cannot be expected that there will be any clear-cut inter-class differences. This problem has been rightly stressed also by Emler and Dickinson (1985), who suggested that to reduce the effects of free-floating information, studies should compare social groups occupying different living spaces as far as possible (e.g., children of different socioeconomic status living in different parts of the city, and who go to schools of different kinds and quality).

In actual fact, completely different but comparable groups are never available in a field study. To get around this problem, one could create an artificial environment in which the effect of particular information on selected subjects could be examined, as in experimental research on learning, or in empirical studies on curriculae. However, in the field of economic ideas few studies have been carried out using such strategies (for an example of experimental research, see Berti et al., 1986; for an example of curricular study, see Ajello et al., 1986a; Kourilsky, 1981).

Another way would be to take into more detailed account the specific con-

tents of children's reasoning about economic facts, feeding back to them the same kind of problem but referring to diverse situations. This is necessary above all to ascertain whether the children's ideas are linked solely to the content peculiar to the questions. This was the strategy used by Piaget from the time of his early studies on representation of the world (1926) in which, for instance, when trying to outline the development of artificialism, he asked children to indicate the origin of various things: mountains, night, rain, etc. Since Piaget was interested in seeing if there was any convergence between children's answers, he chose things about which they were unlikely to have any verbal information, and with which they had all had the same kind of experience. In this way environmental effects are cancelled out, and light is shed on the subjects' growing ability to arrive at explanations of these phenomena. Also with regard to economic ideas, in many instances when tackling general problems, researchers have asked children questions on specific examples. For instance, we ourselves (Berti & Bombi, 1981), in studying children's ideas concerning the remuneration of work, have asked them to tell us who pays workers, farmers, bus drivers, etc. Or, when investigating their ideas concerning price differences of goods we asked questions such as: "Do this watch and that book have the same price or not?"; "Between this oil painting and this poster, is one more expensive than the other?", etc. The recurrent aspects of the answers were revealed by analysis, without going into the reasons for any differences. This was done, as we said earlier, to make the identification of general trends in development the primary aim of research into the child's economic world.

Nevertheless, any differences between the answers offered in relation to specific examples can be analyzed in order to highlight those aspects of the solution that are facilitated or hindered by information available in the environment. Implicit in this strategy is the adoption of a cognitive-developmental point of view in which development is treated as the interaction between the environment and the child's gradually changing cognitive structures. In such a perspective it is also to be expected that the "weight" of the available information will vary according to the child's age and information processing capacity. Consequently, any study of the development of economic knowledge applied to different contents will have two interrelated purposes: (1) to see whether the child's conceptions change with age by passing through hierarchically structured levels, and whether these conceptions subsequently recur in relation to different contents; and (2) to see whether there are any differences in the *rate* at which children pass from one level to another, when the problems refer to facts of which the children may have quantitatively and qualitatively different experiences.

HYPOTHESES AND THE RESEARCH METHOD

On the basis of the above premises, an investigation was conducted of the cognitive representations of the production and distribution of various goods, among Italian children living in an urban area. The investigation was then repeated one year later, this time using children living in a small mountain village.

The subjects and their environment. The urban sample was composed of 80 children, ten boys and ten girls for each of the following age groups: 4-5 (kindergarten), 6-7 (first grade), 8-9 (third grade), and 10-11 years (fifth grade). In the curriculae of these grades in contemporary Italian schools, no formal teaching of economic concepts takes place, although it cannot be ruled out that some information about the production and distribution of goods is actually present at school. However, if it exists, it is only incidental and cannot be expected to play a significant part in the children's school experiences. Therefore, the main sources of children's economic knowledge are their direct observation of the environment, and information extracted non-systematically from adults' conversations, as well as from the mass media. All the urban children in the study were of lower-middle-class background, and lived in a peripheral quarter of a north Italian city with a population of about 200,000. On the whole, the environment of these children could be considered fairly uninformative regarding the problem of the origin of goods. Their neighbourhood has no factories or craftsmen's workshops, and the only relevant experience the children were certain to have had was that of purchasing something at one of the numerous shops in the area.

The mountain village sample had the same composition regarding social class and number of each sex at each age level. However, their environment was quite different from that of the urban children. The village (located in the eastern part of Italian Alps) has its main economic resource in timber from the surrounding woods. The children therefore had had the opportunity of witnessing a complete productive cycle, i.e., from cutting timber to the construction and sale of craftwork. Furthermore, many of their parents were involved in activities related to the processing of wood, such as lumberjacks, carpenters, sawmill workers, and craftspeople. One further aspect in which this environment differs from the urban one is the large number of houses with vegetable gardens, which enabled the children to observe how fruit and vegetables are grown.

The interview contents and associated difficulties. The urban sample was interviewed about the origin of three objects: an item of clothing, a glass, and a peach. These objects were chosen since they satisfied a number of requirements. All three could be included in the children's conception of goods (see also Burris, 1983) because they are small and can be transported around and are frequently seen in shops. Furthermore, they are consumed fairly quickly (the fruit is eaten, the clothes wear out, and the glass may be accidentally broken). The children were therefore certain to see them bought again. Finally, these goods undergo various degrees of transformation between the producer and the consumer: the primary product (peach) is sold in its natural form and human inter-vention is involved only in growing and harvesting it, but the two secondary sector products are the result of a series of operations carried out on raw materials. In the case of the glass (the material of which is the result of a chemical process that completely transforms the appearance of the raw material), these operations are particularly complex and the child has little or no access to them. For clothing, the spinning of natural fibers (such as wool, silk, or cotton), the weaving of fabric, and cutting and sewing clothing are merely physical re-arrangements that are easier to understand than chemical transformations of a substance.

Hypotheses

In both samples, and for each object examined, we expected that different ideas would emerge and could be ordered into hierarchical levels clearly related to age, as in other fields of children's economic ideas (Berti & Bombi, 1981). In view of the peculiar nature of the goods chosen, we expected the development of ideas on the distribution of glasses and peaches to proceed synchronically in urban children, for whom only the end point of the production chain of these goods is accessible through direct experience. A few differences were expected in the case of the clothing, which can be produced also on a small scale (at home, tailors' shops, etc.). Finally, we expected that the natural origin of the peach would be understood before that of the manufactured items, and that of the latter two, the origin of the clothing materials would be identified before that of the glass.

In the case of the mountain village sample it was decided to add a wooden chair to the list of goods considered, in order to investigate the children's conceptions of a typical object of the local economy, made out of a material with which they were quite familiar. These children were expected to have correct ideas both about the people involved in producing and distributing this object, and on the natural origin of the material of which it was made. The question was also raised as to whether they would generalize and extend their knowledge of such goods to the other products included in the investigation.

Procedure

The interview structure was the same for each object. The experimenter began by asking the child how one would get hold of a glass (or a peach, clothes, or a chair). The children usually answered that the object could be found in the home, or that it had to be bought. The question was then put as to how the child's parents or the shopkeeper had managed to procure it. These questions were continued until the child responded with "I don't know," or else referred to someone who had made the object. At this stage it was inquired which materials had been used to make it and where they came from. In the case of the peach, the interview ended if the child mentioned that it was picked off a tree. Each child was interviewed separately in a room set aside by the school. Interviews were all recorded and transcribed verbatim.

Classification of Answers

Children's answer were classified into two separate level sequences, one referring to the type and number of economic roles believed to be involved in producing and distributing the product ("distribution chain"), and the other to the conceptions of how the objects were produced and, if applicable, to the origin of their materials ("production chain").

As far as the *distribution chain* of the goods was concerned, four different types of answer to the question "How do you get a glass (peach, clothes, chair)?" were found. Some children merely asserted that the object was either found or made in the home, without mentioning any economic role. This type of answer was considered to be the most elementary and was assigned to level 1. The children who mentioned only the economic role of the shopkeeper, stating that the goods were bought in shops, received the slightly

higher ranking of level 2: when asked how shopkeepers got the goods they sell, these subjects replied that they simply "had them," or that they bought them at another shop. Other children mentioned not only the sale of the goods but also their production, although attributing them to a single person, sometimes described as a shopkeeper and sometimes as a craftsperson. Since two functions have now been perceived, i.e., selling and producing, these answers were given a higher rating of level 3. Finally, several children made a distinction between producing and selling, attributing the two different activities to separate persons: the shopkeeper buys the goods from someone who makes them, with or without a wholesaler or transporter acting as middleman. This was considered to be the most sophisticated response to the interview question and was rated as level 4.

The answers concerning the *production chain* were ranked according to three levels, one of which was further subdivided into two nominal categories. Children who made no mention of productive activities, merely stating that the goods in question were to be found in the home or the shop, were assigned to level 1. Level 2 comprised all the children who realized that the goods had to be produced by somebody, whether at home or outside it, but could not identify any raw materials. This awareness of a production stage, despite the child's inability to trace the human activity back to the natural raw materials, was displayed in two ways that we considered as qualitative variants of the same level. One group of children, assigned to level 2a, was unable to give any answer other than a laconic "I don't know"; others, assigned to level 2b, explained that products were made by using material from other manufactured goods, such as rags for the clothes, pieces of glass for the glass, or other fruit or juice for the peaches. Finally, the children who mentioned raw materials found in nature and not produced by previous human activity were assigned to level 3.

Scoring

The sequences were rated by two independent judges, who made a blind examination of the interview transcripts. For each child, these judges were asked to assign two levels, one for the understanding of the distribution chain and the other for the production chain, for each of the objects mentioned in the interview. The assessments of the two judges were in agreement in 88% of cases.

Statistical analysis. The scores were subjected to several statistical analyses, both within and between the samples:

1) Spearman's rank order coefficient between the children's age group and their scores in the questions on the origin and production of each object was calculated.

2) A comparison was made of the scores obtained by each child for all possible object pairs, in order to see whether there was any systematic trend to give more sophisticated answers for any particular object. The sign test was used for this purpose.

3) Comparison between the two samples was performed using chi square and the Fisher Exact Test.

ECONOMIC ROLES IDENTIFIED IN THE DISTRIBUTION CHAIN

We shall first present the results on children's ideas of the distribution process. A detailed description will be given of the various types of answer, with each level illustrated with interview excerpts. Later, it will be seen how the urban children's answers and those of the mountain village children are distributed with reference to the various objects and the results of the statistical analyses.

Level 1. The goods are found in the home. The children who were considered to operate at this level did not mention any economic subject or activity outside the family, claiming that the goods were found in the home or made by their parents. Luca (aged 4 years 5 months) gave this type of answer for all the objects included in the interview:

Luca (4:5): What do you do to get a peach? - I don't know - What does Mummy do to get a peach? - She didn't make them -She didn't make them? -She didn't make them, she has them - What do you do to get a glass? - They give it me - Who gives it you? - Mummy - And what does Mummy do to get it? - She has them- Where? - In the kitchen - And if there aren't any glasses in the house what do you do to get them? - You make them - Who? - Mummy - And how? - I don't know - And what do you do to get clothes? - She makes them - Who? - My Mummy.

Thus, Luca just states that the peaches are in the house without having any idea how they got there. In other typical replies at this level (given especially by the children of the mountain area sample) the parents are said to get the fruit by picking it directly from the tree:

Nadia (5:0): What do you do to get a peach? - You eat it - But what do you do to get it? - Mummy takes it from the trees - And where are the trees? - Just on the other side of my field - And if the trees weren't there what would you do to get a peach? - You'd take one from the cellar.

About the origin of the chair, only one child said that his father made it. In the other answers that we ranked at this level the children merely stated that they did not know how this object was obtained.

Level 2. The products are in the shop. For children at this level the products in the house are known to come from the shops where they were bought. They do not know of any economic activities apart from buying and selling: some do not know how the products arrived in the shop, others do not even seem to understand the problem since they continue to repeat that the merchandise is found in the shop; finally, others state that the shopkeeper buys them in another shop or at the market, without ever referring to production.

Annalisa (4:5): What do you do to get a peach? - Go and buy it - Where? - At Luciana's - What does Luciana do to get the peaches? - I don't know.

Silvia (4:6): What do you do to get clothes? - (no answer) - These jeans for example, what did you do to get them? - Mummy bought them - Where? - In a shop - And what did the man in the shop do to get these jeans? - A lady put them there - And what did the lady do to get them? - She had them in a room - What room? - Where the clothes are - And where were they before being in the room? - In the drawer.

Mauro (4:0): What do you do to get a glass? - They sell them everywhere - How do you

mean? - In the shops - What do the people in the shop do to get them? - They bought them - Where? - I don't know; they have them.

Silvia and Mauro do not seem to worry at all about the source of the shopkeeper's products. However, other children state that the shopkeeper also has to buy them and they depict a kind of "chain of shops" in their answers:

Alberto (4:0): What do you do to get a glass? - From the man who sells glasses - And what does he do to get them? - He goes to the other one - What other one? - He goes and buys them from another one - And what does the other one do to get them? - With big big boxes; he puts them down and then he takes them to the other one - To put them down what does he do to get them? - He has a long long ladder; he goes up with the glasses and he puts them down - And where does he get the glasses? - I don't know.

Some answers given by children from the mountain region regarding the chair also belong to this level:

Simone (4:3): What do you do to get a chair? - You buy it - Where do you buy it? - At the shop - What does the man in the shop do to get the chairs? - They take them to him - Who? - I don't know.

Level 3. The seller is the producer. Replies at this level contain the idea that the person who sells the merchandise also makes it. The idea of manufacture is also extended to the peach but only by some city children. However, in the case of the fruit the prevailing idea at this level is that the greengrocer picks it from a tree:

Elisabetta (6:1): What do you do to get a peach? - They make it - How do they make it? - With fruit juice or also with oranges - And how do they do it? - They make the peel with flour and then they put it on and the peach comes out - And who makes the peaches? - The man who sells them in the shop.

Antonella (4:5): What do you do to get a peach? - You buy it in the shop - And what does the man in the shop do to get the peaches? - He takes them from the trees.

Barbara (8:6): What do you do to get a glass? - You go and buy it - Where? - In a shop - And how does the shopkeeper get it? - With glass - What do you mean? - He has pieces of glass and he makes them - How does he make them? - He glues them all.

Elisabetta (6:1): What do you do to get clothes? - You buy them - Where? - In the shops - And what do the people in the shops do to get them? - They buy the material and make them.

As regards the chair, we have added to this level the replies in which the children mention an artisan who makes and sells the chairs:

Fabio (5:7): What do you do to get a chair? - Buy it - Where? - From the carpenter - And what does the carpenter do to get the chairs? - He makes them with wood and nails.

Level 4. The shopkeeper and the producer are separate. At this level children state that the shopkeeper buys the merchandise from someone who produces it. The producer is sometimes depicted as a single individual who works alone, sometimes as an organized group such as a factory. Some children also introduced intermediaries between the producer and the shopkeeper. It was not considered necessary to distinguish between these replies and the others and to assign them

to a separate level because there were so few of them. The contrast between the children who depict the producer as a single individual and those who depict the producer as a factory was extremely clear in the replies given by Alessia and Massimiliano:

Alessia (4:6): What do you do to get a glass? - You buy it - Where? - In the shop - And what does the man in the shop do to get it? - He buys them from a man who makes them - And what does the man do to make them? - He goes around with a bag and puts all the glasses in it, then he goes home and fixes them.

Massimiliano (6:8): To get the glasses, the shopkeeper goes to the factories where they make them - What do they do to make them? - With the machines.

Federica (9:1): What do you do to get a chair? - You buy it or you go to the carpenter who makes it for you - Where do you buy it? - From a shop which sells furniture or from the carpenter - And what does the shop do to get the chairs? - They take them by lorry where they make them, where there are a lot of carpenters who make chairs in one carpenter's shop.

And here is one of the rare cases in which, as well as the retailer and the producers the intermediaries are also mentioned:

Daniela (10:2): The clothing shopkeeper buys them in bulk - And the ones who sell in bulk? - They go to the factory where they make them.

Finally, in respect to the peaches, some children in this level stated that the shopkeepers buy them at the market where the sellers get them by picking them off the trees, while others maintained that the shopkeepers are supplied by a lorry driver.

Arianna (5:10): The greengrocer buys the peaches in the market - And how do the people in the market get them? - They wait for them to come on the plants and then take them to the market -.

This is how Silvia (8:3) describes the way greengrocers are supplied:

Because there are lots of lorries that come from where the peach trees come from, and so they take them to the shops and sell them - And how do the people with the lorries get the peaches? - Because they have peach trees.

Similarities and Differences Among Development Sequences Referring to the Different Objects

We shall now examine the answers given by children of different ages about the production of various objects, beginning with the city group.

Table 1 shows the distribution of answers over the levels 1-4. It is seen that, for all three objects, only a small number of children in the lower age levels envisage no economic role or mention only the sale of the goods. Most preschoolers already have an idea of the function of producing goods, although this function is largely attributed to the shopkeeper in person, rather than to a distinct economic role. The identification of a producer distinct from the retailer is the principal modification occurring between age groups, and is complete by the age of 10-11. The data show that, for all three objects, the transition from one level to another takes place gradually as children grow older. In fact, there is a significant correlation between age and level (p<.001 for all three objects; clothing item: rho = .63, glass: rho = .43, peach: rho = .57). The progression does not, however, take place at the same rate for all three objects.

Table 2 shows that answers of the same level are more often given for the two manufactured items, than for either of these items considered together with the peach. The sign test was carried out to see whether the children who gave answers of different levels for various pairs of objects were more advanced with respect to one of the objects. The results show that considerably more advanced answers are given for the glass than for the clothes or the peach. Comparison of clothes and peach reveals no significant differences.

TABLE 1

URBAN CHILDREN'S ANSWER LEVELS ABOUT THE DISTRIBUTION CHAIN
OF CLOTHES (C), GLASS (G) AND PEACH (P)

Age	4-5			6-7			8-9			10-11			Total		
	C	G	P	C	G	P	C	G	P	C	G	P	C	G	P
Answer levels															
1. No economic roles	3	1	2	1	0	0	0	0	0	0	0	0	4	1	2
2. Seller	5	5	5	4	5	2	3	0	0	0	0	0	12	10	7
3. Who sell, makes	9	7	10	10	6	16	3	10	12	2	2	5	24	25	43
4. Producer	3	7	3	5	9	2	14	10	8	18	18	15	40	44	28
Total	20	20	20	20	20	20	20	20	20	20	20	20	80	80	80

TABLE 2
NUMBER OF URBAN CHILDREN GIVING ANSWERS AT THE SAME OR DIFFERENT LEVEL
ON EACH PAIR OF CONSIDERED OBJECTS
(PROBLEM: DISTRIBUTION CHAIN)

	Pairs of objects		
	Clothes-Glass	Clothes-Peach	Glass-Peach
Higher on the first object	7	22	28
Same level on both objects	56	44	40
Higher on the second object	17	14	12
Sign test significance	$p < .05$	n.s.	$p < .05$

TABLE 3
MOUNTAIN CHILDREN'S ANSWER LEVELS ABOUT THE DISTRIBUTION CHAIN OF
CLOTHES (C), GLASS (G), PEACH (P) AND CHAIR (CH)

levels	C	G	P	Ch	C	G	P	Ch	C	G	P	Ch	C	G	P	Ch
1 No roles	8	4	7	6	1	2	1	0	1	1	3	1	0	0	1	0
2 Sellers	6	12	6	3	4	5	3	3	1	1	0	0	0	0	0	0
3 Who sells, makes	3	3	4	10	7	5	7	14	6	3	4	9	9	3	1	15
4 Producer	3	1	3	1	8	8	9	13	12	15	13	10	11	17	18	5
Total	20	20	20	20	20	20	20	20	20	20	20	20	20	20	20	20

Examination of the distribution of answers of each level in the different ages (Table 1) indicates where differences occurred in ideas of the origins of the three objects. The most widespread idea regarding the peach is that the greengrocers themselves pick it from the tree, and/or grow it. Ideas for the glass and the clothes are more differentiated, and the number of level 4 answers rises with age: more rapidly for the glass; only after the age of 8 for the clothes. This reveals that many children envisage only a shopkeeper-producer for the peach, whereas they already make a distinction between the person who makes the glass and the person who sells it. Comparison of the glass and the clothes reveals primitive answers only for the clothes from a number of children from age 4 to 7 years. Comparison of the clothes and the peach shows that the presence of these low-level answers for the clothes is compensated for by the large number of level 3 answers for the peach.

One may wonder why the idea of the greengrocer producing or harvesting the fruit is so widespread. One answer is suggested by the results of other studies carried out on city children. A study of the ownership and functions of various means of production has revealed that younger children are convinced that the countryside belongs to everybody, and that anyone can go there to pick the fruit (Berti et al., 1982). When children become aware of farmers as holding a distinct economic role, they attribute no productive function to them, believing that plants grow by themselves and that the only tasks are to watch over them and every so often harvest the fruit and vegetables to eat or take to market (Ajello et al., 1986b; Berti and Bombi, 1981; Berti et al., 1982). It thus seems that children readily associate agricultural activity with that of retailing fruit and vegetables, because they do not consider the former a real job.

We shall now examine the answers given by children from mountain areas. Their distribution is shown in Table 3. In the case of the peach, the glass and the clothes, the preschoolers' answers are concentrated in levels 1 and 2. Only in the case of the chair do a majority of the younger children mention a productive function, which is attributed to a craftsperson who either sells directly or supplies the shopkeeper. As the age increases, there is a gradual transition from primitive to more developed levels. By the age of 10-11, these children are also able to distinguish the producer from the seller. There is a significant correlation between answer levels and age (p<.001; clothes: rho = .48; glass: rho = .66; peach: rho = .56; chair: rho = .43).

As with the urban children, comparison by *pairs* of objects again reveals a tendency to give answers at the same level (Table 4). The sign test shows no significant differences with respect to the clothes, glass, or peach. In fact, the advanced and backward answers (for each object considered in turn) cancel each other out. Comparison of the answers for these objects with those for the chair, however, reveals that the latter are systematically of a lower level. Table 3 shows that, in the mountain group, the majority of children of all ages give level 3 answers when asked to identify the distribution chain of the chair, while level 4 answers are sooner or later reached for all the other objects. This only partly confirms the hypothesis we have put forward. In fact, fairly advanced answers are given for the chair before any of the other objects. However, the children remain at level 3 in the case of this object, while progress continues with respect to the distribution chain of the other items.

Comparison of City Children With Children From Mountain Areas

We shall now examine, object by object, the sequences of development in the children from the two environments. In order to compare the distribution of the answers in the different levels, the children were divided into only two age groups: from 4 to 7 and from 8 to 11. In a few cases, it was necessary to combine some levels, as illustrated in Table 5.

For the smaller children, significant differences are revealed between the city and mountain groups in the cases of the

TABLE 4
NUMBER OF MOUNTAIN CHILDREN FROM ANSWERS AT THE SAME OR DIFFERENT LEVEL ON EACH PAIR OF CONSIDERED OBJECTS (PROBLEM: DISTRIBUTION CHAIN)

| | Pairs of objects | | |
	Clothes-Glass	Clothes-Peach	Glass-Peach
Higher on the first object	15	10	16
Same level on both objects	47	50	46
Higher on the second object	18	20	18
Sign test significance	n.s.	n.s.	n.s.

	Clothes-Chair	Glass-Chair	Peach-Chair
Higher on the first object	21	26	32
Same level on both objects	50	40	35
Higher on the second object	9	14	13
Sign test significance	$p < .05$	$p = .058$	$p < .01$

TABLE 5
COMPARISON OF ANSWER FREQUENCY AT EACH LEVEL GIVEN BY URBAN AND MOUNTAIN CHILDREN (PROBLEM: DISTRIBUTION CHAIN)

4- to 7-year-old children

	clothes		glass		peach	
	U	M	U	M	U	M
level 1	4	9	1	6	2	8
level 2	9	10	10	17	7	9
level 3	19	10	13	8	26	11
level 4	8	11	16	9	5	12
Total	40	40	40	40	40	40

8- to 11-year-old children

	clothes		glass		peach	
	U	M	U	M	U	M
level 1	0	1	0	1	0	4
level 2	3	1	0	1	0	0
level 3	5	15	12	6	17	5
level 4	32	23	28	32	23	31
Total	40	40	40	40	40	40

glass (Chi square = 7.38, df. 2, p<.05) and the peach (Chi square = 12.81, df. 3, p<.01). As regards the peach, most city children mentioned a shopkeeper-producer, while the answers given by the mountain group are far more scattered over the various levels, and often mention a producer as a role distinct from the greengrocer. It is our opinion that these differences arose from the greater familiarity of rural children with agricultural activities, which enabled them to distinguish the farmer from the shopkeeper more easily. When they did not give level 4 answers, through their inability to connect the two roles, they said that their parents pick fruit from their own orchards (level 1), or mention only the sale of the goods (level 2). In the case of the glass, on the other hand, the distribution of answers revealed greater concentration of the mountain group on the two lower levels, which mentioned no productive activity.

Considered in overall terms, the conceptions of the mountain children aged 4 to 7 with respect to the origins of the clothes, glass, and peach differ from those of the city children by referring less to shopkeeper-producers and more to distinct producers (as in the case of the peach) or shopkeepers who only sell (as in the case of the glass). Table 2 has already indicated that the idea of producers who also sell what they themselves make is very widespread among the mountain children in the case of the chair. Furthermore, they call these producers by their proper name, identifying them as carpenters. Why is it that, in spite of their familiarity with this role from their local economy, these children form the idea of someone who produces and sells other manufactured goods less frequently than the city children, for whom the shop-

keeper is the most familiar role? In our opinion, it is their very awareness of the differences between an artisan's workshop and a shop that prevents the mountain children from imagining a shopkeeper making glasses from pieces of broken glass picked up in the street. Not knowing how the shopkeeper obtains goods, they prefer to answer, "I don't know," or say that the shopkeeper, in turn, buys them from a shop. The city children, on the other hand, form the idea of a "shopkeeper-producer," not because it corresponds to anything they themselves have experienced, but because it enables them to give a sensible answer to the problem of where the goods come from. For the very reason that they have constructed this role themselves with only a vague idea of how it functions, they can easily apply it to other spheres.

For the older children, the differences between the two groups tend to narrow, disappearing for the glass and peach, but found for the clothes (Chi square = 4.71, df. = 1, p<.05). This time, however, a role-figure who both produces and sells is mentioned more often by the mountain group children. In this case too, a corresponding producer exists, i.e., the tailor.

The various differences observed between children from cities and from mountain areas can, in our opinion, be traced back to one basic difference. The mountain children elaborate concepts that fit the real situation, and do not attempt to explain events without sufficient information. On the other hand, the city children tend to fill the gaps in their direct experience with imaginative elaborations. In the next section, we shall see if the data regarding the production and origin of raw materials follow the same trend and give further support to the interpretation we have put forward.

THE PRODUCTION AND ORIGIN OF RAW MATERIALS

We shall now use some examples to have a closer look at the children's ideas regarding the production and origin of raw materials.

Level 1. No idea about production. At this level we find the children who see no problem at all in the origin of goods, but say that they have always been in the house or the shop, or that they do not know where they came from. No examples of this type of answer are given since they are the same as those illustrating levels 1 and 2 in the previous sequence.

Level 2. Production exists but it is not known how it is carried out. Children at this level mention productive activity, but are unable to say what materials are used. Some merely answer, "I don't know," or say that the objects are made by machines, without mentioning any materials, or that the materials are bought in a shop (type *a* answers).

> Massimiliano (6:0): Glasses are made in factories - How do they make them? - With machines - And what else? - With glass - How do they get the glass? - They make it - How do they make it? - They make it with special machines; you press a button and the glass comes out.

> Maura (9:1): The dressmaker makes clothes out of material - How does she get it? - She buys it from the material man - And how does he get it? - He buys it - Where? - ..... - How does the man who sells the material get it? - He makes it - How does he make it? - With thread - And how do they get the thread? - They make it - What do they make it with? - I don't know.

Answers of this level are also given for the chair, even though the mountain group children have direct knowledge of woods and trees:

> Carlo (6:9): The carpenter makes chairs out of wood - How does he get the wood? - I don't know, perhaps God sends it down from heaven for him.

Other children say that the objects are made out of used materials, without realizing the circularity of this explanation. Those who make clothes must therefore obtain rags, and those who make glasses need a supply of broken glass. These children often use the verbs "mend" or "repair" instead of "make." Only the city children give answers of this type also for the peach, which they claim is made from other kinds of fruit (type *b* answers).

> Elena (4:10): The shopkeeper has a special machine for making glasses - How does it work? - It mends glasses, puts them back together - What are the glasses made of? - Of glass - How does he get the glass? - He goes to a man who gives him glasses - And how does this man get them? - With a machine - What is this machine like? - It's got a hand that puts them back together - Puts what back together? - The broken glasses.

The children of this level all have the same idea of the way in which the person who produces glasses obtains the pieces of glass:

> "There's a man who goes around with a sack where he puts all the pieces of broken glass. Then he takes them all home and mends them." (Alessia, 4:7). "They find the broken glass in the rubbish dumps and put it back together" (Laura, 4:6). "They find the glass on the ground and stick it together." (Lorenza, 6:4). "They buy lots of

empty bottles that nobody needs and then smash them all with a hammer." (Elisabetta, 6:2).

This is how the people who make clothes get the material:

Manuela (6:3): How do they make the material? - They get lots of rags and make material and then make clothes - Where do they get the rags? - A man brings them with a lorry. He goes round the houses and asks people to give him their old rags. Then he puts them in his lorry and takes them away.

Simone (4:8) - How does the dressmaker get the material? - She's got all these old clothes that are no good, so she undoes them and makes new ones.

As already mentioned, answers of this type are also given for the peach, but only by city children. In describing the previous sequence, we have already seen how Elisabetta (6:1) thinks that peaches are made of oranges. Other children mention melons and apricots.

Level 3. Production is the transformation of things existing in nature. The children say that people use things existing in nature to produce the objects. The precision and correctness of their answers can differ, as is shown by the examples given below regarding the glass. The criterion adopted in order to define this level was not the correctness of the answer, but the awareness that manufacturers use material not generated by their own activities:

Elena (8:0): Glasses are made of ice; they take a knife and a hammer and then make a circle where they put the ice, I don't know exactly how, and then cut it - How do they get the ice? - With these moulds, or with a bowl. They put the water in there and wait.

Then with the shape of the bowl they make a cup - What is the glass made of? - Of glass, but the ice dries off after just like glass.

Cristiano (6:8): How do the men in the factory get glass? From the chimneys of the volcano.

Roberto (7:7): Glass is made of crystal: Where do they get the crystal? - From the mountains - What is there in the mountains? - There's iron . . . like a mine.

Monica (10:1): Glass comes from minerals. For instance, white minerals that go into the factory where they divide them up and get the stuff that makes glass.

When asked about material, children of this level mention sheep, silkworms and textile fibers of vegetable origin:

Walter (8:3): They get wool from sheep, then cloth . . . that's made . . . with a needle and thread, with sewing machines I think, and cotton . . . I don't know.

Irene (10:2): Some stuff, like linen and cotton, they get from flowers; the linen flower, for instance, is blue; cotton is grown in the fields, in India and other countries; wool comes from sheep.

At this level, the children answer that fruit is found on the trees and wood for chairs comes from logs.

Table 6 shows the distribution of answers given by city children over the three levels described above. It may be seen that the development sequence differs according to the object in question. While the majority of children of all ages correctly indicate the natural origin of the peach, such an origin is mentioned for textiles by the majority of children aged from 8 to 9, and for glass by those aged from 10 to 11.

TABLE 6
URBAN CHILDREN'S ANSWER LEVELS ABOUT THE PRODUCTION OF CLOTHES (C), GLASS (G) AND PEACH (P)

Age	4-5			6-7			8-9			10-11			Total		
Answer level	C	G	P	C	G	P	C	G	P	C	G	P	C	G	P
1.No production	5	5	5	5	4	2	3	0	0	0	0	0	13	9	7
2. Don't know	15	15	2	15	14	5	6	15	2	2	5	0	38	49	9
3. Raw materials	0	0	13	0	2	13	11	5	18	18	15	20	29	22	64
Total	20	20	20	20	20	20	20	20	20	20	20	20	80	80	80

TABLE 7
NUMBER OF URBAN CHILDREN GIVING ANSWERS AT THE SAME OR DIFFERENT LEVEL ON EACH PAIR OF CONSIDERED OBJECTS (PROBLEM: GOODS PRODUCTION)

	Pairs of objects		
	Clothes-Glass	Clothes-Peach	Glass-Peach
Higher on the first object	13	3	3
Same level on both objects	58	42	35
Higher on the second object	9	35	42
Sign Test significance	n.s.	$p < .001$	$p < .001$

TABLE 8
MOUNTAIN CHILDREN'S ANSWER LEVELS ABOUT THE PRODUCTION OF CLOTHES (C), GLASS (G), PEACH (P) AND CHAIR (CH)

Age	4-5				6-7				8-9				10-11			
Levels	C	G	P	Ch	C	G	P	Ch	C	G	P	Ch	C	G	P	Ch
1 No production	7	15	8	6	5	7	4	4	1	2	3	0	0	0	0	0
2 Don't know	11	5	1	3	10	10	0	6	3	12	0	1	7	11	0	0
3 Raw materials	2	0	11	11	5	3	16	10	16	6	17	19	1	39	20	20
Total	20	20	20	20	20	20	20	20	20	20	20	20	20	20	20	20

These differences are reflected in correlations between age and answer level and in the results of the sign test given in Table 7. Spearman's correlation coefficients, while always significant (p<.001), differ according to the object in question (rho = .38 for the peach, .69 for the clothes and .63 for the glass). Table 7 reveals that many children give the same type of answer for the two manufactured items, and the answers of different type are scattered at random. The answers for the peach, on the other hand, are more advanced than those for the clothes or glass.

The answers given by children of the mountain group are shown in Table 8, and follow a similar pattern. Here we see that recognition of natural origin occurs first for the peach, then for wood, then material, and finally for glass. Answer levels for all objects are significantly correlated with age (p<.001). Correlation is, however, higher for answers regarding the three manufactured items (clothes: rho = .53; glass: rho = .63; table: rho = .47) than for the peach (rpb= .39).[1]

Comparison by pairs of answers given for the clothes, glass, and peach reveals that numerous children express ideas of the same level, and that this happens especially in the cases of the clothes and the glass (see Table 9). Here too, as in the city group, ideas regarding the peach are more advanced than for the clothes or glass. Unlike the city children, whose ideas regarding the two manufactured items do not differ significantly, the ideas of the rural children are more advanced for the clothes than for the glass. Comparison of answers given for the chair with those for each of the three other objects reveals that the number of children giving the same type of answer for the peach and the chair is much higher than for the other two objects. Moreover, the sign test shows that the few answers of different level given for the peach and the chair are distributed at random. Answers given for the chair are, however, more advanced than those for the clothes and glass.

The order in which the children of the two groups recognize the existence of raw materials for different types of object corresponds overall to what the complexity of the transformations inherent in the production of each led us to expect. The only exception is provided by the fact that the city children's answers for the glass were not significantly less advanced than for the clothes, which is not easy to explain.

Comparison of City and Mountain Group Children

Initial comparison of the two groups as regards ideas of production reveals significant differences only for younger children and only in the case of the glass (Chi square = 8.9, df = 1, p<.01). Table 10 shows the distribution of answers over the three levels and the way in which levels were combined when necessary in order to calculate the Chi square.

It can be seen that the ideas of the two groups regarding the production of the peach and clothes follow the same lines. The origin of the fruit is correctly indicated by the majority of children by the age of 7, and level 3 answers are given by

---

[1] In the case of the peach, since all but one of the answers were distributed over only two levels, point-biserial coefficient of correlation was calculated by giving a value of 0 to all level 1 answers and to the one level 2 answer, and a value of 1 to the others.

TABLE 9
NUMBER OF MOUNTAIN CHILDREN GIVING ANSWERS AT THE SAME OR DIFFERENT
LEVEL ON EACH PAIR OF CONSIDERED OBJECTS (PROBLEM: GOODS PRODUCTION)

	Pairs of objects		
	Clothes-Glass	Clothes-Peach	Glass-Peach
Higher on the first object	32	7	4
Same level on both objects	44	42	30
Higher on the second object	4	31	46
Sign test significance	$p < .001$	$p < .001$	$p < .001$

	Clothes-Chair	Glass-Chair	Peach-Chair
Higher on the first object	1	45	10
Same level on both objects	52	35	62
Higher on the second object	27	0	8
Sign test significance	$p < .001$	$p < .001$	n.s.

TABLE 10
COMPARISON OF ANSWER FREQUENCY AT EACH LEVEL GIVEN BY URBAN AND
MOUNTAIN CHILDREN (PROBLEM: GOODS PRODUCTION)

4- to 7-year-old children

	clothes		glass		peach	
	U	M	U	M	U	M
level 1.	10	12	9	22	7	12
level 2	30	21	29	15	7	1
level 3	0	7	2	3	26	27
Total	40	40	40	40	40	40

8- to 11-year-old children

	clothes		glass		peach	
	U	M	U	M	U	M
level 1	3	1	0	2	0	3
level 2	8	10	20	23	2	0
level 3	29	29	20	15	38	37
Total	40	40	40	40	40	40

practically all children aged 8-11. Both mountain and city groups go from level 2 answers, which predominate among the younger children, to the level 3 answers generally given by the older. In the case of the glass, however, the mountain group starts from a more backward level. The youngest of them do not even mention production. By the age of 8-11 years, however, the economic knowledge base been built up and there are no longer significant differences between the two groups.

Greater differences emerge on examination of the frequency of the two types of level 2 answer. The mountain group rarely mentions the recycling of already existing material, and never in the case of the peach. These ideas are, however, often found in the city group, especially for the glass. Table 11 shows that differences between the two groups are always significant in this case (clothes: Chi square = 4.59, p<.05; glass: Chi square = 23, p<.001; peach: Fisher Exact Test, p<.005). All these results show that city children have a greater tendency to use imagination, and supports the hypothesis previously put forward as to why the idea of a "shopkeeper-producer" is so widespread in the urban group. Their limited experience of productive activity is precisely what enables city children to imagine

someone picking up bits of broken glass in the street and sticking them together to make glasses, or making clothes out of rags. In the case of the mountain children, their familiarity with timber, tree-felling, and the transformation of logs into planks, gives them a more precise idea of production, which they cannot easily generalize and apply to other fields. This acts as a brake on their imagination. As they do not know what material glass and cloth are made of, they simply admit it. This may be seen when they only mention the sale of the goods, without imagining the shopkeeper or anyone else sticking bits together.

CONCLUSIONS

The data presented enable us to answer the questions underlying our study. Are the sequences we have described really stage-like? What role does the environment play in the development of children's conceptions of the chain of production and distribution of goods and the origin of raw materials?

The sequences we have suggested make it possible to classify all the answers given by children of different ages and localities, both in regard to the roles making up the chain of production and

TABLE 11
COMPARISON OF FREQUENCY OF TYPE (a) AND (b) ANSWERS GIVEN BY URBAN AND MOUNTAIN CHILDREN ABOUT THE PRODUCTION OF CLOTHES, GLASSES AND PEACH

	clothes		glass		peach	
	U	M	U	M	U	M
2a	18	23	12	29	2	1
2b	20	8	37	9	7	0

distribution of goods, and in regard to the raw materials required for production. Age and answer level are always significantly correlated. It appears that in most cases, children give answers of the same level for more than one object. This shows that the levels distinguished by us are found in different sample groups and for different subjects, and thus supports the idea that the child gradually constructs concepts of increasing complexity and adequacy for this aspect of the economic world. However, the different frequencies of some types of answer according to the object in question and the child's environment lead us to wonder whether the sequences are made up of steps that each child must follow, or whether particular environmental circumstances can modify the process and allow the child to bypass certain stages.

With respect to the origin of goods, the sequence we have described is characterized by two different aspects derived from distinct psychological processes. The first is the growing number of economic functions and activities that the child connects at different stages in a chain of distribution. Many scholars, who start from different theoretical premises, acknowledge that in the course of cognitive development the child constructs increasingly complex and integrated structures, linking a growing number of operations or pieces of information. There is much to support this point of view, both in the sphere of social cognition and the sphere of physical or logico-mathematical knowledge (see Case, 1985). This aspect of our sequence can thus be regarded as deriving from fundamental psychological processes, and therefore as universal.

The second aspect characterizing the sequence is that it follows in reverse order the stages that goods follow in the

real world from production to consumption. The children initially mention no economic role, but say that the objects are in the house or are made by their parents. Shopkeepers are mentioned only later, and producers last of all. This aspect of the sequence is not derived from any psychological structure, but simply reflects the type of experience available to children of all ages in urban industrial societies. There may therefore be greater or lesser variations in environments that differ from this one. In urban areas, where the child is constantly in contact with the phenomenon of retail selling but can seldom observe productive activity, the first step towards reconstruction of the chain of production and distribution is necessarily recognition of the role and functions of the shopkeeper. We have seen that a large number of city children take this first step at 4-5 years of age.

The next step is to link the functions of producing and selling. Our results indicate different ways of achieving this. In some environments, such as the mountain village considered here, children are in contact not only with shopkeepers but also with artisans, who combine the functions of production and selling. When asked about the origin of goods produced by artisans, these children obtain a correct solution from their own direct experience. In other environments (such as our city district) the children have little or no familiarity with this kind of role. The solution they arrive at is not therefore derived from their observation of artisans and workers, but from their awareness that a productive phase is necessary, although they are unable to attribute this to any role other than the familiar shopkeeper. The "advantage" enjoyed by the mountain group is, however, relative. It must be borne in mind that, for all the goods now produced only or mostly in factories (the majority), their knowledge of craftspeople does not enable them to give correct answers. When asked about such objects as the glass, the mountain children, just like their city counterparts, are forced to draw conclusions going far beyond the evidence of their own eyes. They do, however, know one thing more than the city children, i.e., that there are two types of sellers, those who make their own goods and those who do not. Their ability to distinguish the two roles makes them less inclined to offer imaginative solutions, such as the "shopkeeper-producer" of glasses.

Recognition of the functions of production and retail selling still does not make it possible to construct a relatively faithful image of modern society, characterized as it is by the division of labor. A further step towards this is to recognize the specific nature of these two functions, and to distinguish to some extent a role characterized by production from one characterized by selling. This only happens at an age when children are no longer tied to their own direct experience, but are able to process verbal information and thus to extend their knowledge outside their immediate environment by adding details to the ideas of the economic world from books, television, and school. Our study has revealed that differences between the two groups tend to disappear gradually as children grow older and more capable of using "free-floating information," in which respect there is no significant difference between an Alpine village and a city on the plains of Northern Italy.

To conclude, the sequence of the chain of distribution we have delineated appears to be characteristic, especially in the first levels, of city children. There-fore, in our opinion, it should be found more or less the same not only in the type of level, but also in the rate of transition from one level to another for all children from this type of environment. In environments where artisans are numerous, diversification is to be expected in the sequence according to the goods under consideration. There will also be children who immediately identify the artisan as a role on the same level as the shopkeeper, and subsequently distinguish between producers and sellers without forming the idea of a "shopkeeper-producer."

It has been seen that an important stage in understanding the chain of distribution is the recognition that goods exist because someone makes them. Piaget's study of the child's representation of the world (1926) reveals that younger children see no problem regarding the origin of the things around them. They ask themselves "where things come from" but not "how they began," as if they have always been in existence. Piaget calls this way of thinking "diffuse artificialism" and traces it back both to the cognitive characteristics of the small child (egocentrism) and to social factors. The child is accustomed to depend on parents who satisfy all its needs, and therefore finds it natural that the world should be equipped with everything one requires. This type of attitude is reflected in the most primitive answers given as regards production: the objects are in the house, or in a cupboard that the shopkeeper takes them out of; apples are "in the orchard," and those without an orchard get them from the cellar; the glasses are in the sideboard, and when they break you get more from the cupboard.

Seeing the problem of the origin of objects does not mean being able to solve it. According to Piaget (1926) "diffuse artificialism" is followed by "mythological artificialism," which is characterized by the idea that natural elements such as lakes, mountains and stars originated in human constructive activities, coupled with imaginative conceptions of the way in which this came about. Similar conceptions were found during our study, such as the idea that the materials used to make clothes, glasses, and even peaches were themselves produced by human activity. Children with these ideas seem completely incapable of recognizing nature as the source of what human beings merely transform. These imaginative elaborations are not, however, found with the same frequency in the two environments under consideration. While the city children were naively convinced of their ability to solve the problem even without all the necessary data, direct experience of productive activity made the mountain children aware of the fact that raw materials are necessary, and made them cautious in cases where they could not distinguish the raw materials involved. We see that an important function of direct experience is that of making the child more prudent. Awareness of the limitations of their knowledge makes them less willing to fill the gaps with inferences that do not strike them as very plausible.

REFERENCES

Ajello, A.M., Bombi, A.S., Pontecorvo, C. & Zucchermaglio, C. (1986a). Teaching economics in the primary school: The concepts of work and profit. *International Journal of Behavioral Development,* in press.

Ajello, A.M., Bombi, A.S., Pontecorvo, C. & Zucchermaglio, C. (1986b). Understanding agriculture as an economic activity: The role of figurative information. *European Journal of Psychology of Education,* in press.

Berti, A.E., & Bombi, A.S. (1981). *Il mondo economico nel bambino.* Firenze: La Nuova Italia.

Berti, A.E., Bombi, A.S. & De Beni, R. (1986). Acquiring economic notions: Profit. International *Journal of Behavioral Development, 9,* 15-29.

Berti, A.E., Bombi, A.S., & Lis, A. (1982). The child's conceptions about means of production and their owner. *European Journal of Social Psychology, 12,* 221-239.

Berti, A.E. & De Beni, R. (1986). *Logical and mnemonic prerequisites for the concept of profit.* Paper presented to the Second European Conference on Developmental Psychology, Rome, Italy.

Burris, V.L. (1983). Stages in the development of economic concepts. *Human Relations, 36, 9,* 791-812.

Case, R. (1985). *Intellectual development from birth to adulthood.* New York: Academic Press.

Connell, R.W. (1971). *The child's construction of politics.* Carlton, Vic.: Melbourne University Press.Connell, R.W. (1977). *Ruling class, ruling culture.* Melbourne: Cambridge University Press.

Danziger, K. (1958). Children's earliest conceptions of economic relationships (Australia). *Journal of Genetic Psychology, 91,* 231-240.

Duveen, G. & Shields, M. (1984). *The influence of gender on the development of young children's representations of work roles.* Paper presented to the First European Conference on Developmental Psychology, Groningen, Netherlands.

Emler, N. & Dickinson, J. (1985). Children's representation of economic inequalities: The effect of social class. *British Journal of Developmental Psychology, 3,* 191-198.

Furth, H.G. (1980). *The world of grown-ups.* New York: Elsevier.

Goldstein, B. & Oldham, J. (1979). *Children and work: A study of socialization.* New Brunswick, N.J.: Transaction Books.

Hong Kwan, T. & Stacey, B. (1981). The understanding of socio-economic concepts in Malaysian Chinese school children. *Child Study Journal, 11,* 33-49.

Jahoda, G. (1979). The construction of economic reality by some Glaswegian children. *European Journal of Social Psychology, 9,* 115-127.

Jahoda, G. (1983). European "lag" in the development of an economic concept: A study in Zimbabwe. *British Journal of Developmental Psychology, 1,* 113-120.

Jahoda, G. & Woerdenbagch, A. (1982). The development of ideas about an economic institution: A cross-national replication. *British Journal of Social Psychology, 21,* 337-338.

Kourilsky, M. (1981). Economic socialization of children: Attitude toward the distribution of rewards. *The Journal of Social Psychology, 115,* 45-57.

Leahy, R.L. (1981). The development of the conception of economic inequality: Descriptions and comparisons of rich and poor people. *Child Development, 52,* 523-532

Leahy, R.L. (1983). Development of the conception of economic inequality: II. Explanations, Justifications, and concepts of social mobility and change. *Developmental Psychology, 19,* 111-125.

Leiser, D. (1983). Children's conceptions of economics. The constitution of a cognitive domain. *Journal of Economic Psychology, 4,* 297-317.

Piaget, J. (1926). *La représentation du monde chez l'enfant.* Paris: P.U.F.

Stacey, B. (1982). Economic socialization in pre-adult years. *British Journal of Social Psychology, 21,* 159-173.

Strauss, A. (1952). The development and tranformation of monetary meaning in the child. *American Sociological Review, 17,* 275-286.

Strauss, A. (1954). The development of conception of rules in children. *Child Development, 25,* 193-208.

Chapter 12

Formal Operational Thought
and the Moroccan Adolescent

Douglas A. Davis

INTRODUCTION

In this chapter I report some of the results of an investigation of problem-solving and cognitive development among adolescents in a Moroccan town. The cognitive data were collected as part of a comprehensive cross-cultural study of adolescence in a variety of national settings. The Moroccan portion of this study is the subject of a forthcoming book by Susan Schaefer Davis and myself. The larger study (entitled the Harvard Adolescence Project) involved ethnographic participant-observation as well as structured interviewing and cognitive testing. Here, I will discuss only the results of the more narrowly cognitive testing in relation to the cultural, community, and personal context in which these young Moroccans performed the tasks given. My intention is thus to combine presentation of a particular contribution to the cross-cultural literature on cognitive development with a more general discussion of the problems that have beset the search for universal factors in the devel-

opment of psychological abilities. The result will be neither a conventional presentation of empirical research on a particular aspect of development, nor a traditional ethnographic treatment of a non-Western community, but a combination of both.

This chapter will first briefly discuss the cross-cultural psychological literature on the development of formal-operational and post-conventional reasoning. After describing the Moroccan field setting in which the ethnographic observation and systematic testing were done, I will present the results of tests of problem-solving and block design administered to a sample of young people in Morocco, showing the effects on their performance of sex, age, and years of formal schooling. Finally, I will discuss and elaborate on these findings by drawing on semi-structured interviews with some of the subjects in the larger study, using the latter discussion to raise general questions about the adequacy of existing cross-cultural models of development.

273

CULTURE, COGNITION, AND ADOLESCENCE

The major cognitive change alleged to occur during the adolescent years involves the emergence of what Piaget has called "formal operations" (Inhelder & Piaget, 1958; Piaget, 1972). Formal operations are reflected in increased ability to reason hypothetically independently of concrete situations, and to describe one's own reasoning processes. In the samples studied by Inhelder and Piaget, formal operations were said to become established between the ages of roughly 11 and 15. Piaget noted, however, that the rate of progression through the developmental stages described appeared to vary from culture to culture (Inhelder & Piaget, 1958, pp. 337-347). He also acknowledged that while formal operational reasoning is in principle independent of the content to which it is applied, empirical studies have indicated individual and cultural differences in the contexts in which such reasoning is displayed. It was thus reasonable to assume that the wide range of sociocultural settings in which our data for the Harvard Adolescence Project were collected would show divergences from the bulk of the U.S. and European developmental literature in the levels and rate of achievement of various cognitive performances.

The Harvard Adolescence Project

The research on which our account of "Zawiya" (the name we shall here give the Moroccan town in which the data reported below were collected) is based was conducted as part of a cross-cultural and interdisciplinary study of adolescence in seven cultural settings under the auspices of the Department of Anthropology at Harvard University. The Harvard Adolescence Project was designed by Beatrice and John Whiting and Irven DeVore, and co-supervised by a group of Harvard scholars from the fields of cultural and biological anthropology, cognitive and personality psychology, and education. This project continued a long involvement of the Whitings and their students in cross-cultural studies, constituting what has been called the "Field Guide" approach (Campbell & LeVine, 1970).

The general goals of the Adolescence Project were to sample cultures representing widely varied levels of complexity, ecological setting, and ethnic/religion background, and to study the related physical, psychological, and social maturation of a group of young people between puberty and adulthood in each of these settings. While the studies undertaken were methodologically complex, and while each has evolved partially independently of the others, certain theoretical questions as well as a set of core methods were shared. These included the definition and testing of a sub-sample of adolescents from several of the settings on two cognitive measures: a test of logical problem-solving through the elimination of alternatives, developed by Edith Neimark (Neimark & Lewis, 1967); and the standard Kohs block-design subtest of the WISC. These were selected because they each had been shown to be strongly related to both maturation and intelligence in the Western literature, and because each seemed relatively free of cultural content. The settings studied included an Inuit settlement in the Canadian Arctic, an Aboriginal settlement in northern Australia, a Thai fishing village, two Ijo-speaking towns in southern Nigeria, a Kikuyt community in Kenya, a

Romanian farming town, and the town of "Zawiya" in central Morocco. I will briefly review the cross-cultural literature before presenting our own findings.

Keating (1980), in a critical discussion of the literature concerning cognitive development in adolescence, notes deep and quite pervasive disagreement about both the extent to which Piagetian "formal operational" thought has been demonstrated and the extent to which it *can* be demonstrated, given the complexity and the inadequate specification of the alleged components of reasoning. Commenting on this literature, Kagan (1972, p. 90) notes that "the Western mind is friendly toward the construction of discrete, abstract categories, each with its special set of defining characteristics." This "prejudice" Kagan contrasts sharply with the preference of the Chinese for viewing nature and experience as part of a "contained and continuous whole." The latter position is probably closer to that of non-Western peoples generally. As Kagan suggests, the psychology of the West conceives of discrete developmental stages as natural, and it purports to discover evidence of stage-specific behaviors. The most influential twentieth century theories of personality development (those of Freud and Erikson), of cognitive development (Piaget, 1932, 1972), and of moral reasoning (Kohlberg) all treat psychological functioning as stage-specific. The consequences of such assumptions have recently become the subject of important criticisms (cf. Gilligan, 1982).

Some of the developmental literature has specifically addressed the concept of a "releasing mechanism" for the next stage of cognitive development. In a study using the Embedded Figures Test (Witkin et al., 1962) with a population of rural and urban Moroccans, Wagner (1978) attempted mathematically to partial out the effect of schooling on the EFT, and found that the predictiveness of both age and the rural-urban ecological variable largely disappeared. Education may function, Wagner suggests, as a releaser variable for a variety of cognitive performances.

Cross-Cultural Piagetian Research

In a general review of this literature, Dasen (1972) noted that the bulk of the cross-cultural Piagetian work has been "descriptive" rather than "experimental." Most studies have found some support for the qualitative stages described by Piaget, but cultural factors typically appear to affect the rate of development.

Much of the cross-cultural research on the development of formal operations has shown cultural differences in the levels of reasoning displayed by members of various cultures, with schooled Western samples consistently showing superior performance. Cross-cultural sex differences have also been demonstrated, with male subjects tending to score higher on a variety of measures of formal operational reasoning. Douglas and Wong (1977), for example, found that a sample of American 13- and 15-year-olds scored higher on three Piagetian formal-operational tasks than did a sample of similarly aged Chinese youth, and that males performed better than females. Chinese females had the lowest scores on each of the tasks.

Cross-Cultural Research
On Moral Reasoning

While the first data to be reported here were concerned with an abstract measure of formal operational reasoning rather than with social cognition, the possible relevance of this cognitive domain to social cognition was a concern of the Harvard Adolescence Project. The most widely cited cross-cultural literature on social cognition concerns the dimension of moral judgment as articulated by Kohlberg and his associates (Kohlberg, 1964, 1971; Kohlberg & Gilligan, 1971). Kohlberg's work has important implications for developmental psychology generally, since the internalization of cultural values is a topic with cognitive-learning, personality, and neuropsychological implications. His treatment of moral reasoning draws heavily on Piaget's stage theory of the development of genetic epistemology, and similar difficulties have attended its cross-cultural application.

In a current review of the literature on the cross-cultural universality of Kohlberg's stages of social-moral development, Snarey (1985, p. 202) finds "striking support" for many of Kohlberg's assumptions, and also great difficulty discovering "post-conventional" moral cognitions in non-Western settings. As Snarey notes, one key assumption made by Kohlbergian research has been that the full range of moral stages (pre-conventional, conventional, and post-conventional) be present in all cultures.

However, while the full range has been demonstrated repeatedly for Westernized urban societies both in Europe and elsewhere, *no* study reviewed by Snarey found evidence of Stage 4/5 or Stage 5 moral reasoning in a non-urban, non-Western setting. Salili, Maehr, and Gillmore (1976) compared evaluations of described moral and achievement situations by Iranian children ranging in age from seven to 18

years. They found roughly similar overall stages in the evaluation of moral situations. Iranian subjects, however, seemed to expect more moral behavior from persons of higher described ability than did similarly aged Americans; seemed more ready to view described competence as an inherent good; and seemed more ready to reward effort regardless of outcome of a described activity. Salili et al. suggest that cross-cultural variations in such factors as the relative importance of ascribed social status may be important constraints on subjects' behavior in moral-judgmental tasks.

Using a new manual calling for matching responses to criteria judgments, Nisan and Kohlberg (1982) compared the stage levels and sequences of village and urban Turkish subjects between the ages of 10 and 28, with earlier work on Western populations. They argue that their results support the claim for structural universality in moral judgment. Village subjects showed a slower rate of development than city subjects, used lower levels of reasoning on all dilemmas presented, and tended to stabilize at Kohlberg's Stage 3 (Conventional). They also tended (regardless of stage) to justify their decisions in terms of social norms. In contrast, older city subjects were more likely to relate their positions to principles of justice. Nisan and Kohlberg suggest that the "conventionality" of the village subjects' responses may have stemmed from the continued presence of a strong moral consensus in the village setting, and they argue that "the social ecology of the small village does not seem to call for the broader, generalized system perspective which is the hallmark of Stage 4" (1982, p. 875).

It was therefore with the ambitious and mixed goals of discovering formal-operational thinking in the narrower sense, and of relating it to more contextual thinking about social and personal dilemmas, that we set out for Zawiya in January, 1982.

Neimark's Problem-solving Task

Neimark, who developed the problem-solving task used in our own research (Neimark, 1964), noted that subjects' calculated strategy scores for performance on the eight-problem task correlated significantly with the rated quality of their verbal descriptions of the strategy used (Neimark, 1975b), as well as with mental age (Neimark, 1967). The task used involves matching a pattern concealed under a set of eight shutters arranged in a circle to one of a set of eight patterns of white and black dots (Neimark & Wagner, 1964; Neimark & Lewis, 1967).

The optimal strategy for solving such a problem involves reducing uncertainty by one bit per move through selection of a shutter position, at which half the still-eligible patterns have a black, and half a white, dot. Each optimal move thus discovers one binary feature of the concealed pattern, and this has the effect of reducing uncertainty by half with each shutter-choice. The results to be reported below express test performance as an average "strategy score," expressed in the average content in bits of the subject's moves: 1.00 represents a perfect three-move solution to each of the eight problems in the test proper; 0.65 represents random performance. Mean performance among American subjects tested by Neimark increased from roughly 0.75 at age 10 to over 0.90 by age 17 (Neimark, 1967, p. 112).

Zawiya

All four of the field sites in which roughly comparable data to those to be presented here (Romania, Morocco, Canadian Inuit, and Thailand) were collected are non-urban traditional communities, and three are also non-Western. In two of these settings (Romania, Morocco) a sample of adolescents were in addition to the Neimark testing asked a set a questions concerned with social cognition and moral values. These data (for the Moroccan case I will be briefly discussed below. More information about the domain of moral reasoning in these settings is provided in the monographs concerned with adolescence in each of the field sites making up the Harvard Adolescence Project.[1]

The community in which the ethnographic data presented below were collected has been described in detail by Susan S. Davis (1982). It is a large, traditional Muslim, semi-rural community of about 11,000 citizens (1980 census) in north central Morocco only a few miles from a small city built during French colonialism. Susan Davis and I returned to Zawiya during ten months of 1982 as one of the field teams of the Harvard Adolescence Project. We had lived in the same neighborhood a decade before. The focus of our ethnographic interviewing, testing, and observation was roughly 50 families living in one neighborhood, and in particular their 150 children who were between the ages of nine and 21 at the time of the study. During eleven months of fieldwork in 1982 we lived in this neighborhood and took part in many of

---

[1] These are being published as separate volumes in the series Adolescents in a Changing World, Rutgers University Press.

its public and semi-private activities such as weddings and circumcisions. We collected physical growth measurements and background family, educational, and travel data on over 100 adolescents. We also interviewed two dozen teenagers and young adults at length about their experiences and feelings toward family, friends, and self. These interviews typically included both the "social cognition" questions reported below and the presentation and solicitation of "moral dilemmas." Neimark's problem-solving task was administered during the summer vacation of 1982 to a sub-sample of 65 adolescents, and the Kohs block test was given to 46 of these in December of that year.

COGNITIVE TESTING

Testing Situation

The Zawiya sample for Neimark's problem-solving task included 65 young people, 31 males and 34 females. Testing was carried out late in the 1982 summer school vacation. Test administration was by the author or by Susan Schaefer Davis, assisted by Hamid Elasri, a male schoolteacher from the neighborhood.[2] All explanation and prompting was delivered in colloquial Arabic, and all testing was in a semi-private room in the researchers' house. Since the flavor of this testing may be important in interpretation of the results, I quote briefly from my fieldnotes concerning the testing experience:

---

[2] Test materials and a computer program for calculation of strategy scores were prepared by Mitchell Ratner and Ann-Mari Gemmill, who conducted the Romanian study in the Harvard Adolescence Project. Ratner is preparing his results for publication in the *Adolescents in a Changing World* series.

[26-Aug-82] *Formal testing*. After two days and about eight runs, the special vocabulary for the Neimark is getting clear. We have just tested two sons in the same family, and the older made no errors at all and could give a clear explanation of the rationale (i.e., that he should eliminate half the remaining possibilities each time), while his 13-year-old brother was essentially random even by the end and after a great deal of prompting by my assistant Hamid. The older brother is a strong student in fifth year of science, while the younger has flunked three years, so age and intelligence are probably confounded.

[28-Aug-82] With most of the sample males between 11 and 16 tested, it appears the age at which most have the ability on which success at the Neimark depends is much older than in the U.S. At least half the subjects never really get the idea that there is a correspondence between the picture covered by the shutters and the problem alternatives, such that one can eliminate possibilities steadily. We have had to remind several at *each* move to cover the *dis*-similar and not the similar dots, and roughly a third of subjects make mistakes until the end on which alternatives a shutter move entitles them to cover. We also are encountering a whole range of Third World distractions: older and younger sibling tagging along, previous subjects trying to kibbitz, wedding parties passing the house with loud music, our daughter's preschool group reciting Arabic or playing in the courtyard, a goat wandering into the house.

Correlational Results: Neimark Task

Despite these difficulties, which gave us in a few days a profound respect for the complications of cross-cultural testing, we were able to discover significant correlates of performance on this and the block-design test. While we took pains

TABLE 1
COGNITIVE TEST RESULTS FOR ZAWIYA ADOLESCENTS

Sex	N	Neimark	Mean Age	Mean Schooling
Males	31	0.686	15.5	5.3
Females	34	0.610	15.4	4.0

to test roughly equal numbers of male and female adolescents at about the same ages, we did not attempt to match numbers of years of schooling for the two groups. Summary data for the sample are given in Table 1.

The average age of males tested was 15.5 (range 12.5-20.5 years), and that of females 15.4 years (range 11.3-21 years). The 31 males who completed the Neimark test had successfully completed an average of 5.3 years of schooling (range 3-9 years), while the 34 females had an average of 4.0 years (range 0-10 years). Thus, while the mean Neimark test score for females (0.610) is significantly (p<.01) lower than that for males (0.686), this is almost certainly due at least in part to their lower average schooling. Girls in Zawiya are still only about half as likely as boys to continue beyond elementary school, although roughly equal proportions begin the five-year elementary school program.[3] It should also be noted that the Moroccan school system is very competitive, with a very high failure rate (almost one year for every two attended, in the Zawiya sample) and a difficult standardized examination for passage to secondary school.

As expected, the variables of age, completed years of schooling, and performance on Neimark's problem-solving task were correlated, and the pattern of correlations was quite different for males and females (see Table 2). The most striking difference is that age and years of schooling are not significantly correlated for females tested. Secondary schools have been built close to Zawiya only in the past few years, so only recently have increasing proportions of girls been continuing beyond the first few years of elementary school. As a consequence, the older teenage girls tested in 1982 were not on the average more educated than their younger neighbors and sisters. The significant correlation of years of schooling with Neimark performance indicated that the small group who were more schooled were indeed better able to complete the task than their school-dropout agemates. For males, age and schooling were strongly correlated, and it is therefore not surprising that both age and schooling show significant positive relationship to Neimark performance.

When the strategy score is treated as a simultaneous function of sex, age, and schooling using multiple regression analysis, the effect of age is statistically significant (p<.01); that of years of schooling is marginally so (p<.10); and that of sex is still significant (p< .05). That is,

---

[3] Roughly one-third of the secondary-school age children in the study neighborhood were still enrolled in 1982. Schooling data reported here are for the number of years passed by each individual.

TABLE 2
INTERCORRELATIONS OF NEIMARK WITH AGE AND SCHOOLING

	Schooling	Strategy
Males (N = 31)		
Age	.74***	.37*
Schooling	—	.49**
Strategy Score		—
Females (N = 34)		
Age	.14	.45**
Schooling	—	.21
Strategy Score		—

*p < .05.   **p < .01   ***p < .001

older, more schooled, and male subjects tended to do better on the test even when the other effects were statistically controlled. These results are consistent with those of other researchers, in that performance on any measure of Piagetian formal operations is expected to increase sharply with age (Hollos, Leis, & Turiel, 1986; Neimark & Lewis, 1968). Formal schooling appears also to be a key contributor to test performance. The poorer performance of girls tested is, as suggested above, probably due primarily to the fact that fewer of them (15%, compared to 39% of males) had reached the secondary school level at which formal reasoning is taught, although it is also possible they were more anxious at being questioned by males. Even among male subjects, however, the average level of performance was not much above chance. I kept detailed notes on the way each subject approached the task, and I was in several cases startled to note that a boy who was a skilled card or checkers player (both skills tapping similar problem-solving abilities) was utterly confused by the Neimark test.

Correlational Results: Kohs Block Task

For the block design task, the results show even more clearly the critical role that formal schooling can play, despite the smaller sample size for this study. The average score for the 24 females that we tested (18.6) was not significantly different from that of the 22 males (20.0). While age and years of successfully completed schooling were both moderately correlated with block design performance, when both variables were included in the regression analysis only years of schooling contributed signifi-

TABLE 3
INTERCORRELATIONS OF KOHS BLOCKS WITH AGE AND SCHOOLING

	Schooling	Kohs
Males (N = 22)		
Age	.75***	.40*
Schooling	—	.48**
Kohs	—	
Females (N = 24)		
Age	.24	.30
Schooling	—	.34*
Kohs	—	

*p < .05 **p < .01 ***p < .001

cantly (p<.05). The deletion of two female subjects who had had *no* schooling increased the strength of this finding (p< .01). The intercorrelations of the Kohs block design task with age and schooling for both male and female subjects are depicted in Table 3.

These results appear to confirm the strong role of structured schooling in establishing even modest levels of achievement on standard measures of cognitive performance. To more fully understand the possible applications of cognitive capacities to real (or at least moderately realistic) situations, we relied on semi-structured interviews with a subset of neighborhood youth. This attempt involved both discussions of moral dilemmas and/or presenting subjects with a modified version of the "Heinz" dilemma used by Kohlberg, and the administration of a set of questions requiring logical thought or

generali-zation from a concrete situation. The latter set of questions were modeled closely on a set used by Mitchell Ratner in his research in a Romanian town as part of the Harvard Adolescence Project.

Our own set of questions consisted of the following:

Social Cognition Questionnaire

A. Hypotheticals

1. What would happen if a sheep didn't have feet?
2. What would happen if only boys were born in Zawiya?
3. What would happen if the buses and trains no longer ran?
4. Now can you make a question that begins, "What would happen if?"?

B. Exhaustion of Possibilities

1. A family has a goat. One night the goat didn't come home. Can you explain why this might happen? Might there be another explanation? Another? [Three explanations were asked for.]

2. There once was a farmer who always would plow with two different mules. One day he would use the brown and the black, another day the brown and the white, and so on. If he had 3 mules, how many days could he plow without using the exact same pair twice? What if he had 4 mules? And if he had 5 mules?

C. Counterfactuals

1. People began to use cars in 1900. Sultan Moulay Ismail lived in the 17th century. Is it possible that in a Meknes museum where they keep old things so that we now may see them there is a car that Moulay Ismail used?

2. One person builds his house of brick, and another builds his house of stone. Is it possible for a house of brick to be heavier than a house of stone? [If no: What if the brick house were much larger?]

3. Three farmers met at the market. Each had a sheep to sell. Farmer A looked at the sheep of B, and he thought to himself, "My sheep is larger than B's, I'll get a higher price." Later Farmer C looked at the sheep of A and thought, "My sheep is larger than A's, I'll get a higher price." Then Farmer B looked at the sheep of Farmer C, and he thought to *himself*, "My sheep is larger, I'll get a higher price." What do you think? Is it possible for all the farmers to be right in what they believed?

4.a) Let's say there is a village called "Duwwar Zwin" and in Duwwar Zwin there are only black cows. On the way to Duwwar Zwin you met a woman from there and she said she had a cow at home. Would you know what color her cow was? What color?

b) On another day, you met on the road a woman from a neighboring village, called "Duwwar Xayb," and she told you she has a cow at home. Would you know what color her cow was? What color? Why?

c) If you happened to meet a black cow on the road, would you know for sure what village it was from?

d) And if you happened to meet a brown cow on the road, would you know for sure what village it was from? What village?

e) If the answer is "no": would you knw for sure what village the cow could *not* be from?

D. Social Counterfactuals

1. Is it possible for a schoolteacher to teach something that isn't true?

2. Is it possible for a father to tell a lie to his child?

3. Is it possible for a policeman to steal?

4. Is it possible for a wife to be very dear to her husband and [yet] he beats her?

5. [A question used by Ratner concerning whether a person could be both a Christian and a Communist was skipped.]

6. Is it possible for there to be a mother whose children are not dear to her?

7. Is it possible there is a religious scholar who studies the Koran and is married, and [yet] he goes out with [other] women?

8. Is it possible for a judge to put an innocent man in jail?

Nine males and 13 females between the ages of 11 and 21 were asked these questions late in the fieldwork year as part of a general round of interviewing concerning their attitudes and experiences. As a rough way of capturing the expected increase in sophistication during this age range, I simply noted the number of questions that elicited a clear "right" answer (e.g., "Yes," to "Is it possible for a house of brick to be heavier than a house of stone?"). For this group of subjects, the number of correct responses to the social thought questions was significantly correlated with years of successfully completed schooling (r =.45, p < .025). This effect appears to have been produced solely by the male respondents: however, when the data are dichotomized by sex, both age and school effects are significant for males while neither is for females. The correlation matrices for these social thought questions are presented in Table 4.

It seems plausible that this effect too is a consequence of the lower persistence of females into secondary school, and indeed, schooled subjects mentioned classroom parallels to some of the questions. The *manner* of responding to these questions showed the effects of schooling in a striking way for several of the male subjects. For example, three boys in secondary school puzzled over the mule-combination question, then asked for paper and pen and drew Cartesian products, explaining that they had learned this in math class!

For the last set of questions, concerned with whether various role models may behave inconsistently with their roles, I simply noted the number of times each subject responded "yes." This number increases with age and schooling, but the correlations are significant only for male subjects, among whom older youth gave more affirmative answers.

Individual subjects produced a number of responses that are of special interest in the context of social reasoning in Zawiya (and perhaps in other traditional communities). Younger children tended to answer each "social counterfactual" question in the negative: a teacher couldn't

TABLE 4
INTERCORRELATIONS OF SOCIAL THOUGHT WITH AGE AND SCHOOLING

	Schooling	Number Correct	Number Yes
Males (N = 9)			
Age	.47	.61*	.94*
Schooling	—	.85**	.42
Number Correct		—	.64*
Number Affirmed			
Females (N=13)			
Age	.26	.19	-.35
Schooling	—	.25	.11
Number Correct		—	.02
Number Affirmed			—

*p < .025.   **p < .001

teach a falsehood, a policeman can't steal. Older adolescents not only realized that such generalization could easily be false in a particular instance, but they also frequently couched their answers in terms of a realistic (if rather cynical) awareness of the tenuousness of moral behavior. Thus, 19-year-old Abdelaziz pointed out when asked whether a teacher could teach something that wasn't true that the teacher might teach something he himself believed (giving fortune-telling as an example) but which was not really so. He illustrated this principle with a quotation from the Koran condemning fortune-telling. Indeed, older adolescents often responded to the questions about whether authority figures could violate their trust with variations on, "Are you kidding?" When 18-year-old Kabiri was asked whether a judge could jail an innocent man he said, "Yes. Think how many innocent men are in jail." Several younger boys and girls, however, gave a simple "no" to all seven of these social counterfactual questions. Only one, a girl of 12.5, thought it was possible for a woman's children not to be "dear" to her, and she said this might be because her husband hit her because of their behavior.

WESTERN METHODOLOGY, ZAWIYA REALITY

These, then, are some illustrative results of an attempt to evoke adolescent cognitive judgments in a non-Western traditional setting. As important as any inferences about the validity of Western theories of development to which these findings might be applied, however, is the lesson concerning the *methodological* requirements of such research. Such work will, I believe, necessarily require toler-

ance for variations in testing procedures: samples that are small and non-random, and a mixture of numerical analysis and single-case explication which offends the clear distinctions most of us learned in graduate school. The fundamental tension I am describing is between rigorous and replicable methods involving *grouped* data, and a clinical/ethnographic style of selecting and presenting *case histories*. Accordingly, I have moved in this account, as in the book manuscript from which these results are partly extracted (Davis & Davis, forthcoming), from an account of a regression analysis of cognitive test data for a sample of 65 Zawiya subjects (themselves a sub-sample of the 150 neighborhood sample) to a more "clinical" attempt to understand the reasoning of several members of that first sample.

Moral Reasoning in Zawiya

We also asked our clinical informants about moral dilemmas, both ones posed by us and ones arising from their own recent experience. The results are impossible to summarize adequately here, but several aspects of social self-perception were clearly illustrated by their responses.

We posed the problem Kohlbergians have often used (cf. Kohlberg, 1973); the dilemma of a man whose wife is dying of a disease for which the only medicine is controlled by a druggist who demands more money for it than the man can raise. We did not, as has been usual in Kohlberg's research, ask directly whether the man would be justified in stealing the medicine, but rather asked our adolescent informants to suggest what he should do. It was striking to us that Zawiya adolescents typically did not mention the possibility of the man's *stealing* the drug until all other options had been exhausted. Most often it was suggested that he could surely reason with the druggist and get him to take payment over time, or that relatives would lend the necessary money.

We also asked each subject to suggest a moral dilemma of his or her own, and the responses gave us some insight into personal styles and preoccupations. Several secondary school male students responded by recalling instances in which a friend wanted to copy their work in school. These examples were discussed, not in terms of universalizing conceptions of the general good ("What would happen if everyone cheated?"), but rather in terms of a realistic assessment of the relative interpersonal cost of disappointing a friend or of being punished by a teacher. Abdelaziz, when asked to make up a dilemma, said, "You might know somebody who's fleeing the police and comes to your house. If you tell the police they'll send him to prison for 12 years, and people will say you did a bad thing; but if you don't tell the police might punish you, perhaps with three years in prison." In this "prisoner's dilemma" imagined moral question, as in his real example concerning school, Abdelaziz casts the issue in terms of whether to follow a societal rule and both hurt a friend and suffer community censure, or to break the law and be severely punished. Such responses do not earn Abdelaziz membership in the highest Kohlbergian stages, but they reflect vividly the actual content of Zawiya ethics.

Formal thinking, informal thinking. Here, for example, is 'Abdelkhalq, a boy of 13 at the time we talked. 'Abdelkhalq had six years attendance at school behind him, three of which he passed. I had first asked him for a personal example from the previous year in which he had not

known what was the right thing to do, and he could think of no example. I then posed the modified "Heinz" dilemma, and got the following answer (transcribed from notes taken during the interview):

> He should give him (the druggist) half, and then work to get the rest of the money. [And if he doesn't have the money?] Borrow. [And if he's tried everything and can get only half the money, should he steal the medicine or leave his wife without?] He should steal. [Why?] So his wife will live. [But is the druggist also in the right?]

This last question seemed hard for 'Abdelkhalq to understand. He struggled with it and finally said of the druggist, "Yes, he's right too." My next question concerned "moral behavior" in school:

> [Do kids sometimes copy in class?] Yes, lots. [What does the teacher do?] Well, our French teacher is very tough, and she hits the kids with a hose. [But do kids say it's OK to copy?] If it's their friend. Otherwise they get angry. Older kids even pay to copy.

The immediately following question is one I have puzzled about for years in relation to Morocco:

> [If you see a boy who's nice and quiet at home but hits others with stones in the street, why do you think that is? 'Abdelkhalq repeats my question, and I ask "Any idea why?"] No. [But say, why is he nice at home?] So his father will say, "He's nice." Then if he hits a kid in the street his father will say, "Mine's a good boy, he doesn't hit."

What are we to make of this as moral self-reflection? There are of course two very different readings for the (hypothetical?)

boy's motives in behaving with careful correctness in front of his father. It seems obvious that we could take this to be evidence of a cynical or of a naively "concrete" and "conventional" way of behaving in each situation in a manner that minimizes personal loss and wins approval of parents or peers. On the other hand, Abdelkhalq's motives, while not ignoring the crass advantages of such behavior in the not-unlikely event his father has to defend him in public (or at least order his older brothers to do so), may be more complex. He may indeed begin to believe that he is what he shows himself to be in front of Dad, that this is the social role he will grow into and make his own. We can hardly judge on the basis of this small behavior sample, but I have known Abdelkhalq's older brothers for years and I think *they* have undergone such a maturational process.

Abdelkhalq had helped us in our research six months previously by locating and bringing to our house for testing the younger boys and girls included in the cognitive sample.I asked him what he had done with the fifty dollars I had paid him at that time. He told me he still had the money, and that he planned to buy new trousers and shoes but they were expensive in the fall. Do we credit him with foresight and self-restraint in this instance, or assume that his parents or oldest brother have impounded the money? I don't know the literal answer, but it seemed to me he was expressing a personal belief. More importantly, his answers make sense in the context of Zawiya, where boys need street toughness and at least the appearance of good behavior at home to make their way in an uncertain world where too few resources are claimed by too many young people (half the Moroccan population is under 18 years of age).[4]

CONCLUSION

We began interviewing and testing in Zawiya with good reason to believe that the youth there would not perform as Western subjects have, both because of limitations of the tests developed for U.S. and European use and because of lower levels of schooling in Zawiya. We do not believe the low average scores of persons tested in Zawiya or other non-Western settings can be used to infer differences in native ability. From long association with the adults of Zawiya, I can assure readers that they reason as subtly about their social world as do Westerners about theirs. They do not, however, typically express this social intelligence in easily recognizable expressions of the formal didactic or syllogistic thinking Piagetians have described; and this "failure" seems to me primarily due to the low level of Western-style formal schooling in Zawiya. These results are thus consistent with Scribner's (1976) observation concerning the critical effect of schooling on the emergence (or at least the display) of Piagetian formal operations:

> In all cultures, populations designated as "traditional" or "nonliterate" have just somewhat better than a chance solution rate across all types of problem material . . . Within each culture there is a large discrepancy in performance between schooled and non-schooled. With schooling, there is little between-culture variation in performance for the cultures studied. (pp. 5-6)

The teen years in Zawiya are clearly a time of changed self-perception, and indeed of the formation of a newly sophisticated sense of oneself as a social

---

[4] Morocco's per capita Gross Domestic Product was $71-l in 1982, the year these data were collected (United Nations, 1983).

actor. The successful older adolescent will be aware how he or she comes across to others, will have a clear conception of how one's own behavior is judged by the context in which it occurs and by the company one keeps, and will know how to enlist the support of neighbors and to avoid conflict. While these skills may not translate into skilled performance on standardized tests, they are indicative of a well-honed intelligence which allows the Moroccan adult to see a wide range of possible motives and consequences of one's own and others' actions, and to take moral considerations into account in a practical way (cf. Rosen, 1984). Despite their often impoverished circumstances, the youth of Zawiya aspire to a much more affluent life, perhaps one taking them far beyond the scope of their semi-rural community and family ties. While they view many of the traditional practices of their parents with ambivalence, they remain on the whole committed young Muslims and proud Moroccans. Indeed, they fit very well a picture of adolescence as a time of tension between rampant optimism and sometimes self-contradictory thinking about how to achieve goals. What they fail to show in formal reasoning in structured tests, or in the classroom, they can often demonstrate with great subtlety in their relations with peers and family. Living with them helps us appreciate that there is still much to learn about the social imbeddedness of reasoning. As Inhelder and Piaget (1958) have observed:

[T]here is more to thinking than logic. Our problem now is to see whether logical transformations fit the general modifications of thinking which are generally agreed — sometimes explicitly but often implicitly — to typify adolescence (p. 335).

Like other cross-cultural studies of the development of formal thinking, these Moroccan results suggest only a partial and attenuated movement through the stages delineated by Piaget, Kohlberg, and other Western theorists. It does seem fair to say that when given material of more obvious relevance to *their own* goals and problems, Zawiya youth often respond with a subtlety one would not predict from their performance on imported structured tests. I believe some of the lessons to be learned from such work are obvious: let us understand the goals and dilemmas actually occurring in non-Western settings and build some of our measures around them and let us, as Valsiner (1984) has suggested, learn to see the person-setting *interaction* as the necessary focus of our investigations.

ACKNOWEDGMENTS The comparative research on which this paper is based was made possible by grants from the National Institute of Mental Health (#MH 14088) and the William T. Grant Foundation. I am grateful to Susan S. Davis and Jaan Valsiner for comment on an earlier draft.

REFERENCES

Campbell, D.T., & Levine, R. A. (1970). Field-manual anthropology. In R. Naroll & R. Cohen (Eds), *Handbook of method in cultural anthropology*. New York Columbia University Press, 366-387.

Dasen, P.R. (1972). Cross-cultural Piagetian research: A summary. *Journal of Cross-Cultural Psychology, 3*, 23-40.

Davis, S.S. (1982). *Patience and power: Women's lives in a Moroccan village.* Cambridge, MA: Schenkman.

Davis, S.S., & Davis, D.A. *Presenting the Self: Adolescence in a Moroccan town.* Rutgers University Press, forthcoming.

Douglas, J.D., & Wong, A C. (1977). Formal operations: Age and sex differences in Chinese and American children. *Child Development, 48,* 689-692.

Hollos, M., Leis, P.E., & Turiel, E. (1986). Social reasoning in Ijo children and adolescents in Nigerian communities. *Journal of Cross-Cultural Psychology, 17,* 352-374.

Inhelder, B., & Piaget, J. (1958). *The growth of logical thinking from childhood to adolescence.* New York: Basic Books.

Kagan, J. (1972). A conception of early adolescence. In J. Kagan & R. Coles (Eds.), *Twelve to sixteen: Early adolescence.* New York: Norton.

Keating, D. P. (1980). Thinking processes in adolescence. In J. Adelson (Ed.), *Handbook of adolescent psychology.* New York: Wiley-Interscience.

Kohlberg, L. (1964). Development of moral character and moral ideology. In M.L. Hoffman and L.W. Hoffman (Eds.), *Review of child development research* (Vol. 1). New York: Russell Sage Foundation.

Kohlberg, L. (1971). From is to ought: How to commit the naturalistic fallacy and get away with it in the study of moral development. In T. Mischel (Ed.), *Cognitive development and epistomology.* New York: Academic Press.

Kohlberg, L. (1973). Continuities and discontinuities in childhood and adult moral development revisited. In L. Kohlberg, *Collected papers on moral development and moral education.* Moral Education Research Foundation, Harvard University.

Kohlberg, L., & Gilligan, C. (1971). The adolescent as a philosopher: The discovery of the self in a post-conventional world. *Daedelus, 100,* 1051-1086.

Neimark, E. D. (1964). Information gathering in diagnostic problem solving as a function of number of alternative solutions. *Psychonomic Science, 1,* 329-330.

Neimark, E.D. (1967). The development of logical problem-solving strategies. *Child Development, 38,* 107-117.

Neimark, E.D. (1975). Intellectual development during adolescence. In F. D. Horowitz (Ed.), *Review of Child Development Research* (Vol. 4). Chicago: University of Chicago Press.

Neimark, E.D. & Lewis, N. (1968). Development of logical problem-solving: A one year retest.*Child Development, 39,* 527- 536.

Nisan, M., & Kohlberg, L. (1982). Universality and variation in moral judgment: A longitudinal and cross-sectional study in Turkey. *Child Development, 53,* 865-876.

Piaget, J. (194; [1932]). *The moral judgment of the child.* Glencoe, IL: The Free Press.

Piaget, J. (1972). Intellectual evolution from adolescence to adulthood. *Human Development, 15,* 1-12.

Rosen, L. (1984). *Bargaining for reality: The construction of social relations in a Muslim Community.* Chicago: The University of Chicago Press.

Salili, F., Maehr, M., & Gillmore, G. (1976). Achievement and morality: A cross-cultural analysis of causal attribution and evaluation. *Journal of Personality and Social Psychology, 33,* 327-337.

Scribner, S. (1976). *Modes of thinking and ways of speaking: Culture and logic reconsidered.* Unpublished manuscript.

Snarey, J. R. (1985). Cross-cultural universality of social-moral development: A critical review of Kohlbergian research. *Psychological Bulletin, 97,* 202-232.

Valsiner, J. (1984). *'Intelligence' as person-environment interaction in structured action contexts.* Paper presented at the symposium Changing Conceptions of Intelligence and Intellectual Functioning, XXIII International Congress of Psychology, Acapulco, Mexico.

Wagner, D.A. (1978). The effects of formal schooling on cognitive style. *Journal of Social Psychology, 106,* 145-151.

Witkin, H.A., Dyk, R.B., Faterson, H.F., Goodenough, D. R., & Karp, S. A. (1962). *Psychological differentiation.* New York: Wiley.

Conclusion

General Conclusion

Towards Culture-Inclusive Developmental Psychology: Overcoming Epistemological Obstacles

Jaan Valsiner

This book has entailed three general messages. First, it elaborates the need for developmental psychology to become culture-inclusive (as opposed to a mere cross-cultural research paradigm). Second, several contributions (especially Chapters 2, 4, and 12) address the difficulties that Western research practices encounter when efforts are made to apply them in a Third World context. Methodology that honored the cultural traditions of these societies would make developmental psychology culture-inclusive in its international dissemination. However, there is no need for a developmental psychologist who is eager to make her (or his) discipline culture-inclusive to travel to far-off places to accomplish that goal. Research in Western cultural contexts needs to be culture-inclusive along similar linese.

The third message may be less prominent than the other two: the *need to develop novel methodology that would afford empirical research in culture-inclusive ways*. This is perhaps the most difficult to fulfill out of the three. It is not too difficult to prove that culture-inclusive developmental psychology is needed — almost any example of the mismatch between existing developmental research and the reality of child development in specific contexts should suffice (see Valsiner & Benigni, 1986). It is equally easy to turn our empirical interest towards the study of our own culture. However, the traditional ways of conducting empirical research are poorly fitted for actual integration of culture and child development, and our theoretical thinking has to wrestle with several epistemological difficulties.

CULTURE AND CHILD DEVELOPMENT: SOME EPISTEMOLOGICAL OBSTACLES

The first obstacle involves the difficulty of considering cultural context and child development in an interdependent manner. Here we encounter a particularly complex version of the old "figure-ground problem": in our analysis of the "figure" (child development) is is easy to pay less attention to the "ground" (the culturally organized environment that provides support for development and guides it towards a goal). In the case of a culture-inclusive approach, the actual *interaction* of the figure and ground needs to be studied. Chapters 1 and 7 of this book provide one possible direction that may prove useful in this respect — description of the structural organization of a culturally relevant adult-child interaction setting (getting dressed, displaying "bye-bye"), paired with a qualitative longitudinal description of the emergence of novel behavioral phenomena.

The methodological emphasis on qualitative rather than quantified research methodology does not constitute a return to "soft science" — a breach in faith that most psychologists are highly afraid of. Qualitative methodologies are as valid ("scientific," as that label is often used) as quantitative ones (Kvale, 1983), and often even more so (see Sorokin, 1956, for an active criticism of "quantophrenia" in Western social sciences). Qualitative (structural) methods are appropriate if these are created so as to fit the dynamic, constantly changing nature of developmental phenomena.

This latter requirement — that there be a fit with the changing nature of phenomena — constitutes another epistemological obstacle to the use of qualitative methodologies. The majority of available kinds of such methods are ill-suited for dealing with the high variability that is the rule in the developmental process (see Valsiner, 1987, Chapter 5). That variability is high both within a developing organism (see Chapter 1, this volume), and between different developing systems (see Chapters 7 and 9). Theoretically, high variability — both intra-systemic (within the developing organism over time) and inter-systemic (between different organisms) — is expected due to the open systems nature of development (Valsiner, 1984). Therefore, any qualitative (structural) methodology that is to be usable in culture-inclusive developmental psychology needs to preserve information about variability. In essence, such methodologies need to be *structural-dynamic* in their nature. Examples of the use of combinatorial strategies to characterize the holistic structure of the phenomena provide a possible path along which to make sense out of variability (e.g., family relationships in polygamic families — chapter III). The structural organization of the psychological functions of the child and his or her cultural environment need to be described as they undergo transformation, and as they become reorganized into novel structural forms (see Basov, 1929).

Nevertheless, a structural-dynamic account of the variability inherent in the process of development introduces a new epistemological obstacle — not every variable aspect of a child's relationship with the cultural environment contributes to the process of development. It is often the case that some infrequent events may have a dramatic impact on development, whereas many variable and frequent happenings in the child's life (e.g., particular behavior of the mother while dressing the child — Chapter 1; or circumstances of showing social courtesy — Chapter 7) may be largely of peripheral relevance for children's development as a whole. There are no *a priori* empirical criteria for deciding which aspects of variable behavioral and cognitive phenomena are relevant. Therefore, empirical research that is not guided by an explicit theory is likely to search for developmentally relevant phenomenology in a haphazard way. In contrast, theory-driven empirical research efforts would derive "data" from the existing phenomena in accordance with the particular theory, and would never use all the information available in the phenomena (see Chapter 1). Different culture-inclusive theoretical systems derive data from the phenomena in different ways, dependent upon the way in which the theoretical system is set up. It is probably neither possible nor necessary to arrive at a single culture-inclusive theory of child development.

TOWARDS CULTURE-INCLUSIVE DEVELOPMENTAL PSYCHOLOGY

The reader of this book has been exposed to different efforts, from the sides of both developmental psychology and cultural anthropology, to make our understanding of child development more explicitly culture-bound. Culture-inclusive developmental psychology utilizes the concept of culture as the organizier of children's development in their particular environments. It is not equivalent to the cross-cultural psychological research tradition, which simply uses culture as an index variable in its empirical investigations. Rather, it is a descendant of Lev Vygotsky's cultural-historical approach, which has become rather well known to Western psychologists in the last decade. However, the theoretical implications and further development of this approach, have not been charted out in detail. Making developmental psychology culture-inclusive constitutes one small step in this direction. It is the hope of all contributors to this volume that the reader will arrive at a better understanding of different phenomena of psychological development, as they are intertwined with culture. Developmental psychology would cease to be developmental, if it were to deny its own development as a scientific discipline. It is that development to which this volume makes a humble contribution.

REFERENCES

Basov, M. (1929). Structural analysis in psychology from the standpoint of behavior. *Pedagogical Seminary and the Journal of Genetic Psychology, 36,* 267-290.

Kvale, S. (1983). The quantification of knowledge in education: On resistance toward qualitative evaluation and research. In B. Bain (Ed.), *The sociogenesis of language and human conduct* (pp. 433-447). New York: Plenum.

Sorokin, P. (1956). *Fads and foibles in modern sociology and related sciences.* Chicago: Regner.

Valsiner, J. (1984). Two alternative epistemological frameworks in psychology: The typological and variational modes of thinking. *Journal of Mind and Behavior, 5, 5,* 449-470.

Valsiner, J. (1987). *Culture and the development of children's action.* Chichester: Wiley.

Valsiner, J., Benigni, L. (1986). Naturalistic research and ecological thinking in the study of child development. *Developmental Review, 6,* 203-223.

Name Index

Subject Index